AF871901

The Swedish Conflict of Laws

The Swedish Conflict of Laws

by

HILDING EEK

Carl Lindhagen Professor of International Law
in the University of Stockholm

MARTINUS NIJHOFF / THE HAGUE / 1965

ISBN 978-94-011-8714-5 ISBN 978-94-011-9552-2 (eBook)
DOI 10.1007/978-94-011-9552-2

Copyright 1965 by Martinus Nijhoff, the Hague, Netherlands. All rights reser-
Softcover reprint of the hardcover 1st edition 1965
ved, including the right to translate or to reproduce this book or parts thereof in any form.

Bok- och Reklamtryck AB, Stockholm 1965

To Helen

Preface

The purpose of this book is to present to lawyers outside Sweden an introduction to Private International Law as applied in Sweden. As in the original Swedish version, *(Internationell Privaträtt. Metod och Material,* Stockholm 1962), emphazis is put on the structure and functioning of conflict law, and the book does not attempt to present a comprehensive survey of Swedish conflict rules. A résumé of these rules has, however, been included in the English edition.

The author wants to express his thanks to those who have helped to make possible the publication of this book. Generous support was given by the Swedish State Council for Social Science Research. Dr. Stig Strömholm, Uppsala, prepared the translation into English of the original Swedish text. Some alterations were subsequently made in the English version, including minor deletions of material which had appeared in the Swedish original and the addition of some new material, including the whole of present chapter IV. The English text as a whole was finally revised by the author with the help, in the case of chapters I, IV, V and part of chapter II, of Mrs. Helen Moats Eek (Ph.D., University of Chicago) and, in the case of chapter III and part of chapter II, of Mr. Richard Cox (B.Sc.Econ (Hons.), F. R. Econ. Soc.). Valuable assistance, particularly in the preparation of the bibliography and the index, was given also by Mr. Lars Lindgren (LL.B), amanuensis at the Institute for International Law of the University of Stockholm.

Stockholm, May 1965

Hilding Eek

Contents

Note on Swedish Legal Material

The texts of Swedish statutes and ordinances in force on 1 January of a given year are published annually in *Sveriges rikes lag.* This semi-official compilation is the main collection of laws used by lawyers. It is referred to in the present work as *the Statute-Book.* As this book does not, however, include all statutes and ordinances, reference is also made from time to time to the official and complete publication which has appeared annually since 1825, entitled *Svensk författningssamling* and cited in this book as *S. F. S.* Legislative material (travaux préparatoires) is found in 1) *Statens offentliga utredningar,* cited as *S. O. U.*, a series which contains reports preparatory to legislation submitted to the King in Council by committees or experts appointed by him; 2) Royal propositions to the *Riksdag* (the parliament) containing draft enactments and explaining their motivation; 3) reports by the legislative committees of the parliament. After the adoption of new legislation, this material appears in abbreviated form in the second volume of the annual publication, *Nytt juridiskt arkiv* (cited as *N.J.A. II.*). This publication, however, deals in substance only with legslation of special importance and contains bare references to other new enactments.

The first volume of *Nytt juridiskt arkiv* (cited *N. J. A.)* contains abstracted reports concerning the most important decisions by the Supreme Court and notes referring to all other decisions by the Court. *Regeringsrättens årsbok* (cited *R. Å.)* is a similar annual publication reporting decisions by the Supreme Court of Administrative Justice. Some cases from courts of appeal are reported in a special section of the periodical *Svensk juristtidning* (cited *Sv. J.T.).* A few older cases are quoted from *Schmidts Arkiv* and *Naumanns tidskrift* (cited *N. T.),* periodicals which long ago ceased to appear.

At the end of this book the reader will find a table of cases. Swedish cases are generally not cited by reference to the names of the party or parties but only to the publication where a case is reported and the year of publication. Citations to reports in *N. J. A.* also indicate the page where the report begins. Notes in *N. J. A.* are referred to by their number and letter, for example 1951 *N. J. A.* C 733. A case reported in *R. Å.* is referred to by the symbol (number or number and letter) given to it in the publication.

Scandinavian legal periodicals are cited not by numbers and/or volumes, but only by the year of publication. The abbreviations of the their titles used in this book will be found in the list of abbrevations. This list also includes abbreviations of works, both foreign and Swedish, to which frequent references are made. At the end of the book, immediately before the Index, a special bibliography will be found which contains the full titles of all printed books and articles in the Swedish language referred to in this book. It should be mentioned, however, that in the book, references sometimes are made to unsigned notes in legal periodicals. Such notes do not figure in the bibliography.

A complete and systematic bibliography of Swedish legal writing for the years 1865 to 1956 was published in Stockholm in 1957 by Mr. Justice Nils Regner; a supplement covering the years 1957 and 1958 was published in *Sv. J. T.* 1959 (pp. 406 ff.), another covering the years 1959 and 1960 in *Sv. J. T.* 1962 (pp. 93 ff.) and a third covering the years 1961 and 1962 in *Sv. J. T.* 1963 (pp. 677 ff.). A *Scandinavian Legal Bibliography,* containing translations into English of the titles of works in Scandinavian languages, was published in Uppsala in 1961 as No. IV of *Acta Instituti Upsaliensis Iurisprudentiae Comparativae;* its editor was Professor Åke Malmström. *Scandinavian Studies in Law* — a yearbook published in Stockholm since 1957 under the auspices of the Faculty of Law of Stockholm University — contained in Volume 5 (1961) a bibliography entitled "Swedish Legal Publications in English, French and German", compiled by Dr. Lars Frykholm. The list covers the years 1935—1960.

Some Abreviations Used in this Book

Actes	*Conférence de la Haye de droit international privé: Actes.*
A.J.I.L.	*American Journal of International Law*
Arminjon	P. Arminjon, *Précis de droit international privé* I—III. 2nd ed., Paris 1947—52.
Batiffol	Henri Batiffol, *Traité élémentaire de droit international privé.* 2nd ed., Paris 1955.
Beckman	Nils Beckman, *Svensk domstolspraxis i internationell rätt.* Stockholm 1959.
Borum	O. A. Borum, *Lovkonflikter.* 4th ed. Copenhagen 1957.
B.Y.I.L.	*British Yearbook of International Law*
Clunet	*Journal du droit international*
Dennemark	Sigurd Dennemark, *Om svensk domstols behörighet i internationellt förmögenhetsrättsliga mål.* Stockholm 1961.
Dicey	A. V. Dicey & J. H. Morris, *Conflict of Laws.* 7th ed., London 1958.
Eek	Hilding Eek, *Om främlingskap.* Stockholm 1955.
Ehrenzweig	Albert A. Ehrenzweig, *Conflict of Laws, Part one: Jurisdiction and Judgments.* St. Paul, Minn., 1959.
Frankenstein	Ernst Frankenstein, *Internationales Privatrecht.* Berlin 1926—35.
Gihl, *Lois*	*Torsten Gihl,* "Lois politiques et droit international privé." *Recueil des Cours,* Leyden 1953.
Gihl, *Principer*	Torsten Gihl, *Den internationella privaträttens historia och allmänna principer.* Stockholm 1951.
Gihl, *Studier*	Torsten Gihl, *Studier i internationell rätt.* Stockholm 1955.
Goodrich	H. F. Goodrich, *Handbook on the Conflict of Laws.* 3rd ed., St. Paul, Minn., 1949.
Hambro	Edvard Hambro, *Jurisdiksjonsvalg og lovvalg i norsk internasjonal kontraktsrett.* Oslo 1957.
Hassler & Nial	*Internationell privaträtt,* efter föreläsningar av professor Åke Hassler. Andra upplagan, reviderad efter föreläsningar av professor Håkan Nial. Stockholm 1941.
Hjerner	Lars A. E. Hjerner, *Främmande valutalag och internationell privaträtt. Studier i de offentligrättsliga lagarnas tillämplighet.* Stockholm 1956.
Hult	Phillips Hult, *Föräldrar och barn enligt svensk internationell privaträtt.* Stockholm 1943.
I.C.J.	International Court of Justice
I.C.L.Q.	*International and Comparative Law Quarterly*

J.B.L.	*Journal of Business Law*
J.F.F.T.	*Tidskrift utgiven av Juridiska Föreningen i Finland*
Karlgren	Hjalmar Karlgren, *Kortfattad lärobok i internationell privat- och processrätt.* 2nd ed., Lund 1960.
Lewald	Hans Lewald, *Règles générales des conflits de lois.* Bâle 1941.
Liber amicorum	*Liber Amicorum of Congratulations to Algot Bagge.* Stockholm 1956.
Melchior	Georg Melchior, *Die Grundlagen des deutschen internationalen Privatrechts.* Berlin & Leipzig 1932.
Minnesskrift	*Minnesskrift utgiven av juridiska fakulteten i Stockholm vid dess femtioårsjubileum 1957.* Stockholm 1957.
Ne.T.I.R.	*Nederlands Tijdschrift voor internationaal Recht.*
Nial	Håkan Nial, *Internationell förmögenhetsrätt.* 2nd ed., Stockholm 1953.
Niederer	Werner Niederer, *Einführung in die allgemeinen Lehren des internationalen Privatrechts.* Basel 1954.
N.I.R.	*NIR. Nordiskt immateriellt rättsskydd.*
N.T.I.R.	*Nordisk Tidsskrift for International Ret.*
Nussbaum	Arthur Nussbaum, *Principles of Private International Law.* New York 1943.
Pillet	Antoine Pillet, *Traité pratique de droit international privé.* Paris 1923 & 1924.
Raape	Leo Raape, *Internationales Privatrecht.* 4th ed., Frankfurt a. M. 1954.
Rabel	Ernst Rabel, *The Conflict of Laws. A Comparative Study.* Vol. I, 2nd ed., Chicago 1958; Vol. II, 2nd ed., Chicago 1960; Vol. III, Chicago 1950; Vol. IV, Chicago 1958.
Rabels Z	*Zeitschrift für ausländisches und internationales Privatrecht.*
Recueil	*Recueil des Cours.* Académie de droit international.
Reuterskiöld	C. A. Reuterskiöld. *Handbok i svensk privat internationell rätt.* 2nd ed., Uppsala 1912.
Schmitthoff	Clive Schmitthoff, *The English Conflict of Laws.* 3rd ed., London 1954.
Schnitzer	Adolf F. Schnitzer, *Handbuch des internationalen Privatrechts,* I and II. 4th ed., Basel 1957—58.
Strömholm	Stig Strömholm, *Torts in the Conflict of Laws.* Stockholm 1961.
Stv.T.	*Statsvetenskaplig tidskrift.*
S.Y.I.L.	*Soviet Yearbook of International Law.*
S.Ö.	*Sveriges överenskommelser med främmande makter* (the Swedish treaty series).
T.f.R.	*Tidsskrift for Rettsvitenskap.*
T.S.A.	*Tidskrift för Sveriges advokatsamfund.*

U.f.R.	*Ugeskrift for Retsvaesen.*
Undén	Östen Undén, *Internationell äktenskapsrätt enligt gällande svensk lag.* Lund 1922.
Wolff, *Deutschlands*	Martin Wolff, *Das internationale Privatrecht Deutschlands.* 3rd ed., Berlin 1954.
Wolff, *Private*	Martin Wolff, *Private International Law.* 2nd ed., Oxford 1950.

Chapter I
Introduction

§ 1. Basis and Function of Private International Law. Terminology

The rules of Swedish law, whether written, customary or embodied in the decisions of courts, have developed and been formed to govern matters of concern to Swedes, and affairs within Sweden. They are made for us.[1] As a result of international intercourse, however, it sometimes occurs—and more often in these days than in earlier times—that Swedish courts and other authorities are confronted with questions which relate to the business of foreigners or are otherwise connected with foreign countries. Such questions may concern events or happenings or facts which have been examined by foreign courts. The application of "Swedish" rules to such cases may sometimes appear unreasonable or senseless. Since foreign rules concerning succession, liability in tort, legal obstacles to marriage, etc., are not the same as ours, the application of our rules to a case connected with a foreign country may also be unjust and, therefore, repugnant to those general principles of law and of legal protection for the individual which are at the root of our legal system as a whole.[2] The function of the particular rules of private international law is to ensure rational and just solutions in cases containing foreign elements or otherwise connected with foreign countries.[3]

[1] Cf. Gihl, *Principer,* pp. 9 ff.

[2] "Jeder Staat hält sein Privatrecht für das gerechteste, weil er es sonst nicht erlassen und beibehalten hätte. Trotzdem kann es ungerecht sein, wenn ein Staat sein vermeintlich bestes Privatrecht anwendet." Kegel in *Festschrift Hans Lewald,* Basel 1953, at p. 270.

[3] In *I.C.J. Reports* 1958, at p. 94, Sir Hersch Lauterpacht states: "The purpose of private international law is to make possible the application, within the territory of the State, of the law of foreign States. This is an object dictated by considerations of justice, convenience, the necessities of international intercourse between individuals and indeed, as has occasionally been said, by an enlightened conception of public policy itself." *Vide* also Carswell in 8 *I.C.L.Q.* (1959) pp. 268 f.

The need for special rules applicable to external matters has been met partly by the introduction into the legal system of certain rules of substantive law concerning, on the one hand, aliens and their legal relations *(law of aliens)* and, on the other hand, the legal relations of Swedes abroad; also partly by the creation, by legislation and judicial decisions, of *choice of law rules*. The function of the latter rules is to indicate what country's substantive law is applicable. As an illustration, the rule embodied in chapter 1 of the Swedish Act of 1937 concerning international questions with regard to the estates of deceased persons, lays down that matters of succession from persons who were not Swedish subjects at their death are governed by the law of the state of which the deceased was a citizen. This rule means that where a person was, at his death, an alien, the administration of the estate and the distribution of assets to the beneficiaries are to be performed in accordance with the succession rules of the country of which the deceased person was a citizen and not be governed by the rules in the Swedish Inheritance Code which would otherwise be applied in Sweden. In a sense, choice of law rules are the core of private international law. However, as we shall show in greater detail in the following chapters, there is in actual practice a close interplay between choice of law rules and some of the rules belonging to the law of aliens. Rules of both these kinds—which can be put together under the heading *external rules* or, possibly, conflict rules—are treated in private international law. Both categories are found side by side in legislation on external matters. Chapter 4 of the 1904 Act on international questions concerning marriage, infancy and adoption, contains, for instance, rules in sections 1—3 dealing with the appointment of guardians for minors, i.e. enactments belonging to the law of aliens, whereas section 5 contains a choice of law rule under which Swedish courts, when confronted by questions concerning the effects of infancy of interdiction, shall disregard Swedish substantive law in this field and apply the law of the country where a guardian or committee has been appointed. Among rules which are not choice of law rules in the proper sense but are nevertheless essential for solving problems of private international law, the rules of international procedural law are particularly important, especially with regard to the jurisdiction of Swedish courts and the recognition of foreign judgments.

Private and Public International Law

Both the law of aliens and the rules intended to solve conflicts between different legal systems are part of national law. Under the prevailing opinion, each country is, at least in principle, at liberty to frame its private international law at its own discretion.[5] In other words, private international law is not governed by public international law.[6] However, the liberty of states in this respect is not unbounded. In the first place, they are bound by conventions. Moreover, there are principles in the general law of nations which impose certain obligations on all states. Thus it is established that aliens are entitled to the protection of the law. They must be granted legal capacity and access to the courts of justice. Certain status relations must be recognised.[7] States must take into account the reasonable legal interests of aliens as well as the interests of foreign powers.[8] Too far-reaching tendencies to let the law of the *forum* country prevail, refusals to assume jurisdiction or expressions of a general hostility to aliens in the framing of conflict rules may cause other states to take counter-measures. Even if in no case has a state based a claim against another state on the character of the latter's rules of private international law,[9] the application of such rules in individual cases may result in international litigation.[10]

[5] Cf. Gihl, *Principer*, pp. 287 ff.

[6] Vide, however, Hambro in *Ne.T.I.F.*, 1950, pp. 132 ff.

[7] Cf. below at pp. 53 f.

[8] This idea is expressed in a polemic form by Lepaulle: "Le législateur français ne peut pas plus, en fait, dire que le mariage d'un Chinois en Chine sera régi par la loi française dans sa forme, qu'il ne peut ordonner aux Français de marcher sur l'eau." See Lepaulle, *Le droit international privé, ses bases, ses normes et ses méthodes*, Paris 1948, at p. 36.

[9] Cf. Nussbaum, *Principles of Private International Law*, New York 1943, p. 25 with note 26 and Lipstein in 27 *Transactions of the Grotus Society*, (1942), pp. 142 ff. *Vide* also *Survey of International Law*, United Nations Publications, Sales No.: 1948. V. 1, pp. 29 f.

[10] An illustration (taken from a field governed by an international convention, however) is the so-called *Boll case* between the Netherlands and Sweden, which was decided by the International Court of Justice on 28 November 1958. It concerned the question whether Sweden had committed an infringement against the Hague convention of 1902 on guardianship through the fact that Swedish authorities had taken care of a Dutch girl for so-called "protective education." *I.C.J. Reports* 1958, p. 55. Cf. also Petrén in *Sv.J.T.* 1959, pp. 201 ff., and Eek, *Sv.J.T.* 1959, pp. 561 ff., also note 227 below at p. 157.

It should also be pointed out that private international law is influenced by changes occurring in public life and in the structure of the community. This is exemplified by the re-emergence in Europe of the principle of domicile at the expense of the principle of nationality. It is obvious that people nowadays to a greater extent than at the turn of the century reside outside the countries of which they are citizens, and it is a consequence of this that the domicile is gaining in importance. Moreover, the very idea of nationality has become looser. Thus in the European Economic Community of six continental states, the principles of private international law hitherto accepted (including the principle of nationality) seem to need reexamination and even investigation of the radical solution of a uniform private law seems indicated.[11] Logical consequences of these developments are the introduction of new and "international" methods of construction in municipal courts of justice and the need for common and supranational courts of last instance in the field of private law. This means that problems which at present are dealt with by private international law as a branch of municipal law, have become the concern of public international law. The traditional approach towards conflicts of law must be modified and will, perhaps, gradually disappear. Among the facts which influence this change are the new kinds of relations—often framed upon the model of private law—between international organizations or between such organizations and states or individuals.

Terminology

Both Swedish and foreign works on private international law make use of a special terminology. The specific terms of this branch of legal science are, in some cases, indispensable instruments for the expression of distinctions which are not found in *internal* law (as distinquished from national *external* law). Other terms may have no such claim to necessity but are explained by the fact that legal writing in this field has an impressive age and is essentially international. It is possible, perhaps even probable, that we could do without a number of these terms and that they ought to be avoided in the interest of lucidity. Since revolu-

[11] In art. 3 of the Rome treaty of 1957 which is the basis of the European Common Market it is stated that one of the tasks of the organisation is to remove differences between the national legal systems in so far as it is necessary to make the common market work.

tions in the field of terminology seem predestinated to fail, however, we must very largely observe the rules of traditional vocabulary. At any rate, knowledge of that vocabulary is a necessary condition for the successful study of works dealing with private international law.

In Swedish legal usage, the subject is called "private international law" *(internationell privaträtt)*. Some writers prefer to put only choice of law rules under that heading, but such a limitation cannot be reconciled with the practical need for studying also what we have called rules of the "law of aliens" together with choice of law rules;[12] furthermore, in the Swedish universities, the subject, "private international law", also comprises international procedural law, while international criminal law, i.e. the question of the territorial applicability of Swedish criminal law—or rather the extension of the claim of Swedish law to inflict punishments—is considered, for teaching purposes, a branch of criminal law.

In the conflict of laws, the law of the country where the court is sitting is called *lex fori.* From the point of view of the City Court of Stockholm, *lex fori* is Swedish law as a whole. In the terminology of private international law, the law of the *forum* is composed of substantive rules and choice of law rules. The latter are purely formal inasmuch as they only indicate from what legal system the court shall take those substantive rules upon which the decision of actual litigation shall be founded.

The term *lex causae* is not uniformly used. In the present book, it serves to denote the substantive rules applicable in the case at issue. In external or international litigation, the first task is to look for the applicable rules of law, which is found by means of a choice of law rule. Once the latter has been selected and it indicates that the applicable law, say in a tort action, is the law of the country where the injury occurred, it follows that if the injury occurred in England, English law is the *lex causae.*

A number of special terms refer to the so-called connecting factors; like other terms, generally Latin, and indicating different *fora,* these words will be introduced in their due place in the following chapters. However, we cannot postpone a few words on the term *statute,* which has hung on in private international law ever since the Middle Ages.

[12] Some writers distinguish between choice of law (or conflict) rules, on the one hand, and "substantive" or "material" rules of private international law on the other. See von Overbeck in *Ne.T.I.R.,* 1962 pp. 362 ff.

In that period, Roman law was recognised in Northern Italy as a common legal system, but in addition to this, the various states or cities had their own particular laws, *statuta*. Statute, then, means law or enactment (cf. the English term "statute" in other connections). The question of the territorial applicability of the particular laws or enactments, was raised, and within the common system of Roman law, the postglossators invented a system for the decision of such questions. Laws concerning property *(statuta realia)* were valid only within the territory of the state from which they emanated, where the property was supposed to be found, whereas laws concerning legitimacy and other personal matters *(statuta personalia)* were supposed to follow, as it were, the person concerned wherever he went. A court of justice at Bologna, exercising jurisdiction over a citizen of Modena, had to apply the laws of Modena in questions concerning personal matters. These rules, which were developed into a vast system,[13] had their rationale in the prevailing community of law. The nearest parallel which can be found at the present time are rules on the applicability of municipal bye-laws and "interprovincial law" (see below, at pp. 8 f.). However, the statute theories were succeeded and transformed by the doctrine of private international law after the end of the Middle Ages, when the earlier legal community had been replaced by a number of equal national legal systems. We are not going to discuss these transformed statute theories. It is sufficient for present purposes to state that by the middle of the 19th century, they had had their day in court. What remains, however, is the term "statute" which means simply the applicable law. Thus, where a writer refers to the "statute of debts" this implies nothing beyond the "applicable law in legal relations based upon debt," and similarly, the "personal statute" is the law applicable to questions concerning personal status or relations, etc. It must be admitted that the term "statute" can occasionally facilitate discussion, e.g. where a writer wants to express the idea that the applicable law in a relationship based upon debt ("the statute of debts") shall not necessarily be applied to all questions arising in actual litigation. "The

[13] In conflict literature, reference is often made to the *famosissima quaestio* whether the primogeniture rule of the English law of succession was applicable to property left abroad by a deceased Englishman. If the essential contents of that legal rule were the mention of the heir-at-law, it was a personal statute and as such applicable everywhere; but this was not the case if the emphasis of the rule lay upon the property as such. Cf. e.g. Nussbaum, *op. cit.*, p. 11.

statute of debts," in this case English law, is not necessarily called upon to settle questions concerning the formal validity of a contract; it is enough, under the rule *locus regit formam actus,* that the formal requirements of the law of the place outside England where the contract was concluded have been observed. Nor is English law always applicable to questions concerning the mode of payment, which are usually decided under the law of the place of payment. It is customary to say that the principles discussed deal with the limitation, field of application, or scope, of the statute of debts.

A few more questions of terminology will be touched upon although at first glance they may seem trivial. Where a "Swedish judgment" is referred to, we mean a decision rendered by a Swedish court of justice. Similarly, a "foreign judgment" is delivered by a foreign court. What is relevant is the nationality of the authority concerned, not the country in the territory of which the judicial decision was rendered. Thus an "English judgment" may emanate from an English court sitting outside the territory of England. This distinction becomes more apparent if applied to an action by an administrative authority, e.g. the celebration of marriage. We use the term "Swedish marriage" for marriages solemnized by Swedish authorities, not only in Sweden but also abroad, under the rules of Swedish law (chap. 1, sec. 8 of the Swedish Act on international questions concerning marriage, infancy and adoption, 1904).[15] In the Swedish conflict rules on bankruptcy, an important distinction is to be drawn between Swedish and foreign bankruptcies and between Scandinavian and non-Scandinavian bankruptcies.[16] A "Scandinavian" (other than Swedish) bankruptcy is a bankruptcy decreed in Denmark, Finland, Norway or Iceland if the court assumes jurisdiction on the ground that the debtor is domiciled in the country of the court (cf. sec. 14 in the Act on the effects of Scandinavian bankruptcies, 1934). With regard to arbitral awards, a different distinction has been made. Section 1 of the Act on arbitral awards, 14 June 1929, contains special rules determining whether an agreement to submit to arbitration shall be regarded as Swedish or foreign. The agreement is regarded as foreign if the arbitral procedure shall take place outside the country even though the agreement was concluded in Sweden.

[15] The possibility of a "foreign" marriage within Sweden is presupposed in the 1904 Act. Cf. below 238.

[16] Cf. Nial, pp. 97 ff.

Under section 5, an arbitral award shall be regarded as foreign if it was made abroad.

It should finally be pointed out that in legal writing the term "inter-provincial law" is occasionally used. The word is used about states with several legal systems or complex legal systems,[17] where—to use the language of chapter 7 : 1 of the Act on international questions concerning marriage etc., 1904—"different laws are in force . . . in different areas." In some, but not all such states, there are uniform interprovincial (inter-state, inter-cantonal, inter-local etc.) rules which fulfil, within the territory of the state concerned, the same function as private international law in the relations between states. It should be remembered that in th United States a federal private law exists only in some fields, and that each of the states of the union has its own system of private law. Nor is there any federal system of law to regulate the conflict relations between the states. On the other hand, the legal systems of the various states contain conflict rules resulting chiefly from decisions of state courts. A court sitting in the state of New York—even if it is a federal court—makes use of the conflict rules developed in New York to determine the question whether the law of New York or e.g. that of Vermont is applicable in a given case. These rules which, from a historical point of view, are inter-state rules, are equally applicable where the question is, say, whether Swedish law or the law of the state of New York shall be applied to a given case. In Spain, on the other hand, the *Codigo civil* contains both international and interprovincial conflict rules; the civil code is applicable only as a secondary source of law in Catalonia, Aragon, Navarre, Biscay and the Balearic Islands, which have retained their autonomy in the field of private law and live in accordance with their *consuetudines*.[18] Thus the existence of several legal systems is not a feature particular to federal states.

The term "interpersonal law" has been used for rules which may be resorted to where certain groups of persons within one state are subject to special systems of rules. Interpersonal law is intended to define the field of application of each such system. India provides an illustration of a country where different rules of private law are applicable to different categories of persons according to their religion. In modern

[17] Cf. Arminjon in *Recueil* 74 (1949, I) and Beitzke in *Revue hellénique de droit international,* 1955, pp. 131 ff. Cf. also below, pp. 137 ff.

[18] Niederer, p. 98. As to Denmark, *vide* Borum, pp. 6 ff.

Greece, the general civil code of the country is not applicable to the Mohammedan population as far as personal and family matters are concerned; in these respects, Islamic law prevails.[19]

Intertemporal law is a term used to denote those rules which are applied when old laws are replaced by new legislation. Nowadays, such questions are usually dealt with at the time of the promulgation of a new enactment. In some countries there are constitutional rules for the solution of these problems. In themselves, such questions have nothing to do with private international law. However, questions of time play an important part in the conflict of laws.[20] Conflict rules normally contain, or presuppose, an element of time, and occasionally it is necessary to face the question what regard shall be paid to changes introduced after a certain moment into the applicable foreign law.[21]

§ 2. The History of Private International Law in Sweden

A. BEFORE 1900[22]

The problem of the legal position of foreigners and their property and affairs was raised early in history. In the most remote days foreigners were dealt with in an arbitrary fashion. According to Theodor Mommsen the situation in Rome in the days of the Kings was such that what a *civis romanus* took from a foreigner was "ebenso recht erworben wie die am Meeresufer aufgelesene herrenlose Muschel."[23] But the development of trade and intercourse made it imperative for all communities to establish legal protection of visitors from abroad and their property. It was done in the first stages through the adoption of special rules relating to foreigners (the law of aliens) and later through the application by national courts of rules of law of foreign countries to matters closely connected with the countries concerned.

[19] Arminjon, *op. cit.*, pp. 158 ff. Cf. below, p. 159, note 5.

[20] *Vide* the large monography Gavalda, *Les conflits dans le temps en droit international privé,* Paris 1955.

[21] As for this problem, cf. below pp. 99 f., 125 ff. and 145 ff.

[22] Cp. Eek in *Mélanges Séfériades,* Athens 1961, pp. 29 ff. and Eek in *Revue hellénique de droit international,* 1961, pp. 3 ff.

[23] Mommsen, *Römische Geschichte,* I, 5th ed., Berlin 1868, pp. 157 ff.

In Sweden as elsewhere problems created by increased intercourse and travel across frontiers seem to have been approached at first by special legislation for aliens. Both in the Provincial Codes of the 13th and 14th centuries and in the first national Codes of law for the rural areas and the boroughs, from about 1350, we find rules about foreigners (substantive rules).

There is reason to look into the personal and territorial applicability of any legal rule. Some enactments are explicitly concerned with certain groups of people or events within a certain area; quite often, in international or external cases, it is necessary to determine whether a certain rule, e.g. an enactment taken from foreign law, *is intended* for general application or for application limited in one way or another.[24] It is quite possible that in Sweden as in other countries, the rules of law were, in the earliest times, applicable only to those who belonged to a certain tribe, etc.[25] It would seem, however, that by the middle of the 15th century, when King Christopher's amended version of the Rural Code of Laws was issued, the principle later to be known as the principle of territoriality had been accepted in Sweden.[26] Only Swedish law was applicable to the national territory and to the inhabitants. It should be remembered that any person domiciled in Sweden was then a subject of the King, even if he had moved in from abroad.[27] It is likely that

[24] Cf. below, pp. 63 ff.

[25] Montgomery, *Handbok i Finlands allmänan privaträtt,* vol. I, 1899, p. 145, and Malmström in *Rättsvetenskapliga studier ägnade minnet av Phillips Hult,* 1960, pp. 352 f.

[26] According to the Danish writer H. Federspiel, *Den internationale Privatret i Danmark,* 1909 (at pp. 44 ff.), the reason why the problems of territorial limitation of laws were not observed in early days was that there were so many laws to choose between: rural laws, borough laws, national laws, canon law, etc. The judge applied the law he knew "without much bothering about the question whether it was territorially applicable or not." It was only after legal unity had been achieved that the notion of the "sovereignty of the law within its territory" gained the position of a real maxim of legislative policy. This point of view may contribute to the explanation of a prohibition in King Christopher's amended version of the Swedish Code of Laws for the rural areas of "the introduction of outlandish law into the Kingdom, to the detriment of the common people," and also the later prohibition (in the Code of Laws, 1734), against invoking foreign law in Swedish decisions; in an earlier period, it had been possible to use Roman law as a secondary source of law.

[27] As late as 1809, Swedish citizenship could be acquired by taking up a domicile in the Kingdom. *Vide* the historical notes in Blomberg, *Om svenskt statsborgarskap,* 1891, pp. 33 ff.

Swedish law was considered applicable also to foreign visitors without domicile in the Kingdom, but it must be kept in mind that the special rules concerning the treatment of foreigners were part of Swedish law. It was no derogation from the principle of territoriality that it might occasionally be necessary to make a choice between various Swedish enactments, e.g. between the rules of the Code of laws for the rural areas and those of the Code for the boroughs.[28]

In a community where relations with other countries are in a process of development, it soon appears that a body of rules exclusively belonging to the category "law of aliens" is not sufficient to solve all external legal problems. We must therefore ask when Swedish judges and other lawyers first gave any attention to the possibility of, and need for, solving these problems by admitting the application of foreign law or of substantive rules borrowed from such law.[29] In the 16th and 17th centuries, there are occasional expressions of the idea that foreign law could, as it were, ask for admission and application.[30] Thus, in a Royal decree of 29 March, 1682, the question is discussed whether a Swedish lady's dower in the estate of her husband, a Swedish noble-

[28] Ekström (in *Sju internationellt privaträttsliga uppsatser,* 1920), pp. 42 ff. rejects the idea of drawing conclusions applicable to the conflict of laws from the rules of this "interlocal" law. It should be pointed out, however, that in an early 18th century commentary, Abrahamsson's *Landslagen* (the Code of Laws for rural areas), 1726, p. 315, it is stated, with regard to the fields of application of rural and borough law, that real property abroad "is distributed among the heirs according to the law of the place where the property is."

[29] It is particularly interesting to compare the development of English law in this field with the evolution in Sweden. *Vide* Sack, *Conflict of Laws in the History of English Law,* 3 Law: A Century of Progress 1835—1935, New York & London 1937. As for the development in Northern America, cf. Nadelmann, "Some historical notes of the doctrinal sources of American conflict law," in *Ius et Lex,* Basel 1959.

[30] The fact that all special laws had been cleared away and the judge thereby deprived of any possibility to choose between different groups of national rules may have supported the idea that in cases of a very particular kind, the rules of foreign law could be convenient to use. Federspiel quotes *(loc. cit.)* a Danish judgement from 1594 where a choice of law is at least discussed. It concerned a document by which a man domiciled in Sweden had given his wife a share in his real estate in Danmark; according to the judgment, Danish law was exclusively applicable to the formal validity of the document. Federspiel, however, does not want to draw the conclusion that in other matters, e.g. concerning matrimony or contract, Danish courts would at that time have applied Danish law exclusively.

man, should be determined otherwise than in accordance with the provisions of the law of Sweden; the answer was in the negative. Section 1 of the Statute of Wills, 1686, admitted the application of foreign law in certain cases. In his treatise on Swedish civil law, a work from 1729, the great jurist Nehrman states that when "litigation arises within the Kingdom about agreements concluded between private persons in foreign countries, or about property belonging to foreigners but situated in the Kingdom, the litigants utsually invoke foreign laws."[31] He thereupon rejects the statute theories, showing that he was acquainted with them, and recommends the application of Swedish law. "For the law has usually no effect outside the territory." However, he also establishes a number of exceptions from this proposition, e.g. with regard to contracts or wills made abroad or to inheritance from persons who had lived and died in a foreign country.

The Judicial Procedure Code, 1734, contains a provision (chap. 21, sec. 3) about the decisions of courts which may seem to interrupt the development mentioned above; it is laid down that "foreign law must not be invoked therein, nor must foreign languages be used." Did this mean a prohibition against a custom which, to judge from Nehrman's statement, had already been adopted by the courts? The late Professor Reuterskiöld has assumed that to be the original implication of the enactment.[32] However, a less severe view was held by the 18th century lawyer Stobaeus in a dissertation as early as 1768,[33] and later writers have also rejected a construction of the relevant section of the Judicial Procedure Code according to which that provision would imply an unconditional prohibition against the application of foreign law.[34] The specific purpose of the provision was to prevent the basing of Swedish decisions upon Roman law. Later legislation did not adopt the principle of prohibiting foreign law. The Statute on bills of exchange, which was enacted in 1748, contains some references to foreign law. Another early illustration may be given: a Royal decree of 13 November, 1795,

[31] Nehrman, *Inledning till den svenska jurisprudentiam civilem,* 1729, p. 69.

[32] Reuterskiöld, *Inledning till den svensk-internationella obligationsrätten,* 1899, pp. 24 f.

[33] Joannes Stobaeus, *Tentamen juridicum de legibus peregrinis,* 1768, pp. 8 ff. It should be pointed out that in his *Tillägg* (Addenda), 1746, Nehrman mentions the new enactment in chap. 24 sec. 3 of the Code of Procedure without modifying his earlier opinion. Cf. also Flintberg, *Lagfarenhetsbibliotek,* vol. 4, 1801, p. 606.

[34] *Vide* for instance Kallenberg, *Svensk civilprocessrätt* I, 1923, p. 97.

according to which the question whether divorced spouses were "free to contract a new marriage" should be answered with at least some regard to foreign law. The background was that a court in Stockholm had granted a divorce between two French spouses who were Roman Catholics and had given both of them the right to enter into a new marriage. The vicar apostolic had protested against this judgment.[35] The applciation of foreign law was also becoming visible in the decisions of courts.[36] Authority against a rigid interpretation of chapter 24 of the Judicial Procedure Code has been found in the often cited decision in the Filén inheritance case of 1832.[37] This action concerned the right to inherit from a Swede deceased in county Demerary, British Guyana, and it is stated in the decision that "the plaintiff's alleged right to a portion of the estate of Jonas Filén (must) be judged under the law which is proved to have been in force in the country where the aforesaid Filén had his domicile and his real estate at the time of his death."

By the middle of the 19th century no doctrine of the conflict of laws in the proper sense of the word had been developed in Sweden, and it is difficult to draw any conclusions as to the theoretical positions of courts from those decisions which have been reported.[38] In the world at large, the middle of the 19th century was the time when a modern doctrine of the conflict of laws came into being. A pioneer work of great importance, particularly in Europe, was Savigny's treatise "Über die räumliche und örtliche Geltung der Gesetze" (vol. VIII of his *System des heutigen Römischen Rechts,* 1849). Savigny argued, *inter alia,* that the law of the forum country should not be granted preference

[35] *Vide* Flintberg, *op. cit.,* vol. 2, 1797, pp. 136 f.—On the other hand, the principle of territoriality was often maintained with severity. In a Royal Letter to the Göta Court of Appeal, 1771, it was held that no secular punishment could be inflicted upon an unmarried female who had had sexual intercourse with a Danish officer and become pregnant. The reason was that the woman, who was "born a Norwegian subject" had committed the offence abroad, "for which reason no punishment is set out in the general Code of Laws." A striking contrast is found in a decision of the Supreme Court from 1960 (1960 *N.J.A.* 430) where a Swede was punished in Sweden under the Swedish Traffic Offences Act for negligence committed on the highway when driving his car between Hirschhorn and Eberbach in Germany.

[36] Schmidt, *Arkiv,* vol. IV, p. 400; *N.T.* 1864, p. 499.

[37] Schmidt, *Arkiv,* vol. III, p. 301.

[38] In a contract case from 1820 (Schmidt, *Arkiv,* vol. XV, p. 97) the Supreme

over foreign law *a priori,* that the various legal systems should be considered as equal and that the system of private international law should be framed in accordance with a principle which the writer gave the following formulation:

> "Bei jedem Rechtsverhältnis muss dasjenige Rechtsgebiet aufgesucht werden, welchem dieses Rechtsverhältnis seiner eigentümlichen Natur nach angehört oder unterworfen ist, worin dasselbe seinen Sitz hat."

In the English-speaking countries, the publication of Story's *Commentaries on the Conflict of Laws,* 1834, was a decisive event in the development towards a modern conception of private international law. According to Story, the reason why courts sitting in one country applied the law of another country was to be found "in mutual interest and utility, in a sense of the inconvenience which would result from a contrary doctrine, and from a sort of moral necessity to do justice, in order that justice may be done to us in return." There are undoubtedly great differences between Savigny and Story.[39] Neither can be exempted from criticism, and such criticism has been put forward from many quarters. Nor did the two writers clear the decks completely of older doctrines, although Savigny is commonly represented as the destroyer of the statute theories, and the learned debate is still going on in conflict literature. However, the reasonable approach to the problems as such and

Court held that a contract concerning a loan "which had been concluded under the protection of Prussian law by persons who were then Prussian subjects, and also the promissory note founded upon the aforesaid contract and now invoked in support of the demand for enforcement of the claim should be considered, as to their conditions and effects, in the light of that law." The case concerned limitation, and the Prussian period of limitation, which was longer than that laid down in Swedish law, was applied in favour of the plaintiff. It is possible that the decision is influenced by the so-called doctrine of vested rights which had been put forward by the Dutch writer Huber. (Vide Gihl, *Principer,* in particular pp. 145 ff. Huber is mentioned by Wilde in his *Sueciae historia pragmatica,* 1731, p. 20.) The influence of the doctrine of vested rights can be traced, it would seem, to a statement by the 19th century lawyer Naumann to the effect that a party must be allowed "to prove, by means of rules of foreign law, legal relations created abroad which such party wants to enforce in this country." *N.T.* 1864, p. 711. Cf. also the *exposé des motifs* of the Swedish Legislative Commission draft of a general Civil Code, 1826, p. 270.

39 It should be noted, however, that Savigny refers to Story in his work.

the realism—at least by the standard of the period—of the ideas developed in the two works must have been attractive.[40]

The influence of Savigny's doctrine in Sweden may be found in the writings of Schrevelius, Professor of Private Law in Lund about the middle of the 19th century. In the first edition of his textbook *Lärobok i Sveriges allmänna nu gällande civilrätt,* I, 1844, he mentioned only briefly the "sphere of application" of legislation, and set out a few exceptions to the rule that Swedish courts must not "apply any other law than that of the land." In the second edition of the same work (1851), his attitude was completely changed. The main rule, it is now stated, quite regardless of the provision in chapter 24 of the Judicial Procedure Code, is "that the law of a country should not always and exclusively be applied" (pp. 35 ff.). It is necessary, Schrevelius continues, "in each particular legal relation to find the locality to which it belongs according to its nature and where it has, as it were, its seat, from which it obviously follows that the law applicable in that place should be used." This seems almost a copy of Savigny.[41] It must be assumed that Schrevelius' rather lengthy statements, in the second and third editions of his standard work, concerning the "sphere of application" of national law had some effect on the views of Swedish lawyers in questions belonging to this field of the law. In 1876, J. Kreuger submitted an exhaustive account of Swedish conflict rules in a chapter concerning "the legal position of aliens with regard to private law" in his work *Hufvuddragen af utländingars rättsförhållande i Sverige.*[42] Kreuger appears to have been acquainted with the theorists

[40] Cf. Gutzwiller, *Der Einfluss Savignys auf die Entwicklung des internationalen Privatrechts,* Freiburg 1923.

[41] It should be observed that in the preface of his first edition, 1844, Schrevelius refers to Savigny, "from whose writings I gratefully admit to have learned much." At this time, however, Savigny had not yet published the work with which he was to introduce a new epoch in the history of private international law. In the same preface, Schrevelius refers to the great Danish lawyer Ørsted whose writings he had, in his own words, "made much use of." However, he does not seem to have used Ørsted's paper "Over de grundsaetninger hvorefter vore domstole kunne tage fremmede love i betragtning" (On the principles according to which Danish courts may take foreign law into consideration), in *Eunomia* 1822, where Ørsted levelled decisive criticism against the statute theories before Savigny. Ørsted's pioneer contribution is now beginning to be noticed also outside Scandinavia. *Vide* e.g. Korkisch in 23 *Rabels Z.* 1958, pp. 604 f.

[42] It is interesting to note that Kreuger (at p. 15) announces the transition from

of private international law from the older Italian and Dutch schools to Savigny, Story and others, including the leader of the new Italian school, Mancini.[43] Modern foreign theories were also of great importance for Reuterskiöld when he, at the turn of the century, began his systematic presentation of Swedish private international law. From the same period, further evidence can be found showing that the conflict of laws was becoming an independent subject of teaching and an independent field of legal science in Sweden.[44] Towards the end of the 19th century it is possible to find occasional judicial decisions in which the application of foreign law is discussed in a relatively modern manner,[45] and from about 1910 a new method begins to characterize the thinking and writing habits of courts. It is also obvious that there was a considerable legislative interest in the problems of private international law. Sweden participated in the second Hague Conference, 1894, and its representative found, with regard to the decisions of the first conference, that he could "constater que la jurisprudence suédoise est conforme à la plus grande partie des résolutions prises." Questions of private international law were discussed at the eighth Inter-Nordic jurists' conference in 1896 and at the annual meeting of the Swedish Bar Association in 1902.

We have arrived at our own period.

the principle of domicile to the principle of nationality: "We consider nationality to be the proper basis in most cases where domicile has so far been decisive."

[43] Kreuger finds Savigny's theory "somewhat nebulous" and contents himself with stating, quite undogmatically, that "in particular cases, the nature of things calls for the application of this or that law" (p. 14).

[44] In Professor Winroth's many works from this period, accounts of "international legal relations" are regularly included. In Finland, Montgomery dealt with the "local limitations" of laws in some detail in his *Handbok i Finlands allmänna privaträtt,* part one, 1889, where he referred to international theories; in *Finlands gällande civilprocessrätt* I (first ed., 1905) Wrede discussed the "local applicability of procedural law." In Norway, there are Synnestvedts book *Le droit international privé de la Scandinavie,* which appeared in Paris in 1904, a chapter on international procedural law in Hagerup's *Den norske civilprocess* I (first ed. 1895—1901) and a paper by Boye in *T.f.R.* 1902, pp. 46 ff. In Denmark, the conflict of laws was discussed by Ørsted in 1822 (*vide* note 41 above) and, in great detail, by Scheel in *Privatrettens almindelige Deel.* I, 1865.

[45] 1879 *N.J.A.* 185; 1905 *N.J.A.* 146.

B. INTERNATIONAL COOPERATION

It is now clearly realised that the conflict of laws is not governed by supra-national rules or by rules or principles belonging to the law of nature, but is part of national law. At the same time, however, this branch of the law has become remarkably international in the sense that legislatures and judges in various countries have found that international cooperation is necessary to reach satisfactory solutions of those practical legal problems which arise through international intercourse. Private international law in the twentieth century is characterized by extensive international cooperation intended to create uniform conflict rules. Sweden has taken part in this cooperation, and as a consequence, statutes have been adopted which contain rules agreed upon in conventions most of which have at considerable number of parties. To some extent, therefore, Sweden has a written system of conflict rules. Although Sweden has denounced certain conventions in the course of the years, and an important body of rules has been created by the decisions of courts, the continuing development of private international law in Sweden, as elsewhere, is still primarily dependent on the internationally organized efforts to find legislative solutions to problems in the field.

As a result of international cooperation, uniform rules—both conflict rules and substantive rules—have been adopted. The importance of uniform substantive rules is that they are a means of realizing what has been called "conflict avoidance." Where two or more states agree upon an identical choice of law rule, the approach is different; then a conflict between laws of the states concerned is normally solved in the same way wherever the case comes up and the dispute is decided under the same substantive rules. It is generally stated that this result is the aim of international cooperation in the field of private international law.

If an Englishman, in London gives a member of his club a horse kept in Paris, by oral promise, the donee is not likely to succeed in securing, by an action in an English court of justice, an injunction for the donor to deliver the horse. The case is governed by the *lex actus,* i.e. the law of the place where the promise was given. The English court therefore applies English law, and, under English law, a mere promise of a gift would probably not cause title in the property to pass to promisee. If the English promisor had been sued in a French court, however, the *lex situs,* i.e. the law of the place where the property was to be found at the critical moment, would seem to be decisive. Thus the French conflict rule is not the same as in England, and the French rule leads to the application of French substantive rules.[46] If these were not identical to the English rules—if the promise could be considered binding—the action about the horse would be decided differently in France and in England. In Sweden, on the other hand, English law would be applied—provided that the Swedish courts would take jurisdiction in the case[46]—under a third conflict rule which implies the application of the donor's national law. If, on the other hand, the countries concerned had agreed upon a conflict rule, the English and the French courts would normally apply the same substantive rules when deciding the case. Agreements about uniform conflict rules would create greater security in international intercourse and reduce the possibilities of what is called in American conflict literature "forum-shopping."

In family law, also, the divergencies between national conflict systems produce unsatisfactory results. If an Englishman leaves property in Sweden at his death, the assets are distributed under the English law of succession, which is applicable according to a Swedish conflict rule to the effect that questions concerning succession are governed by the law of the state of which the deceased person was a subject, whereas in English law it is at least the general principle—a reservation should be made for what is called *renvoi* (cf. pp. 175 ff below)—that property left in England would be distributed according to Swedish law if the deceased Englishman had been domiciled in Sweden. Equally unsatisfactory are the divergent rules in different countries with regard to jurisdiction in matrimonial cases (divorce and separation) and the restrictive rules of national legislation regarding the recognition of foreign judgments. These questions have been the subject of international discussion and international agreements. It should be remembered that legal provisions on these matters are substantive rules. The Inter-Nordic conventions and the legislation based upon them demonstrate how such rules may serve the avoidance both of conflicts and of the inconsistencies which often result from the fact that even choice of law rules with an identical wording may be construed and applied diffe-

[46] Cf. Batiffol, p. 651.

rently by the courts of different countries. There is, for example, a provision concerning jurisdiction in the Royal Ordinance of 31 Dec. 1931 on international questions concerning marriage, adoption etc., that determines in which Nordic country a given divorce case shall be taken up; furthermore, conflicts are avoided through section 9, under which each country shall apply its own law when trying divorce questions. It has not been possible, however, to bring about an Inter-Nordic allocation of jurisdiction, and a corresponding *lex fori* principle, all over the field; it has been necessary to make use of uniform choice of law rules in some cases (cf. sec. 3 of the Royal Ordinance referred to above).

Sweden has participated in most of the conferences on matters of private international law which have taken place in the Hague since 1893. Moreover, Sweden is a party to conventions elaborated by international organizations or upon their initiative e.g. League of Nations, United Nations, Council of Europe. The Inter-Nordic system of conventions is particularly important. Finally, there are bilateral conventions between Sweden and other countries of some importance for the conflict of laws. It should be mentioned, moreover, that Swedish lawyers have participated in the elaboration of draft conventions within the *International Law Association,* which was created in Brussels in 1873.[47]

The Hague Cooperation

The first conference in the Hague took place in 1893. It had been preceded by several unsuccessful endeavours by the Italian jurist and statesman Mancini to bring about a universal convention concerning uniform conflict rules and also by preparatory work within the *Institut de droit international.* In the Netherlands it was T. M. C. Asser, a friend and collaborator of Mancini's who succeeded, after the latter's death, in convincing his Government of the advantages of taking the initiative for a conference. An invitation to a conference in 1874 did not meet with any response, but at the conference convened in 1893, many states were represented; Sweden was not among them, however. A second conference, in which Sweden participated, took place in 1894. There fol-

[47] The *International Law Association* usually holds a conference every second year and issues a printed report after each conference. Work of interest in the present context is also performed by the *Institut de droit international* (created in 1873) and reported on for in an *Annuaire* which is, however, chiefly devoted to public international law.

lowed conferences in 1900 and 1904. The fifth conference was held in 1925,[48] the next one followed in 1928.[49] The work was resumed after the Second World War and the seventh, eighth, ninth and tenth conferences were held in 1951,[50] 1956[51], 1960[52] and 1964 respectively. In 1951, the cooperation in the conferences assumed a formal character: a special statute for the Hague conference on private international law was adopted, which, inter alia, provided for the establishment of a permanent bureau. At the conferences after the Second World War, England, which had earlier refrained from taking part in the Hague cooperation, participated, and in 1956 and 1960, the United States was represented by observers. Delegates from some twenty states were present in 1956 and 1960.

As far as Sweden is concerned, it had not by 1963 carried out any revision of its private international law as a consequence of the last five Hague conferences.[53] On the contrary it has freed itself from the conventional obligations in the field of family law which derived from the earlier conferences. This disengagement does not mean, however, that the cooperation in the Hague has been, or will in future be, unimportant for the development of private international law in Sweden.

The conferences in 1896 and 1905 resulted in conventions on certain matters pertaining to the law of civil procedure. As a consequence of the 1896 convention, Swedish legislation was adopted in 1899; it was later replaced by the procedural enactments which are found, in the yearly editions of the Statute-Book, after chapter 35: 14 of the Judicial Procedure Code. The 1905 convention, a substitute for that of 1896, has now been replaced by the convention of 1954.[54]

The conference in 1900 resulted in three conventions signed in 1902. One of them concerned divorce and separation[55], and rules from it are

[48] *Vide* Stenbeck in *Sv.J.T.* 1926, p. 438.

[49] *Vide* Ekeberg in *Sv.J.T.* 1928, p. 113.

[50] *Sv.J.T.* 1952, p. 163.

[51] *Sv.J.T.* 1957, p. 73.

[52] *Sv.J.T.* 1961, pp. 71 f.

[53] The convention of 1 March, 1954, on certain questions in the field of civil procedure has been ratified by Sweden. *Vide Royal Proposition* No. 13, 1957. However, it is only an amended version of the 1905 convention.

[54] Cf. note 53 above. The 1896 convention is found in *S.F.S.* 1899, No. 34, and the 1905 convention in *S.F.S.* 1908, No. 30.

[55] *S.F.S.* 1904 No. 27, p. 10. Cf. 1905 *N.J.A.* II, No. 5, and *Royal Proposition* No. 21, 1904.

found in chapter 3 of the Swedish Act of 1904 on international questions concerning marriage etc.; however, in 1933, Sweden gave notice of its denunciation of the convention, followed in 1934 by certain amendments the 1904 Act.[56] The two other conventions concerned conflict of laws in regard to marriage[57] and guardianship of minors.[58] These conventions also served as the basis for rules on the same matters in the 1904 Act. On 29 November, 1958, Sweden gave notice of its denunciation of the conventions, which took effect from 1 June, 1959.

At the Hague conference in 1904, conventions were elaborated—they were not signed until the next year—on the effects of marriage on the rights and duties of the spouses in their personal relations and on the property of the spouses,[59] and on interdiction and similar measures of protection.[60] The first convention caused the adoption of the Act concerning certain international questions with regard to the legal effects of marriage, 1912, while the latter one, to which Sweden acceded as late as 1924, resulted in chapter 5 of the 1904 Act, which was enacted in 1924. In 1960, Sweden gave notice of its denunciation of the conventions to take effect from 23 August, 1962.

The seventh Hague conference in 1951 elaborated a convention concerning the law applicable to international sales of movables; it was ratified by Sweden in 1964.[61] On the other hand, the Swedish delegation could not support the draft conventions on the recognition of foreign companies and other corporations and on avoidance of conflicts between the principles of domicile and nationality.[62] At the 1951 conference, agreement was further reached on a draft which was to become the 1954 convention on civil procedure.

The 1956 conference carried on the work towards a regulation of questions concerning international sales of movables; the problems of jurisdiction were also dealt with. Two draft conventions on these matters were elaborated. The conference also discussed, and worked out draft conventions on, the applicable law in actions concerning alimony

56 *Vide S.Ö.* 1934, No. 25, 1934 *N.J.A.* II, p. 423 and 1933 *N.J.A.* II, p. 712.

57 *S.F.S.* 1904, No. 27.

58 *S.F.S.* 1904, No. 27, p. 19.

59 *S.Ö.* 1912, No. 6. Cf. also 1912 *N.J.A.* II, p. 55 and *Royal Proposition* No. 58, 1912.

60 *S.Ö.* 1924, No. 31. Vide also 1924 *N.J.A.* II, p. 217.

61 *Vide* Nial, pp. 55; same author in *Liber amicorum,* pp. 155 ff.; Nial and Dennemark in *SvJ.T.* 1955, pp. 81 ff.

62 See Borum in *Liber amicorum,* pp. 16 ff. and Wortley in *Festschrift Hans*

to children and the recognition and enforcement of judgments and orders on such alimony.

Three convention drafts resulted from the 1960 Hague conference; they deal with the abolition of the requirement of diplomatic and consular authentication of foreign documents, the form of wills and the applicable law in questions concerning protection of children. The enforcement of foreign judgments and problems with regard to adoption etc. were also discussed.

The Inter-Nordic Conventions

The Inter-Nordic conventions in the field of private international law were adopted in the nineteen-thirties.[63] They are: (1) a convention on matrimony and related matters, 1931[64]; (2) a convention on enforcement of alimony orders, 1962[65]; (3) a convention on recognition and enforcement of judgments, 1932[66]; (4) a bankruptcy convention, 1933[67]; and (5) a convention on deceased persons' estates, 1934[68]. The conventions have been followed up by legislation in Sweden and in the other Nordic countries. An account of Swedish legislation in this field will be given below in the chapter dealing with the sources of private international law as now in force.[69]

Lewald, pp. 407 ff.

63 A systematic account of the Inter-Nordic conventions is given by Allan Philip in *Recueil* 1958, pp. 245 ff.

64 *S.Ö.* 1931, No. 19. Cf. also *S.Ö.* 1954, No. 2 and *Royal Proposition* No. 206, 1953.

65 *Sv.J.T.* 1962 p. 588. The convention replaced an earlier agreement from 1931. *S.Ö.* 1931, No. 20 and 1954, No. 8.

66 *S.Ö.* 1933, No. 6.

67 *S.Ö.* 1934, No. 8.

68 *S.Ö.* 1935, No. 17.

69 The *travaux préparatoires* of the system of conventions are found in the reports of the Standing Royal Commission on Legislation containing draft statutes on certain international questions (*S.O.U.* 1929, No. 12 and 13, 1931, No. 9 and 1933, No. 1 and No. 35). Vide also 1932 *N.J.A.* II, pp. 376 and 489, 1933 *N.J.A.* II, p. 1 and 1935 *N.J.A.* II, pp. 1 and 352. The conventions are commented by Bentzon in *T.f.R.* 1934, pp. 336 ff. The conventions on matrimony and alimony are discussed by Ekeberg in *Sv.J.T.* 1929, pp. 508 ff. On the alimony convention, vide further Walin, *Barnens ställning enligt föräldrabalken*, 1953, pp. 196 ff.— Another result of Inter-Nordic cooperation is the protocol on mutual legal assistance, 26 June 1957 (See note 94 below.) It should be mentioned that the

Other International Cooperation

The League of Nations initiated cooperation in the field of private international law. The first results were the Protocol of 24 September 1923 on Arbitration Clauses and the Convention of 26 September 1927 on the Execution of Foreign Arbitral Awards.[70] The present Swedish Act on foreign arbitration agreements and arbitral awards, 1929, is based upon these international agreements. As a result of a conference organized by the League of Nations in the Hague, a convention was adopted on 12 April 1930 on certain questions relating to the conflict of nationality laws as well as a protocol relating to military obligations in certain cases of double nationality. These agreements were ratified by Sweden some years later.[71] In 1930 and 1931, conventions on uniform bills of exchange and cheque legislation were signed in Geneva.[72] As complete unity could not be attained, and also for other reasons, the principal conventions were accompanied by conventions for the solution of conflicts between different national laws in the fields of bills of exchange and cheques.[73] In each of the two Swedish statutes on bills of exchange and cheques, 1932, conflict rules are embodied in the chapters on the relations with foreign legislation. These rules are applicable also to states which are not parties to the Geneva conventions, inter alia, the Anglo-Saxon countries.[74]

The United Nations has also participated in the endeavours to bring about conventions. Mention should be made of the following agreements made under the auspices of the United Nations and particularly important from the point of view of private international law: the con-

Inter-Nordic convention system is continuously developing through close cooperation between the Ministries of Justice of the five countries.

[70] *S.Ö.* 1929, No. 27, *S.Ö.* 1929, No. 28 and 1931, No. 32; also 1929 *N.J.A.* II, p. 69. The protocol and the convention will be replaced by a new convention elaborated under the auspices of the U.N. *Vide Sv.J.T.* 1958, pp. 616 f. and below, pp. 240.

[71] *S.Ö.* 1937, No. 9. Cf. Eek, pp. 53 ff. It should be remembered that Sweden has ratified the convention of 20 February 1957 on the nationality of married women which has been elaborated within the U.N. and signed the U.N. convention of 7 November 1962 on the minimum age for the conclusion of marriage.

[72] *S.Ö.* 1933, No. 26 and *S.Ö.* 1933, No. 29.

[73] *S.Ö.* 1933, No. 27 and *S.Ö.* 1933, No. 30.

[74] Cf. Ekeberg in *Sv.J.T.* 1930, p. 497.

vention on presumption of death with regard to missing persons, 6 April 1956 (not ratified by Sweden), the convention relating to the status of refugees, 28 July 1951,[75] and the convention relating to the status of stateless persons, 28 September 1954, (ratified by Sweden 1965). The United Nations produced a convention of 20 June 1956 on the enforcement of alimony decrees which was ratified by Sweden in 1958.[76] The Council of Europe has brought about patent law conventions, ratified by Sweden in 1957 and a European convention on extradition, ratified by Sweden in 1959.[77] The convention text which has served as basis for the Swedish Act on liability for damage due to the exploitation of atomic energy was concluded by the O.E.E.C. on 29 July 1960. The Swedish statute is in force until 31 December 1965 when a new Act also modelled upon the convention will replace it.[78]

In addition to the legislative work, more or less closely connected with conflict of laws, which takes place at the international level, *inter alia* within the United Nations and other international agencies, Sweden's bilateral treaties also deserve mention. Among these, the convention with Switzerland, 15 January 1936 on the recognition and enforcement of judgments and arbitrary awards may be of particular interest.[79] The recognition of foreign judgments would seem to be a question where it is easier to reach solutions step by step through bilateral treaties than to proceed through general conventions. However, Sweden has not continued this course. Other bilateral treaties are agreements on substantive rules, answering, upon the whole, to the description of the law of aliens given above; thus, no conflict rules are included. As an illustration of agreements of immediate importance for Swedish private international law, mention should be made of the treaty with France, 8 April 1949, on *inter alia* administrative aid for the collecting of tax

[75] *S.Ö.* 1954, No. 55. Cf. *Royal Proposition* No. 134, 1954.

[76] *Vide Royal Proposition* No. 138, 1958, *Sv.J.T.* 1956, p. 536 and *T.S.A.* 1956, pp. 152 ff.

[77] *Vide* the surveys of Lidgard in *Sv.J.T.* 1962, pp. 233 ff. and of Essén in *Sv.J.T.* 1963 pp. 507 ff. and more particularly about the convention on extradition, *Royal Proposition* 139, 1958.

[78] *S.O.U.* 1962, No. 14. On the Brussels conferences 1961 and 1962 and the 1963 Vienna convention on civil liability for nuclear damage *vide* Nordenson in *Sv.J.T.* 1963, pp. 559 ff.

[79] *S.Ö.* 1936 nr 10. *Vide* further 1937 *N.J.A.* II, p. 1 and Dennemark in *SvJ.T.* 1937, pp. 329 ff.

arrears;[80] the treaty occasioned an Order in Council, 14 March 1952, with special rules on the estate in Sweden of French citizens domiciled in France at the time of their death. Another example is the legal assistance conventions with France, 7 March 1956[81] The various conventions, many of them Inter-Nordic, on social benefits and social security as well as various agreements on the right of aliens to settle and to trade within the country are important elements of the Swedish law of aliens.[82] From a historical point of view, the general friendship, trade and sailing treaties have had a highly important function in breaking down the very restrictive attitude which prevailed in earlier days with regard to the right of aliens to enter, trade and work in the Kingdom. In this way, the treaties prepared the ground for a modern private international law.[83]

C· INTERNAL DEVELOPMENT OF THE CONFLICT OF LAWS

The importance which international cooperation has had for formation of Swedish private international law in the present century does not mean that internal progress has been lacking. In the field of legislation mention should be made of the 1937 Act on international questions concerning deceased persons' estates; this, however, was not entirely a product of Swedish legislation since it was created in cooperation with Finland in order to bring about uniform general conflict rules in addition to those embodied in the Inter-Nordic convention on deceaced persons' estates.[84] In the course of the work on the 1937 Act, the conflict rules in the first chapter were characterized as a "codification of the law as already in force"; even if they were only this they nevertheless provided a needed clarification of the content of the law in the field.[85]

It has been characteristic of the 20th century that questions of private international law have been increasingly noticed and discussed by legal writers. In court, the number of cases containing an international

[80] *S.Ö.* 1951, No. 19 and No. 20.

[81] *Royal Proposition* No. 100, 1956.

[82] *Vide* list in the Calendar of the Swedish Ministry for Foreign Affairs.

[83] See Matz in *F.T.* 1950, pp. 217 ff.

[84] The *travaux préparatoires* are found in *S.O.U.* 1936, No. 24, *Royal Proposition* No. 7, 1937, and 1938 *N.J.A.* II, p. 205.

[85] *S.O.U.* 1936, No. 24, p. 60. Cf. Ramel, *Studier i svensk internationell arvsrätt,* 1930, passim.

element has increased, but not to such an extent that the trend of decisions can furnish any clear picture of a development in one direction or another. It should be observed, however, that the so-called *Gold Clause* case (1937 *N.J.A.* 1) marked a break-through for the *individualizing method* of determining the applicable law in disputes concerning contracts having an international element; this would seem similar to the finding of the "proper law" as understood in English conflict law.[86] When analysed against the background of earlier decisions, the judgment also gave some support to the view that, at least in principle, an explicit selection of the applicable law by the parties is a connecting factor of decisive importance in that branch of the conflict of laws which deals with contracts. Another case which should be mentioned is 1949 *N.J.A.* 724 which accepted the recognition of clauses referring actions arising out of the contract to a foreign jurisdiction. The decision is in harmony with the view that the choice of law by the parties should be accepted.[87] In family law, there is a tendency worth mentioning; i.e., the principle of nationality is gradually being replaced by that of domicile, which was abandoned towards the end of the last century.[88] Sweden's denunciations of the Hague conventions may have been inspired by a wish to facilitate the further advancement of the principle of domicile.[89]

§ 3. Sources of Swedish Private International Law

A. LEGISLATION

It has already been pointed out that the conflict of laws comprises two main types of rules: choice of law rules and such substantive rules as may be called "external" because they deal with the specific legal problems of foreigners (law of aliens) or otherwise with facts connected with foreign countries. The distinction made here will be discussed in greater detail in the following chapter. At present we should only point out

[86] Nial, pp. 37 ff.; Bagge in *T.f.R.* 1937, pp. 158 ff.; Dennemark in *Sv.J.T.* 1943, pp. 675 ff.; Hjerner, particularly pp. 199 ff. Se also below p. 267 f.
[87] Cf. Karlgren, p. 165; Eek, p. 134 and in *Sv.J.T.* 1957, pp. 179 f.
[88] *Vide* Folke Schmidt in *Festskrift för Ekeberg,* 1950, pp. 453 ff. and in *The International Law Quarterly* 1951, pp. 43 ff.
[89] Vide *Sv.J.T.* 1960, pp. 71 ff.

that the distinction cannot serve as a basis for a survey of the statutory material. The main Swedish statutes in the field of private international law contain both choice of law rules and substantive rules, among them certain procedural provisions. The rules in other enactments dealing with private international law usually—but not always—have the character of substantive rules. Moreover, it is occasionally unclear whether, or to what extent, a provision is intended to prescribe the application of foreign law in certain cases and is therefore a choice of law rule rather than a rule of substantive law.[90] Consequently, the following survey of legislation enumerates—without regard to the distinction between choice of law rules and substantive rules—first the statutes on international family law, and then the legislation on international property law and international procedural law. Finally, mention is made of a number of other statutes or single provisions in Swedish legislation which are of importance from the point of view of private international law. The survey also contains information concerning the legislative material relating to the more important enactments.

Family Law

General Rules

(a) The Act on international questions concerning marriage, infancy and adoption, 8 July 1904.

The Act is accompanied by supplementary regulations; these are contained or indicated in the Statute-Book, and so is the Act on the celebration of marriage by Swedish authorities abroad, 12 November 1915.

Travaux préparatoires: 1905 *N.J.A.* II, No. 5; *ibid,* 1916; p. 313; 1917, p. 516; 1921, p. 741; 1924, p. 657; 1932, p. 476; 1933, p. 712; 1934, p. 423; 1947, pp. 334 and 340; 1950, p. 165; and 1959, p. 194.

(b) The Act concerning certain international questions with regard to the legal effects of marriage, 1 June 1912, and schedules attached thereto.

Travaux préparatoires: 1912 *N.J.A.* II, p. 55 and *ibid.* 1921, p. 334.

(c) The Act concerning international questions with regard to de-

[90] *Vide* e.g. the Act on the right of foreign companies to do business in Sweden, 3 June 1955, sec. 4. Cf. further pp. 60 ff. below.

ceased persons' estates, 5 March 1937, with the schedules set out or indicated in the Statute-Book.[91]

Travaux préparatoires: 1938 *N.J.A.* II, p. 205.

(d) Chapter 1: 3 and chapter 9: 3 in the Inheritance Code (which deal with the right of aliens to come into property in Sweden by succession).

(e) Transitional legislation 27 November 1964 for the facilitation of divorce and separation in certain cases. (See below pp. 248 f.) Royal Proposition No. 168, 1964.

Inter-Nordic Rules

(a) The Royal Ordinance on certain international questions with regard to marriage, adoption and infancy, 31 December 1931, with the schedules set out in the Statute-Book.

Travaux préparatoires: 1932 *N.J.A.* II 1932, p. 376 and *ibid.* 1954, p. 1.

(b) The Act on the estates of deceased Danish, Finnish, Icelandic or Norwegian subjects domiciled in Sweden, 1 March 1935.

Travaux préparatoires: 1935 *N.J.A.* II, pp. 352 and 409; *ibid.* 1938, p. 259.

(c) The Act on public control of the administration of the estates of deceased Danish, Finnish, Icelandic or Norweigian subjects before the distribution of assets, 1 March 1935.

Travaux préparatoires: 1935 *N.J.A.* II, p. 419.

(d) The Act on the estates of persons domiciled in Denmark, Finland, Iceland or Norway, 1 March 1935, with schedules.

Travaux préparatoires: 1935 *N.J.A.* II, p. 415.

Property, Contract and Economic Legislation

(a) The Act on international sales of movables, 29 June 1964. (Cf. Royal Proposition No. 149, 1964).

(b) Sections 79—87 of the Bills of Exchange Act and sections 58—65 of the Cheques Act.

(c) The Act on certain restrictions on the right of acquiring realty, mines or shares in certain companies, 1916; the Act on the right of foreign insurance companies to do insurance business within Sweden,

[91] Another enactment which should be mentioned is the Order in Council of 25 Sept. 1952 (set out after chap. 18 of the Parents and Children Code) on the duty of Swedish authorities to give information to British consulates in certain cases.

1950, section 5 (*S.F.S.* 1950, No. 272); the Act on the right of foreign companies to do business within Sweden, 1955, section 4.
(d) The Currency Act, 1939, and the Currency Ordinance, 1959; Act on the performance of obligations of payment abroad in certain cases, etc. (the Clearing Act), 1934.
(e) The Act on liability for damage caused by atomic reactors (Atomic Liability Act), 1960, sec. 15 (Cf. *Royal Proposition* No. 140, 1960).[92]

Procedural Legislation

Jurisdiction

(a) Chapter 10 of the Judicial Procedure Code and the enactments set out after chapter 10: 21 of the Code in the Statute-Book.
(b) The Act containing certain provisions on foreign state vessels, 1938 (set out after chap. 26 of the Judicial Procedure Code) and the Act on special privileges for certain international organisations, 1962.[93]
(c) Chapter 15: 4 of the Marriage Code, chapter 20: 1—5, 9, 14, 15, 24 and 30 of the Parents and Children Code.

Procedure

(a) The Order in Council on the application of the Legal Aid Act (19 June 1919), 18 April 1935; other enactments relating to legal aid set out after chapter 18 of the Judicial Procedure Code in the Statute-Book.
(b) Chapter 33: 11 of the Judicial Procedure Code (on service of writs and other documents abroad) with an Order in Council, 24 November 1933, on service of documents in Sweden at the request of foreign authorities and schedules attached thereto.
(c) Chapter 35: 2 of the Judicial Procedure Code (about proving the contents of foreign law).
(d) Enactments attached to chapter 35: 12 and 14 of the Judicial Procedure Code dealing with the taking of evidence in Swedish actions

92 Cf. above, p. 24.

93 Mention should also be made of the Act on the exemption of certain aircraft from provisional orders of seizure or injunctions, 1939, set out after sec. 195 of the Execution Act, 1877.

in foreign courts and the taking of evidence for foreign actions in Swedish courts.[94]

Travaux préparatoires: 1947 *N.J.A.* II, p. 211.

(e) The Act on the duty of foreign subjects to produce bail for costs and damages in actions before Swedish courts, 19 November 1886, and enactments attached to the Judicial Procedure Code.

Travaux préparatoires: 1886 *N.J.A.* II, No. 7 (pp. 17 ff.) and 1956 *N.J.A.* II, p. 384.

Enforcement of Foreign Judgments etc.

(a) The Act on the enforcement in certain cases of the decisions of foreign courts (on costs), 6 March 1899, and enactments attached thereto (set out after section 37 of the Execution Act).

(b) The Act on foreign arbitration agreements and arbitral awards 14 June 1929 (after section 46 of the Execution Act).

Travaux préparatoires: 1929 *N.J.A.* II, p. 69.

(c) The Act on the enforcement in Sweden of alimony decrees granted in Denmark, Finland, Iceland or Norway, 1962, and an Order in Council on the enforcement in Denmark, Finland, Iceland or Norway of alimony decrees granted in Sweden, 1962. Both are found after section 37 of the Execution Act.[95]

Travaux préparatoires: 1932 *N.J.A.* II, p. 489, *ibid.* 1954, p. 22 and *Royal Proposition* No. 158, 1962.

(d) The Act on the recognition and enforcement of judgments delivered in Denmark, Finland, Iceland and Norway, 2 December 1932, after section 37 of the Execution Act.[96]

[94] *Vide* S. Falk in *Sv.J.T.* 1959, pp. 708 f. on the protocol signed by Sweden, Denmark and Norway on 26 June 1957 concerning mutual assistance in legal matters. Sweden's international agreements on this topic are found in *S.F.S.* 1962, No. 2.

[95] Cf. above, note 65.

[96] It should be pointed out that provisions on enforcement of judgments and settlements concerning damage caused by reindeer are laid down in an Act of 20 June 1919 containing provisions for the implementation of the convention between Sweden and Norway on the right of nomadic Lapps to pasture reindeer, 5 February 1919. The convention was denounced by Norway, 15 June 1962.—Moreover, under the Convention on water rights between Sweden and Norway, 11 May 1929, judgments and decisions rendered in certain questions of water rights in Norway and no longer subject to appeal there may be enforced as final decisions by Swedish courts. *Vide* Act of 20 December 1929 on the validi-

Travaux préparatoires: 1933 *N.J.A.* II, p. 1.

(e) The Act on the recognition and enforcement of judgments delivered in Switzerland, 27 March 1936 (*S.F.S.* 1936, No. 79).

Travaux préparatoires: 1937 *N.J.A.* II, p. 1.

(f) The Act on the accession of Sweden to the international agreements on carriage of goods by rail, etc., 4 March 1955, sections 4—8.

(g) The Order in Council (30 October 1958) on the application of the convention concerning enforcement of alimony decrees abroad, 20 June 1956 (*S.F.S.* 1958, No. 522).

Travaux préparatoires: Royal Proposition No. 138, 1958, and B 17, 1958. 1958 *N.J.A.* II, p. 452.

(h) The Act on the collection in certain cases of foreign tax arrears or other public dues, 15 June 1935 (after the Collection of Taxes Ordinance in the Statute-Book) and an Act of the same date on collection of foreign tax arrears or other public dues by means of deduction from wages or pensions (after chapter 4 of the Execution Act).

Bankruptcy

(a) The Act on the effect of declarations of bankruptcy made in Denmark, Finland, Iceland or Norway, 6 April 1934 (set out in the Statute-Book after the Promulgation Decree of the Bankruptcy Act).

The Act is completed by several enactments which are found at the same place in the Statute-Book, among them the Act containing provisions on bankruptcies which comprise property situated in Denmark, Finland, Iceland or Norway, 6 April 1934, and the Act on recognition and enforcement of certain foreign decisions rendered in connection with bankruptcy administration, 6 April 1934.

Travaux préparatoires: 1935 *N.J.A.* II, p. 1.

Other Legislation

Under the present heading we shall indicate some additional sets of rules which, on the whole, fall outside the field of private international law but which may have to be taken into account in cases with foreign elements. The rules concerned belong to special fields of law. While choice of law rules occasionally appear, the main purpose of the rules

ty within Sweden of the water right Convention between Sweden and Norway, (*S.F.S.* 1929, No. 404).

surveyed is not to regulate conflicts but to settle questions of substantive law.

Carriage of Goods

In maritime law, air law and the law of the carriage of goods there are both written and unwritten choice of law rules as well as substantive rules with a bearing on international actions. For example, the Act from 1955 on the accession of Sweden to the 1948 Convention concerning international recognition of rights in aircraft contains conflict rules. Further illustrations are furnished by some provisions in the Air Communications Act, 1957, and the rules on the Swedish nationality of vessels in sections 1 and 5 of the Maritime Code. However, conflicts are very largely avoided by unified legislation and standardized contract forms.[97] In the teaching of law at the Swedish universities, these questions are dealt with under the heading of civil law. However, several problems in the fields of shipping, air traffic and communications in general fall within the domains of both private and public law; a characteristic feature is that rules in these branches of the law are largely found in conventions.[98]

Copyright, Patents, Marks and Designs

In these fields solution of external problems has been sought through the extensive use of conventions. By this means conflicts have been avoided and a kind of *droit unioniste* has been created, composed in part of uniform rules and in parts of rules providing for national treatment of foreigners. Mention should be made of the enactements which are reproduced in the Statute-Book after the Acts, 30 December 1960,[99] on copyright in literary and artistic works and on copyright in photographic pictures, and also of an Order in Council from 1953 containing provisions on the protection granted to foreign patents, designs

[97] *Vide* Schmidt *et al., Huvudlinjer i svensk frakträtt,* 1962, *passim,* and Schmidt, *Föreläsningar i sjörätt,* pp. 13 ff.

[98] Cf. Eek, p. 161. On aerial law, *vide* Grönfors, *Om trafikskadeansvar utanför kontraktsförhållanden,* pp. 342 ff., same author in *Festskrift till Herlitz,* 1955, pp. 107 ff. and in *T.f.R.* 1957, pp. 54 ff.; also short notices in *Sv.J.T.* 1953, pp. 193, 594 and 747; 1955, p. 664 and 1959, p. 712. On the international cooperation initiated in "space law," *vide Sv.J.T.* 1959, p. 713 and 1960, pp. 634 f. Sweden signed, in 1962, the Paris Convention on the establishment of the Organization for European Space Research.

and trade marks as a consequence of Sweden's accession to the revised Paris Convention for the protection of industrial property, 1883.[100]

Fiscal Law

Under this heading, section 72 of the Local Income Tax Act, 1928, should be mentioned; it refers to agreements for the avoidance of double taxation. There are many such agreements.[101]

Criminal Law

In this field, we refer to the legislation on extradition,[102] and to the relevant provisions of the Criminal Code on persons subject to Swedish criminal jurisdiction. These enactments may occasionally assume importance in conflict questions, e.g. in tort actions.[103] When considering the question whether an action has been committed, or an event has occurred "within the country," some attention must also be

[99] On the historic development within this field, *vide* Eberstein, *Den svenska författarrätten*, 1, 1923, pp. 83 ff.; *S.O.U.* 1956, No. 25, pp. 34 ff. and 50 ff. *Royal Proposition* No. 134, 1960, pp. 12 ff.; *Royal Proposition* No. 176, 1960 pp. 8 ff. Cf. also *Sv.J.T.* 1960, pp. 563 f. and 1962, p. 328. On so-called *droits voisins* see Bergström in *N.I.R.* 1960, pp. 132 ff. Sweden ratified the Universal. Copyright Convention in 1961 and the International Convention for the Protection of Performers, Producers of Phonograms and Broadcasting Organizations in 1962.

[100] Se further Godenhielm, *Utländsk och internationell patenträtt*, 1953; same author "Internationellt privaträttsliga frågor inom patenträtten," *N.I.R.* 1956, pp. 53 ff., and the discussion held at the ninth Inter-Nordic conference for the protection of industrial property, *N.I.R.* 1956, pp. 259 ff.; also von Zweigbergk in *N.I.R.* 1961, pp. 97 ff. On the Lisbon Conference, 1958, for a revision of the Paris convention, vide *N.I.R.* 1958, No. 4, and *Sv.J.T.* 1959, pp. 211 f. See also Ljungman in *N.I.R.* 1961, pp. 33 ff. on the revision of the Hague Convention, 1925, on international registration of designs and models. On European cooperation in the law of patents, *vide* von Zweigbergk in *N.I.R.* 1960, pp. 1 ff. and in *N.I.R.* 1962 pp. 231 ff. Cf. also Wirner, *Wettbewerbsrecht und internationales Privatrecht*, Munich 1960.

[101] Vide Sandström, *Svenska dubbelbeskattningsavtal i vad de avse skatt å inkomst eller förmögenhet*, 1949, and Geijer, *Om beskattning i Sverige vid in- och utflyttning samt vistelse i utlandet*, 1959. Cf. below p. 78.

[102] On the European convention concerning mutual assistance in criminal actions, to which Sweden has acceded, vide *Royal Proposition* No. 48, 1961.

[103] Cf. Nial, p. 79, note 2. *Vide* further Agge, *Den svenska straffrättens allmänna del i huvuddrag*, I, 1944, pp. 68 ff., Eek, pp. 118 ff. and *S.O.U.* 1953, No. 14, pp. 436 ff.

paid to the enactments which are found in the Statute-Book after the Act on the limits between public and private waters, 1950.

Mention should also be made of the uniform legislation on co-operation between Denmark, Finland, Iceland, Norway and Sweden for the enforcement of judgements rendered in criminal actions which came into force in 1963. It superseded a convention of 1948 and a Swedish Act of the same year.

Public Law

In this branch of the law, particular mention should be made of the Swedish Nationality Act, 1950, and the enactments found in the Statute-Book in connection with that statute.[104] Administrative rules on the diplomatic protection of Swedes abroad may also assume some interest.[105] The legislation on population registers is of considerable importance for international family law.

The Act on the legal position of aliens, 1954, ("Aliens' Act"), with the various minor enactments attached thereto, also belongs in the field of public law,[106] and so do a great number of statutes and single provisions in various enactments, partly connected with international conventions, which deal with the right of aliens to do business, receive social benefits etc. Such enactments can be found in the Statute-Book by means of the alphabetic index.

Spheres of Application of Family Legislation

In the survey of family legislation above, the enactments were grouped under the headings "General Rules" and "Inter-Nordic Rules". In fact, within the field of international family law, Sweden operates with two systems of rules. Where a disputed question arises, it is always necessary first to make clear whether it belongs to the general or the Inter-Nordic system. The two groups of rules embodied in the Swedish law are so different that it is impossible to describe the Inter-Nordic rules as mere exceptions from the general rules on family law. The latter is

[104] *Vide* Wahlbäck and Nordström, *Lagen om svenskt medborgarskap,* 1952; Sundberg, *Förvärv och förlust av svenskt medborgarskap,* 1953, and Hellberg in *Sv.J.T.* 1956, pp. 624 ff.

[105] *Vide* Eek in *Festskrift till Halvar Sundberg,* 1959, pp. 87 ff.

[106] *Vide* Björling and Lindencrona, *Utlänningslagen jämte dithörande författningar,* 1955.

the case formally, but in actual fact, the two systems are juxtaposed as independent and different sets of rules.

The general rules are embodied in the Acts of 1904, 1912 and 1937. The Inter-Nordic rules are found in the Royal Ordinance of 1931 and in those statutes which have been enacted as a consequence of the Inter-Nordic Convention on the estates of deceased persons, among them the Act on the estates of Nordic subjects domiciled in Sweden, 1935.

Although the 1904 Act is founded upon conventions, it was made universally applicable.[107] As revised, however, the Act in chapter 7, section 5, paragraphs 1 and 2, authorizes the King in Council to make exceptions. The authorization in the second paragraph was used in support of the adoption of special rules on infancy and interdiction (lunacy) "in so far as relations with" states which are parties to the Convention on interdiction, 1905, are concerned. The authorization in the first paragraph is applicable to agreements with Denmark, Finland, Iceland and Norway concerning rules which diverge from the 1904 Act "with regard to the subjects of the Contracting Parties". The Swedish Ordinance of 1931 is founded upon a convention and contains exceptions from the 1904 Act. If a question can not be decided under the 1931 Ordinance, it falls under the 1904 Act.[108] The boundary between

[107] The extent of the obligations assumed under the law of nations is defined in the concluding articles of the Conventions, which are not always easy to interpret.

[108] In the text, we discuss the sphere of application of the 1904 Act only in relation to the Inter-Nordic special rules. There is, however, a more general question, viz. whether a matter of family law of the type dealt with in the Act is at all "external" and thus liable to fall under the Act. In this sense, the sphere of application is determined by a construction of the text, which orders the application of foreign substantive rules instead of Swedish law in certain specified situations. As an illustration, mention may be made of the provisions in chap. 3, all of which except secs. 5, 6 and 7 on recognition of foreign divorce decrees, deal with divorce and judicial separation between "foreign subjects"; it must be noticed that under chap. 7 sec. 2 spouses may be considered, for the purposes of the Act, as "foreign subjects" although one of them is a Swedish citizen. To those who are not "foreign subjects," Swedish law is applied. In the present writer's view, therefore, it cannot be correct to apply in any case the rule in chap. 3, sec. 2, second para. of the 1904 Act also in divorce actions between spouses who are both Swedish citizens when the matter is brought before the courts. The contrary view is held both by Undén (pp. 76 ff.) and Karlgren (p. 116 note 2). According to these writers, a divorce decree could not be granted, although there were grounds for it under Swedish law, if the spouses had become Swedish citizens by naturalization, and the ground for divorce was a fact that had occurred before

the systems is therefore drawn by means of an examination of the manner in which the Inter-Nordic "exceptional rules" determine their own field of application.

When the 1912 Act was introduced, the Swedish legislator was not prepared to make those principles from the Hague Convention, 1905, which are embodied in the Act, generally applicable. Thus it is stated in the preamble that the King is authorized to decree the application of the Act "on condition of reciprocity". The Act, in section 2: 10,—where the application of the *Convention* is referred to—consequently restricts its applicability in such manner that "the Convention shall not be applicable if it would follow from its provisions that the law of any State not party to the Convention would have to be applied." In a special Order in Council, 1912, the King in Council decided that the Convention's rules "as given in the Act of 1 June 1912" should be put in operation. It was set out in the Order what states besides Sweden were parties to the Convention; the intention was perhaps to indicate that the Act must be applied in all cases where it would be the law of one of the parties (now Germany, Italy, the Netherlands, Poland, Portugal and Rumania) which would, as a result, govern.[109] In a later Order it was stated that the Convention should no longer be applicable to France, which had given notice of denunciation. Thus, from the point of view of legislative technique, the 1912 Act also embodies special, exceptional rules which presuppose that other "general" rules exist and are applicable to cases falling outside the sphere of application of the Act which, however, is difficult to define. At the time of the adoption of the Act it was hard to state with any certainty what the general principle of Swedish law was with regard to the legal effects

the naturalization and did not constitute a divorce ground under the law of their earlier home country. In our view, this case is not "external" and there is no reason to draw analogical conclusions from the conflict rules of the Act that would mean that certain Swedish citizens would come into a special situation from the point of view of matrimonial law. It should be observed, however, that although Sweden has maintained the principle of nationality, the legal effects of marriage with regard to proprietary rights may be governed by foreign law although both spouses are Swedish subjects. This result, when it occurs, is due to the rule in sec. 1, subsec. 2 of the 1912 Act, where it is laid down that changes of the nationality of either or both spouses after marriage has been contracted has no effect upon the applicable law in this respect. Cf. below, pp. 151 ff.

[109] It is also possible that the convention would be applicable only to spouses who are citizens in a state party to the convention.

of marriage, and it would be even more difficult today to attempt a survey of "general" rules outside the 1912 Act. It seems that in reality this Act embodies the general Swedish rules.[110] Karlgren states that "the principles established by the Act would seem to be widely applicable by analogy to other states" besides those which are parties to the Convention.[111] However, the Inter-Nordic rules on the legal effects of marriage—which are found in the Royal Ordinance of 1931—are different from those laid down in the 1912 Act.

The rules of the 1937 Act have been given universal applicability. This statute also grants the King in Council the right to introduce certain exceptions from the statutory rules upon agreement with foreign powers. This power was once used in a limited extent, as the result of an agreement with France. As for the Nordic countries, it is expressly stated in the 1937 Act that special rules, viz. those embodied in the 1935 Act, are applicable to the estates of Nordic citizens domiciled in Sweden.

The field of application of the main 1935 Nordic Act appears from section 1 of the Act. The Act is applicable to questions of intestate succession, wills, administration of estates, dissolution of the matrimonial community of property and distribution of assets in deceased person's estates in those cases where the deceased was a Danish, Finnish, Icelandic or Norwegian citizen and domiciled in Sweden at the time of his death. Of course, a Nordic citizen may leave property in Sweden without being domiciled in this country at his death. If such person was domiciled in another Nordic country, the estate falls under the rules of the Act of 1 March 1935 on the estates of deceased persons who were domiciled in Denmark, Finland, Iceland or Norway. In other words, the Convention and the Acts contain a complete system of rules applicable to those cases where a citizen of one of the Nordic countries dies domiciled in any of these states.[112] On the other hand, if a Norwegian who leaves property in Sweden was domiciled in Paris or Toronto at his death, the case falls outside the scope of the 1935 legislation. The general rules contained in the 1937 Act will have to be applied.

[110] Cf. 1931 *N.J.A.* 495, discussed below, pp. 151 ff.

[111] Karlgren, p. 37; cf., however, Undén, pp. 109 ff.

[112] The provisions of the convention and the statutes respecting wills are not quite exhaustive. (Cf. Bentzon in *T.f.R.* 1934, pp. 339 and 360 ff.) It may occur, therefore, under certain circumstances, that a question concerning the estate of a deceased citizen of one of the Nordic countries domiciled in Sweden must be

According to its introductory provisions, the Royal Ordinance adopted in 1931, concerns questions of marriage, adoption, and guardianship. Its rules shall be applied "in relation to Denmark, Finland, Iceland and Norway." These words merely contain a general indication of the field of application of the Ordinance. To determine whether a particular case belongs to the Inter-Nordic system, the various single rules must be consulted. Thus it appears from section 3 that the Ordinance is applicable to the legal effects of marriage upon the proprietary rights of the spouses if each was a citizen of a Nordic state at the time of marriage and they thereupon took up domicile in such a state. If any of these requirements is not fulfilled, the 1912 Act is applicable instead. The same distinction is drawn with regard to marriage settlements and decrees for the dissolution of the matrimonial community of property. On the other hand, the rules of the 1931 Ordinance are applicable to divorce actions as soon as the spouses are citizens of a Nordic country. As for annulment, section 10 makes the applicability of the Ordinance more restricted. Both the criterion of nationality and that of domicile are used to determine the applicability of the 1931 enactment to adoption and guardianship. In other words: the spheres of application of

decided under "general" rules of private international law. In sec. 9 of the 1935 Act it is laid down that the will of a person "who was, at his death, a citizen in a signatory state and domiciled in such state" shall be held formally valid if it was made in accordance with the law of that signatory state, where it was written or where the testator was domiciled or had citizenship at the time of making. The language of the Act seems to imply that a will made in Belgium and in accordance with the formal requirements of Belgian law by a Dane domiciled in Sweden would not be held valid if the formal conditions of Danish or Swedish law had not been fulfilled. In fact, however, this case cannot be considered to be dealt with in the 1935 Act; the question of validity must therefore be answered in the light of "general" rules, i.e. chap. 1, sec. 4 of the 1937 Act, where it is provided that a will shall be considered formally valid if made in accordance with the law of the place where the document was made or of the state of which the testator was a subject. The converse construction of the 1935 Act would imply a discrimination which cannot have been intended. (Cf. Bentzon, *op. cit.*, på 362, Borum, p. 134, and Philip in *Recueil* 1958, p. 313.) The importance of the enactment in the 1935 Act is that in Inter-Nordic relations it admits the validity of a will also where it was made in accordance with the formal conditions of the country where the testator was *domiciled* at the time of making. Thus if a Dane domiciled in Iceland has made a will in accordance wih the formal requirements of Icelandic law when on a visit to Stockholm the will shall be considered formally valid even if Swedish and Danish formal rules have not been observed; this would not be the case under "general" rules.

the Inter-Nordic rules now discussed are determined by means of an analysis of the text in each case. If the conditions set out in the text are not fulfilled, e.g. with regard to citizenship or domicile, the Ordinance of 1931 is simply not applicable, and the general rules in the 1904 or 1912 Acts must be applied.

B. JUDICIAL DECISIONS

The decisions of courts assume a particular importance in the law of conflicts where legislation is scarce. In many departments of private international law, and especially in the fields of contract and property in general, conflict rules have been developed through precedents.

However, it is not easy to determine the value of a court decision as a precedent. In other fields of the law, there is written, relatively modern and complete legislation, which is usually based upon good *travaux préparatoires*. Law-making follows a considered programme of legislative policy and rests on a traditional system of legal concepts. Judicial decisions here play the important rôle of clarifying the details of an area the rough outlines of which are already known, and of leading legal development towards a destination which is largely known. Thus, when rendered in the fields of statutory law, judicial decisions have a final character. They make clear, e.g., what is meant in chapter 11 : 3 of the Marriage Code, where the "resumption" of married life between spouses who have been granted a decree of separation is referred to (1939 *N.J.A.* 48; 1945 *N.J.A.* 260 and 1947 *N.J.A.* 359). They give a precise meaning to the words "within thirty days before" a petition for adjudication in bankruptcy was filed (sec. 30 of the Bankruptcy Act; 1955 *N.J.A.* 441). In private international law we have to do without the firm foundation which, in other fields of law, is made up of statutes, established concepts and a legislative programme resting on generally accepted policy. The territory is not explored, and the relatively few isolated decisions which have been rendered cannot serve as connecting links between well-known mileposts. Precedents do exist, since courts have been confronted by problems which, as in duty bound, they have had to decide upon. If the courts always try to find the reasonable decision *in casu,* then these decisions must seem, from the point of view of later judges looking for precedents, little more than traces in the sand which the wind blots out. If, on the other hand, the decisions of courts constitute a free creation of law according to the method described by Gény as *libre recherche scientifique,*[113] then they should be considered almost as legislative enactments and carry considerable authority. There are certainly decisions of both kinds, but courts have but occasionally or imperfectly, been able to pay any regard to their own wish to lay down the law for the future as distinct from the need for reaching a just decision in a concrete action. It follows from this antithesis that precedents must be interpreted with the greatest caution in those cases where the court has had to "find the law" without any guidance from written law or custom. In those cases where judicial precedents in the field of private international law are based upon a construction of statutes, they should also be interpreted cautiously; for frequently—in fact, usually—they are interpretations of expressions in enactments which the lapse of time appears to have made obsolete.

We have, when making the foregoing remarks, had Swedish case law, Swedish judicial decisions in mind. It is an essential point to remember when studying Swedish decisions that the doctrine of *stare decisis* is not a part of Swedish law. The Supreme Court is not bound by its own previous decisions, nor are lower courts legally obliged to apply, in their decisions, a "law" previously laid down by the Court in a similar or even identical case. The Supreme Court is, of course, anxious to be consistent and the lower courts normally follow its decisions.[114] But the very fact that it is not the task of the Supreme Court to develop or elucidate the law by distinguishing cases from one another but only to decide the case actually *sub judice,* explains why the Court shows reserve towards "unnecessary" comments on the law bearing upon matters outside the case. A Danish writer has said that, whereas in doubtful cases courts outside Scandinavia often formulate their grounds as a syllogism in which both the applicable rule of law and the facts sub-

[113] On this problem, vide O. A. Germann, "Zum Verhältnis zwischen Rechtsquellen und Rechtsfindung," in *Festschrift Hans Lewald,* Basel 1953, 485 ff.

[114] It could be said of Sweden today, as was said by Baron Hume of Scottish law at the end of the eighteenth century: "The authority of precedents as a part of our law certainly is not established but . . . they ought to have much weight . . . A judge on this account will often decide according to precedents in preference of his own opinion, though he will not be guilty of a breach of duty if he swerves from them." Quoted from T. B. Smith, *The Doctrine of Judicial Precedent in Scots Law,* Edinburgh 1952, pp. 9 f. Cf. Schmidt, "Construction of statutes," *Scandinavian Studies in Law* 1957, p. 167.

sumed under the rule are established, Scandinavian courts often do not mention the rules of law they have had recourse to. They seem to mention only the facts that seem relevant. "The reader is left to find out for himself which contact is decisive *prima facie,* which rule applies."[115] Even such far-reaching reticence can be understood with respect to the courts in a country where the "need for certainty," which according to Goodhart is both the cause and the justification for the English doctrine of precedent,[116] is satisfied by the system of codification. But in the very special field of private international law, where statutory regulation is less complete than in the field of private law in general and where the existing written rules are to a large extent outmoded and difficult to construe, a less reticent attitude on the part of the courts would be desirable. Some of the cases which will be discussed later seem to bear out this statement.

Most decisions referred to in the present book and included in the table of cases were rendered by the Swedish Supreme Court. It must be pointed out, however, that judgments from the courts below may also be of considerable interest. Particular importance must be attached to the decisions of the Stockholm Court of Appeal on questions concerning the recognition of foreign divorce decrees and the granting of *exequatur* to foreign judgments under special enactments. In the field of family law, the decisions of the city courts in the largest cities are often valuable sources.[117] The habits of construction developed by the various authorities which deal with the registration of inhabitants have hardly been studied at all. Administrative practice by other authorities is also likely to provide information about the "living law".

Nor are foreign decisions devoid of interest. In many countries, the situation is identical with that prevailing in Sweden. Questions come up in practice to which no attention has been paid in written law or which in many different ways present unforeseen complications. The courts have had to make decisions, and the way in which these problems have been dealt with abroad may provide some guidance for the treatment

[115] Lando, "Scandinavian conflict of law rules respecting contracts," 6 *American Journal of Comparative Law,* (1957), pp. 7 f.

[116] Cf. Goodhart, "Precedent in English and continental law," *Law Quarterly Review,* Vol. 50, pp. 40 ff.

[117] *Vide* e.g. Rosén, "Något om utländska dödförklaringars giltighet," *Sv.J.T.* 1959, p. 43.

of similar questions in Sweden. Lastly, decisions by international judicial bodies may also be of interest.[118]

Surveys of decisions in the field of private international law have been published in *Svensk Juristtidning:* 1937, pp. 374 ff. (for the period 1931—1935); 1942, pp. 399 ff. (for the period 1936—1940); 1950, pp. 35 ff. (for the period 1941—1948) and 1956, pp. 401 ff and 1961, pp. 646 ff. (for the period 1949—1960). Court practice is examined by Beckman in *Svensk domstolspraxis i internationell rätt,* Stockholm 1959. For the purpose of teaching, hectographed casebooks have been published by Malmström[119] and Eek[120]

C. LEGAL WRITING

Swedish writing in the field of private international law is not very extensive. Even if an increased interest in the theoretical treatment of the conflict of laws has been apparent lately, it is hardly possible to find a continuous scientific discussion, a *doctrine* in the French or German sense. It is also obvious that the views upon the fundamental questions of this branch of the law have changed, and that within Swedish conflict literature, at least before Professor Torsten Gihl published his first works, it was impossible to find the conscious endeavour to confront diverging theoretical opinions with each other which helps towards the creation of a legal *doctrine* in the proper sense. It is likely that the courts met with some difficulty when they tried, with the assistance of legal writing, to follow a definite course in their decisions.[121]

There are few systematic surveys of private international law in Swedish legal literature. In the fields of contract, property and commercial law, however, there is Nial, *Internationell förmögenhetsrätt,* 2 ed. 1953. Mention should also be made of Michaeli, *Internationales Privatrecht* (in German), 1948. Karlgren, *Kortfattad lärobok i internationell privat- och processrätt,* 1960, is chiefly intended for use in teaching. In his *Föräldrabalken,* 1952, Mr. Justice Walin deals with

[118] *Vide* Niederer, pp. 107 ff.

[119] *Samling av uppsatser och rättsfall för studiet av internationell privaträtt,* Uppsala 1955.

[120] *Rättsfallssamling i internationell privaträtt,* Stockholm 1962.

[121] Cf. on the influence of legal writing upon the decisions of courts below, pp. 106 ff.

international questions concerning the personal relations between parents and children, infancy and interdiction.

It is not uncommon that older works must also be consulted in order to get a perspective upon the problems under consideration. For this purpose, the whole field of private international law may be studied in Reuterskiöld, *Handbok i svensk privat internationell rätt,* 2 ed. 1912. Early works on family law are Undén, *Studier i internationell äktenskapsrätt,* I and II, 1913, and a more recent survey by the same author, *Internationell äktenskapsrätt,* 1922. Special sections in works on internal private law should also be consulted.

Swedish conflict writing comprises few scientific monographs. Hult, *Föräldrar och barn enligt svensk internationell privaträtt,* 1943, and Hjerner, *Främmande valutalag och internationell privaträtt,* 1956, do however belong to this category. Ramel's treatise *Studier i svensk internationell arvsrätt,* 1930, deals with the law of succession as it was before the introduction of the 1937 Act. Strömholm, *Torts in the Conflict of Laws,* 1961, has a comparative purpose.

There is no systematical survey of the whole field of international procedural law. This subject is discussed *passim* in Kallenberg's great textbook on procedure, *Svensk civilprocessrätt,* and in other general works on civil procedure and articles on special questions. A pioneer work and a systematic study of an essential part of the international law of procedure is Mr. Justice Dennemark's work on the Swedish rules of jurisdiction, *Om svensk domstols behörighet i internationellt förmögenhetsrättsliga mål,* 1961.

Fundamental theoretical problems are analysed by Gihl in *Den internationella privaträttens historia och allmänna principer,* 1951, and in *Studier i internationell rätt,* 1955. A special problem in the theory of conflict law—the question of classification, to which we shall return later on—is dealt with by Malmström in *Det s. k. kvalifikationsproblemet inom internationell privaträtt,* 1938. In later years, a theoretical debate of some intensity concerning fundamental problems has been going on in Scandinavian legal periodicals. Several papers in the *Liber Amicorum of Congratulations to Algot Bagge,* 1955, are of great interest.

Detailed information about available conflict literature is found in Mr. Justice Regner's great bibliographical work *Svensk juridisk bibliografi,* 1957. When making use of a work on the conflict of laws, the reader must always keep in mind from when it dates; the foreign sources referred to in the work may also contribute to the finding of an answer to the question how up to date the author's views are. Among the relatively few Swedish writers, the reader will soon be able to distinguish between those who are apt to give their works a practical, sometimes political, character, and those whose main interest is theoretical, i.e. the delineation of those legal phenomena which are commonly treated under the heading of private international law.

In the foregoing section of the present chapter we pointed out that foreign court decisions may sometimes be of use when trying to find solutions to conflict questions in Sweden, as the problems often are the same. It is only natural to make use of the total body of international experience. This statement is also true about foreign conflict literature. It may be particularly helpful when penetrating problems of a general order. Even if the Swedish Supreme Court rejected the doctrine of *renvoi* in the decision 1939 *N.J.A.* 96, it is by no means impossible that questions of *renvoi* may recur again. If so, it is natural for a Swedish lawyer to go to foregn writers for information about the topic. The same may be said concerning the question of the binding force of foreign judicial decisions; this problem is discussed, or at least touched upon, in Swedish legal periodicals, but study of foreign writing is indispensable for a full elucidation of the subject.

The number of works from other Scandinavian countries is not considerable. However, mention should be made of Borum, *Lovkonflikter,* 4 ed., 1957, which deals with Danish law, Ekström, *Sju internationellt privaträttsliga uppsatser,* 1920, which refers to conflict law in Finland, and—to some extent—in Sweden. In Norway Hambro has published *Jurisdiksjonsvalg og lovvalg,* 1957, a comparative work which is interesting because attention is paid to the interrelation between private international law and procedure. Recent works in Denmark are Philip, *Studier i den internationale selskapsrets teori,* 1961, and Lando, *Kontraktstatuttet,* 1962.

D. CONVENTIONS

A great number of conventions are important in one way or another in deciding international cases and in *jurisdictio voluntaria.* The most important conventions have already been discussed in the historical survey above or have been mentioned in the survey of written sources of private international law. The texts of treaties are found in the official series *Sveriges överenskommelser med främmande makter* (S.Ö.), where all treaties ratified by Sweden since 1912 have been published. Earlier treaties were published in *Svensk författningssamling* (S.F.S.). The texts of treaties can also be studied in the propositions requesting parliamentary approval. A list of treaties is found in the Calendar of the Royal Ministry for Foreign Affairs, where bilateral and multilateral agreements with other states, which are still in force, are listed chronologically. The information supplied by the Calendar is completed by accounts of new treaties in the yearly publication *Documents of Swedish Foreign Policy,* published in English by the Ministry for Foreign Affairs.

Treaty texts in addition to those ratified by Sweden are found in international treaty series. Nowadays, particular importance can be claimed by the *United Nations Treaty Series,* which contains agreements registered with the Secretariat; under article 102 of the Charter of the United Nations every treaty and every international agreement entered into by a member state shall be registered. This obligation is not always observed, however. In addition to the publication of texts, the United Nations issues periodical registers of treaties and monthly surveys of registrations. A serial calendar is also published containing information about ratifications or other accessions to multilateral conventions; its title is *Status of Multilateral Conventions of which the Secretary-General Acts as Depositary.*

With the ratification of a convention by Sweden and its coming into force—two dates which need not coincide—Sweden has a duty under the law of nations to observe the rules of the convention. Where these demand that a certain legal principle shall be applied by Swedish courts (or other authorities) whether it be a choice of law rule or a provision of substantive law, a statute or other instrument is usually enacted in Sweden to secure the application of the rule embodied in the international agreement. It might be argued, under these circumstances, that judges ought to be free from the task of examining the rules embodied in the convention; their canon should be the statutory text. It seems natural to assume that the legislature had seen to it that the convention is covered by the enactment in such manner that the duties arising out of the convention will be fulfilled if the internal enactment is applied. In actual practice, however, it appears that it is not always possible, and not even advisable, for the judge to stick merely to the language of the

Swedish legislation. In particular, it should be noted that such Swedish statutes as are based upon conventions have a specific function which must be considered when applying these statutes. If several states agree upon the adoption of a certain conflict rule or of uniform substantive rules, e.g. those embodied in the "Hague Act,"[122] the purpose of the agreement is that a certain type of dispute in private international law or maritime law shall be settled in the same way irrespective of the nationality of the court trying the action. Consequently, all courts in the states concerned should apply rules based upon the convention in the same manner. This presupposes an international method of construction; in a text founded upon a convention, the meaning of words is not necessarily exactly the same as in a purely internal enactment. Results of statutory construction which would seem obvious when deciding an internal case may also be questionable, and it is self-evident that the greatest caution must be observed when interpreting expressions of the kind exemplified by "apparent good order," "reasonable delay," "due care," "good faith", etc. This fundamental problem is not always clear to courts in all countries, and the directions embodied in national legislation do not always furnish any guidance in this respect. In some countries, however, e.g. in England, courts seem to have realized that the construction of a statute which comprises uniform international rules must be performed with due attention to the common interest of the signatory states in attaining real uniformity. In *Stag Line v. Foscolo Mango,*[123] which concerned the construction of an English statute, the Carriage of Goods by Sea Act, 1924, where the Hague rules are embodied, Lord Macmillan made the following statement on this question of principle:

> "It is important to remember that the Act of 1924 was the outcome of an International Conference and that the rules in the Schedule have an international currency. As those rules must come under the consideration of foreign Courts it is desirable in the interest of uniformity that their interpretation should not be rigidly controlled by domestic precedents of antecedent date, but

[122] The term "Hague Act" means the Act issued on 5 June, 1936, as a consequence of Sweden's accession to the international convention on bills of lading, 1924. The Hague Act amounts to a translation of the convention.

[123] [1932] A.C. 328, 350.

rather that the language of the rules should be construed on broad principles of general acceptation."[124]

In order to construe Swedish rules which have an "international currency" owing to the fact that they are based upon conventions, it is obvious that courts have to consult these international agreements. They must be regarded as sources of law in the administration of such rules.

Conventions as Sources of Law

Swedish courts regularly study the *travaux préparatoires* of statutes, including the convention texts, which are usually reprinted in Government propositions and elsewhere. Sometimes, these conventions furnish important guidance towards their own construction. Some examples may be taken from the so-called *Boll* case.[125] It does not appear from the Swedish Act on international questions concerning marriage, infancy and adoption, 1904, that the duties of guardians as set out in the Act concern both what is called guardianship in modern Swedish terminology, i.e. the representation of the infant in economic matters, and the duty to take care of the infant's person, but it appears from article 6 in the 1902 Convention; when construing and applying the 1904 Act, this fact must be taken into consideration. Nor does it appear from the Act that the obligation under the law of nations to apply the Convention is limited by the general provision in article 7 concerning "tous les cas d'urgence." This provision creates a possibili-

[124] Cf. Schmitthoff in *Law and Contemporary Problems,* Summer, 1956, pp. 434 ff. A conscious and consistent endeavour towards construction in an "international spirit" may be found in those contracts—it is true that they are not conventions—which were concluded in 1954 between the Government of Iran, the state-owned Iranian oil company, one Dutch, one British, one French and five American oil companies, on the exploiting of the Iranian oil-fields. Article 46 in the contract runs thus: "In view of the diverse nationalities of the parties to this Agreement, it shall be governed by and interpreted and applied in accordance with principles of law common to Iran and the several nations in which the other parties to this Agreement are incorporated, and in the absence of such common principles, then by and in accordance with principles of law recognised by civilized nations in general, including such of those principles as may have been applied by international tribunals." *Vide* Jessup, *Transnational Law,* New Haven 1956, pp. 14 f.—On a similar clause in the Iranian-Italian oil agreement of 1957, *vide* E. H. Wall in 7 *I.C.L.Q.* (1958), pp. 736 ff.

[125] *Vide* note 10 above.

ty to do what Swedish authorities actually did in the *Boll* case, but this possibility is not referred to in the 1904 Act; there the exception emboided in the Convention merely influenced the drafting of a rule in chapter 4: 3 second paragraph (the appointment of a temporary guardian with limited authority in urgent cases).

It is not always enough to read the convention text, however. It follows from the fact that Swedish statutory rules are sometimes intended to have an "international currency" that it may be necessary to take one step further and consider the *travaux préparatoires* of conventions. These are not always as easy to find for a judge as the text itself. From the Hague cooperation, however, there are *Actes* and *Documents* printed in the Hague since the first conference in 1893; similarly the preparatory material of conventions which have been drafted under the auspices of international organizations is regularly included in the documents or publications of such organizations.[126] Further, it may be advisable and practical for the judge to study the decisions of courts in the other member states on matters dealt with in the convention.[127] National courts of justice cannot avoid this troublesome task as long as states do not establish common courts for the decision of cases where uniform legislation is applicable.[128]

Swedish courts seem to pay increasingly great attention to the necessity of interpreting legislation based on conventions in an international spirit. Among reported Supreme Court decisions, particular mention should be made of 1955 *N.J.A.* 661, which concerned the validity of a general so-called invoice clause in a bill of lading under the Hague Act.[129] It appears from the very full dictum of Mr. Justice Romanus that international sources had been consulted to a very considerable extent. By way of introduction, Justice Romanus states that when con-

[126] *Vide* Eek, *Studiet av folkrätt,* pp. 62 ff. Cf. Eek, *Socialpolitiken inför internationellt forum,* 1951, pp. 96 ff.

[127] The need for such comparative studies has been one of the reasons for the creation of *Nordisk Domssamling,* a series of reports from all the Scandinavian countries. *Vide op. cit.,* first year (1959), pp. 1 f.

[128] Cf. Ellilä in *Sv.J.T.* 1959, pp. 351 ff. on the need for an Inter-Nordic advisory body on judicial matters. Vide further *Nordisk utredningsserie* 1961, No. 6 (Joint Nordic commission report series) and *Sv.J.T.* 1962, p. 501.

[129] Vide also 1951 *N.J.A.* 319, 1953 *N.J.A.* 488 and 1962 *N.J.A.* 305. A case of some interest is also 1954 *N.J.A.* 573, where the Supreme Court attached importance to the opinion prevailing in English law when construing a standard charter-party.

struing the Convention—which was what the Court had to do *in casu* —"attention should be paid not only to the *travaux préparatoires* but also to such opinions on the meaning of the Convention as had been expressed in foreign legislation, judicial decisions and writing." It has been argued that it would not be advisable to make this decision the basis of general conclusions with regard to the question to what extent Swedish courts construe conventions with the help of an international perspective.[130] That Swedish courts do give attention to conventions must be admitted, however; it is also noticeable that legal writers emphasize more than has been the case hitherto the necessity of construing and applying rules based on conventions in an international manner.

Difficulties arise, however, when trying to find the principles of construction applicable to conventions. In the first place, this is a problem for the law of nations: how shall the nature of the obligations assumed by a state which has acceded to a convention be determined? As the case may be, such construction of conventions is a task for the states themselves, for international courts and similar bodies or for national courts of justice. Thus the legal *milieu* in which various questions of construction are decided is heterogenous. Writers on the law of nations do not give much guidance. Their opinions vary within a field comprising the most divergent solutions: on the one hand, it is recommended that since conventions are contracts between states, the methods of construction with regard to internal contracts developed within these states should be used, on the other hand it has been suggested that a so-called teleological method be resorted to.[131] It should be pointed out, however, that the United Nations International Law Commission, which has worked on codification of the "law of treaties" for a number of years, in 1964 examined also examine the problem of construction of conventions. It should further be observed that the questions of this kind which have regularly been brought before national courts of justice, i.e. those which concern various rules of uniform private law, are clearly different, in the typical cases, from the questions arising where other conventions are concerned. It does not seem impossible to attain a more farreaching international harmony on the judicial method applicable to questions in the first group mentioned than that applicable to the second group. No attempt will be made here to give

[130] Grönfors in *Sv.J.T.* 1957, p. 19.

[131] See Gihl, *Huvuddragen av den allmänna folkrätten,* 1956, pp. 204 f.

a recipe for the interpretation of conventions. Two points should be made, however: first, the *travaux préparatoires* of multilateral conventions are not at all comparable to the legislative material used by Swedish courts in other connections, and must be handled with the greatest caution, particularly when they belong to conventions created at international conferences.[132] Secondly, there is a problem which may occasionally confront a national court of justice, namely when one of the parties argues that a choice of law rule based on a convention should be set aside since it would result in application of a law incompatible with the public policy of the *forum.*[133]

Disharmony between Conventions and Statutes. Direct Application of Conventions

So far we have been discussing the construction and application of Swedish law as based upon conventions. In these cases, there is a Swedish source to be consulted in the first place, and the convention with its *travaux préparatoires* comes into consideration only as an auxiliary source intended to make possible, or facilitate, an application of the Swedish statute in the spirit of the convention.

An entirely different situation occurs where Sweden is bound by a convention but no Swedish enactment embodying the conventional rules has been passed, or where the provisions of a convention which is binding under the law of nations do not harmonize with the rules of a Swedish enactment. We shall not engage in the discussion about the "dualistic" and "monistic" schools of thought in public international law or about the conclusions drawn by either school with regard to the relation between a duty binding upon a state under the law of nations and the municipal law of such state. The question we shall put is another, viz. whether Swedish public law contains a principle under which courts and other authorities have to consider a convention as a source of municipal law even where no internal legislation has been passed, or whether such application of international agreements pre-

[132] On the reasons for this, cf. Grönfors, *loc.cit.,* at p. 20. *Vide* also Hjerner, pp. 37 ff., on the construction of article VIII of the Statute of the International Monetary Fund, and Dölle in 26 *Rabels Z.* 1961, pp. 4 ff. on conventions drafted in more than one language.

[133] Cf. Eek in *Sv.J.T.* 1959, pp. 571 ff. on the question whether the law of nations admits arguments of public policy against the performance of a treaty obligation.

supposes a specific enactment (so-called "transformation"). There are no written rules on this subject in the Swedish Constitution or in any other enactment. However, a few judicial decisions support the view that no transformation is required and that conventional rules should be applied by the courts even in the absence of enactments to that effect.[134] In Swedish legal writing, statements by Undén and Sundberg can be cited in favour of this view.[135] Legislative practice does not contradict their opinion; it would seem that considerations of a purely practical nature have determined the question whether internal legislation is to be adopted as a consequence of conventions.[136]

Thus it may occur that a court or other authority has to apply conventional rules directly. The first prerequisite for such application is obviously that the convention has been brought to general knowledge; in Sweden, this is regularly performed by pulication in the treaty series, *Sveriges överenskommelser med främmande makter*. In actual practice, immediate application is not very frequent and need not carry with it insurmountable difficulties. An entirely different situation exists where a Swedish statute and the rules of a convention are incompatible. The constitutions of many states contain rules relating to this problem, usually to the effect that municipal law must surrender to the conven-

[134] 1892 *N.J.A.* 377 and 1930 *N.J.A.* 78. The case 1955 *N.J.A.* 661, which has already been discussed above, also provides some support.

[135] Undén, *Studier i internationell äktenskapsrätt* I, 1913, pp. 3 f.; Sundberg, *Lag och Traktat*, 1942, pp. 49 ff. The opposite opinion is held by Eng in *N.T.I.R.* 1938, pp. 101 ff.; the writer states that whereas treaties were earlier considered as "statutory instruments" in the sense of Article 47 of the Constitution of 1809, this is no longer the case. *Vide* also Gihl, *Principer,* pp. 296 f., where the public law problem is not considered, however. Hassler and Nial, on p. 13, attack Undén's opinion with the argument that the authorities of a state "must obey its laws when they are enacted in the order provided for by the Constitution." Mr. Justice Beckman, on p. 40, states: "The fact that Sweden has acceded to a convention is something to which Swedish courts are not normally bound to pay any attention unless municipal enactments have been passed on the topic." The word "normally" seems to indicate that the writer does not find any constitutional obstacle to the immediate application of a convention.

[136] Cf. Sundberg, *op.cit.,* pp. 42 ff. Eng's conclusions from legislative usages are too far-reaching (*op.cit.,* pp. 101 ff.) The fact that practical considerations have prevailed and occasionally resulted in imperfect statutory rules would rather seem to support the interpretation that both the Executive and the Legislature have taken a stand against the idea of the necessity of "transformation" Cf. e.g. the relation between the Extradition Act, 1913, and the conventions on the same matter with Norway, 1907, with Denmark, 1913, and with Finland, 1923.

tion, but there is no written rule on this question in Swedish public law. Whereas the statements of Undén quoted above implied that the convention must be granted precedence, Mr. Justice Beckman has said that "under an old rule" internal law remains the victor. [137] This view is not shared by Sundberg.[138]

In actual practice national courts confronted by such conflicts tend to make conventional and statutory rules harmonize by means of ordinary methods of construction. It is presumed that the statutory rule was not intended to be incompatible with the treaty rule.[139] In some cases, however, such harmonizing constructions have been out of the question. This is particularly obvious where a national enactment clearly seems to require the non-application of certain provisions of a convention, which are, in themselves, binding under the law of nations.[140] When discussing these matters in Swedish law, it is customary to refer to the case 1925 *N.J.A.* 655. The Royal Railway Board had ordered, in obedience to a Royal decree, that the freight for goods dispatched to certain railway stations in Denmark should be paid at the Swedish station from which the goods were sent. This rule was incompatible with the provisions of the international agreement on carriage of goods by rail, 14 October 1890, to which Denmark and Sweden had acceded. As a consequence of the order issued by the Railway Board, a person had had to pay freight in Swedish crowns for that part of carriage which took place in Denmark. He instituted an action to recover an amount corresponding to the difference in rates of exchange. The Supreme Court unanimously held that "by using the services of the Swedish railway administration for the transport concerned, the plaintiff had submitted to the conditions established by the King in Council for such transport irrespective of the question whether these conditions were in harmony with the provisions of the international convention on carriage of goods by rail". It is highly doubtful that this isolated

[137] Beckman, *loc. cit.*

[138] Sundberg, *Folkrätt*, 2 ed. 1950, p. 15.

[139] Cf. Eek, p. 33 with note 4. Grenander (*op.cit.*, pp. 84 f.) gives the following example from Norwegian law: "When the limitation convention was incorporated into Norwegian law, the legislator forgot to make a corresponding alteration in the rules on collision liability in Art. 222 of the Norwegian maritime code. In case of collision the ship would, in spite of the convention rules, form the limit of the shipowner's liability. The Norwegian Supreme Court, however, interpreted the legislation in accordance with the convention rules."

[140] *Vide* the examples given by Grenander, *op.cit.*, pp. 77 and 83.

forty-year old decision can be regarded as authority for the view that the King in Council is entitled under the Constitution to decree that some part or parts of a valid convention shall not be applied.[141] It even seems probable that today, the result of an action identical to the case from 1925 would be different. The 1925 decision should further be compared with 1953 *N.J.A.* 488; here a provision adopted in 1944 amending the Water Act, 1919, was set aside as being incompatible with art. 8 in the 1929 Convention between Norway and Sweden on the right to waters flowing through both countries. If, on the other hand, in an individual case, it were quite clear that a certain legal provision was actually intended to prevent the application of a convention, it would be hard to argue that such provision would unconditionally be void of effect. Under the Constitution such a provision could be adopted by the Government without the requirement of parliamentary approval, and would simply express the Government's opinion that for one reason or another the convention was no longer in force.[142]

E. THE LAW CF NATIONS

On various occasions, Swedish courts have based their decisions upon rules of the law of nations which have been considered part of the law of Sweden without any formal "transformation." In the decision 1942 *N.J.A.* 65, for instance, there are judicial *dicta* which imply that in questions concerned with the basic principles of public international law—here the rules relating to immunities—Swedish law coincides with the law prevailing in countries with a cultural tradition similar to Sweden's unless there are quite convincing reasons for assuming the contrary. In 1946 *N.J.A.* 65, the Supreme Court invoked "principles of public international law" which—it was stated—"are applicable also under the law of Sweden." The case concerned criminal jurisdiction.[143]

[141] Cf. Hassler and Nial, p. 14.—In *Lag och traktat,* p. 61, Sundberg states that it is possible "that the legal relationship between the railway and the freighter was considered from the aspect of private law." However, the author further holds that "by this decision, the Swedish courts must be considered to have taken the position that an internal enactment shall take precedence over an earlier treaty."

[142] Cf. Eek in *Stv.T.* 1954, p. 388.

[143] Cf. Eek, pp. 124 f.

Thus the general law of nations must be included among the sources of private international law. This is true particularly in respect of the immunity rules. However, certain principles embodying a "civilized" standard for the treatment of aliens must also be observed; they comprise protection of property, access to courts, recognition of status etc.[144]

[144] Eek, *op.cit.*, pp. 81 ff. and 129 ff. and in *Scandinavian Studies in Law*, 1959, particularly at pp. 42 ff. Notice also the situation in the cases cited by Hjerner in *Sv.J.T.* 1956, pp. 26 ff.

Chapter II
The Material

§ 4. General Observations on the Nature of the Material

In the present chapter we shall deal with the material of private international law, i.e. the various types of rules within this branch of the law; among these rules we have already made a distinction between choice of law rules and provisions belonging to the "law of aliens." A more convenient term for the latter category may be "external substantive rules," since it does not only comprise rules about aliens but the most varied kinds of rules applicable to legal relations which have some connection with foreign countries, e.g. legislation on currency or prohibiting Swedish citizens from contracting marriages abroad "unless entitled to marry under Swedish law" (chap. 1, sec. 1 of the Act on international questions concerning marriage etc., 1904). In actual practice, there is a close relation between the various types of rules which are relevant in actions (and other legal matters handled by courts or other public agencies) having some connection with foreign countries, i.e. what we have called external or international legal matters.

Analysis of the structure of the various types of rules would seem essential to their classification. Some times, however, it may be difficult to assign a rule to one or the other category. At any rate, opinions may differ concerning the group to which it belongs. The reason for this is that strictly speaking the difference is not found in the rules themselves but rather in two different functions. Rules fulfilling the purely formal function of providing for the application of substantive rules from a foreign legal system are choice of law rules, whereas rules which have the function of deciding external questions immediately are external substantive rules. It may happen that the significance of a legal rule, its intended function, does not appear very clearly, or that the rule could function in different ways. As a consequence difficulties may arise in the application of the law. Some examples follow.

If an alien (who is not a citizen of a Nordic state domiciled in one of these states) applies to a Swedish court of justice for an order of adoption, the first question which the court has to answer is whether such an alien is entitled to adopt in Sweden. This is a problem dealt with in the Swedish substantive rules on foreigners; it is the type of rule which belongs to the "law of aliens." The answer is found in chapter 6, section 1, of the 1904 Act, according to which an adoption is permissible if it is "valid" in the state to which the alien belongs, i.e. of which he is a citizen. The Swedish courts, however, have added one more condition: an alien who is not domiciled in Sweden is not entitled to adopt in this country. From the aspect of legal technique, however, this rule appears in the form of a jurisdiction rule: a Swedish court does not consider the application if the alien has no domicile in Sweden.[1] When this question belonging to the law of aliens has been answered in the affirmative, the conflict question arises: under what law shall the application for an adoption order be tried? Shall the conditions laid down in Swedish law (chap. 4 of the Parents and Children Code, 1949) be applied, or shall the court use substantive rules from the applicant's or even the child's national laws? In fact, Swedish courts apply Swedish law, although this is not clearly prescribed in the 1904 Act.[2] But if the applicant, or the child, is an alien, there is, as already mentioned, one further condition for an order of adoption in addition to those set out in the Swedish Parents and Children Code, viz. that the "adoption is valid" (the order of adoption will be recognized) in the state or states of which the applicant and/or the child is a national. Is the latter condition a conflict rule which orders the application of the conditions for adoption embodied in foreign private law? That is not really the case. The Swedish court does not really apply foreign law. It simply accepts an authoritative statement from the Swedish Ministry for Foreign Affairs or from an authority in the alien's home country to the effect that the order of adoption will be recognized there. The rules of the foreign legal system on recognition are not necessarily based upon its substantive adoption rules; they may also have the same form as the Swedish rules, i.e. require the permission of the government.[3] If

[1] 1947 *N.J.A.* 164.

[2] Cf. 1950 *N.J.A.* 379 and Walin, *Föräldrabalken,* 1952, p. 562. Hassler, *Internationella adoptivförhållanden,* 1923, seems to hold a different opinion; *vide* e.g. pp. 51 ff.

[3] That is the case e.g. in Finland, *Sv.J.T.* 1942, pp. 551 f. On these questions *vide* Hallenborg in *Sv.J.T.* 1939, pp. 600 ff. and more recently, *Internationella adoptionsärenden,* Acts of the Swedish Foreign Office, New Series II: 14,

the applicant cannot produce an official statement that the order will be recognized or formal permission by a competent authority in his home country, he has not fulfilled the additional substantive condition laid down by Swedish law with regards to aliens, and his application must be refused. It is possible, however, that he can produce evidence of a rule in his national law providing that a foreign order of adoption will be recognized if the conditions for adoption embodied in the legislation of the home country have been observed. In such a case a Swedish court might have reasons for considering the question whether the facts of the case are such that an order of adoption would be granted in the alien's home country. The 1904 Act, however, does not directly prescribe such a course of action. On the other hand, if the order is not granted because some condition of foreign law has not been fulfilled, the ground for refusal is that under these circumstances a Swedish order of adoption would not be recognized, and that a condition in the 1904 Act which belongs to the law of aliens has not been fulfilled. If the examination resulted in the finding that both the Swedish and the foreign conditions were fulfilled and if the order were consequently granted, it would be based, in principle, upon the law of aliens as embodied in the rule in the 1904 Act. It should be admitted, though, that the situation arising in this case is so peculiar that it might also be described as a simultaneous application of Swedish and foreign adoption rules. The term "application of law" may be understood in more than one sense, and opinions may differ concerning the permissibility under the 1904 Act of the course which the court would have been following had it considered that in a certain situation the provision in the Act could fulfill the function of a choice of law rule.

The case reported in *Sv.J.T.* 1947 p. 22 illustrates the difficulties arising where such a function is ascribed to the rule. The action concerned the adoption of a Greek girl by Swedish spouses. It appeared from a statement by the legal department of the Swedish Ministry for Foreign Affairs that Greek law contained no explicit rule on the validity of an adoption outside Greece, that in the opinion of Greek legal writers the adoption would probably be recognized in Greece if the conditions of Greek law were observed, and that one of these was that the adopter

Stockholm 1961; the survey has been elaborated by L. Kellberg. On the practice of the Government in questions concerning permission for Swedes to adopt or to be adopted abroad, *vide* Wisén in *Sv.J.T.* 1961, pp. 741 ff., criticism by Eek, in *Sv.J.T.* 1962, pp. 751 ff. and reply by Wisén in *Sv.J.T.* 1963 pp. 49 ff.

must be at least fifty years old. One of the Swedish spouses had not reached that age, and the order was therefore refused by the city court on the ground that the adoption would not be valid in the state to which the child belonged. The Court of Appeal, where the matter was brought by the spouses, seems to have taken for granted that in the absence of a Greek legal rule on the recognition of an adoption of a Greek infant abroad, the Court had to examine the substantive Greek adoption rules; at least, the Court did not cite the opinion of the Greek scholars or any other Greek source in support of an assumption of an unwritten rule to this effect. The Court, in its decision, stated that one of the conditions of the Greek adoption rules had not been fulfilled since one of the spouses had not attained the age of fifty, but nevertheless concluded: "Under the circumstances found in the case and in consideration of the fact that the adoption is obviously in the child's interest, it must be assumed that it will be recognized in Greece." On these grounds, the order of adoption was granted. It is possible that the Court of Appeal considered that it had applied Greek law and used the rule in the 1904 Act (chap., 6, sec. 1) as a choice of law rule.[4] It seems more

[4] In the report, there are certain references to Hassler, *Internationella adoptivförhållanden,* which support this assumption. That writer often (e.g. pp. 45 f., 53) uses language which must be understood in the sense that the rule providing that a Swedish order of adoption may be granted only if it is recognized in the home country of the foreigner concerned is a choice of law rule by which the Swedish court shall apply the substantive rules on the conditions for an order of adoption in the personal law of the alien. This opinion is probably due to a misunderstanding of a statement by the Standing Royal Legislative Commission in the *travaux préparatoires.* Hasser writes (on p. 53) that the Commission "seems to have envisaged a cumulative application of both Swedish law and the foreign law applicable to the personal status of the alien." What the Commission has said, however, is only that the courts should observe the conditions laid down in foreign law for the *recognition* of the adoption. (*Vide* 1917 *N.J.A.* II, p. 518). —Hassler further holds that there is no difference in principle between a case where a Swedish court tries an application for an order of adoption in which an alien is engaged and a case where the King in Council (on hearing the Ministry of Justice) decides whether consent shall be granted to an adoption abroad where a Swedish citizen is concerned. The writer means (p. 49) that the latter decision shall depend upon the question whether the "conditions embodied in Swedish law" for an adoption to be granted are fulfilled or not. For the purpose of the examination in both cases, Hassler goes on to state, is "to secure the application of Swedish law with regard to the conditions of the intended adoption." In the present writer's opinion, the purpose of the recognition rules seems rather to be the prevention of situations where a person's status (adopted or not; adopter or

natural, however, to say that the Court of Appeal considered the statutory rule concerned a substantive provision and, in its construction, reduced the scope of the requirement of validity in the child's home country as a condition for an order of adoption; in fact, that requirement was not only reduced, it was set aside in favour of certain principles of Swedish law applicable to children.[5]

This example from the Swedish law of adoption concerns a case where it may be subject to serious discussion whether a statutory rule can serve, from a technical point of view, as a choice of law rule even though it has the appearance of a substantive provision; moreover it is open to question whether such use of the rule is permissible. Similar examples can be found in other fields of the law. In certain cases, the

not) is considered differently in different countries with which the person in question has some connections. It seems that the practice of the Ministry of Justice has followed the quasi-judicial method advocated by Hassler in a way which, in our view, is unfortunate (*vide* Wisén in *Sv.J.T.* 1961, pp. 741 ff.). However, the King's consent to an adoption abroad is not legally bound by the requirements for a Swedish adoption laid down in the Parents and Childrens Code, 1949. It is a question of administrative expediency. Considerations of the child's probable interests (if it is a Swede), and of the applicant's age and status (if that party is a Swede) may influence the decision. But it seems utterly purposeless to try to impose the whole set of substantive adoption rules in Swedish law on the foreign country where the adoption is to take place. Such a course of action only prevents international legal intercourse and favours no Swedish interests. The increasing influence of the principle of domicile provides further arguments against a nationalistic enforcement of Swedish adoption principles as an obstacle against the creation of adoptions under the law of foreign countries where Swedish citizens are domiciled.

[5] Our inerpretation is supported by the fact that the Court of Appeal rather loosely "assumed" that the adoption would be recognized in Greece; these words are put into the decision merely to comply with the actual *language* of the Act. Undoubtedly the decision is incompatible with the principle embodied in the enactment: that changes of status with regard to aliens shall be allowed only in so far as it is clear that they are recognized in the home country of the persons concerned.—It should be pointed out that the report in the *Sv.J.T.* does not contain any statements on the child's religion. The adoption rules of Greek private law are not applicable to the Mohammedan population. A Greek court does never allows an adoption of a person belonging to that category, since the institution of adoption is not only unknown to Moslem law but even clearly incompatible with the fundamental views of Moslem religion, under which an adoption cannot under any circumstances serve the "interests" of children. *Vide* decision from 1957 reported in *Revue Hellénique de Droit International,* 1958, pp. 164 ff. Cf. also above, p. 23.

problem also arises whether a legal provision is really a choice of law rule. The legislation on Swedish nationality contains substantive rules which determine who is to be considered a Swedish citizen. These provisions assume importance for the application of certain choice of law rules and therefore serve as answers to preliminary questions in relation to these rules, or as elements in their drafting. Thus, under the 1937 Act (chap. 1, sec. 1), "the right of intestate succession in the estate of a Swedish subject is governed by Swedish law," whereas the national law of the deceased is applicable if he was not a Swede. Notwithstanding the importance which nationality rules thus have for the law of conflicts, they cannot in themselves be regarded as choice of law rules.

Certain other provisions fulfil a similar function. In some cases the question is uncertain. An illustration will be given.

Corporations registered in Sweden are considered to be "Swedish", whereas such bodies incorporated abroad are "foreign" corporations. This distinction is important as an element in a number of choice of law rules in which it is laid down that such questions concerning limited companies as their legal personality, the right of representing them, the personal liability of shareholders, etc. are governed by the law of the country of incorporation which is called the "personal law" of the company. When it is said that a limited company incorporated in Sweden "is subject to Swedish law," this statement is founded upon this idea of a "personal law", in addition to the fact that those enactments in Swedish company law which are inspired by public policy considerations are applicable to such corporations.[6] This does not mean, however, that certain legal questions concerning Swedish companies—in particular with respect to contracts with an international element concluded by such companies—may not be governed by foreign law under Swedish choice of law rules.

In recent legislation, however, a provision should be noticed, which is found in section 4 of the Act on the right of foreign companies and other associations to do business in Sweden, 1955; in that provision it is laid down that with the authorization of the King in Council, a foreign enterprise may engage in its trade in Sweden through a subsidiary with independent management. That provision is worded as follows:

[6] Cf. Nial, p. 75.

"In respect of such subsidiary, the foreign corporation has to observe Swedish laws and statutory instruments. In all legal questions arising from the business of such subsidiary in Sweden, the corporation shall be subject to Swedish law and have a duty to submit to the jurisdiction of Swedish courts and to the decisions of Swedish authorities."

This provision should be compared with section 5 in the Act on the right of foreign insurance companies to do business in Sweden, 1950:

"In all legal questions arising from their business, foreign insurance companies engaged in the insurance trade in Sweden are subject to Swedish law and have to submit to the jurisdiction of Swedish courts and to the decisions of Swedish authorities."

The latter provision has served as the model for the rule in the 1955 Act.[7] The 1950 provision had been taken over from an Act on the same subject adopted in 1903; that Act, in its turn, had been taken almost verbatim from the 1886 Order in Council (sec. 3) on the conditions upon which foreign insurance establishments are allowed to do business in Sweden. The *travaux préparatoires* contain no information about the precise meaning of the statement that in legal questions arising from business in Sweden, foreign corporations "shall be subject

[7] Cf. *Royal Proposition* No. 87, 1955, p. 30.

[8] The Order in Council, 1886, was founded upon a proposal by a private association, the Insurance Society, founded in 1875, and upon an official report delivered by A. Sjöcrona who had been ordered to draft statutory instruments for the regulation of the insurance trade. In order to make it easier for the insured to enforce his claims, Sjöcrona suggested a rule to the effect that in all legal questions arising from the insurance business, foreign companies should have to submit to the jurisdiction of Swedish courts and to the decisions of such courts. A provision on this subject is embodied in Sjöcrona's draft. In its final text, however, the Order in Council of 1886 contained the additional words that the establishment should be "subject to Swedish law." In the published *travaux préparatoires* of the Order in Council, no reasons are given for this addition or modification—if it was intended as a modification *(Royal Propositon* No. 1, 1886, Ministry of Finance, pp. 44 f.). In the *travaux préparatoire* of the joint Inter-Nordic bill which became the 1903 Act, it is stated that the drafters wanted to ensure that "a foreign company shall be subject to Norwegian, Danish or Swedish law with regard to insurance contracts concluded in one of these countries with a subject of that country." (*Vide* Skarstedt, Lagen *om försäkringsrörelse m. m.,* 1918, p. 291). This statement is not wholly unequivocal, but it is of some interest to find that "business in Sweden" as a condition for the applicability of Swedish law seems to imply both that the contract of insurance has been concluded in Sweden and that the insured is a Swedish subject.

to be "Swedish." Its "personal law" is the law of Sweden. According the provision is no more than a statement, *ex tuto,* of the fact that Swedish public control rules are applicable to the business of a subsidiary within the realm and that such subsidiary is considered, in a general way, as a "Swedish" enterprise from a legal point of view. This would mean that in all cases where the "nationality" of a corporation is of importance for conflict purposes, the subsidiary shall be considered to be "Swedish." Its "personal law" is the law of Sweden. According to this construction, the provision does not, at least not in itself, determine the applicable law. That "Swedish law" to which the company "is subject" comprises also Swedish choice of law rules. Under the alternative construction the provision is really a provision on the choice of law in that it lays down that Swedish courts are not allowed to apply foreign substantive rules when deciding actions concerning the subsidiary, e.g. litigation about the construction of contracts concluded by the subsidiary within Sweden,[9] even in cases where the general choice of law rules of Swedish law would prescribe the application of foreign law, and in spite of the fact that these choice of law rules would be applied if the contract had been concluded by a purely Swedish company.

In Denmark, Professor Borum accepts the first alternative in construing a similar provision in section 77 of the Danish Limited Companies Act.[10] There is some support for this interpretation in a statement contained in the Swedish Government bill which became the 1955 Act,[11] but in another place in the bill, the correctness of the second construction seems to be taken for granted: "Swedish law shall . . . be the law applicable to the contract."[12] This distinction may seem academic since the normal result of the so called individualizing method of determining the law of the contract would be that a contract made in Sweden by a company which should be regarded as Swedish would be

An important condition for the applicability of the provision is obviously that the contract is really connected with business "within Sweden." *Vide,* on the meaning of the corresponding enactment with regard to foreign insurance companies, 1940 *N.J.A.* 62 and the earlier decisions 1920 *N.J.A.* 130 and 1923 *N.J.A.* 202; cf. also note 8 above.

[10] Borum, p. 183.

[11] *Royal Proposition* No. 87, 1955, p. 30.

[12] *Ibid.,* p. 56.

recognized as having its centre of gravity in Sweden.[13] However, the question assumes considerable importance when it must be decided whether a choice of law by the parties shall be recognized. Unquestionably, a Swedish company is at liberty to select a foreign law to govern a contract concluded within Sweden; such choice of law will normally be respected by Swedish courts. Suppose that the chosen law is the law of England, the other party to the contract is an Englishman, and delivery of goods or payment shall be performed in England. In these cases, does it follow from section 4 in the 1955 Act that the subsidiary of a foreign company is barred from making such agreement on the applicable law as is open to Swedish companies?[14] It is possible that the correct answer is that the position of the subsidiary is exceptional in that the permission to do business in Sweden is regarded as a special privilege and that the provision in section 4 is a control measure or one for the protection of Swedish interests.[15] However, the problem does not seem to have been analysed sufficiently by the drafters of the Act. Section 4 like other similar provisions undoubtedly gives rise to problems when the courts have to apply it.

By way of concluding the present section, which only serves as an introduction to the material, the attention is drawn to the importance of observing the territorial and personal limits of the applicability of national law. The application of chapter 5 in the Swedish Workers' Protection Act, 1949, is limited to certain persons: the chapter deals with "the employment of women." The 'Hague Act' (p. 58 above) is limited from a territorial point of view. According to its introduction it is applicable to carriage of goods by sea *from* Sweden to a foreign state. Where goods are transported *to* Sweden, the Act only covers transport from states which are parties to the International Convention relating

[13] Since contracts of insurance are so-called "mass contracts", i.e. concluded without individual variations between one company and a great number of persons, the presumption of Swedish conflict law that the domicile of the company determines the choice of law leads to the application of Swedish law.

[14] Similarly, the subsidiary would be barred from such contracts referring to foreign jurisdiction as Swedish limited companies are allowed to make, and possibly also from entering clauses on arbitrations abroad in their contracts. According to Borum *(loc. cit.)* there is no obstacle to arbitration clauses which discard the jurisdiction of courts.

[15] *Vide* Hassler and Nial, pp. 167 f., on the provision in insurance legislation; choice of law by the parties is not allowed since the legislation is intended to give insured Swedish subjects a benefit.

to Bills of Lading, 1924. Transport within the Nordic countries are excluded from the field of application of the Act. In other cases, an act or a single statutory provision contains no explicit statement on its sphere of applicability. Such cases give rise to a question: where the contrary is not stated, is a Swedish enactment applicable to all men, all things, and all events, irrespective of the location of such men, things or events, only the matter is brought before a Swedish court? The problem may be illustrated by a few examples. In chapter 9: 10 of the Swedish Commerical Code, there is a provision on the interest which a debtor has to pay if he does not observe the day of maturity of his debt. To judge from the language of the provision, it is not limited to Swedish debtors or creditors or the promissory notes issued or payable in Sweden. It must be assumed that the applicability of the rule is unlimited in principle, and that in actual practice, a Swedish court will refrain from using it only *where it follows from a choice of law rule* that Swedish law shall not apply in a specific action concerning interests for overdue debts which is brought before a competent Swedish court. In other cases, is is possible to find an implicit or hidden personal or territorial limitation in a legal provision. The Royal Ordinance on registration of titles to real property in court, 1875, refers to "anyone who acquires a title to real property" without any limitation, but what is meant is obviously only realty in Sweden. It is true that the Workers' Protection Act, 1949, concerns work performed "within Sweden," but the proper meaning of that expression in the Act cannot be established without some reflection.[16] According to section 1 of the Domestic Servants' Act, 1944, the Act is "applicable to contracts in which an employee undertakes to perform work, chiefly of a domestic character, in the employer's household." Is the Act specifically limited to work performed in Sweden or is it applicable, at least in principle, also to service outside Sweden (e.g. a Swedish servant's work for a Swedish family on a holiday trip abroad) provided only that Swedish private international law does not require that the legal relations of the parties are to be determined by foreign law?[17] The question whether there is an implicit

[16] According to Olsson and Starland, *Arbetarskyddslagstiftningen,* 1951, p. 19, Swedish territory for the purpose of the Workers' Protection Act includes Swedish ships on the high seas or in foreign ports. *Vide loc.cit.* about work on board Swedish aircraft and motor vehicles outside the country.

[17] Even if that were the case, however, the Swedish Act might claim observance. Cf. pp. 227 below.

or hidden limitation to the applicability of an enactment may always be raised, and it is important that the problem not be forgotten.[18]

Distinctions of this kind become important particularly when foreign law is applied. If a foreign enactment is limited in personal or territorial respects, it may be that according to its own wording it is not applicable to the case at bar. This question is particularly likely to arise with regard to foreign statutory provisions which establish prohibitions or control measures and fall on the border between private and public law. A foreign rule limiting the capacity of certain persons or bodies to receive testamentary bequests which, in principle, is applicable within Sweden, (chap. 1, sec. 9 of the 1937 Act) may be restricted to property situated in the country where such legislation is in force. Nullity rules in American law for the purpose of controlling transactions with negotiable instruments may define their own spheres of application in such a way that they have no bearing on certain litigation, for example in Swedish courts even though American law is otherwise *lex causae* in such actions.[19] We have chosen these examples as a warning. Where foreign law is applicable in principle, it is easy to overlook the fact that a certain rule must nevertheless be disregarded since it is subject to an implicit or hidden personal or territorial limitation. When this has been ascertained by a Swedish court, and the rule is duly set aside there has none the less been an application of foreign law, since the non-application of the rule follows from the foreign *lex causae*.—A different situation exists where a court refrains from applying foreign confiscatory legislation on the ground that such laws are "territorially limited." In such a case the claim to applicability of the foreign law may be well founded and the finding of the court merely constitutes a

[18] In principle, the Swedish Penal Code is universally applicable, but special rules limit the claims for applicability of Swedish penal provisions. On the other hand, penal rules in special enactments are often applicable only to acts committed in Sweden or by Swedish subjects. *Vide S.O.U.* 1953, No. 14, pp. 436 f., and 1960 *N.J.A.* 430; also Öhrbom in *Tidsskrift for Kriminalvidenskab* 1961, pp. 79 ff.

[19] On these so-called "blue sky laws" *vide* Louis Loss," The Conflict of Laws and the Blue Sky Laws," 71 *Harvard Law Review* (1957—58), pp. 219 f. Loss states that "in the blue sky cases the buyer typically alleges the violation of a particular statute, which often happens to be the forum's, and the question is not whether that statute applies in the face of some other governing law but simply whether it applies at all as a matter of statutory construction." Vide further Verzijl in *Ne.T.I.L.* 1961, p. 3 ff. Cf. also 1937 *N.J.A.* 261, at pp. 149 f. below

translation into the language of legal speculation of the fact that it does not want to render services to foreign powers in matters of confiscation.

§ 5. External Substantive Rules

A. THE LAW OF ALIENS, ETC.

In Sweden private international law as a branch of legal science is chiefly concerned with choice of law rules. The existence of many substantive rules belonging to the law of aliens must, however, be taken into consideration.[20] Where the problem is to determine the "personal law" of a negro girl aged six months and found in Sweden, at Arlanda airport, under circumstances which exclude any knowledge about her origin and *antecedentia,* it may be of some use to read the last words of section 1 in the Swedish Nationality Act, 1950, where it is laid down that "foundlings who are found within the country are considered to be Swedish citizens until the contrary has been proved." Above all, the rules of the law of aliens which are applicable within the fields of family law, contract and property must be taken into account for purposes of private international law; in the teaching of that subject, these rules are indeed usually given attention. Is an alien entitled to take a bequest under a will, and if so, upon what conditions? Is an alien entitled to adopt an infant or to acquire shares in a limited company? These are questions which must be put and answered.

Is Swedish legislation in this field exhaustive? Are there possibly unwritten rules or principles which carry restrictions upon the rights of aliens? These questions are likely to receive different answers from one case to another. Although the general trend of Swedish legislation concerning aliens is towards equal treatment of Swedes and foreigners and this legislation normally follows the form of prohibitive rules, it is unsafe to conclude that whatever is not explicitly prohibited for aliens is allowed on the same conditions as for Swedes. This conclusion might be justifiable in questions pertaining to the general law of persons or the defence of individual legal interests in general. Thus it might be

[20] In Sweden the law of aliens has never been considered an independent subject of study. An attempt towards this was made, however, by Kreüger in his work *Hufvuddragen af utländingars rättsförhållanden i Sverige,* 1876. Notice also Reuterskiöld in *Clunet* 1906.

argued that foreigners are entitled to inherit on the same terms as Swedes" even if there were no explicit rule to this effect in chapter 1 : 3 of the Inheritance Code, 1958.[21] In contract and property, particularly in those branches which are closely connected with regulation of trade, it is advisable to observe greater caution, and occasionally the historical development in the area concerned must be considered in deciding a question.[22] It should further be noted that the law of aliens is based upon conventions to a considerable extent, that the applicable provisions may be found in little known enactments which have been introduced as a consequence of conventions, that aliens from different countries are not necessarily treated in the same manner, and that conventions in this field are characterized by a special technique, which must be taken into consideration.[23]

There are obviously cases which require the application of rules belonging to the law of aliens but do not raise any conflict questions. Such

[21] The provision in chap. 1, sec. 3 of the Inheritance Code can be explained historically; it replaces chap. 15, secs. 1 and 2, in the original Inheritance Code, 1734. Moreover, it has the function of authorizing the King in Council to establish exceptions from the rule of equality as a measure of retaliation.

[22] In its original wording the Ordinance on the Freedom of Trade, 1864, did not at all mention justistic persons and was undoubtedly applicable only to physical persons. For a long time, it was subject to doubt whether a foreign company was or was not entitled to do business in Sweden. Although there was no explicit prohibition, it was held that no such right could be claimed. After the present sec. 32 was added in 1955 and after the introduction of the Act on the right of foreign companies and other associations to do business in Sweden, 1955, where subsidiaries are entitled to business transactions with the King's leave, it is quite clear, however, that the word "alien" in secs. 25 and 26 of the Ordinance on the Freedom of Trade must be interpreted, at least in principle, as a term comprising also foreign corporations. (On the defence of foreign corporation interests in spite of the earlier rules, *vide* Nial in *Festskrift till Herlitz,* 1955, pp. 238 ff.)—Under an Act from 1919 which constitutes an amendment to the Partnership Act, 1895, an alien requires the permission of the King in Council to be entitled to join a Swedish partnership. Is it permissible to conclude from this limited prohibition rule that an alien is entitled to join what is called a "simple partnership," i.e. an association without joint and several liability for debts, or to act as a sleeping partner not expressly named in the firm or articles of association? The question should probably be answered in the affirmative. Cf. Nial, *Om handelsbolag och enkla bolag,* 1955, pp. 63 f.

[23] *Vide* Eek, pp. 165 ff.

cases may concern private law, i.e. be treated as civil actions.[24] However, those cases where both external substantive rules and choice of law rules are involved are of particular interest. We have already mentioned the preliminary problem whether an alien has any right to adopt, to be appointed a guardian, etc. Rules belonging to the law of aliens may, however, be of importance also at later stages of an action. If as the outcome of an action concerning intestate succession before a Swedish court, an alien is granted a share in a Swedish ship, and if as a consequence of this transfer of title the ship ceases to be a Swedish ship, the alien will be compelled under a provision of section 5 of the Maritime Code to assign to a Swedish citizen a share in the ship of sufficient size for the ship to remain Swedish. The exchange regulations, which should be considered as external substantive rules, may also intervene as a corrective and thus influence the outcome of an action; this may serve as a further illustration of the combined application of several types of rules.[25] Another example is the substantive rule appearing in section 8:1, last sentence, of the 1934 Act on bankruptcy comprising property in other Scandinavian countries which involves a special regulation of the priority of payment and constitutes an exception from the choice of law rule in the sentence preceding it.

B. INTERNATIONAL PROCEDURAL LAW

The rules of international procedure belong to the category of external substantive rules. Proceedings before Swedish courts are governed by the Judicial Procedure Code.[26] The function of international proce-

[24] In 1953 *N.J.A.* 99, the validity of a contract of association was put into question. The decisive problem was whether the relationship between the parties was to be considered as a partnership or as that form of cooperation known in Swedish law as a "silent partnership," where the sleeping partner is undisclosed and the business is conducted as if it were the other party's property. The Supreme Court found that the contract was an agreement on a regular partnership; as such it was void, since the contract had been made without such authorization for aliens to join Swedish partnerships as is required under the 1916 amendment to the Act on partnerships and simple partnerships, 1895. Cf. Nial, *Om handelsbolag och enkla bolag,* pp. 63 f. and p. 438.

[25] Vide further below, pp. 224 ff.

[26] It should be noticed that in some cases, foreign procedural rules may assume importance in Swedish courts. Thus it is laid down in an Order in Council from 1909 (to be found after chap. 33 of the Judicial Procedure Code in the Statute-

dural law, therefore, is not to indicate the foreign law which is applicable to certain questions but to solve special problems created by international intercourse. These rules concern the position of aliens in Swedish procedure: the duty of bail for costs which may be imposed upon them, their right to legal aid, etc. Further there are rules on mutual assistance between states in legal matters, i.e. on such assistance as shall be granted foreign authorities in this country and the manner in which Swedish authorities shall call for the assistance of foreign authorities.[27] The general attitude to foreign judgements and decisions by other public authorities is particularly important in international procedural law. The rules on Swedish international jurisdiction or the "competence" of Swedish courts are also of fundamental importance. These rules determine whether Swedish courts shall admit an action which does not appear to be "Swedish" or chiefly Swedish. Like other provisions in the field of international procedure, these rules are not concerned with the question of the applicable law. They do not deal with the question under what national legal system an action "belongs" but simply determine whether the matter is actionable in a *Swedish* court or not. As will be pointed out presently, the existence or absence of a foreign court which has jurisdiction in the case may assume some importance when answering this question.

Certain procedural rules are based upon concepts and distinctions of private law. Thus it is laid down in chapter 11: 1 of the Judicial Pro-

Book) that service of writs in Sweden at the request of foreign authorities shall be performed, "where it is feasible," in a manner different from that prescribed by Swedish law if that is explicitly asked for in the request.—The Act on the taking of evidence in actions in foreign courts, 1946, embodies Swedish rules on the procedure which is to be observed where evidence is taken, but under sec. 7, foreign law shall be applied in some cases: "If the law of the state where the foreign court sits grants the person who shall be examined or perform some action the right to refuse to answer in circumstances other than those specified by Swedish law, such person is entitled to that privilege." (Cf. Ekelöf, *Rättgång* I, 1957, p. 53 on the duty of secrecy). Notice also sec. 8 in the 1946 Act.—The fact that Swedish courts recognize evidence taken abroad on their account, admit declarations upon oath to prove claims in bankruptcy before foreign courts (sec. 119 of the Bankruptcy Act) or recognize service abroad under the law of the foreign country where the writ is served hardly constitutes an execption to the principle that procedure in Sweden is governed by Swedish law. Cf. von Seth in *Sv.J.T.* 1919, pp. 95 f.

[27] On assistance by foreign courts and service of writs abroad, *vide* Persson in *Sv.J.T.* 1953, pp. 487 ff. Cf. Blix, *Statsmyndigheternas internationella förbindelser,* Stockholm 1964, pp. 139 ff.

cedure Code that "any person may be a party to an action at law." While the capacity of any individual, Swede or foreigner, to sue or be sued is incontestable, the question whether an association has legal personality, i.e. whether it may have rights or duties and act as a party to an action, is determined by rules of private law, and it is for the choice of law rules to indicate the applicable foreign legal system. Chapter 11 : 2 of the Judicial Procedure Code, where associations are admitted as parties to actions in so far as they have been granted legal personality, contains an implicit reference to that system. The concluding paragraphs of chapter 11 : 1 and 2 contain provisions on the capacity of parties to engage in litigation. These provisions refer to the rules of private law on infancy, interdiction, and bankruptcy and on the representatives of associations with legal personality. This is another field where choice of law rules may prescribe application of foreign law. In neither case, however, is it correct to state that questions concerning the capacity to be party to an action or to appear without a representative are determined by application of foreign law which replaces rules of Swedish *procedural law*. However, it is laid down in chapter 11 : 3 of the Judicial Procedure Code that an alien who is not capable of acting in court on his own behalf under the rules of his home country is nevertheless entitled to engage in litigation in Sweden if he fulfils the requirements of Swedish law in this respect.[28]

The fact that as a general principle, Swedish courts apply only their own procedural rules does not exclude the application of such foreign rules as are considered procedural in the country where they are in force, but not in Sweden, in actions where the substantive law of such foreign country is applied.[29] Occasionally, however, it may be difficult to state what is procedural from the point of view of Swedish law. In principle, no other kinds of evidence than those allowed under the Judicial Procedure Code can be admitted; on the other hand, all kinds of evidence admissible under Swedish law may be used. Thus if foreign procedural law only admits documentary evidence for the proving of debts below a certain amount, Swedish courts will have to determine whether this rule is procedural and as such merely in-

[28] On the reasons for this rule, *vide S.O.U.* 1938 No. 44, p. 159.—On foreign rules relating to the binding force of judgments, cf. below, pp. 85 ff.

[29] Cf. below, pp. 170 f.

tended to relieve courts of justice from too much work—in which case it is of no interest in Sweden—or whether it should be understood, for the purpose of Swedish courts, as a substantive condition for the existence of a debt, i.e. a formal rule of private law which has to be observed once the legal system embodying such rule has been recognized as *lex causae*.[30] As for legal rules on the value of different kinds of evidence, the principle of free evaluation is maintained in actions before the Swedish courts; this means, in the language of chapter 35: 1 of the Judicial Procedure Code, that "upon careful examination of all facts brought into the action, the court shall decide what has been proved." This is true even where the procedural law of the legal system which serves as *lex causae* is based upon a set of legal rules on evidence which exclude certain sources of knowledge or determines the relative value of different sources of knowledge ("two perjurors = full evidence"). On the other hand, substantive rules on presumptions, the burden of proof and the evaluation of evidence should be observed. In Swedish law, rules of this kind are found in section 6, the Sale of Goods Act, 1905, which creates a presumption in favour of the correctness of invoice prices where the buyer does not protest within a fixed period, and in chapter 6: 9 of the Code of Marriage, where it is laid down to what extent private documents made by spouses on their respective property are entitled to faith against either party's creditors.[31] It is not always easy to draw a limit between these two kinds of rules.[32] In strict reasoning, *procedural*—as opposed to substantive —periods of limitation in Swedish law should always be observed, whether embodied in the Judicial Procedure Code or not, even where the action concerned would be tried under foreign law if it were admitted to trial. Thus it might be argued that the rule in chapter 2: 1 of the Parents and Children Code, 1949, on the limitation of actions concerning legitimacy should be enforced by Swedish courts even though foreign law were applicable to

[30] Cf. Kallenberg, *Svensk civilprocessrätt* I, 2 ed., 1923, pp. 104 f., and Graulich, *Principes de droit international privé*, Paris 1961, pp. 46 f.

[31] *Vide* Kallenberg, *op.cit.*, p. 105. Cf. Ekelöf, *Rättegång*, I, 1957, p. 53; Borum p. 187.

[32] Cf. Bolding, *Bevisbördan och den juridiska tekniken*, 1951, especially at pp. 128 ff. and also Strömholm in *T.f.R.* 1960, p. 435.

the question of legitimacy as such. In one decision, however, the Supreme Court has taken the opposite view; a possible explanation is that the limitation rule has been considered so closely connected with the legitimacy rules, the substantive character of which has never been contested, that the first-mentioned provision has been classified in the same way.[33]

In a later case (1962 *N.J.A.* 123) concerning legitimacy, the courts applied Italian law as the child and its mother and the husband of the mother (at the time of the birth of the child) were Italian citizens. It was too late for the father to initiate proceedings under Italian law and also under Swedish law. The action of the child, represented by its mother, was not admitted as under Italian law only the father and his heirs are entitled to initiate proceedings concerning legitimacy. This Italian prohibition was thus qualified as substantive. It can be added that at the time of the action the father was a Swedish citizen, that the marriage had taken place in Sweden, that the mother was originally a Finnish citizen but naturalized Italian by the marriage, that all three parties were domiciled in Sweden and that the mother had for several years been living with another man who had declared himself father of the child. This, it seems, would be a case where the applicable Italian law could have been disregarded as contrary to Swedish *ordre public*. A legal rule prohibiting a person from having a court decide on his personal status (legitimate or not) appears as contrary to the basic principles of Swedish law.

International Jurisdiction

It would seem to be a view of long standing in Swedish law that the *forum* rules of the Judicial Procedure Code and of other statutes also embody provisions on the international jurisdiction or "competence" of Swedish courts. If a *forum* could be found under these rules, the Swedish court thus indicated would also have jurisdiction regardless of the foreign connections of the action; at any rate, the existence of a

[33] 1953 *N.J.A.* 4. Vide also Karlgren, p. 177. It should be noticed that in the decision 1932 *N.J.A.* 339, the courts admitted the action of a husband, charging the illegitimacy of his wife's child, to trial, but dismissed it on the ground that the period of limitation had expired.

forum under internal rules was a fundamental condition for international jurisdiction and consequently, if no *forum* could be found under internal procedural law, an action was not triable in Sweden.[34] In fact, Swedish courts of justice seem to have been strongly inclined to follow this line of reasoning when discussing their own "competence." In the course of time, however, this view has gradually been abandoned.[35] Nowadays, the question of international jurisdiction is considered to be untouched by statutory provisions—with some exceptions which will be discussed presently. The modern opinion is obviously supported by the fact that in some branches of family law, *forum* rules are framed in such manner that they cannot possibly determine the international jurisdiction of Swedish courts. Thus chapter 20: 3 of the Parents and Children Code, 1949, contains *forum* rules for actions concerning the paternity of illegitimate children; in addition to this, however, it is laid down in chapter 20: 14 that if the other provisions of the Code do not indicate any *forum,* such actions may be tried by the City Court of Stockholm. This cannot mean that the City Court has jurisdiction to try all paternity suits in the world; on the other hand, there is no reason to consider international jurisdiction only in the light of the provisions in chapter 20: 3 of the Parents and Children Code.[36]

In the field of family law there are a few written rules on international jurisdiction. They are due to conventions signed in the course of the Hague cooperation or the Inter-Nordic collaboration and consequently based, as long as these conventions are in force, on obligations binding upon Sweden under public international law. Other conventions may influence the framing of Swedish competence rules, and certain principles of the law of nations—on immunity and denial of justice —are relevant, but apart from these subjects public international law keeps silent. The *jus gentium* contains, in the view of the present writer, no system of rules intended to confer international competence upon

[34] *Vide* Reuterskiöld, pp. 42 ff.; Kallenberg, *op.cit.,* vol. I (1923), pp. 101 and 326; Gärde et.al., *Rättegångsbalken,* 1949, pp. 82 f.

[35] *Vide* Dennemark, pp. 48 ff. Cf. Karlgren, pp. 159 f., Beckman, p. 8, and Ekelöf, *Rättegång,* I, 1957, pp. 52 f.

[36] In the decision 1957 *N.J.A.* 430, where a paternity suit was brought against an Afghan student with whom the plaintiff had had sexual intercourse on several occasions in San Francisco, the Supreme Court decided the question of jurisdiction upon grounds which were completely different from those resorted to by the courts below, which apparently based their decisions upon chap. 20, sec. 3 of the Parents and Childrens Code. Cf. also 1956 *N.J.A.* 410.

the courts of justice of the various nations.[37]

It is customary in Swedish legal writing to make a distinction between functional, material and local aspects of the competence of courts and other public authorities.[38] A court has *functional* competence in a given case if it follows from its position in the hierarchy of instances that the case shall be tried there. As regards *material* competence, the problem is to decide whether a case is of such *character* as to fall under the jurisdiction of this or that judicial or administrative body. *Local* competence, finally, is founded upon the relation between an action and the territorial sphere (jurisdiction) of the court. It is obvious that when discussing whether a case is or is not such as to be triable in Swedish courts, the problem concerns the *material* competence of these courts. The competence of foreign courts is not taken into account and the underlying considerations are essentially domestic: they merely indicate in what cases the courts of this country take any interest at all in, or offer their services for, the decision of actions with foreign connections. If such action is considered, under the rules on Swedish international jurisdiction, a matter for the courts of this country, the next question will be: what court within the country is the "proper *forum?*"[39] Now, and only now, we arrive at the question of the distribution of cases between different courts under internal procedural law. It is chiefly a question of local competence; it concerns what are traditionally called the "*forum* rules."[40]

Apart from some provisions in the field of family law, international jurisdiction is not governed by any statute. This fact raises the question by what method it is possible to decide whether a given case falls under the jurisdiction of Swedish courts. It is customary to state that the problem is largely solved "by analogous application of the

[37] *Vide* Eek, pp. 129 ff.

[38] *Vide* Ekelöf, *Rättegång,* I, 1957, p. 63; Hassler, *Civilprocessrätt,* 1956, pp. 93 ff.

[39] From the point of view of procedural technique, however, it is probable that the question of local competence is raised before that of international jurisdiction.

[40] It is not impossible, however, that a certain case falls under Swedish international jurisdiction but is triable by authorities other than the ordinary courts of justice under internal rules on the material competence of Swedish courts.

forum rules."[41] However, in the field of family law we have already pointed out that the possibility of finding a Swedish *forum* does not justify the conclusion that the courts of this country have international jurisdiction. The rationale of the principal rules on local competence may be examined, but it is no more than reasonable caution to treat each kind of problem in family law separately and to pay attention both to the basic principles of conflict law and to such legislation as actually exists, *inter alia,* enactments which do contain rules on international jurisdiction with regard to certain matters (e.g. on divorce, chapter 3: 1 of the 1904 Act and section 7 of the Inter-Nordic Royal Ordinance of 1931).

The general rules of Swedish law on the proper *forum* in civil actions —which are also of some importance for family law,[42] although in that branch of the law, special *forum* rules are very largely in force—are found in chapter 10 of the Judicial Procedure Code. Under section 1 of that chapter, the competent court for civil actions in general is the court which has jurisdiction over the place where the defendant is domiciled. The domicile of limited companies or other associations endowed with legal personality is where the board has its seat. It is a simple and permissible analogical conclusion from these rules that actions against foreigners domiciled in Sweden *prima facie* fall within the jurisdiction of Swedish courts. It should be pointed out, however, that the Swedish concept "domicile" is neither as complex nor as firmly established as the corresponding English term. In particular, changes of domicile are admitted without the application of the severe criteria used in English law. Upon the whole, the Swedish term for domicile (*hemvist*) may be more adequately translated by "permanent residence." Where the term "domicile" is used below this special meaning must be kept in mind.

It is further laid down in chapter 10: 1 of the Judicial Procedure Code that if a person has no known domicile within or outside Sweden, an action may be brought against him in the court of the place where he is resident. If the defendant is a Swedish citizen whose residence is outside Sweden or unknown, an action may be brought in the court having jurisdiction over the place where such person had his last known domicile or residence. "Residence," for the purpose of these

[41] Ekelöf, *Rättegång,* I, 1957, p. 53.

[42] Cf. 1950 *N.J.A.* 464 and an older decision, 1936 *Sv.J.T.* p. 27.

rules, need not be permanent: mere physical presence is sufficient. It follows from these provisions that an alien who is present in Sweden cannot be sued in the court having jurisdiction over the place in Sweden where he is found if he has in fact a known domicile abroad. By analogical application of these principles to the question of international jurisdiction we arrive at the conclusion that it is not a sufficient condition for the international jurisdiction of Swedish courts that an alien who has a known domicile abroad stays in Sweden. On the other hand, it should not be assumed that an action against an alien staying in Sweden and having no known domicile abroad can always, without exception, be brought in this country.—Under chapter 10: 3 of the Judicial Procedure Code, a person who has not a known domicile within Sweden may be sued where property belonging to him is located, provided the action concerns an obligation of payment. The obvious analogical conclusion on the international jurisdiction level is that Swedish courts are competent to try actions against foreigners concerning payment of money as soon as the defendant has property in this country and regardless of his domicile. The plaintiff's interest in a decision which can be executed effectively also speaks in favour of this rule; in all cases where foreign judgments are unenforceable in Sweden, that interest can be satisfied only by a Swedish decision.[43] Under chapter 10:4 of the Judicial Procedure Code a person who does not have a known domicile within Sweden but who has undertaken or otherwise incurred an obligation may be sued where such obligation was undertaken or otherwise incurred. This rule on the *forum contractus* obviously admits an analogy for the purpose of international jurisdiction. Under chapter 10: 8, actions based upon torts may be instituted in the court of the place where the tort was committed or the resulting damage occurred. By analogical reasoning, Swedish courts have international jurisdiction where an act causing damage has been committed within this country or the injury following from such act has occurred here even though the person against whom recovery is claimed is an alien and possibly also domiciled and resident abroad.

In his work on the international jurisdiction of Swedish courts,[44] Mr. Justice Dennemark has undertaken a thorough examination of these problems in the light of the provisions embodied in chapter 10 of the Judicial Procedure Code. In this connection, it is sufficient to point out

[43] Cf. below, pp. 84 ff.

[44] *Vide* above, p. 43.

that in actual practice, the analogical application of these provisions is based, as it were, on the provisional hypothesis that where a Swedish *forum* can be found under chapter 10 of the Judicial Procedure Code, Swedish courts have international jurisdiction. However, it is often necessary to consider, *inter alia,* the rationale of internal *forum* rules in ascertaining whether there are reasons not to assume jurisdiction in spite of the fact that a *forum* can be found under these rules. On the other hand, it may occur that strong reasons speak in favour of an assumption of jurisdiction although no competent court can be found under the Judicial Procedure Code, chapter 10. In these cases, it has been stated, the task would be "to find a *forum* . . . by means of a construction of the relevant enactment."[45] To give an illustration, let us suppose that an action is instituted against a person who is resident in Sweden to recover rent for real property situated abroad. It does not seem possible to find a *forum* under chapter 10 of the Judicial Procedure Code since it follows from sections 10 and 17 that the court having jurisdiction over the place where the realty is situated has an exclusive competence to try, *inter alia,* claims for rent with regard to the property, and that the parties are not allowed to agree upon submitting to the jurisdiction of any other court. Occasionally, however, there may be special reasons for accepting Swedish jurisdiction in such a case.[46]

[45] Karlgren, p. 160, note 3.—A somewhat different situation is treated by the present writer in *Om främlingskap,* pp. 133 ff., and more recently in *Scandinavian Studies in Law,* 1959, particularly at pp. 42 ff., where the decision 1948 *N.J.A.* 805 is referred to. In this case, it was possible to apply the auxiliary rule in chap 15, sec. 4 of the Marriage Code, under which the City Court of Stockholm is competent to exercise jurisdiction in matrimonial cases when no other *forum* is available, but the international jurisdiction rule in chap. 3, sec. 1 of the 1904 Act on international questions concerning marriage etc. was a bar to the trial of the action. In our view, general principles of public international law created an obligation to put a *forum* at the disposal of the parties in this case. Cf. Dennemark, pp. 60 ff.

[46] *Vide* the exemplary decision of the Stockholm Court of Appeal in 1958 *Sv.J.T.* 13. The Court considered the question upon the assumption that Swedish law did not provide any "proper *forum.*" However, Mr. Justice Dennemark has argued (at pp. 211 ff.) that the *forum rei sitae rule* in chap. 10, sec. 10 of the Judicial Procedure Code only concerns realty *in Sweden* and therefore does not affect the validity of the general *forum domicilii* rule in actions concerning foreign land.—On the rationale of the internal *forum* rule with regard to land, *vide* Ekelöf, *Rättegång,* II, 1958, pp. 213 ff., and Hassler, *Civilprocessrätt,* 1956, pp. 101 ff.

If so, a *forum* must be put at the disposal of the parties, and in our example the natural choice would be the court within the jurisdiction of which the defendant has his domicile or residence.

As regards cases where the assumption of jurisdiction should be declined even though a competent court can be found under internal *forum* rules, it should be recalled that the law of nations contains immunity principles which exclude—with some exceptions—actions against foreign states, foreign sovereigns and members of foreign diplomatic missions. In these cases, public international law constitutes a bar to the jurisdiction of Swedish courts.[47] Similar restrictions may follow from obligations under international treaties.[48] It may also be that in some instances the law of nations does not allow Swedish courts to take cognizance of questions concerning the validity of foreign administrative decisions.[49] Apart from considerations of public international law, however, Swedish courts have adopted the principle of not trying claims founded upon foreign legislation in the field of public law, whether such claims are raised by a state or a private person.[50] Thus it is likely that the foreign tax claims which were raised in the cases 1914 *N.J.A.* 409 and 1924 *N.J.A.* 635 would not have been held cognizable even if such claims had fallen within the jurisdiction of ordinary courts of justice under internal Swedish law.[51] The same rule is applicable to other claims based upon public law rules; and an action by a foreign state concerning, for example, the enforcement of foreign exchange or clearing laws should not be heard.[52] However, difficult prob-

[47] *Vide* Karlgren, pp. 169 ff., Beckman, pp. 8 ff., Hjerner, pp. 323 ff. and the literature referred to by these writers. Among Swedish writing on the problems of immunity in public international law, mention should be made of an article by H. Strömberg in *N.T.I.R.* 1958.

[48] Notice the Act on exceptions from the normal jurisdiction of Swedish courts with regard to certain actions between the master and crew of foreign ships, 1952 (after chap. 10, sec. 21 of the Judicial Procedure Code in the Statute-Book).

[49] Karlgren, p. 162. Cf. Dennemark, pp. 104 ff.

[50] Vide Dennemark, pp. 92 ff.

[51] The collection of foreign taxes is based upon international conventions. *Vide* the enactments attached to the Act on the collection in certain cases of foreign tax arrears or other public dues, 15 June 1935 (after the Collection of Taxes Ordinance in the Statute-Book) and above, p. 33.

[52] Cf. the opinions of Lind and Söderlund, JJ., in 1954 *N.J.A.* 268. In an action instituted by the Bulgarian State in the Stockholm City Court in 1957, which

lems may arise, *inter alia,* because the line drawn between public and private law in traditional legal theory is both debatable and fluid; thus the classification of a claim may be open to discussion.[53] A refusal to take cognizance would seem justified only in those cases where the public character of the claim (its being based upon legislation in the field of public law) is quite clear. Thus if a private person claims recovery of taxes which he has paid on another person's account, the action ought to be admitted; foreign fiscal law may have determined the amount of taxes collected, but it does not constitute the ground of the claim.[54] Other cases where Swedish courts may refuse to take jurisdiction although a Swedish *forum* can be found are those in which Sweden has no legal interest. This idea was particularly developed by Mr. Justice Dennemark in the work previously referred to (pp. 173 ff). Already in an earlier study, he had illustrated the problem by an example in which "two aliens domiciled abroad but temporarily resident within the country have concluded a contract which shall be performed abroad."[55] It is obviously

concerned the same problem as was dealt with in the 1954 case, the plaintiff asked for an order by the court to the effect that an amount of money belonging to the defendant, a former Bulgarian merchant called Takvorian, and deposited with a Swedish public authority, should be transferred to the Swedish-Bulgarian clearing account in favour of the National Bank of Bulgaria. Under Bulgarian currency legislation, Takvorian had a duty to effect that transfer, and it was also claimed that he had undertaken to perform it when granted an export permit for tobacco. Although the claim of the Bulgarian State would seem to imply an immediate enforcement of public law rules on currency, the court admitted it to trial; the action was not sustained, however (*vide* below, p. 206, note 111). Upon appeal, the Stockholm Court of Appeal (decision 10 June 1960) refused to take cognizance of the action of the Bulgarian State. "Since it was essentially raised in the public interest of a foreign State," it could not be tried by Swedish courts. The Supreme Court affirmed this decision, 1961 *N.J.A.* 145. *Vide* further Dennemark, pp. 100 ff.

53 Cf. 1933 *N.J.A.* 486 and 1935 *N.J.A.* note A 257. Cf. also 1909 *N.J.A.* 638.

54 *Vide* Nial, pp. 117 ff.; Hjerner, pp. 248 ff. Cf. further below, pp. 205 ff.

55 Dennemark in *Sv.J.T.* 1950, pp. 38 f. Cf. Eek, p. 133 and Karlgren in *SvJ.T.* 1956, p. 401. In judicial decisions and legal writing, occasional statements can be found which seem to express the view that Swedish courts are not competent to try cases in which it is impossible to arrive at a judgment ordering, for instance, the payment of money which can be enforced within the country. In the decision of the Stockholm City Court referred to above (note 52) it is stated, not very clearly, "that in principle, the administration of justice cannot be extended

possible to find a great number of examples where the interests of Swedish justice are in no way engaged and where jurisdiction should therefore not be assumed.[56] Quite apart from the *forum rei sitae* rule concerning realty in chapter 10: 10 of the Judicial Procedure Code, it might be justifiable to state, at least as a general principle, that the special character of actions about foreign land excludes such cases from the jurisdiction of Swedish courts; as a rule, the courts of this country should be considered as *forum non conveniens.* Chapter 10: 11 of the Judicial Procedure Code creates a possibility for the plaintiff to institute an action at the *forum rei sitae* where his claim has some connection with real property but does not belong to the categories of claims enumerated in section 10. In addition to this possibility, however, he can also proceed in other courts. It may well be asked whether the fact that the real property concerned is situated abroad would not result in the exclusion of Swedish jurisdiction even though the defendant could be sued in Sweden under one or more of the *forum* rules in chapter 10 of the Judicial Procedure Code (secs. 1, 3, 4 or 6).[57]

In one case, 1949 *N.J.A. 724,* the assumption of jurisdiction was declined on the ground that the parties had inserted into the bill of lading upon which the action was founded a clause to the effect that any action based on the bill of lading should be brought in the courts of England. Obviously, certain conditions must be fulfilled for clauses providing for submission to the jurisdiction of foreign courts (which means, correspondingly, avoidance of the

beyond the power of the state." It is quite possible, however, that a party has a reasonable interest in having his action tried even if it is impossible to obtain execution of the judgment in Sweden; the Swedish decision may be enforceable in a country where execution can be secured. In fact, "the power of the state" is more extensive than its power to execute judgments. Cf., moreover, 1957 *N.J.A.* 430 where jurisdiction was held to exist (it is true that the case fell within the field of family law) on the ground that the plaintiff had a strong interest in having his right protected, although the possibility of enforcement against the defendant must be considered insignificant. It should also be noticed that in England the principle, once introduced by Dicey, that the assumption of jurisdiction presupposes the possibility of an "effective judgment" is no longer maintained. *Vide* Dicey & Morris, *Conflict of Laws,* 7th ed. London 1958, pp. 27 f.

56 Dennemark, pp. 173 ff.

57 Cf. Dennemark, pp. 214 f.

jurisdiction of Swedish courts) to be recognized and have the effect that Swedish courts refuse to take jurisdiction.[58] Where that is the case, however, we have a further example of a situation where jurisdiction is not entertained, although a Swedish *forum* can be found. Similarly, submission to the jursidiction of Swedish courts should be accepted only on certain conditions.[59] But problems may certainly arise where the submission clause does not indicate a specified Swedish court but only "a Swedish court of justice", and no Swedish *forum* rule is found applicable; however, it cannot be simply assumed that submission is invalid in such cases since chapter 10: 16 of the Judicial Procedure Code, where the conditions for the validity of agreements on jurisdiction are set out, only refers to internal cases. If the parties make an agreement providing for submission to Swedish jurisdiction after the action has already been instituted, such agreement should be recognized if fulfilling the conditions applicable to submission clauses made before the suit. On the other hand, it is doubtful whether analogical conclusions with regard to international jurisdiction may be drawn from chapter 10: 18 of the Judicial Procedure Code, where it is laid down that in most cases (with some specified exceptions) an action which has not been brought in the "proper" *forum* is nevertheless cognizable in the court where it was introduced if the incompetence of the court is not pleaded in due time by the party having an interest in such plea.[60] It may be objected against an application of this principle to questions of international jurisdiction that such questions concern the "material" rather than the "local" competence of courts. It seems that the court must examine *ex officio* the question whether it has international jurisdiction although in

[58] *Vide* the opinion of Mr. Justice Karlgren in 1949 *N.J.A.* 724; Eek, p. 134, note 2, Welamson in *Sv.J.T.* 1953, pp. 683 ff. The question has been thoroughly considered by Dennemark, pp. 307 ff.—The case 1962 *N.J.A.* 354, concerns the question of the presence of an agreement to submit to foreign jurisdiction. The case seems to confirm the principle followed in the 1949 case.

[59] Karlgren, p. 165. Hambro states (at p. 70) that "a submission to the Norwegian courts is always permissible." *Vide* further Dennemark, pp. 251 ff.

[60] *Vide,* however, Karlgren, pp. 165 f. Cf. Dennemark in *Sv.J.T.* 1950, p. 39 and the decisions 1928 *N.J.A.* 149, 1942 *N.J.A.* 385 and 1962 *N.J.A.* 305.

many cases the explicit joint wish of the parties may be considered a sufficient ground for assuming jurisdiction.[61]

Since written rules on jurisdiction do not exist, considerations of legal policy undoubtedly exercise a particularly strong influence upon the development in practice of principles of international jurisdiction. As we have already pointed out, these considerations are one-sided in so far as the competence of foreign courts—i.e. the distribution of competence between different jurisdictions—is usually not taken into consideration and the essential question is whether the interests of Swedish justice are in any way engaged. There is now, however, a tendency to

[61] Mr. Justice Dennemark has returned to this question in his work on international jurisdiction (at pp. 294 ff.). As for chap. 10, sec. 18 of the Judicial Procedure Code he initially determines its general implications as follows: "A court which is not competent under the general jurisdiction rules may try an action if the defendant has engaged in pleadings against the plaintiff's plea as such —i.e. entered an appearance without objections against the competence of the court *in limine litis*—and if the action does not belong to any of the types set out in chap. 10, sec. 17 of the Judicial Procedure Code." On the question of international jurisdiction, Dennemark arrives at the conclusion (at p. 301) that the rule in chap. 10, sec. 18, is analogically applicable in so far as the fact that the defendant enters an appearance without reservations implies *in principle* a right for the court to adjudicate upon the action although it would not otherwise have been triable in Sweden. The principle is subject to certain exceptions; thus the court has always to "refuse *ex officio* to admit an action which is not at all triable in the Swedish courts under the principles of international procedure acknowledged in this country" and furthermore, an action must not be tried in certain other cases, e.g. where the parties are not entitled to dispose of the action under the *lex fori* or where the litigation is not sufficiently connected with the *forum* country. Mr. Justice Dennemark's theories seem to imply that if the defendant does not raise any objection against the competence of the court in an action with international aspects, the court must nevertheless always examine the question of jurisdiction in order to determine whether it shall not refuse to entertain the action by application of one of these exceptional rules; unlike the solution of similar problems for internal purposes, this examination must be performed without the support of written rules. It would seem most proper to describe the situation in the following manner: the question of international jurisdiction must always be examined *ex officio* but in some cases jurisdiction can be based on the will of the parties under those unwritten rules of Swedish law concerning jurisdiction which the court has to apply in its *ex officio* examination. In our view, the analogical applicability of chap. 10, sec. 18 of the Judicial Procedure Code cannot be accepted, nor do we accept the opinion that jurisdiction can be entertained upon the mere fact that the defendant enters an appearance without objecting to the competence of the court.

give wider scope to legal policy considerations. Thus the fact that no foreign court can actually be found to take jurisdiction in an action which is of importance for an individual may cause a Swedish court to accept jurisdiction whether it is called for under the rules of public international law or not.[62] Conversely, the existence of an available foreign *forum* may be an argument against jurisdiction. In the decision 1949 *N.J.A.* 724, the Supreme Court declined to exercise jurisdiction on the ground that the parties had made a contract of submission to British courts; it was stated that obviously "a competent court for the trial of the action can be found in England." Incidentally, the decision shows the connection between jurisdiction rules and the principles governing recognition of foreign judgments. If it is held that a certain matter should not be tried in Sweden, since the decision would more properly be rendered, for one reason or another, by a foreign jurisdiction, the consequence *ought* to be that a judgement by a competent court within such jurisdiction should be recognized in Sweden.

There is also a connection between jurisdiction rules and choice of law rules. If jurisdiction cannot be exercised, no choice of law issue is present. It is natural that where the question of jurisdiction is subject to doubt, courts actually pay some regard to the result which an action would have, were it heard and substantive provisions applied belonging to the law of the country indicated by choice of law rules. Moreover, there may be reason for giving particular consideration to the question whether a Swedish judgment can count upon recognition abroad. This is particularly true in the field of family law. Decisions which create changes of status or modify family relations should not be rendered unless they can be recognized in countries with which such status or family relations have an important connection in real life.[63] If jurisdiction is nevertheless accepted broadly, it is only reasonable to grant foreign law extensive application, perhaps making recognition abroad easier. From the point of view of legislative policy, the connection between juris-

[62] In actual fact, such considerations may very well have exercised a decisive influence upon the outcome of the case 1948 *N.J.A.* 805, (cf. above, note 45). However, the *ratio decidendi* of the Supreme Court was framed as an expression of a general principle; this produced the result that lower courts in later actions accepted jurisdiction without examining whether foreign courts were available, and this development in its turn resulted in certain modifications in the practice of the Supreme Court. See more fully Eek in *Scandinavian Studies in Law* 1959, pp. 23. ff. A later decision is 1960 *Sv.J.T.* p. 30.

[63] Cf. Eek in *Sv.J.T.* 1957, pp. 535 ff.

diction, recognition of foreign judgements and choice of law is obvious, particularly if international cooperation is taken into account, but this question would seem to need further study.[64]

Foreign Judgments[65]

If it is stated that a foreign judgment is "recognized", this expression refers to the fact that the judgment is held equal to a decision by a Swedish court. In principle, a recognized judgment is entitled to the same effect as a Swedish judgment; it creates a *res judicata* and, if needs be, it shall be enforced by execution.[66] It should be noticed, however, that a formal examination of the order for which execution is claimed always takes place in execution proceedings.[67] Since it is obvious that this examination is more difficult in the case of foreign judgments than where Swedish (or Nordic) decisions are concerned, it is reasonable and in no way incompatible with the principle of recognition that a special examination procedure is instituted with regard to foreign judgments; the outcome of this examination is normally the granting of *exequatur* ("let him execute") or affirmation. It is a question of expediency whether such examination shall be instituted, by what authority it shall be undertaken and what amount of care shall be re-

[64] Cf. Borum, pp. 185 ff.—In the Inter-Nordic convention system, jurisdiction rules are consistently used for "conflict avoidance." Thus in divorce actions the jurisdiction is determined by Inter-Nordic rules and decrees granted by courts in any of the Nordic countries are recognized within the whole area covered by these conventions. Choice of law problems are avoided by making the *lex fori* applicable. This method, however, presupposes a considerable affinity between the countries affected, with regard to their basic principles of law. It seems to have been used in conventions concluded by the Societ-Union with *inter alia* Czechoslovakia, Poland, Bulgaria and Rumania. *Vide S.Y.I.L.* 1958 (Moscow 1959), p. 254 ff.

[65] Foreign decisions in bankruptcy are disregarded in the following discussion, as are also enforcements of foreign tax decisions.

[66] The binding effect also means that the correctness of the actual decision—as opposed to the *ratio decidendi*—must not be questioned. This means, amongst other things that a foreign judgment by which an adoption is created and which is entitled to "recognition," in Sweden actually implies a number of other consequences; e.g. alimony claims based on the adoption must succeed in Swedish courts, provided that the *lex causae* creates a duty to pay alimony on the ground of adoption. Cf. also 1950 *N.J.A.* 464, where an American divorce decree had to be considered "valid" and the Swedish court therefore had to apply those rules in the *lex causae* which concerned alimony to divorced spouses.

[67] *Vide* Hassler, *Utsökningsrätt,* 1950, pp. 98 ff.

quired. For the execution in Sweden of a final and binding Swiss judgment in the field of private law as provided for by sections 8—11 of the 1936 Act on Swiss judgments, an *exequatur* procedure in the Stockholm Court of Appeal is required.

There is some variation both in *exequatur* procedure and in the conditions for *exequatur* established by different acts. In principle, what is intended is a formal examination based upon *criteria* taken from the *lex fori,* and it is important that no trial of the substantive correctness of the foreign decision is undertaken. This would betray the whole purpose of the procedure. Occasionally, however, the authority granting *exequatur* may have to consider the contents of foreign law. Under section 4 : 3 of the Act from 1936 mentioned above, one condition for the recognition of a Swiss judgment, for instance on matters of family law, is that such judgment does not constitute application of a "law which contains provisions incompatible with that law which would have been applied under the conflict rules of this country" (viz. Sweden). Thus the Swedish authority entitled to grant *exequatur* may have to compare the contents of the substantive law which has been actually applied with the dispositions of the legal rules which would have been applicable under Swedish conflict rules.[68] Under section 5 of the same Act (subsec. 6) a judgment shall be considered to have been delivered by the proper court if the defendant had such representative in Switzerland as Swiss law requires. Thus an examination of Swiss law may be necessary, but it is required that such examination be based upon the presumption that the decision of the Swiss court is in harmony with the law of Switzerland. Nevertheless, this provision undoubtedly foresees some sort of application of foreign law in the *exequatur* procedure. No absolutely clear line can be drawn between this procedure and that of conflict law in general. Under chapter 1 : 6 of the 1904 Act, foreign marriage celebrations are recognized in Sweden if the formal requirements of the *lex loci* have been complied with. In this respect, it is likely that a document by an authority in the country of solemnization, or simply a marriage certificate, will be accepted as proof.[69] So far, the rule in chapter 1 : 6 of the 1904 Act appears to be a substantive rule on recognition which prescribes a purely formal examination, performed, incidentally, by administrative authorities.[70] But

[68] Cf. 1957 *N.J.A.* 207; Beckman, pp. 64 f. and Eek in *Sv.J.T.* 1959, pp. 576 ff.
[69] Cf. Undén, p. 31.
[70] *Vide* 1954 *R.Å.* No. 33.

the question whether a marriage has been solemnized validly may be raised as a matrimonial dispute; in that case, the substantive merits of the plea of formal validity may be tried, and the formal rules of foreign law *(lex loci celebrationis)* determine the Swedish decision, in which the rules of the foreign legal system will also be used for the purpose of deciding whether non-observance of such formal rules cause the nullity of the marriage or have some other consequence. If, on the other hand, the marriage has been solemnized in due form, it is nevertheless possible for the question of annulment on substantive grounds to be raised in Sweden (chap. 2 of the 1904 Act).

What has been said in the foregoing paragraphs relates to those cases where foreign judgments are recognized under statutory provisions (pp. 30 f above). Apart from such cases the main rule—with the exception of status decisions—is that foreign civil judgments are *not* recognized. They are considered not to be enforceable without an explicit statutory rule.[71] On the strength of some early decisions,[72] it was held that foreign judgments should be completely disregarded in this country. In a later decision, 1935 *N.J.A.* 611, however, a certain importance as evidence was attached to a foreign judgment.[73] Still it has sometimes been argued in Swedish legal writing that since a foreign judgment may be considered to have some sort of "binding effect", it could serve as the basis of a decision in Sweden; thus an order for execution could be obtained by a kind of summary proceeding.[74] This has been considered particularly reasonable in cases where under the Swedish rules on international jurisdiction no Swedish court would have been available, e.g. in an action concerning foreign land or where the parties have validly submitted to foreign jurisdiction. It may be assumed, however, that the lower courts are not inclined to

[71] Hassler, *Utsökningsrätt,* 1960, pp. 65 f. Olivecrona, *Utsökning,* 1955, pp. 33 f.

[72] 1894 *N.J.A.* 96; 1910 N.J.A. 594 and—although less downright—1913 *N.J.A.* 326. Cf., however, the earlier decision in *Naumanns Tidskrift,* 1871, p. 495.

[73] Cf. also 1954 *R.Å.* No. 31, where in actual fact Danish criminal judgments were granted some importance and also Hambro's example (on p. 121) of the actual effects in Norway of a foreign judgment.

[74] *Vide* Welamson in *Sv.J.T.* 1953, pp. 686 f. Cf. Undén in *Sv.J.T.* 1933, pp. 105 ff., Karlgren, pp. 187 ff. and Reuterskiöld, pp. 70 f. Cf. the analysis in Olivecrona, *Rätt och dom,* 1960, pp. 246 ff.; on patent questions, *vide* Godenhielm in *N.I.R.* 1956, pp. 69 f.

initiate modifications of the earlier practice.[75]

It is far from clear what is actually meant by the "effect as evidence" which foreign judgments are held to possess under the rule in 1935 *N.J.A.* 611 when produced as prejudicial facts in a new suit in Sweden. In the first place, it should be pointed out that it can hardly be argued that such foreign judgments as cannot even claim "validity" in Sweden under the fargoing convention with Switzerland are entitled to any other "effect as evidence" than that which follows from the general principle of Swedish procedure that the court must always conscientiously hear all information which is produced in the action, including the circumstances attending an earlier suit abroad and the contents of the judgment delivered there. In other cases, i.e., where a foreign judgment is such that it could be enforced if it were Swiss or Scandinavian but has actually been rendered by a court in, for instance, England or France, the 1935 decision assumes importance. In that case, the Supreme Court stated, in its *ratio decidendi,* that the defendant had been ordered by an English judgment, to pay costs to the plantiff. "Against the evidence concerning the English lawsuit produced in the present action," the defendant had not "shown any fact which might cause the claim for recovery of costs to be considerd in any other manner than according to the decision of the English court." The rule contained in this decision has occasionally been described as a rule which reverses the burden of proof, i.e., determines which of the parties has to carry the risk if the judge is not satisfied that a relevant fact has been proved. However, this interpretation of the 1935 case does not seem correct. What is contained in the case is, rather, a rule on the *evaluation* of evidence under which the foreign decision shall be held a correct appreciation of the merits of the plaintiff's claim unless the defendant can produce facts of such character as to rebut the presumption. It is in the nature of things that this principle cannot be interpreted in such manner that the presumption for the correctness of the foreign decision has the same strength in each individual case. It necessarily varies from one case to another. If a French court has rendered a decision under French law—which, according to Swedish choice of law rules, was the *lex causae*—and the proceedings which were followed give rise to no objection on the part of the Swedish court, the presumption appears to possess considerable strength. If, on the other hand, it follows from

75 Sundström in *Sv.J.T.* 1958, p. 358. Cf., however, the decision of the Gothenburg City Court mentioned in *Sv.J.T.* 1957, at p. 179 f.

Swedish conflict law that the substantive rules of Swedish law should have been applied, the presumption does not seem to be defensible at all.

Foreign judgments and other decisions which modify or create a status are generally said to have a special position, even where no international conventions have been concluded and no internal legislation has been passed in this connexion (e.g. as is the case with marriage and divorce). It is argued that such decisions, which do not call for measures of execution, should be recognized, provided certain conditions are fulfilled, viz. that the foreign authority was competent under the principles prevailing in Sweden in the field of international jurisdiction, and that the substantive rules underlying the decision were those indicated by Swedish choice of law rules *("the national test")*. The "recognition" of a foreign status decision means, as just explained with regard to decisions in general, that it is held equal to a Swedish judgment. Thus if a German court has granted a divorce between two German nationals, this decree is recognized (chap. 3, sec. 4 of the 1904 Act). If the question whether the two persons concerned are united in marriage or not is raised in Sweden as a prejudicial question, it is clear, on the basis of the German decision, that the answer is "no". Thus in an action concerning alimony, a Swedish court does not try to find the law applicable to the question whether the parties were married or not. That question has been settled by a binding judgment. On the other hand, if either of the ex-spouses should institute an action against the other party in order to obtain a declaratory judgment to the effect that the marriage still existed, or that it had been dissolved, the question would be decided in the same way as if a Swedish court had granted a divorce decree against which no appeal could be made.[76] Questions dealing with special kinds of relief cannot be discussed here. If a foreign divorce decree is not recognized (cf. chap. 3, sec. 5 of the 1904 Act), the spouses are considered to remain married for the purposes of Swedish law. It is not possible to answer here the question whether in cases of this kind the foreign decision, although not "recognized," may be regarded as being important in some respect.[77] Special problems with regard to the meaning of recognition arise where status relations *of a type unknown* to the *lex fori* are concerned (cf. below, pp. 102 f). Even adoption may belong to this group in certain cases.

[76] Cf. 1956 *Sv.J.T.* 65.

[77] Cp. however below p. 247 f.

No systematic enquiry has so far been made into the conditions maintained in Swedish law for the recognition of foreign status judgments and into the meaning of recognition. An enquiry of this kind would probably have to be undertaken in the form of a number of special investigations, each dealing with a limited subject, such as marriage, adoption, legitimacy.

> "It is difficult to make any definite statement on the present standpoint of Swedish law with regard to the effect of foreign civil judgments in general," says Mr. Justice Beckman in his work *Svensk domstolspraxis i internationell rätt* (p. 29). Forty years earlier, another member of the Supreme Court, Judge Alexanderson, had stated that "to find the real and living law on the problem of direct enforcement of a foreign judgment is, generally speaking, rather a difficult problem."[78] One reason why there has been hardly any development in this field would seem to be that changes in the law, either in practice or by legislation are not possible to achieve without a thorough examination of the theoretical aspects of the whole problem. Certain basic principles seem to exist, however. The need for a special *exequatur* procedure can hardly be seriously questioned. Further, whatever the character of the rules concerning recognition, it would seem that a judgment should not be recognized if this would be incompatible with the fundamentals of the Swedish legal system *(ordre public)*[79]; serious deficiencies in the foreign judicial proceedings, particularly with regard to service of process, should preclude recognition.[80] The recognition of foreign judgments in those cases where no Swedish jurisdiction is available is another acceptable basic principle, while it is far from certain that foreign judgments

[78] Alexanderson, *Under vilka förutsättningar bör verkställighet av dom eller skiljedom, meddelad i något av de nordiska länderna kunna erhållas i de övriga,* 1919, p. 25.

[79] The fact that the judgment itself or the law upon which it is based is incompatible with the fundamental rules of the Swedish legal system should not in itself be an obstacle to recognition. *The enforcement* of a foreign judgment, which orders a man to pay alimony to a second wife in a polygamous marriage, does not seem to be repugnant to the fundamental principles of Swedish law. On the other hand, the execution of a judgment obliging a person to pay gambling debts could be considered incompatible with the public policy of a country where such debts cannot be enforced.

[80] Cf. 1956 *N.J.A.* 337.

should *not* be recognized in those cases where it would have been possible to find a competent Swedish court. In Swedish writing, it is often stated—as if it were an obvious truth, needing no proof —that it is a condition for the recognition of foreign judgments that they have been delivered by the courts of a state where the action could be tried according to Swedish rules on jurisdiction and, moreover, that they are based upon the substantive rules which would be applicable under the Swedish conflict of laws. It is doubtful whether these requirements are well-grounded in substance. The first task in the study of these problems should be to determine the types of decisions for which recognition is commonly sought. A further task would be to examine the actual meaning of recognition, and more particularly execution, in different types of cases. After that, it might be time to decide what is acceptable and what is not. "When rendering a decision, it is necessary not to surrender to this or that subtle theoretical objection, but always to measure soberly the reasonable proportions between what is to be gained in each individual case and what may be lost."[81] Questions of procedural technique would be the next problem in reform. Even an isolated Swedish reform would view point, it is obvious that the present attitude of most states to the recognition of foreign judgments is a serious problem. Upon the whole, this approach is either purely negative or is unsatisfactory in actual practice because, for instance, reciprocity is made a condition for recognition or the *exequatur* procedure, where it exists, is complicated, expensive or entrusted to the courts and framed in such a manner that, in reality, a new trial of the substantive merits of the case *(révision au fond)* may take place.[83] States try to promote international legal intercourse by agreements on identical jurisdiction rules, choice of law rules, or, indeed, uniform substantive legislation, but this work looses meaning if its result may be set aside in each individual case by means of restrictive rules on the recognition of foreign judgments

[81] Alexanderson, *op.cit.*, p. 17.

[82] *Vide in Sv.J.T.* 1961, pp. 149 f., the instructions given to an expert charged with a study on the enforcement of foreign judgments in civil actions.

[83] *Vide* the comparative surveys of Riad, *La valeur internationale des jugements en droit comparé,* Paris 1955 (review in *Sv.J.T.* 1957, pp. 174 ff.) and Nadelmann, "Non-recognition of American money judgments abroad and what to do about it," 42 *Iowa Law Review,* No. 2 (1957).

—rules which are shaped with reference to scholastic speculations or the demands of imaginary national interests. The law on the right of foreign companies to do business is based upon mutual commercial interests. But if a judgment in the country of import A, against an exporting company in country B cannot be executed in the latter country, the interests which are common to both states are injured.[84] In order to avoid these inconveniences, states within the same part of the world have sometimes concluded conventions to the effect that they shall mutually recognize each other's judgments. There are also several bilateral treaties.[85] Furthermore, efforts have been made to reach general international agreement on the problem, particularly through the Hague conferences,[86] the *Institut de droit international* and the *International Law Association.*

Decisions by Foreign Authorities

Questions about the effect of decisions by authorities other than courts of justice should also be mentioned; it should be pointed out, however, that these problems have not been extensively studied and, moreover, refer to highly disparate phenomena. The decisions we are dealing with are those falling within the field of public law, not those taken by administrative authorities on private law relations (*e.g.* decisions on adoption or divorce). Decisions of the latter kind may be treated, upon the whole, in the same way as civil judgments. Some decisions in the field of public law are recognized under international conventions and (or) internal statutory rules. In the absence of such a convention or statutory rule, there is no doubt that a foreign decision

[84] As an example may be mentioned the *Rhein & Mosel Feuerversicherungsgesellschaft case.* This company had been allowed to do insurance business in California. After the earthquake in San Francisco, 1906, the company was held liable by the California courts to indemnify certain insured persons. The German courts refused to recognize the California decisions, because no "reciprocity" was held to exist. The *ratio* was manifestly strained. *Vide* Nadelmann, *op.cit.,* pp. 252 f.

[85] *Vide* Walter Jellinek, *Die zweiseitigen Staatsverträge über Anerkennung ausländischer Zivilurteile,* 1953.

[86] *Vide* Malmar in *Sv.J.T.* 1927, pp. 33 ff.

is not entitled to execution in Sweden. Nor is it likely that Swedish courts will grant a judgment enforceable in this country only on the ground of a foreign administrative decision based upon rules of public law. An action of this kind is not cognizable.[87] But since the distinction between private and public law is unclear, certain problems arise, when the line has to be drawn in actual practice. As a rule, however, foreign administrative decisions do not call for enforcement in Sweden. The problem is rather whether a decision shall be recognized as equal to a corresponding decree by a Swedish authority. In certain cases the answer is obvious. The "personal law" of an association, i.e., in the majority of cases the law of the country of incorporation, is held applicable to such questions as its legal personality, the distribution of powers between its different organs, etc. The incorporation as an administrative decision is thus always "recognized" in Sweden. In fact, this attitude has been so far extended as to embrace the effect of individual nationalization decrees in the country of incorporation upon the legal personality of the nationalized enterprise although Swedsh courts decline to order the enforcement of foreign nationalization laws with regard to property situated in Sweden.[88] Similarly, other administrative decisions may be recognized as a consequence of conflict rules.[89] In these cases, the effect of a *res judicata* is obtained inasmuch as Swedish courts or other authorities do not try questions concerning foreign registrations of associations, trade marks, etc. It is not necessary to invoke, in support of this practice, any "principle of territoriality," the "sovereignty" of foreign powers, or any obligation under the law of nations to respect the foreign "act of sovereignty." Moreover, such arguments might speak just as strongly in favour of the recognition of foreign civil judgments in general as these are public acts, or "acts of sovereignty" in the sense that they imply "a compulsive deci-

[87] Cf. above, pp. 78 f.

[88] Cf. e.g. 1941 *N.J.A.* 317, 1944 *N.J.A.* 264; Nial, pp. 136 ff. and Dennemark in *Sv.J.T.* 1950, pp. 44 f.

[89] Cf. 1933 *N.J.A.* II, p. 23 and 1937 *N.J.A.* II, pp. 26 f. on foreign decisions about the granting of patents, registration of trade marks, registration of firms in trade registers or similar measures.

sion, directed against the losing party and founded upon the sovereignty of a state."[90] In actual fact, various kinds of acts by foreign administrative bodies are "recognized."[91] The reasons for this would seem to be the same as lie at the basis of recognition of foreign judgments. Organized intercourse between states in legal matters necessitates the cooperation which is expressed in recognition. This, however, should not be understood as meaning that administrative decisions are in a favoured class. There may well be cases where the courts of Sweden could, and should, completely disregard such decisions, e.g., on the ground that under Swedish principles, the foreign state had no jurisdiction over the matter concerned (the decision was rendered outside the territory, concerned foreigners, etc.),[92] or that a recognition would be contrary to Swedish *ordre public*. In other words, the problem is one of policy.[93]

§ 6. The Choice of Law Rules

A. THE LEGAL CHARACTER OF CHOICE OF LAW RULES

Conflict Rules are Absolute

In legal writing, a good deal of discussion has been carried on with a view to explaining what actually happens when a court in one country applies rules from the law of another country in obedience to a choice of law rule. It has been argued, particularly by Italian writers, that the foreign rule is applied as a part of the *lex fori:* it is incorporated into that legal system, "naturalized" or "transformed"

[90] *Vide* 1929 N.J.A. II, p. 78. The "public" character of judgments is there invoked as an argument *against* the recognition of foreign judicial decisions. Cf. Karlgren, pp. 189 ff.

[91] Gihl, *Studier,* p. 350. Cf. sec. 5 of the Act with certain provisions on foreign state vessels etc., 1938.

[92] Cf. King in 42 *A.J.I.L.* (1948), p. 826.

[93] Cf. Gihl, *Studier,* pp. 363 ff.; Hjerner, pp. 436 ff. and Schmidt, "Asylrätt för flyktingars förmögenhet," *Sv.J.T.* 1944, p. 609. Cf. also Nial, p. 120 (the footnote).

into an element of the law of the court.[94] As well as this so-called *incorporation theory,* and opposed to it, there is a "*competence theory*", according to which conflict rules are to be considered as rules on the competence of each legal system.[95] The latter theory is hardly realistic; at least, it easily creates the impression that in addition to and above the national legal systems, there exist rules on their competence in relation to one another.

When discussing the incorporation theory, some writers have emphasized that choice of law rules are rules on the sources of law and should therefore be considered as part of public law.[96] Undoubtedly, choice of law rules contain statements to the effect that in certain cases with foreign connections, Swedish law shall be disregarded in favour of a foreign legal system (indicated *in abstracto*). The Swedish legislation on the sale of goods shall be set aside, and in the case at bar, the English Sale of Goods Act may furnish a ground for the decision. The direction contained in the choice of law rule is obviously of the same character as the direction of the enacting formula with regard to the application of rules of internal legislation. This compulsive character of the choice of law rules also appears in the fact that they are held to be applicable *ex officio,* without any claim by the parties. The consequence of this opinion should be that, regardless of the pleadings of parties, the judge should have a duty to inquire whether the case contains such facts as make a choice of law rule applicable; it cannot be held that this duty of investigation is limited to cases falling within the field of family law.[97] It should appear from the decsion what choice of law the court has undertaken.[98] Thus choice of law rules are

[94] *Vide* Ross, *Laerebog i Folkeret,* 3 ed., 1951, pp. 83 f., and Gihl, *Principer,* pp. 324 ff. Cf. Nussbaum, *op.cit.* pp. 76 ff., who argues that "the Italian mode of inquiry is sheer scholasticism productive of sham problems and empty controversies."

[95] *Vide* Borum, p 4, and Niederer, pp. 125 ff.

[96] *Vide* Gihl, *loc.cit.* It should be pointed out that in a Danish work on the sources of law from 1890, Hertzberg's *De nordiske Retskilder,* the author also deals with "the local limitations of laws."

[97] *Contra* Hassler and Nial, p. 53 and p. 56. Cf. Kallenberg, *Svensk civilprocessrätt,* vol. II, 1927, pp. 93 ff.

[98] Obviously, this requirement cannot be given such a scope that the courts would have to indicate without exceptions in what cases Swedish law has been applied. But once the question of the applicable law is present in an action, the court should give an account of the choice of law principles resorted to and the

"absolute" or "compulsory" from the point of view of the court. From the point of view of the parties they may be described as incapable of being set aside by agreement. It is not permissible to make a contract to the effect that a choice of law rule in the *lex fori* shall not be applied, and in actual practice it is highly unlikely that contracts will contain clauses (e.g. in a contract of sale) providing that the choice of law in actions concerning the construction or performance of the contract shall take place in accordance with, e.g., English choice of law rules instead of the private international law of the *forum*.[99]

The opinion that the judge has to apply conflict rules and such foreign substantive rules as follow from these *ex officio,* i.e. regardless of any claim or petition to that effect by a party, may be described as prevailing in Scandinavian conflict literature.[100] It seems obvious where an action concerns such disputed questions as cannot be solved by a simple agreement between the parties, viz. matrimonial causes, legitimacy or filia-

outcome of the choice, so that it is clear what substantive rules have been applied. This is not always the case. A recent illustration is furnished by 1959 *N.J.A.* 456. An Austrian national had married a Swedish woman. After the spouses had been divorced, the husband pleaded that real property situated in Sweden and registered in court in his (Swedish) wife's name belonged to him. It was agreed upon by both parties that under Austrian law, spouses retain full and exclusive property each in his belongings. However, the wife claimed that Swedish law was applicable to the action. The District Court held that since the husband was an Austrian subject at the celebration of the marriage "the questions of matrimonial property raised in the case shall be decided under Austrian law, unless the parties have made an agreement to the contrary." A contract (marriage settlement) was given particular importance by the Court. However, both the Court of Appeal and the Supreme Court left the question of the applicable law aside, and the Courts seem to have based their decision on Swedish rules on the buying of Swedish land through the intermediary of agents acting in their own name (in avoidance of legal prohibitions against foreigners acquiring real property in the Kingdom). Nevertheless, it is far from clear that Austrian rules on the effects of marriage upon the proprietary rights of the spouces with regard to realty were not applicable. Cf. chap. 1, sec. 12, of the 1912 Act.

[99] By a submission to foreign jurisdiction which is accepted in Sweden and therefore means that the action will not be admitted to trial in a Swedish court, the parties can manage to avoid Swedish choice of law rules. Conversely, these rules are chosen by a submission to Swedish jurisdiction. In neither case, however, the choice of law rules of the *forum* have been set aside by contract.

[100] Cf. Karlgren, p. 74, Kallenberg, *Svensk civilprocessrätt,* vol. II, pp. 93 ff.; Borum, pp. 65 ff.

tion cases, disputes concerning custodianship, etc. In these cases, the relevant choice of law rules, as well as that foreign law which is indicated by such rules, must be applied by the judge *ex officio*. With regard to other cases, however, viz. those where the parties may agree privately upon the outcome of the litigation and receive judicial confirmation of such agreement, it is possible to argue that choice of law rules and foreign law should be applied only when demanded by either party. There is hardly any statutory rule which can be invoked in favour of the *ex officio* principle in these cases. In chapter 17:3 of the Judicial Procedure Code, however, it is laid down that in such actions as ar subject to private settlement by the parties, the decision of the court must not be founded upon "facts which have not been invoked by either party in support of his plea". Combined with the enactment in chapter 35:2, under which no evidence is required concerning the rules of law, this provision could be construed to mean that the parties are free to introduce facts—upon which the decision shall be based—while the court has a duty to apply all Swedish rules of law, including choice of law rules, regardless of the claims or other procedural acts of the parties.[101]

Against this course of reasoning a Danish writer, A. Philip, has objected (with regard to *Danish* law) that it can only be accepted upon the same conditions as determine the duty of courts to apply their own—*in casu* Danish—law in general. "It is, however, a condition for the right and duty of courts to apply a rule *not* invoked by the parties that the facts calling for the application of such rule, i.e. those facts the existence of which is presupposed by the rule itself as a condition for its applicability, shall have been included in the statements of either party as being important for the decision of the case"[102] The writer concludes that if neither party claims the application of foreign law, the judge is at liberty to make use of a choice of law rule only if it appears from the facts invoked by either party in support of his claim that the rule in question is applicable.[103] Thus the court shall not make enquiries concerning

101 Cf. Philip in *U.f.R.* 1960, p. 159.

102 *loc.cit.*

103 As an example of a situation of the kind referred to Philip *(loc.cit.)* men-

connecting factors, nor is it free to make use of such factors unless either party has introduced them into the action.

It is conceivable that these arguments can be applied to Swedish law. A statutory authority would be found in the rule in chapter 17: 3 of the Judicial Procedure Code (refered to above): "If the action is such that it may be terminated by a private settlement between the parties, the decision of the court must not be founded upon facts which have not been invoked by either party in support of his plea." The convincing force of this reasoning is perhaps most conveniently tested by an example. It should first be recalled, however, that substantive, not procedural, rules determine whether an action is "such that it may be terminated by a private settlement between the parties". Although it is of importance in various respects for the proceedings in court whether an action belongs to this category or not, and although the terminology used in drawing the distinction is procedural, it is nevertheless true that it is based upon a distinction between rules of substantive law; incidentally, this distinction is not always easy to make.[104] We shall give an illustration. A man, who is a Canadian national, abandons his wife at Quebec and goes to Sweden. The wife institutes an action in Sweden to obtain alimony. She does not formally claim that the law of the province of Quebec be applied, nor does she invoke her own—and the husband's—nationality or domicile in support of any other claim. Under Swedish conflict rules, the law of Quebec must be applied for the purpose of deciding this action. It is considered most just

tions an action about a sale by a Danish manufacturer of an instrument, which shall be used in a foreign country with a climate different from that of Denmark —a fact which is important for the correct construction of the instrument. If the buyer alleges, in support of a claim that he be entitled to cancel the transaction, that the instrument was sold for use in the foreign country, that this must have been understood by the vendor since the buyer was domiciled there etc., those facts (connecting factors) which may result in the application of the law of the foreign country must be held to have been invoked in order to affect the decision in the case, even though they hav not been formally used in support of a claim for such application of foreign law. In this case, Philip means, the court may proceed *sua sponte* to apply the law of the foreign country even if the parties have conducted their litigation as if Danish law were the *lex causae.*

104 *Vide* Ekelöf, *Rättegång,* I, 1957, pp. 40 ff.

and practical that an alimony action between foreign spouses shall be decided in accordance with rules prevailing in what may be called the "legal *milieu*" of the spouses. If the reasoning described above were accepted, however, the court would be prevented from applying the Swedish choice of law rule and, by that intermediary, the law of Quebec. The wife has not claimed the application of foreign law, nor invoked a connecting factor in support of any other claim. In this situation, there seems to be a conflict between that which is prohibited under procedural law and that which is required for the purpose of private international law. Let us suppose, moreover, that where a deserted wife is entitled to alimony the applicable Canadian rules prescribe that the amount should stand in a fixed relation to the husband's income and that a contract whereby a wife entitled to this privilege renounces the whole alimony, or part of it, is a nullity—which means that under Canadian law, the matter is not such as to be subject to private settlement between the parties. Would the Swedish judge really remain ignorant—in a formal sense—about these rules merely because his course of action as dictated by chapter 17:3 of the Judicial Procedure Code would be to pass a decision in accordance with *Swedish* substantive rules, according to which alimony actions between spouses may be settled by agreement. Upon closer examination, however, this opposition between the claim for application of Canadian substantive law embodied in the conflict rule and the reference to Swedish law in the procedural enactment would seem to be more apparent than real. For chapter 17:3 of the Judicial Procedure Code does not purport to solve problems of private international law. As a consequence of this view, we can still maintain the principle that choce of law rules shall always be observed *ex officio*. Chapter 17:3 of the Judicial Procedure Code, which is merely intended to govern a procedural question, will then be construed, in international actions, as a rule to the effect that if the parties are at liberty to settle their litigaton by agreement *under the lex causae,* a decision on the substantive merits of the case must not be based upon a fact which neither party has invoked in support of his claim or as a defence.

The absolute character of conflict rules is in no way modified by the fact that *under these rules themselves,* the parties are sometimes allowed to make a choice of applicable substantive rules. From an historical point of view, the will of the parties has possibly been "autonomous" in mercantile law in the sense that the legal relations between contracting parties have primarily been determined by their will.[105] In contemporary conflict law, however, the will of the parties can be held "autonomus" only where a choice of law rule prescribes, e.g., that the law applicable to litigation in the field of contracts is, in the first place, that law which has been chosen by the parties.[106] Similarly, the private international law of the *lex fori* may allow the parties to undertake a choice of law in court, e.g., by jointly declaring that the action should be decided under the substantive rules of the *lex fori.* This only means that—particularly in certain fields of the law of contract and property—choice of law rules attach decisive importance to the will of the parties as a connecting factor. It does not mean that the parties are at liberty to apply or set aside choice of law rules at their own discretion. It may further occur in private international law that certain provisions open a possibility for the parties to take measures which imply, in actual fact, a choice of law, e.g. chapter 1:2 of the 1904 Act, where it is laid down that an alien wishing to contract a marriage in Sweden is free to prove his capacity either under his own personal law or under any legal system to which that law refers.[107]

In this connection, it should finally be mentioned very briefly that the effects of *amendments* to conflict rules have been discussed in international legal writing. Shall the new or the old rule be applied in an action which is based, e.g., upon a contract concluded before such amendment? The natural answer seems to be that this question must be decided in accordance with the general rules of the *lex fori* on the retroactive effects of new

[105] Cf. Karlgren, *Kutym och rättsregel,* 1960, pp. 45 ff.

[106] Cf. Riezler, *Internationales Zivilprozessrecht,* 1949, p. 492: "Die Parteiwillkür kann darüber, welche Rechtsordnung anzuwenden sei, nur insoweit entscheiden, als die massgebenden Kollisionsnormen ihr diese Freiheit lassen."

[107] Sec. 2 of the 1912 Act on the legal effects of marriage, etc., in international relations would seem to make it possible for third parties to make a choice between Swedish law and that foreign law which, in the situation concerned, must not be invoked "against a third party."

legislation.[108] In Sweden it would seem that when modifications are made in the rules of private international law, special transitional provisions are sometimes both natural and necessary. If no such provisions are enacted, new legislation in this field is likely to have a retroactive effect.[109] It is possible, however, that no such effect would be granted a choice of law rule prescribing that a question which deals with the validity of a contract shall be decided under another legal system than that which was applicable under the choice of law rules as they stood when the contract was concluded.[110] This uncertainty calls for clear transitional provisions. New principles introduced by the decisions of courts are necessarily "retroactive" in their effects; the first time that the *lex rei sitae* was applied instead of the rule *mobilia personam sequuntur,* earlier events were obviously being treated in a new manner.

The "Sphere of Operation" of Choice of Law Rules

As indicated by the term "private international law", choice of law rules have their principal sphere of operation in actions concerning the property, rights and obligations of private persons and their family relations A choice of law rule implies that provisions in the *lex fori* are set aside and *replaced* by substantive rules of foreign law. The Swedish rules on the distribution of a deceased person's estate are replaced, e.g., by German rules, if the deceased was a German national at the time of his death. It is not infrequently stated that the scope of choice of law rules is limited to the field of private law. It

[108] *Vide* Roubier, *Le droit transitoire,* 2 ed. 1960, pp. 562 ff. According to Niederer (at pp. 368 f.) the prevailing opinion in contemporary writing would be that a new conflict rule "kann nur für die *nach* seinem Inkrafttreten entstandenen Rechtsverhältnisse gelten." This, the author means, would be true only where a country has no general "intertemporal" rules and—probably—explicit provisions on the introduction of the amendment are equally absent. *Vide* also Graulich, *op.cit.,* pp. 164 ff.

[109] Cf. 1915 *N.J.A.* 391, the statement of the Council on Legislation in 1916 *N.J.A.* II, p. 324 and the discussion about the retro-active effects of the rules in the 1912 Act in *Royal Proposition* No. 58, 1912, at pp. 22 ff. (Supreme Court) and 41 (the Minister of Justice).

[110] On new legislation in property, torts, and contract, vide Almén & Eklund, *Om köp och byte av lös egendom,* II, Stockholm 1960, pp. 890 ff., and 1911 *N.J.A.* 48.

can hardly be pretended, however, that it would follow from the "nature" of choice of law rules that they cannot claim a more extensive function. Is it not possible then, that the question of replacing Swedish rules of "public law" by foreign provisions could be raised in an action brought to a Swedish court?

An answer cannot be given merely upon the strenght of conclusions from any fixed definition of the term "private international law".[111] The reasons for the distinction between public and private law cannot offer us guidance.[112] It was never intended to solve such problems as arise in a "conflict" between legal systems. It is necessary, therefore, to examine limited fields of law and conclude, in each individual case, on the ground of legislative provisions and judicial decisions, to what extent foreign law is "imported" to replace Swedish rules. We shall find, in the course of such an enquiry, that foreign criminal law is not applied; it must be assumed, however, that when applying the Swedish Criminal Code in criminal actions, certain prejudicial questions may be raised, for the decision of which foreign law may assume importance.[113] As a rule, Swedish procedural law is not replaced by foreign rules. Proceedings in courts and in other agencies are subject to the law of the land. Exceptionally, however, foreign law may be of relevance. If proceedings are instituted for the granting of an *exequatur* of a foreign judgment or if such a judgment is of prejudicial importance in a civil action, the Swedish court must ascertain that the document is really a "judgment" under the procedural rules of the state from which it emanates or that it is no longer subject to appeal, etc. A regular application of conflict rules takes place in those cases where a state adheres to the principle of enforcing foreign judgments upon the conditiòn that they are binding in the country from which they come. When trying whether a person has a deed entitling to immediate execution, the rules of the *lex fori* are then (wholly or partially) replaced by foreign rules even though, in the usual terminology, these are procedural. Foreign fiscal laws, re-

[111] It should be noticed that Professor Gihl's definition in *Lois* (at p. 170) does not admit any such conclusions: "Nous définissons donc cette branche du droit comme l'ensemble des règles du droit national d'un pays, en vertu desquelles les tribunaux de ce pays appliquent des règles de droit étrangères aux rapports présentant un élément étranger."

[112] Cf. Ross, *Om ret og retfaerdighed*, 1953, pp. 246 ff.

[113] Cf. Eek, p. 160, note 3.

quisition rules, etc. are not applied in Sweden, on the ground that no jurisdiction is held to exist.[114] Once an action has been found cognizable, however, the question may arise whether "public-law elements" in the foreign *lex causae* are to be applied.[115] It is further obvious that in some cases a question must be decided in accordance with foreign "public law," and it is far from impossible that this question is the only important element in the whole suit. The question whether a contract between a French municipality and a Swedish vendor is invalid on the alleged ground that the person who signed the contract on behalf of the municipal body had no powers to bind it can hardly answered unless French local government legislation is applied. In a case like this, a rule of "private" international law (a choice of law rule) prescribes the application of French law, as being the legal system of the country to which the municipality belongs.[116] Similarly, the public law of international organizations may be applied, for instance to settle the question of the validity of an agreement between it and a private party.

Thus it is obvious that the sphere of operation of choice of law rules cannot be determined with certainty. It could even be argued that there is nothing to prevent a legislature or courts from laying down conflict rules covering. the whole legal system. The increasing number of international conventions, particularly in the field of administrative law, has in fact resulted in the use of conflict technique also within branches of the law where in earlier days foreign rules were not introduced to replace Swedish provisions.[117]

Rules Incompatible with the Structure of the Lex Fori

It is recognized that within that field of the legal system which is generally considered as private law, foreign rules may be introduced to replace Swedish enactments. It is in the nature of things that these rules differ from their Swedish counterparts; if

[114] Cf. above, pp. 78 f.

[115] *Vide* further below, pp. 206 ff.

[116] Cf. Nial, pp. 78 f.; Eek, p. 158.

[117] Cf. Eek, p. 158, note 6, on payment of workmen's compensation awards by Swedish authorities but in accordance with Norwegian law. In this connection, some interest is also due to that trend of development which is illustrated by the Act on cooperation with other States in the frontier customs control. (Cooperation Act), 1959. *Vide* Jungefors in *Sv.J.T.* 1960, pp. 305 ff.

not, private international law would have no reasonable function. But to what extent are such differences acceptable? This question is usually answered in the chapters devoted to the doctrine of *ordre public* (*vide* below, pp. 197 ff.), according to which certain rules may be rejected as repugnant to the general principles underlying the legal system of the *forum*. It is occasionally argued, however, that "actions concerning rights or legal institutions of a type unknown to the *forum* state" (structurally incompatible institutions) should not be cognizable at the *forum*.[118] This reasoning would seem to imply the idea that Swedish choice of law rules (or those of any given state) only concern legal relations to which at least some sort of counterpart can be found in Swedish private law, and that in other cases it is simply impossible to find anything which could be "replaced" by an imported rule. Those cases, it would follow, would be outside the "sphere of operation" of Swedish choice of law rules. To refuse to try an action in these situations, however, would seem to be contrary to the fundamental principle that the protection of the law shall always be granted. If a Swede engages, in England, to marry an English-woman, but subsequently breaks the engagement, it seems unreasonable for Swedish courts to refuse to take jurisdiction on the ground that breach of promise is unknown to Swedish law, if the lady institutes a suit against him in Sweden, where he is domiciled and has his property. If, on the other hand, the supposedly applicable English rules on damages for breach of promise turn out to be inacceptable, they will have to be rejected under the principle of *ordre public,* and the Englishwoman's claim will be refused in accordance with Swedish law, which does not allow such actions to succeed.[119] It is not justifiable to pretend that a refusal to take cognizance is the necessary solution, because no conflict rule is available for claims based upon structurally incompatible institutions (e.g. dowry or morning gift).

[118] Cf. Karlgren, p. 162. *Vide* Riezler, pp. 223 ff.

[119] This would seem to be the reasoning adopted by Hassler & Nial, at pp. 48 f. The fact that a foreign legal institution is unknown in Denmark, Borum says (at p. 75), is "certainly not sufficient to exclude the use of that foreign law which would otherwise be applicable under the rules of Danish private international law."

There is no insurmountable difficulty in finding a conflict rule concerning, e.g., dowries by comparing the case with existing rules on similar matters, such as alimony to children and gifts *inter vivos* to legal heirs.[120]

Unwritten Choice of Law Rules

We have already recalled the fact that there are both written and unwritten conflict rules. The former are found in statutes. But how can the latter be found? Gihl has often emphasized that "without support in a choice of law rule, there can be no application of foreign law".[121] This dictum creates the impression that it is possible to list the various unwritten choice of law rules before their application is called for. However, the problem is not as easy as that. There are—at least, there have been—jurists who take for granted that a court applies its own law *(lex fori)* and makes exceptions from this principle only in the presence of an explicit statutory rule establishing such exception ("principle of exclusivity").[122] Where this principle is upheld, there is obviously no scope for unwritten conflict rules. If, however, we argue against the advocates of this principle that legislation is not the only source of law and that courts, in Sweden as elsewhere, also take customary rules, "the nature of things" and earlier judicial decisions on similar matters into consideration when searching for rules upon which a judgment can be based, this objection is nevertheless insufficient to furnish an answer to the question *how* unwritten conflict rules are found. If we consider this problem outside the courtroom, as a question about the probable attitude of a court to a certain matter, we find little guidance in that source of law which comes next in turn after legislation, viz. precedents. There are not many decisions which constitute a series. Judgments are scattered, and it is far from always certain that a given decision will really constitute, in the distant future, a strong reason for the courts to adopt the rule expressed in such precedent. The various unwritten conflict rules are therefore difficult to establish with a reasonable degree of

[120] Cf. Lederman in *Law and Contemporary Problem,* 1956, pp. 592 f., and Melchior, p. 80.
p. 80.
[121] *Vide* e.g. Gihl, *Studier,* pp. 357 ff.
[122] On this doctrine, *vide* Ekström, *op.cit.,* pp. 46 ff.

certainty. Nor, on the other hand, can it be argued that no conflict rules *exist* because they have not appeared in the decisions of courts.[123] There are still many fields of the law which are "blanks" from the point of view of private international law; no question of applying foreign law has been raised. Does this mean, however, that "there are no choice of law rules" in these fields? Will courts have to apply the *lex fori* simply because they are barred from laying down a conflict rule which results in the application of foreign law? Obviously not. For however scarce precedents may be, those which exist show at least that when a question arises within any of these "blanks on the map", courts nowadays do consider the question of applying foreign law and often draft (create) a choice of law rule which is thereupon often described in theoretical works as a creation of precedents. This leads to the statement that choice of law rules may "exist" although they have not (yet) taken shape in a judicial decision or an enactment ("latent choice of law rules"). Courts actually conform to a pattern which may be described as follows: in those cases which include foreign elements, Swedish courts proceed—usually at the request of either party—to decide in a preliminary way whether foreign law is to replace the law of Sweden in the action. Although in actual practice the situation does not imply a choice between an unlimited number of legal systems, the decision nevertheless takes the form of an application of an abstract choice of law rule. The ground of this pattern of behaviour, which has been called the "principle of internationality" in conflict literature, is possibly to be found in that "non-objectivated" source of law which the Danish writer Ross calls "the tradition of civilization".[124] Possibly it may be called custom. The pattern is there, however, and may be described as a first rule of private international law. In the imperative, it may be expressed as a rule to the effect that where the contrary does not follow from a statute, *the judge has to choose the applicable law in*

[123] From his thesis—"without support in a choice of law rule there can be no application of foreign law"—Gihl *(loc.cit.)* draws the further conclusion that *e.g.* foreign requisition laws are not applied, since there is no choice of law rule enjoining upon the judge to apply them.

[124] Ross, *op.cit.*, pp. 90 ff. Cf. the quotation from Sir Hersch Lauterpacht above, p. 1. Ekström, (*op.cit.*, pp. 46 ff.) who adopts the principle of internationality, argues that where no positive enactment can be found, the judge has to determine the applicable law "according to such principles as appear just and reasonable in consideration of the character of the case at bar." Cf. also Hult, pp. 4 f.

cases containing foreign elements with due consideration to justice and practical expediency.[125] This duty of the judge has some connection with his duty (discussed at p. 94 above) to apply choice of law rules *ex officio* and to investigate the possible existence of such foreign elements as may put these rules into operation (connecting factors).

The practice of courts assumes a particular importance from the point of view of legislative policy, since the general principle just referred to is not used for the immediate adjudication upon the dispute. It merely constitutes a standard for the choice of the applicable law, and in the decision it is stated that the choice has taken place in accordance with a more precise choice of law rule—in abstract terms—which may be resorted to for the purpose of choosing the proper law in other actions. It is obviously possible that the judge has had to lay down a conflict rule, the general applicability of which he finds doubtful, simply because he has had to arrive at a reasonable outcome of the case he has a duty to decide. As we have already stated more than once, this contributes to the prevailing uncertainty about the content of choice of law rules. On the other hand, the technique applied in these decisions will undoubtedly help to make law.

What then is the character of the material with which the courts "make" conflict rules? Analogies from written law obviously have some importance; but this seems to be decreasing, since the appropriateness of many conflict rules in written law is nowadays subject to discussion. On the other hand, influences from contemporary international legislative deliberations are increasingly making them-

[125] It does not seem very important in what terms this general standard of behavious is expressed. The tenor suggested in the text is based upon the following statement by Nial (p. 117): "At the root of private international law is the idea that legal questions concerning the relations of private persons are most justly and most practically solved if they are submitted to the legal system of that country with which they have their strongest connections and that therefore a national court of justice—which, when confronted by a legal question with foreign elements, is not entitled to refuse to try the matter—shall not in principle give preference to the *lex fori* but apply that legal system which is indicated by the connecting factors of the case under the competence rules of the *forum*." We do not overlook the fact that Nial's statement merely results in the conclusion that the court shall follow its own "competence rules." This observation is not entirely devoid of purpose, as appears from the often blamed fact that the courts of various countries have a tendency to avoid foreign law. It is common to refer to the *vis attractiva* of the *lex fori* or the "homeward trend" of courts.

selves felt. It must further be assumed that legal writing, the "doctrine", is of great importance. In the preface of his *Handbok* (first ed., 1907), Reuterskiöld states that he had of course tried to make use of modern Swedish decisions but that "it would be utterly wrong to base a survey of contemporary Swedish conflict law, where that term has any sense at all, upon these relatively few and often incompatible decisions". "The building of law through judges and judicial decisions", Reuterskiöld affirms, is in fact "nothing but more or less correctly applied legal science." On the basis of Reuterskiöld's theory, Ekström wrote a few years later, with regard to the situation in Finland, that "those not very rare cases in the field of private international law which our courts have had to try have probably generally been decided on the strength of one or another proposition put forward in legal writing—where the decision has not been exclusively founded upon intuition".[126] The main source of Reuterskiöld's theories was von Bahr's *Lehrbuch des internationalen Privat- und Strafrechts* (Stuttgart 1892), which has thus been, as it were, "translated" for the purposes of the Swedish legal *milieu*. It would still seem to be true that Swedish writers very largely resort to foreign theories and thus make them known.

A further basic concept of private international law should be mentioned in this connection, although it concerns the application of conflict rules just as much as their framing. It is that respect shall be paid to "equality" or "mutuality";[127] this means that in principle foreign law is to be treated as equal to the *lex fori*.[128] A further step is taken when it is recommended that the creation of national law in various countries should be adapted to the purpose underlying work on international conventions in the conflict of laws.[129] Due regard must be paid to what Borum calls the "principle of the uniform

126 Ekström, *op.cit.* p. 42.

127 Hult, pp. 17 f.

128 Karlgren (at p. 28) gives the following example of the principle of "equality": "If it is held by Swedish lawyers e.g. that for deciding the question whether a person is an infant or a lunatic his nationality is of importance, this means that the person's nationality must be taken into account not only where a Swedish subject's minority (lunacy) or full legal capacity is concerned (and Swedish law is consequently applicable), but also where the status of a Frenchman is dealt with (and French law is thus applicable)."

129 Cf. above, p. 31.

solution"[130]—Wengler speaks of the "minimum of conflict"[131]—i.e. the drafters of rules should try to frame conflict rules in such a manner that they help to bring about the result that the substantive law actually applied is the same as would have been applied if the case had been tried in a court abroad.

Like other principles proposed by writers for the making of choice of law rules by courts or by legislation, the principles of internationality, equality, or uniform solution as referred to above hardly tell us anything about the desirable contents of choice of law rules *in concreto*. The difficulty of deciding this question and, more particularly, of arriving by international argeement at choice of law rules with the same effect seems to explain in part the suggestions about a "free lawmaking" method which are occasionally put forward in conflict literature. In the law of contract the courts of many countries—including, nowadays, Sweden—try to find the "proper law of the contract" in each individual action. This "individualizing method" can be described almost with the precision of a rule, however: "questions concerning mutual contractual obligations shall be decided under the rules of that legal system with which the action is most closely connected". In the course of time, it will be possible to conclude from the decisions of courts and prevailing mercantile views and customs—which are connected with the practice of courts—that in contracts of type A, connecting factors of type B are given decisive importance, and such conclusions are made easier by the fact that this method makes use of rules applicable *in dubio* to various kinds of obligations; there are resorted to when the weighing of various connecting factors against one another does not produce any result. On this ground, the individualizing method can hardly be called a "free lawmaking": it makes use of a choice of law rule, albeit a flexible one. A more radical method has been suggested by an American scholar, Professor Yntema. Where several legal systems may have a claim to be applied, i.e. where an action is international in its character, he recommends that the judge himself try to find a solution in accordance with "comparative

130 Borum, pp. 35 f.

131 *Zeitschrift für öffentliches Recht,* 1943—1944, pp. 483 ff.

justice"; this result would be attained through a comparison between "the underlying policies of the domestic substantive laws."[132] Considerations of security militate against this solution. Without choice of law rules of at least relative firmness —among them the rule attributing decisive importance to the will of the parties as a connecting factor—the planning of international legal transactions would be impossible. And such planning may well be the most efficient method for conflict avoidance under present conditions.

B. THE STRUCTURE AND CONSTRUCTION OF CHOICE OF LAW RULES

General Remarks

While the following chapter is devoted to the use made of the available material in the conflict of laws—*inter alia* the question how a choice of law rule is brought into function—we shall now consider the structure and elements of choice of law rules, features characteristic of such rules as legal provisions, and their construction. The legal system, we all know, is composed of rules and fragments of rules, instructions, directives—there are many names which may be used—with a structure varying in many respects, although such variations are not always entitled to any particular interest. Choice of law rules, however, present typical and characteristic differences in relation to other legal provisions. This is due to their specific function. If A institutes an action against B and claims that B should pay a sum of money to him, a choice of law rule will not give the judge any guidance—at least not directly—for his decision about A's claim. The conflict rule only indicates those substantive rules upon which this decision shall be based. It assumes importance only when the presence of a foreign elements makes the judge consider the possibility of a choice of law.

The basic formula for conflict rules can thus be simplified into: "X under the rules of Y". This may be illustrated by an example from the

[132] Yntema in *Canadian Bar Review,* 1957, p. 737. Cf. also Beckett in 15 *B.Y.I.L.* (1934), and Cavers, A Critique of the choice-of-law problem, 47 *Harvard Law Review* (1933—1934), pp. 173 ff.

Swedish Act on international questions with regard to deceased persons' estates, 1937. Chapter 1:6 contains the following rule: "Whether a provision in a will is invalid because of error" etc.—(X)—"shall be tried under the law of that country of which the testator was a citizen when the will was made"—(Y). In an actual case it may occur that the estate of a Dutch national has to be distributed in Sweden. One person, P, invokes a will, which gives him the estate. Other claimants, e.g. the deceased's two brothers, contend that the testator, when making his will, was acting on the erroneous assumption that P was his illegitimate son. P admits that this may have been the case but argues that the will is nevertheless valid. Here we are confronted by a series of facts and a disputed claim which, however, is also a fact. In addition to the examination of facts, the court has to consider the problem from the legal point of view. This is where the choice of law rule comes in as an auxiliary element: with regard to matters like that at bar (X) it prescribes the application of the law in the deceased person's home country (Y). Therefore, it is not in the Swedish Inheritance Code that the rules applicable to the decision is to be found in our example. Instead, we try to get information about the rules of Dutch law on the effects of *error in motivis* upon the validity of wills. The first element of the choice of law rule (X) may be called "referring section". The posterior element (Y), we shall call the "connecting section". Questions relating to the referring section of a choice of law rule, its structure, construction, application, etc. are often dealt with in works on conflicts under the heading of "classification", or as the "classification problem". We have found it most suitable to discuss the "classification" questions in different places, particularly in the following paragraphs about the referring section, where policy considerations appear, and below (pp. 164 ff.) in a connection where the choice of law is essentially treated as a practical question, a task for the courts.

A choice of law rule with the same structure as the provision in the 1937 Act discussed above is usually described as *twofold* and *complete* (or *general*), since it sets out the conditions for the application of both *lex fori* and foreign law. It is customary to distinguish this group from *one-sided* conflict rules, which merely contain the conditions for the applicability of the *lex fori*. As an example, a rule in the French *code civil* (article 3, paragraph 3) is often cited; it provides that French law is applicable to questions of capacity even with regard to

Frenchmen living outside France.[133] A rule to the effect that all contracts of a certain kind concluded within a country are "subject to" the law of the land[134] is also of this character. The rule has nothing to say about contracts made abroad. The one-sided conflict rule is certainly not typical if it is assumed, as a characteristic feature of choice of law rules in general, that their function is to indicate in what cases and in what way a court shall set aside its normal and natural course of action—to apply its own law in cases upon which it must adjudicate. From this point of view the "one-sided conflict rule" may be considered an *ex tuto* provision, an explicit prohibition against setting aside the *lex fori* in certan cases.[135] However, even "one-sided" rules fulfil the functions of choice of law rules, for in actual practice, courts often complete them in such a way that they become twofolds rules. Thus it is held in French legal writing that it may be concluded from the above-mentioned provision in the *code civil* that under French law, as a general principle, "la capacité est régie par la loi persoinelle de l'incapable."[136] Finally, writers on private international law occasionally make use of the term "*incomplete twofold conflict rules.*" What is meant are rules which lay down, on the one hand, the conditions for the applicability of the *lex fori* and, on the other hand, the conditions for applying foreign law *in certain cases,* while other cases are left aside. Thus a rule may be introduced on the distribution of the estates of deceased persons who were domiciled in the country where the enactment is in force; it may be laid down in the rule that the nationality of the *de cuius* at the time of his death is decisive, whereas nothing is said about the law applicable to the distribution of the estates of persons not domiciled in the country. The extent to which and the manner in which one-sided or

[133] Cf. chap. 4, sec. 1 of the Swedish Act of 1904: "The rules of Swedish law on guardianship for infants shall be applied also to infants who are Swedish citizens but not dimiciled within the Kingdom."

[134] Cf. above, pp. 60 ff.

[135] In general, courts do not seem to consider themselves bound to invoke any particular rule of private international law in support of their application of the *lex fori.* In legal writing, however, the principle implying that "procedural questions are governed by the *lex fori*" is occasionally described as a conflict rule. *Vide* Malmström in *Liber amicorum,* p. 135, or Hult in *Festskrift tillägnad Halvar Sundberg,* 1959, p. 243.

[136] *Vide* Batiffol, pp. 467 ff.; cf. Niederer, pp. 122 f.

incomplete choice of law rules shall be widened into twofold and complete provisions are problems of statutory construction.[137]

The Referring Section

The judge makes use of a choice of law rule when he has to make a choice between legal systems. Under the rule, substantive provisions of foreign instead of Swedish law shall be applied for the decision of certain questions. It should be pointed out that purely internal law also contains choice of law rules. Let us assume that in an exclusively internal civil action, A raises a claim against B. Both parties produce evidence about those facts which they consider to be relevant for the decision and therefore important elements in the action, and both submit legal arguments in their pleadings. As a basis for his decision, the judge needs a rule which, in Sweden, he usually looks for in a statute. In order to find it, the judge "classifies" (characterizes, subsumes under a category) the dispute. For instance, different substantive rules are applicable to sales of goods *in specie* and to sales of quantities defined *in genere*. In order to know which body of rules is to be applied, the judge examines the facts in the light of a definition in section 3 of the Sale of Goods Act, 1905, which describes the characteristic features of a situation which, in legal language, should be characterized as a sale of a determined quantity as opposed to a sale *in specie*. The rules on real property form a specialized group which is distinct from the provisions on personalty. In this case the "classification" is performed with the help of an Act of 1895 on real property.

This choice of the applicable rules is not always easy but it seems such an obvious stage in the process of statutory construction that in Swedish internal law it is not treated as a special—or as a specially tricky—problem.[138] The choice of law under a conflict rule is subject to the same technique. If A is an alien who made a contract with a Swede, B, in a place abroad, where the contract is also to be performed, the connection with foreign law is obviously of a particular strength. Are the rules of the Swedish Sale of Goods Act, 1905, or the

[137] Cf. Trammer, "Über die sogenannten 'einseitigen Normen' des internationalen Privatrechts," *Rabels, Z.* XXII (1957), pp. 405 ff.

[138] Some problems of this kind are discussed by Ahlander, *Om rätt och rättstillämpning,* Stockholm 1952, pp. 123 ff.

substantive rules of a certain foreign statute on the same topic applicable? The judge finds his answer to this question by considering whether the facts of the case are such that, in legal terminology, the action really concerns a "sale of goods" and not e.g. a "hire of services," and by consulting a choice of law rule which lays down, e.g., that "questions concerning sales of goods" shall be decided, unless otherwise agreed upon by the parties, under the substantive rules of that legal system with which the case is most strongly connected ("individualizing" method or "proper law" theory), the strength of the connection being evaluated in the light of a rule which is applicable in case of doubt and which is not the same as would be applied to a contract on hire of services.

The fact that, whether a conflict rule has been created by precedents or has been laid down in a statute, its "referring section" normally contains a legal concept or a forensic term ("sale", "succession", "estate", "legal effects of marriage", etc). has sometimes been understood to imply that the referring section describes or concerns certain "subjective rights" or legal relationships on which the "connecting section" of the rule subsequently contains substantive dispositions. Among legal writers, von Bar has already attacked this opinion and emphasized that the referring section merely describes pure facts. Any other interpretation is impossible, "denn um zu wissen, ob bestimmte Tatsachen ein Rechtsverhältnis darstellen oder hervorbringen, muß man dieselben an einem bestimmten Gesetze oder Rechte als der massgebenden Norm messen, d.h. zuvor *das* Recht oder Gesetz kennen, von dem sie beherrscht werden, und dies gerade kennen wir einstweilen noch nicht".[139] A comparison with internal rules would seem to be of some interest also in this connection. Such rules may very well be drafted in such a casuistic manner that they contain a description of pure facts to which is attached a direction for the judge's or a private person's course of action in the presence of these facts. Several examples of this drafting technique may be found in the Swedish Code of Laws, 1734: "if a shepherd allows animals to go astray"; "if a man comes drunk to church", "if somebody suffers greatly from another man's house, from water falling from the roof, from darkness, windows, loopholes, water being taken away, or any other prejudice ...". In order to create a legal system

[139] von Bar, *Theorie und Praxis des Internationalen Privatrechts,* 2 ed., 1889, p. 107.

which is more complete and easier to survey as a whole, modern legislators draft their rules in such a manner that their field of application is defined by legal symbols. This is also the case with choice of law rules. Their referring section states what kinds of facts they are applicable to, although they make use of terms from the world of legal concepts; in other words, this part of a chocie of law rule defines the delimitation of the applicability of the rule.

From the point of view of the legislator the question how the referring section should be framed or, to put it more explicitly, what facts shall be covered by the rule, is obviously a question of policy. As far as the judge is concerned, the problem is one of construction, and in textbooks on the conflict of laws, the descriptions of choice of law rules as actually in force also constitute attemps to construe statutory rules or precedents. However, interpretation is also strongly influenced by considerations of legislative policy. This is due, *inter alia,* to the fact that the referring section of choice of law rules is often drafted in a sweeping and occasionally a not very clear way. The applicability, or scope, of a rule—which should result from its construction—therefore becomes a doubtful question which, in many cases, cannot be answered without an enquiry into, and an evaluation of, what must be the reasonable purpose of the rule. This statement is even more true of rules which have been created by precedents. And finally, as we have underlined more than once, the judge may occasionally find himself obliged to "make" a choice of law rule. If so, he may consider proposals put forward by writers, and look for suggestions in foreign law. However, the policy evaluation must be done by the judge himself. It is chiefly based upon the actual case, but it is likely that a judge—just as much as a writer—will pay some regard to what he considers to be the particular function of the rule within the legal system. Obviously this point of view also assumes some importance where the construction of a choice of law rule already made is concerned. The particular function of choice of law rules may imply that the legal terms used for the drafting of such rules have a meaning which differs somewhat from that which they would have in internal rules.[140] It must be emphasized, how-

[140] *Vide* Malmström, *Det s. k. kvalifikationsproblemet inom internationell privaträtt,* Uppsala 1938, particularly pp. 31 ff. and the same author in *Liber amicorum,* pp. 130 ff.; Hult, *op.cit.,* pp. 235 ff.; earlier than these writers, Rabel discussed the problem in "Das Problem der Qualifikation" in *Rabels* Z. V. 1931,

ever, that internal legal systematics and terminology constitute the obviously starting points for the purpose both of drafting and of interpreting the referring section of choice of law rules. Written rules generally deal with questions of a type known to the legislator and described by such terms as "questions of succession", "the mutual rights and duties of spouses in their personal relations", etc. In some cases, the meaning of a statute is not subject to doubt. It is beyond the field where clear solutions are offered by statutes that the constructions of judges and writers assume importance from the point of view of legislative policy; in these cases, such deviations from the normal construction of concepts for the purposes of internal law as were referred to above may be taken into consideration.[141] Occasionally, the internal system of concepts can offer no guidance: we have no substantive rules on e.g. morninggifts, and it seems uncertain under what heading such rules would be put if they did exist; nevertheless, a judge may be faced with the task of "finding" a choice of law rule on such a topic.[142]

In court, the choice of law rules—which are then assumed to be "ready-made" and have the contents of their referring sections determined—are *confronted* with the case actually at bar. The judge has to put the question whether this case, upon which he has to adjudicate, is of such character as to fall within the field of application of this or that choice of law rule in the *lex fori* or whether it falls com-

pp. 241 ff. Cf. further below, pp. 164 ff. on the choice of law in concrete civil action.

[141] Cf. Karlgren in *Sv.J.T.* 1954, pp. 497 ff.

[142] It should also be noticed that choice of law rules may "expire" or loose their applicability because of changes in internal law and legal systematics. One conflict rule which is part of Swedish law as now in force is occasionally described as follows: questions concerning rights *in rem* ("real rights") are usually answered by the law of the place where the *res* is situated, the *lex rei sitae*. Is this statement correct (apart from the important lack of any reference to the element of *time* (cf. below, pp. 126 f.)? Is it not necessary to conclude that since we have abandoned, or at least begun to abandon, the fundamental distinction between rights *in rem* and *in personam* in internal legal systematics as no longer corresponding to the actual facts of the law, it is doubtful whether a choice of law rule may be successfully based upon that distinction? In legal writing, there is no uniform "real statute" *(French: statut réel)* except in chapter headings, and the analysis of writers deals separately with specific questions concerning proprietary rights: immovables, *res in transitu,* the protection of emptors against the vendor's creditors, etc.

pletely outside the operation of conflict rules. The practical consequences of his answer to this question may turn out to be so undesirable that the judge considers himself obliged to revert to the task of interpreting the referring section of the rule concerned. In this way, rules may undergo modifications.

This problem, and a number of others dealing with the application of choice of law rules, have been intensely debated in conflict literature under the name of "classification problems". It is a problem not unknown in international legislative work. Since the referring section of choice of law rules is usually interpreted in each country on the basis of the legal systematics and legal concepts of the *lex fori,* it sometimes happens that the desired result of international conventions, viz. the application of identical substantive rules in the decision of each concrete action regardles of the *forum,* is not always obtained in actual fact. Thus if several states agree upon a choice of law rule to the effect that "questions concerning international sales shall be decided under the *lex debitoris*", it is quite possible that the referring section—"questions concerning international sales"—will be construed differently in states A and B, both signatories of the agreement, so that an action X, which is held to concern an international sale in A, is decided by the courts of that country in accordance with the *lex debitoris,* whereas the courts of B do not consider the case as an "international" sale and may therefore find that it lies within the sphere of application of another choice of law rule which provides for the applicability of e.g. the *lex loci contractus* (which, *in casu,* is another law). In the drafting of conventions, detailed definitions of the meaning of the referring section are often attempted. Resort to this method implies that a highly specialized choice of law rule—the scope of which is consequently limited—is agreed upon.

We have now arrived at another policy question with regard to the drafting of referring sections, i.e. the problem whether conflict rules with an extensive or a limited scope are to be preferred. In international conflict literature, this question is know as the "slicing" *(Spaltung, coupure)* or specialization of choice of law rules. Either the referring section can be framed in such a manner that it covers e.g. all questions which deal with the distribution of a deceased person's estate, or this section can be limited, as the case is in the Swedish Act of 1937 on international questions regarding deceased persons' estates where questions about the formal validity of wills, the capacity to make a will, the essential validity of wills, etc. are subject to special rules. It is possible either to determine the scope of the *lex obligationis* in such a manner that all questions in an action upon a contract are decided under the same legal rules, or to lay down different choice of law rules for such actions, so that one law is applicable to the validity of the contract, another set of rules is applied where the effects of the contract are to be dealt with, and a third law governs questions about the modalities of payment.[143] The prevailing opinion would seem to be that specialization is not satisfactory and that conflict rules should preferably be given an extensive scope.[144] In fact, it is the method of far-reaching "slicing" which has given rise to the lengthy debate which has been going on in conflict literature, particularly about the relations between succession claims and matrimonial proprietary rights. The choice of law rule of country C applicable to "questions of succession" refers to the law of A, whereas the choice of law rule for "matrimonial claims" makes the law of B applicable; as a consequence, the widow X, who had a matrimonial proprietary right in a portion of her husband's estate but no right of succession under the law of A, and who had a right of succession but no proprietary right under the law of B, will be barred from any claim upon her husband's estate if it is distributed in country C where the laws of B and A are "successively" applied, as the conflict term is. For in spite of various recommendations to proceed otherwise found in conflict literature, the usual technique means that where a conflict rule makes e.g. German law applicable to "questions of succession", Swedish rules on "succession"—that concept being defined in accordance with Swedish legal principles—are set aside and replaced by all those rules of German law which, in the Swedish view, deal with "succession", while no regard is paid to such German rules as are considered "matrimonial" from a Swedish angle. In many cases, conflict rules are drafted in such a way that the use of this

[143] Cf. with regard to Swedish law Nial, pp. 46 ff. A "slicing" also results from choice of law rules which are drafted in such manner that questions about *e.g.* obligations shall be determined under the *lex loci solutionis*. In case of mutual obligations, such a rule may produce the result that the vendor's obligations are subject to one law and those of the emptor governed by another legal system ("two laws system"). Cf. Karlgren, p. 105.

[144] Cf. Niederer, pp. 207.

technique must be held to be intended by the makers of a statute. The "problem of classification" which may thus arise through a *successive application* of rules from foreign legal system can only be solved through a reform of conflict rules, as the late Professor Hult has convincingly demonstrated.[145] It is when *drafting* these rules that their consequences must be taken into consideration.[146]

There are cases, however, where good grounds may be invoked in favour of a specialization.

> Thus it may be a rational solution to decide questions concerning the modalities of payment in accordance with the *lex loci solutionis,* as a "subsidiary" legal system, even if the action as such is governed by another legal system.[147] In chapter 1:9 of the Act on international questions regarding deceased persons' estates, 1937, it is laid down that the question "whether a person has capacity to receive a testamentary bequest or to acquire property by intestate succession is decided under the law of the country of which that person is a citizen". Lewald has furnished a striking illustration of the need for this rule which, on the one hand, excepts the question of capacity from trial under the law otherwise applicable to the distribution of the estate and which, on the other hand, is an expression of the principle that questions of legal capacity should be decided under the same law, regardless of the situation in which they arise.[148] Under Spanish law, a child must have been alive outside the mother's body for at least 24 hours in order to be considered as an independent physical person. Suppose that an estate is to be distributed in Sweden in accordance with the rules of Dutch law. Dutch succession rules grant the child of a Spanish mother capacity to acquire property by succession if the child was alive at the time of the death of the *de cuius* even if the child's total life-

[145] Hult in *Festkrift tillägnad Halvar Sundberg,* pp. 247 ff.

[146] In international legislative work, the drawbacks of specialization are avoided by an *international* definition of the referring section, which is intended to replace the various national concepts.

[147] It is more doubtful whether an alien's being a "merchant" or not is a question for his personal law, while the contract of sale for which this question is of importance is governed by Swedish law. This standpoint is defended by Berglund, *Svensk eller främmande lag,* 1946, p. 13.

[148] Lewald, p. 13.

time did not exceed 20 hours. If the question of capacity were not singled out, the child would be held entitled to the property. Thereupon the Swedish administrator or court would distribute the Spanish child's portion in accordance with the legal system indicated by Swedish choice of law rules on intestate succession, i.e. Spanish law. Under Spanish law, however, the child has never been considered as a person and thus cannot be inherited.

In actual practice, a splitting of legal issues by means of specialized choice of law rules is not infrequent. The practical result *in concreto* is that the decision in an action will be passed in accordance with rules from several legal systems, perhaps several foreign legal systems. This is also the case where the referring section of a choice of law rule prescribes a cumulation of substantive rules (*vide* below, pp. 122 f.). This method of creating a *lex causae* with materials from various quarters undoubtedly makes the above-mentioned incorporation theory (pp. 93 f.) appear realistic; it can hardly be stated that e.g. English law is applied where certain elements of the action are at the same time treated in accordance with French law. The *lex causae* rather appears a special law, a composite system created by the operation of choice of law rules. Moreover, certain rules of an absolute character in the *lex fori* are often applied side by side with the *lex causae* (below, pp. 224 ff.).

C. THE CONNECTING SECTION

It has been stated above that the need for choice of law rules is created by the fact that certain cases contain a foreign element. These elements, or the connection between the case and a foreign country, or foreign legal system, oblige the court or other authority confronted by the task of deciding the case to put the question whether it is not suitable, or most consistent with the demands of justice, to apply foreign instead of Swedish law in reaching its decision. The drafter of statutes who frames written conflict rules is faced by the same problem. As already stated, a choice of law rule may be simplified into the formula "X under the rules of Y," where X is the referring section, which we have now dealt with, and Y is the connecting section. The legislative technique used for the framing of choice of law rules both in the process of legislation and in the free creation of law through the courts implies, in its simple and typical form, that a certain element of the case is picked out as decisive for the choice of law, that is as Y. An action may have connections with several countries or legal systems. A Swede domiciled in Spain has died in that country and left property in Sweden; his only relative is a son who is domiciled in London and is a British subject. The Swedish estate is to be distributed in Sweden. A German citizen domiciled in Denmark has left property in Sweden, which is to distributed there. On the choice of law in these cases, it is laid down in chapter 1:1 of the 1937 Act that "the right to acquire property by intestate succession after a Swedish citizen shall be tried in accordance with Swedish law even if the deceased was not domiciled in the Kingdom". It is further provided: "in respect of intestate succession after a citizen of another country the deceased's national law shall be applied." Apart from certain modifications laid down in the ensuing sections of chapter 1 of the 1937 Act, the rule is, consequently, that where the "right to acquire property by intestate succession" is concerned the Swedish choice of law rule picks out the nationality of the *de cuius* (at the time of death) as decisive among various possible connections, points of connection or *connecting factors.* Since more than one connection or connecting factor may be found in the same case, it may be rational to use a special term for that connecting factor which is decisive under a certain choice of law rule, *i.e.* which constitutes the connecting section of the rule. The term *connecting element* could be reserved for this purpose; it should be pointed out, however, that in conflict literature, the terms "connecting factor" and "connecting element" and other similar terms are used indiscriminately, sometimes to denote foreign elements of the action in general, sometimes as a term for the connecting fact which is granted decisive importance under a given choice of law rule. Occasionally, the decisive connecting factor is described as the *localizing element* which, as it were, localizes the case to the sphere of a certain national system of law.

The private international law of a country is characterized by the principles followed in the framing of the connecting sections of choice of law rules. The choice of connecting factors is the decisive policy problem. It is natural, therefore, that for centuries legal writers have given particular attention to the question of the "proper" connection. Writers who thought they could deduce legal rules from principles in the law of nature or conflict rules from the law of nations often chose to submit their conclusions in the form of "principles", which were said to be binding for the creation of conflict law. It must be strongly emphasized, however, that in reality the questions concerning the choice of a connecting factor are *policy problems.*[149] Before making a choice, the legislature—or the judge when acting as legislator—examines a number of questions, such as the effects of a rule framed in this or that manner. In a country like Sweden, the drafter of the rule may well consider that he is bound to find the most adequate and just solutions (cf. above, pp. 105 f.), but in order to arrive at these solutions, he must pay attention to a great number of circumstances, such as the character of international intercourse, the legal rules prevailing abroad, the present rules of his own legal system, etc. When he finally makes his choice, he is free. He is not bound by any "principles" laid down in legal writing. However, through its arguments concerning the "proper" connection conflict literature has elaborated many valuable recommendations for legislators and judges; through its examination of the policy problems involved, the conflict *doctrine* has been of great importance for the evolution of this branch of the law.

Certain "principles" put forward by writers may obviously be used in a theoretical work in order to resume briefly the actual state of the law. Thus it may be stated that the principle of nationality (as opposed to the principle of domicile) prevails in Swedish conflict law. Similarly, it is true that in the Swedish conflict rules on bankruptcy the principle of territoriality prevails, since foreign bankruptcy decisions are usually not recognized in Sweden. The last-mentioned "principle" must be invoked cautiously, however. It is defined in many different ways. Sometimes it is invoked in support of the opinon that certain foreign laws have only a "territorial validity", but it should be observed that the "principle" does not provide any effective help towards understanding which those laws are. Sometimes it serves as an argument for the thesis that rights acquired abroad must be protected as "vested rights." In both cases, remnants of thinking habits which are likely to have their roots in the theory of the "law of nature" are clearly visible: all persons and all actions within a country are "subject" to the sovereign's power; a sovereign "cannot" exercise power *extra territorium;* one sovereign's exercise of power

[149] Cf. Gihl, *Principer,* pp. 394 ff.

"must" be respected by other sovereigns in a particular way, etc. In each individual case, where a "principle" from the conflict *doctrine* is invoked, it is necessary to examine the meaning of the statement where such principle appears: whether it is intended to describe certain fundamental characteristics of the law as actually in force, or whether its purpose is to advocate a certain policy. In both cases, its soundness must be tried.

While a discussion of the connecting section of choice of law rules from the point of view of legislative *policies* would seem to have its proper place in descriptions of the particular rules, this seems the proper moment for a discussion in some detail of the legislative *technique* used in the framing of connecting sections and of certain problems related to the construction of such sections.

Legislative Technique

In its simplest form, the legislative technique implies that a connection with a foreign legal system is effected by means of *one* single fact, as for instance in chapter 1:1 of the 1937 Act, where the deceased's nationality is the connecting factor. In many choice of law rules, however, the connecting section has been framed in a much more complicated way. The terms *cumulative* and *alternative* choice of law rules are used to denote two special kinds of rules in which the connecting section is drafted in a special manner.[150] Rules which make it a condition for the applicability of foreign law that there shall be more than one connecting factor pointing to the same foreign legal system may be considered as cumulative. If the condition of cumulation is not fulfilled, the *lex fori* is applied. Usually, however, the term *cumulative connection* is taken to mean that the connecting section of a choice of law rule prescribes the application of rules from several legal systems. A typical example is furnished by the rule in chapter 3:2 of the Act of 1904. Under that provision, the question whether foreign spouses may be granted a decree of divorce or separation shall be tried under both Swedish law and the law of the country of which the spouses are citizens, and no relief shall be granted unless a ground for divorce or separation is proved to exist under both legal systems. The idea is that the domestic law of the spouses (under the

[150] On so-called *subsidiary* connection, *vide* below pp. 132 ff.; on *subordinate* connection, below p. 136.

principle of nationality) should have a decisive influence but that in deference to established principles of morality, Swedish courts should not grant a decreee of divorce or separation upon a ground which is not considered acceptable in this country. In the second paragraph of the section just referred to it is laid down that if the spouses have had another foreign nationality than that which they possessed when the petition was made in Sweden, it is not permissible to invoke facts which occurred before the change of nationality, unless such facts constitute valid grounds for a decree of divorce or separation in the original home country of the spouses. This provision involves, in actual fact, a cumulation of the rules of three legal systems; the ground is that those who cannot obtain relief in their home country should not try to avoid this obstacle by a change of nationality. As a further example of cumulation the rule applied by English courts in international actions concerning liability in tort may be mentioned; it means that an action in tort will accrue only if the incriminated act abroad would have given rise to liability if committed in England and is not justifiable under the law of the place where it was performed *(lex loci delicti commissi).*

The old adage *locus regit forman actus* or *locus regit actum*[151] is the best-known example of an alternative application of foreign laws. Chapter 1:4 of the 1937 Act contains a rule to the effect that a will shall be held formally valid or validly revoked if it complies with the conditions laid down by the law of the place where the making or revoking was effected or by the law of the testator's country of citizenship. The main rule is that questions concerning wills shall be decided under the law of the country in which the *de cuius* was a citizen. The rule just quoted, however, means that a will shall be considered to have formal validity even if the formal requirements of the testator's personal law have not been fulfilled, provided that the conditions for formal validity of the *lex loci* have been observed. Similarly, it is held to be a fundamental principle in the law of contract that a sale is formally valid if the formal requirements either of the *lex loci* or of the legal system under which the essential validity and effects of the transaction are to be decided were observed at the making of the contract of sale. The rule *locus regit actum* is therefore called facultative. It is resorted to only when it is needed because of a flaw

[151] *Vide,* for more details, Ekström, *op.cit.,* pp. 67 ff.

in the formal validity of a transaction under that legal system which is otherwise applicable.[152] Conflict writing and the legislation of various countries contain further examples of choice of law rules which imply an alternative application of foreign laws.[152]

It must be observed that the alternative or facultative rule does not give a choice to the parties in a suit. It is a conflict provision for the judge, who when trying for instance the formal validity of a will is bound to recognize its validity as soon as the formal requirements of either of the legal systems pointed out as alternatives in the choice of law rule have been observed. In some choice of law rules, however, the connecting section has been drafted in such a manner that it leaves the parties a choice between different laws (elective choice of law rules). Thus a rule on alimony to children may by framed so as to allow the child to invoke that one among a number of legal systems which would produce the most satisfactory result from the child's point of view.[153] A further example is provided by the rule in chapter 1:2 of the Swedish Act on international questions concerning marriage, etc., 1904, where it is laid down that in certain cases the question whether an alien is entitled to contract marriage shall be tried, at his request, in accordance with another law than that of his home country.

In the practice of courts a special technique has been developed for the choice of the law applicable to mutual obligations; in Sweden it is called the *individualizing method*. This method means the application of the law, with which the parties' transaction has the strongest connection. Thus the connecting section has not been given a concrete form; on the contrary, the various connecting factors are weighed against one another. However, in this process, certain rules applicable *in dubio* or general presumptions are resorted to as decisive in those cases where the weighing does not produce any definite result. These auxiliary rules are drafted in the traditional manner; it is laid down, e.g., that *in dubio* actions concerning promissory notes shall be decided under the law of the debtor's domicile *(lex domicilii debitoris)*.

152 In some cases, however, the application of the rule *locus regit actum* is compulsory. This is true about obligations expressed in bills of exchange (sect. 80 Bills of Exchange Act, 1932; cf. para. 3 in the same sect.). I should be pointed out, moreover, that the rule is subject to exceptions. *Vide e.g.* secs. 1 (6) and 2 (2) of the Swedish Act on the legal effects of marriage, 1912.

153 *Vide* Lewald, pp. 25 ff.

154 Cf. further Lewald, pp. 30 f.

Some connections may be called "constant", others "variable".[154] If a choice of law rule states that the law of the place where a contract was concluded, a tortious act committed, or where immovables are situated shall be applied for the purpose of deciding actions of a certain kind, a constant connection is being used. If the contract was made in London, or if the real property is situated in Switzerland, we have been told that English or Swiss law respectively is applicable. But if a choice of law rule refers to the law of the debtor's domicile, the law of the deceased's home country, the law of the flag, or the law of the place where movables are situted *(lex rei sitae)*, it does not provide an exhaustive answer to the question *what* legal system shall be applied, for these connections are variable: a domicile may change, as well as a home country, and movables may be taken from one country to another. Legislative technique therefore makes use of the element of time in order to complete such references. Chapter 1 of the Act on international questions concerning the estates of deceased persons, 1937, contains several examples of this method. It is true that it is not expressely stated that questions concerning the right to come into property by succession shall be decided under the law of the deceased's home country *at the time of his death;* in this place, the time element is implicit. But it *is* stated that questions concerning capacity to make a will shall be tried in accordance with the law of the testator's home country "when the document was made"; it is further set out explicitly that the question whether a testamentary disposition is invalid because of its contents shall be decided under the law of the state of which the testator was a citizen "at the time of his death"; finally, it is stated that the law of the state in which the *de cuius* was a citizen "at the time of the gift" governs the question whether property received by a legal heir from the *de cuius* by way of gift *inter vivos* shall be considered as a part of such heir's portion of the estate received in advance. If the relevant time had not been determined in the last-mentioned rule, it would be uncertain whether e.g. German or Swedish law is applicable for the purpose of deciding the question dealt with in the rule in a case where a naturalized Swede, who was earlier a German citizen, has given his son a gift before the naturalization. Now the determination of the relevant time points to German law as the applicable legal system. On the other hand, it is not stated in the rule that the applicable substantive

[154] Cf. Lewald, pp. 38 f.

rules are those which were in force in Germany at the time of the gift.[155] The time element contained in the conflict rule merely fulfils the purpose of locating the action, as it were, to Germany in a geographical sense.

Where a rule of law contains no time indication or where there is no written choice of law rule, it is the task of the courts of justice to determine the time element which completes the choice of law rule, either by construction of the written rule or, in the abesence of enactments, by their continuous lawmaking. It is hardly possible to advocate any *prima facie* solution.[156] In some cases it may seem reasonable to apply, for instance, the law of the country of which a person was a citizen at the time when the action was instituted; in others it may be rational to place the relevant moment at an earlier stage. In the lengthy discussion of this question—*le conflit mobile* in the language of French scholars—the doctrine of vested rights has also been resorted to.[157] A more realistic argument is based upon the point of view that a person should not be allowed to influence the choice of law, e.g., by changing his nationality or domicile.[158] It has been said that "from the point of view of security, the connection which existed at the creation of a legal relation must usually retain its decisive influence".[159] This course of reasoning has produced as a result the idea that questions concerning the relationship between an buyer of movables and the vendor's creditors should be decided under the *lex rei sitae,* a term which, in this connection, is taken to

[155] On this question of time, *vide* below, pp. 145 ff.

[156] Niederer (at p. 359) emphasizes that the time element must be determined "durch vernünftige Auslegung der Kollisionsregeln." F. A. Mann, in 31 *B.Y.I.L.* (1954), 224, states: "The problem cannot be solved dogmatically. Its solution lies in the interpretation of each conflict rule and in the appreciation of its *ratio.*" The author proceeds, in the following pages, to give some interesting illustrations of various solutions by English courts.

[157] In Swedish conflict writing about this problem, *vide* Gihl, *Principer,* pp. 174 ff., Malmström in *Sv.J.T.* 1953, p. 545, and Karlgren, pp. 23 f.

[158] Lewald (*op.cit.,* at pp. 96 ff.) gives an account of a development of Swiss judicial practice which led to the result that questions concerning men's duty to give alimony to illegitimate children were governed by the law of the imputed father's domicile at the time when the child was conceived. It is stated, in defence of this solution against the objection that the time is difficult to determine, that other methods would make it possible for the father to "déterminer à son gré le droit applicable, en changeant de domicile pendant le cours de la grossesse."

[159] Hassler & Nial, p. 67.

mean the law of the place where the movables were situated *at the time* when the disputed effects of the sale upon the rights of the parties are supposed to have taken place. If another solution were adopted a person would be able to choose the applicable substantive rules by moving the goods from one country to another. Attempts are being made to prevent such "changes of statute", as they are called in Continental law, but only where there are good reasons for it. Both in legislation and in judicial decisions there are examples of choice of law rules in which the time elements has been conceived in such a way that a change of statute is allowed and where measures to that effect by the parties are consequently possible.[160]

The Connecting Factors and their Interpretation

The connections which are selected, for the purpose of choice of law rules, as relevant localizing elements or connecting factors may of course vary considerably. However, conflict law in different countries knows a certain number of typical connecting factors, and this number is limited.[161]

The *will of the parties* has already been mentioned as one connecting factor, and so has the *place where some event has taken place.* On the basis of the last-mentioned principle, the connecting section of various choice of law rules indicates, as *lex causae,* the place where a contract was concluded *(lex loci contractus),* where an obligation is to be fulfilled *(lex loci solutionis),* where a tortious action has been committed *(lex loci delicti)* or where matrimony has been solemnized

160 According to the 1912 Act, the legal effects of marriage with regard to the proprietary rights of the spouses are governed by "the law of the state of which the husband was a citizen at the time of entering into marriage," and changes of nationality in the course of married life has no effect, *i.e.* changes of statute are impossible, but under the 1931 Royal Ordinance, where the same question is governed in principle by the law of that (Nordic) state where the spouses took up their domicile immediately upon marrying, the law of that other Nordic state where both spouses have subsequently taken up their domicile shall replace the legal system of the first domicile country. A change of statute is consequently allowed. Where the effects of transactions performed before the change of domicile are concerned, however, the law of the first domicile is applied.

161 A Swiss writer who has made an inventory of the connecting factors held appropriate by legislatures and courts in various countries, accounts for them under 16 different headings. *Vide* Engel, *La détermination des points de rattachement en droit international privé,* Genève 1953, p. 133.

(lex loci celebrationis). The location of property is the connection pointing out the *lex rei sitae*. The *nationality* of a person has been selected as the proper connecting factor in those cases where the *lex patriae* is applicable, his *domicile* or *residence* where the application of the *lex domicilii* is prescribed. In international maritime law, reference is made to the *law of the flag* for the purpose of deciding certain questions. The connection with the court seized with the action makes the *lex fori* applicable, and certain questions, it is held, should be decided under the law of the country where an adjudication in bankruptcy has been rendered *(lex concursus)*.

In legal writing, a distinction is often made between rules in which the connecting factor is a mere factual circumstance (e.g. a place) and rules where legal terms (e.g. domicile) are used. Here as well as in the referring sections of conflicts rules, however, the legal expressions or terms refer to pure facts.[162] This does not prevent the construction of the connecting factor from being liable to create certain difficulties. What actual *locus delicti* is referred to in a rule applicable to a tortions act where the tortfeasor's act occurred in Louisiana but resulted in an injury in Florida?[163] Where was a contract concluded the acceptance of which was teleprinted in London and received in the same way in Amsterdam?[164] What actual place is meant, where a rule refers to the domicile or residence of a person? There is no difference in principle between these questions and those which may arise in the administration of internal law.

Where the connecting factors of choice of law rules are concerned, however, the task of applying and interpreting the law is often particularly difficult for reasons similar to those which we have already discussed when dealing with the referring section as the "problem of classification". In conflict writing, the question has been posed whether the connecting factor should be interpreted in the light of the *lex fori,* of the *lex causae* or of supranational principles.[165] The law which is to be found—the *lex causae*—is obviously unable to furnish the starting point, and it would seem obvious that the legal systematics, terminology and concepts of the *lex fori* must provide

[162] Cf. above, pp. 113 f., Gihl, *Principer,* p. 397.
[163] Strömholm in *T.f.R.* 1960, pp. 434 ff.
[164] Cf. 1940 *N.J.A.* 354. Cf. Bomgren in *Festskrift till Karl Schlyter* (1949), pp. 64 ff., and Wortley in *Liber amicorum,* pp. 261 ff.
[165] *Vide* e.g. Engel, *op.cit.,* p. 30.

at least the basis for the interpretation of expressions in the connecting sections.[166] However, it is not necessary that the drafter of a choice of law rule, or the judge, who has to answer the question what is actually meant by the connecting factor of a certain rule, should stick strictly to internal concepts. Both are free—wholly or partly—to determine the meaning of the connecting factors in the applicable choice of law rule of the *lex fori* with due consideration of the international function of the rule. The situation is similar to that which has been discussed above with regard to the referring section of choice of law rules.

Certain choice of law give rise to special problems of interpretation. One such problem refers to the term "domicile".[167] It is defined in various forms in different legal systems, and in those countries where it has acquired a precise and well-established meaning, this meaning also determines the construction of such choice of law rules in the law of these countries where domicile is a connecting factor. In Swedish law, however, the term "domicile" as an element in choice of law rules is still not very clear. Our legal system knows several "local criteria", among them the term *hemvist* (originally = "home"; usually rendered in English by "domicile"), which has been developed for the needs of internal law.[168] When construing certain early provisions, e.g. in chapter 3 of the 1904 Act, it is possible that the mere fact of a person being registered as having his *hemvist* in a Swedish parish in the yearly census is sufficient to give him a "domicile" in this contry, although the Swedish term is used in the Act for conflict purposes.[169] In section 5 of the Act on recognition and enforcement of judicial decisions rendered in Switzerland, 1936, a person's domicile *(hemvist)* is defined "the place where the defendant lives with the intention of remaining permanently". Here, then, something more than being included in the census is required. On the other hand, registration in the census is probably not necessary; in the *travaux préparatoires* of the Act, it is stated that "formal grounds

[166] Cf. Gihl, *Principer,* pp. 398 ff.

[167] *Vide* Dennemark, pp. 72 ff. Cp. 1962 *N.J.A.* 547.

[168] *Vide* Eek, pp. 63 ff. It should be pointed out that the term "domicile" in the present book is used both for this Swedish term and, sometimes, for "domicile" in the Anglo-American sense.

[169] Cf. Chap. 7, sec. 3 of the 1904 Act, and chap. 10, sec. 2, (2) of the Judicial Procedure Code.

for the attribution of a domicile" must not be decisive "when considering the question whether a person has a domicile in the sense of the convention".[170] Thus in Swedish law we have to work with a "legal" and an "actual" domicile. Moreover, it is far from clear that either of these concepts must, or should most properly, be used where the meaning of "domicile" outside written conflict rules is to be determined. In chapter 2:2 (2), of the 1904 Act a domicile which has been maintained for at least one year is held relevant for conflict purposes; in the 1931 Ordinance on Inter-Nordic Relations, the minimum period is two years. Is a domicile thus defined *the* "domicile" for the purpose of modern Swedish Conflict of Laws? In other words, does the 1931 Ordinance intend to establish the Swedish concept of domicile? This question cannot be simply answered in the affirmative.[171] Indeed, it seems to be necessary to determine, in the case of each individual conflict rule, what is meant by *hemvist* or "domicile," and where the directions of a statute are not clear it is only natural if the judge looks for guidance in definitions of "domicile" in foreign law. In other words: the meaning of the notion of domicile varies, if not from one case to another, at least from one rule to another. This tendency is stressed by the fact that it may be reasonable to expect, at least as a possibility, some difference between "domicile" for family law purposes and the same term when used in property or contract law; in the latter fields of the law, it is sometimes the personal domicile which must be found, and sometimes the fictious "domicile" of a certain activity. Moreover, special questions arise concerning the domicile of corporations.

The preceding paragraphs have dealt with the determination of *hemvist* or "domicile" as a connecting factor in Swedish conflict law on the basis of our own legal systematics and concepts, which, in this field, are hardly the results of extensive or deep reflexion. In chapter 7:3 of the 1904 Act there is a provision to the effect that where it follows from the statute that the jurisdiction of an authority depends upon the domicile of a

[170] *S.O.U.* 1936, No. 2, pp. 28 f. Cf. The remarks of the Council on Legislation in *Royal Proposition* No. 25, 1936, pp. 13 f.

[171] Cf., however, Gihl, *Principer,* p. 399, and 1932 *N.J.A.* II, pp. 384 ff. On the notion of domicile in the Scandinavian convention system, *vide* A. Philip in *Recueil* 1958, pp. 265 ff. Cp., again, 1962 *N.J.A.* 547.

party within the state of such authority, the question whether the party actually is domiciled in the state "shall be tried under the law of the aforesaid state". The field of application of this rule is not beyond discussion. However, the following statements about its impact seem incontestable. As a condition for the recognition of certain foreign divorce decrees, chapter 3:5 of the 1904 Act stipulates, *inter alia,* that the defendant shall have had his domicile in the country to which such authority belongs. It follows from the above-mentioned provision in chapter 7 of the same Act, that the question to be examined is whether the defendant has had a domicile in the state of the authority and the meaning of domicile shall be determined in accordance with the law of that state. The foreign concept must therefore be studied. Thus, in this case, a connecting factor in a Swedish choice of law rule is *to some extent*[172] interpreted on the basis of foreign law according to an explicit statutory provision. A similar method may be necessary in other cases also. If we are trying to ascertain a person's domicile in order to find the applicable law, the question normally confronting us in a concrete case is whether the person concerned (X) has a domicile in country A or country B, or in A, B or C. If he has domicile in Sweden (A) under Swedish law *(lex fori),* the matter is likely to be settled: Swedish law will be applied even if a domicile can also be found e.g. in England (B), whether under Swedish or English law. If there is no domicile in Sweden, the question arises whether a domicile can be found in B or in C. The starting point for the examination of this problem is likely to be the Swedish notion of domicile, i.e. the enquiry turns upon the question whether X has that connection with B or C which is implied in the concept "domicile" in the Swedish choice of law rule. But since that connecting factor is often difficult to interpret, it is impossible not to attach

172 *To some extent!* From the point of view of conflict law, the rule could also be envisaged as follows: the question whether the defendant had a domicile in the State of the authority shall be decided under the law of that State. The connecting factor, "the law of the State of the authority," does not imply any problems of construction. But the term "domicile" in the referring section obviously cannot be construed in the light of Swedish concepts but must be given a wider sense based upon comparative studies.

some importance to the question whether X is domiciled in B or C according to the local laws. If X is found to have a domicile (in the Swedish sense) in both countries, we have to select one of these domiciles as the "effective" one in order to find the applicable law; for this purpose, it may be of importance that X has a legal domicile (under local law) in B, but not in C. If, on the other hand, X has no domicile (in the Swedish sense) either in A, B, or C, nor in any other country, we must create a connecting factor which can replace the non-existent domicile; this creation is performed by so-called *subsidiary connection.* If X has a legal domicile in England (which may be the case even if he is not a resident of that State and therefore, under Swedish law, cannot be considered domiciled there), this fact may constitute a subsidiary connection.[173]

Certain special problems also arise where citizenship (nationality) is used as a connecting factor. The question whether the construction of the connecting factor as expressed in statutory rules should be based upon the *lex fori,* the *lex causae* or some supranational principle seems highly academic.[174] The legal concept "nationality" is largely identical in the various legal systems and the world is so organized that individuals are usually citizens of a state and of one state only. Therefore it is not particularly difficult to ascertain, by consulting the legislation concerning nationality of a given country, whether a person is a citizen of that country or not. Problems arise if it is found that a person is stateless or is a citizen of several states.[175] A

[173] If no such domicile can be found, however, the law of the place of residence or the *lex fori* must be resorted to by means of subsidiary connection. Cf. Eek, pp. 153 ff. and 63 f.

[174] Cf. the partly incompatible points of view of Lewald, *op.cit.* at pp. 88 ff., and Gihl, *Principer,* pp. 399 f. The statement that public international law leaves each State full liberty to determine the extent of that group of people which is called "citizens," and that other States have to respect this definition of the word does not mean, obviously, that a state is barred from giving nationality as a connecting factor for the purposes of private international law as much or as little scope as the state prefers. *Vide* Eek, "The Administration of Justice in Conflict Cases involving Refugees," *Scandinavian Studies in Law* 1959, pp. 28 ff., 35 and 48 f. Notice also chap. 7, sec. 2 (1) of the 1904 Act.

[175] Special questions arise in the international law of property and contract with regard to e.g. the nationality of corporations or ships.

person who is in possession of both Swedish and foreign citizenship is generally considered by Swedish courts to be a Swedish citizen, even if he is domiciled in the other state concerned.[176] In other cases of double citizenship, the normal proceeding would seem to imply a choice of the "effective" nationality by applying various criteria (domicile, etc.).[177] With regard to persons, who have no *lex patriae,* a so-called *subsidiary connection* is necessary. Usually, it implies that domicile fills the gap following from the lack of citizenship, and that the *lex domicilii* is consequently applied. This was the case in 1939 *N.J.A.* 96.[178] Where a stateless person has no domicile, the law of the place of residence or the *lex fori* will come into consideration by means of subsidiary connection.[179] As a rule the *lex fori* constitutes the last resource, resorted to where no connecting factors can be found for the purpose of conflict rules and where a subsidiary connection is impossible.[180]

In certain cases—dealing with questions of divorce and separation—the situation may be that the spouses are citizens of different states. In such cases, it is laid down in chapter 7:2

176 Cf. Eek, pp. 53 ff.

177 Eek, pp 56 f. Cf. Niederer, pp. 156 ff.

178 In the case 1914 *N.J.A.* 305, decision was based upon the finding of a domicile in Sweden.—Where a person's nationality cannot be determined, he should probably be treated in the same way as an apolite; cf. Raape, p. 120.

179 It is not only in family law or where no *lex patriae* can be found that a subsidiary connection is necessary. Above (at p. 136) we have shown the necessity of subsidiary connection where no domicile can be found. Karlgren (at p. 104) uses the expression "subsidiary *lex causae* for obligations." The solution implied by this term should probably be adopted where the connecting factor of a strict rule on the law applicable to obligations could not possibly be ascertained. However, the "individualizing method" (proper law theory) with its presumptions and rules applicable *in dubio* would seem to render any search for "subsidiary *leges causae* for obligations" unnecessary.

180 Lewald (*op.cit.* at pp. 105 f.) provides the following example: "En droit international privé italien la gestion d'affaires est soumise à la loi du lieu où elle a été accomplie. Or de quelle manière devra-t-on determiner la loi compétente lorsque la gestion d'affaires consiste dans le sauvetage d'une cargaison effectué sans mandat du propriétaire hors des eaux territoriales en haute mer? Étant donné qu'il est impossible de parvenir à une solution an moyen du rattachement prévu par la règle de conflit, il ne restera en fin de compte — à défaut d'un rattachement subsidiaire — que l'application de la loi du for."

of the 1904 Act, the court shall treat the action *as if* both spouses were citizens either of the last state of which both were citizens at the same time or, if such has never been the case, of the husband's home country.[181] This rule should probably be taken to mean that if either spouse is a Swedish citizen and both spouses have previously possessed Swedish citizenship at the same time, Swedish law is applicable. If the husband is a Swede, the same solution will be adopted unless both spouses have previously held e.g. German citizenship at the same time; if so, German law is applicable.[182] If both spouses are stateless, it is easy to modify the rule in the sense that such persons' present *domicile* is used instead of the "present" nationality referred to in the Act. It would also seem possible to combine nationality and domicile in such a way that for instance where the husband has a domicile in Germany and the wife in Sweden, while both have previously been, say, Hungarian subjects, the law of Hungary should be applied. Where refugees are concerned, however, courts may possibly have a tendency wholly to set aside the previous common nationality of the spouses and consider, in our example, that German law is applicable. However, it would be obviously incompatible with the language of the statute to make use of that solution if the wife had acquired Swedish citizenship (chap. 7, sec. 2, second para., of the 1904 Act is assumed not to be applicable) and the husband had been naturalized in Germany.[183]

[181] The Swedish Act on international questions concerning the legal effects of marriage, 1912, contains a similar rule on the legal effects of marriage in personal respect (chap. 1, sec. 9); it is laid down that if in the course of their marriage, spouses become citizens of different countries, the law of the last country of which both were citizens at the same time shall be considered as their national law. Nothing is said, however, about the situation occurring were they have never possessed a common nationality. The reason would seem to be that at the time of the introduction of the Act (and the underlying convention) it was taken for granted that the wife would get the nationality of her husband through the marriage. Thus it was argued by the French delegates in support of using the term "law of the spouses" instead of "the husband's law" in that provision of the convention which corresponds to chap. 1, sec. 2 of the 1912 Act, that at the time of marriage "par le fait même du mariage, les époux ont la même nationalité." *Vide Actes,* 1904, p. 260.

[182] 1929 *N.J.A.* 1.

[183] Some Swedish Supreme Court decisions have been held to imply that cer-

In practice, only one choice of law rule will normally be relevant in a case and it is the connecting section of that one rule which the judge has to construe. In some cases, however, several choice of law rules are applicable. The method of "slicing" choice of law rules (*vide* above, pp. 116 ff) imports that, for instance, questions arising in the same case concerning a surviving spouse's right of succession and his or her proprietary rights in the estate on the ground of matrimonial property law are governed by substantive provisions indicated by different choice of law rules, in which the connecting factors are not identical. As a rule, the texts describing these connecting factors are construed separately, in the light of the system of *lex fori* (as stated above). Sometimes, however, the "slicing" implies that certain questions are singled out for the application of a special choice of law rule, which is called a "subsidiary statute" in relation to the "principal statute" applicable to the action in general. Then, the connecting factor of that Swedish conflict rule which serves to indicate the "subsidiary" *lex causae* may have to be construed on the basis of foreign law. A typical example is the rule according to which questions concerning the modalities of performance of money obligations (e.g. currency or tender) shall be answered in accordance with the law of the place of payment *(lex loci solutionis)*,[184] irrespective of the law applicable to the essential contents of the obligation (the "statute" of the obligation, i.e. the "principal" *lex causae*). However, for the purpose of determining the place of payment in case of disagreement between the parties, the rules of the law applicable to the obligation, not those of the *lex fori*, are observed. Thus if German law has been found applicable to the essential questions of an action concerning a sale in a Swedish court, it follows that it is for the rules of German law to determine *where* payment shall take place. Thereupon, the Swedish conflict rule is applied; it provides that questions concerning the modalities of payment shall be decided under the

tain so-called "*quasi-apolites*" (persons who "do not enjoy the protection of their home state" or only possess a "formal" citizenshop) shall be treated in the same way as apolites and thus be considered to "belong" to that country where they have acquired a domicile. However, the choice of law problem arising with regard to refugees can be solved without having recourse to such fictions. An adoption of the principle of domicile would also contribute to reducing the whole problem. Vide Eek in *Scandinavian Studies in Law,* 1959, p. 23.

184 *Vide* Nial, pp. 48 f.

law of the place indicated by the German rule.[185] If, on the other hand, the *lex causae* of the obligation is Swedish law and the parties do not agree upon the manner of payment—we will suppose that the action concerns a promissory note—the court declares, (section 3 of the Swedish Promissory Notes Act, 1936), that since the creditor lives and does business at Lisbon, payment shall be effected there and questions in respect of the modalities of payment shall consequently be decided under Portuguese law. (This is true even if Portuguese rules on promissory note state that payment shall be performed e.g. at the *locus contractus,* say London, if no special place of payment has been agreed upon.) Niederer calls the method now described "subordinate connection".[186] In what cases this method should or must be resorted to is a policy question.[187]

Many writers, even those who admit that the *lex fori* must be the basis for the construction of terms in the connecting section of choice of law rules, point out that the variations between different legal systems with regard to the method of determining e.g. where the "place" of a contract is situated or what is meant by "domicile", create insecurity and constitute an obstacle to international intercourse. Not even uniform choice of law rules created by means of international conventions are a guarantee of an internationally uniform solution of the question what is the law applicable to a certain action. One of the reasons for this deficiency is that even the connecting section of a uniform choice of law rule is interpreted differently in different countries. The relatively small number of typical connecting factors has encouraged the Swiss writer Engel to undertake an enquiry by which he tries to demonstrate that it is possible to make uniform definitions of connecting factors by means of conventions. This would mean a considerable step along the road towards a conflict law with a universal charac-

185 Similarly, *lex loci solutionis* determines the currency and thereby constitutes the application *in concreto* of the rule under which questions about the qualities of money and its recognition as legal tender are governed by the law of the country where the currency concerned has its origin (the "money statute," *lex pecuniae).*

186 *Vide* Niederer, pp. 205 f.

187 Cf. Nussbaum, p. 171.

ter. "Avant de vouloir que le monde entier parle la même langue, il faut songer à unifier l'alphabet des langues apparentées."[188] This is an interesting technique in international conventions, and a complement to that which implies the drafting of uniform and complete choice of law rules, and it might give some practically valuable results—although by no means such as to constitute a real revolution in international conflict co-operation.[189] Another possibility is the creating of uniform rules in internal substantive law on such points as the definition of the place of contract, etc.[190]

A Special Problem: States with More than One Legal System

By means of the "localizing" effect of connecting factors, choice of law rules indicate the application of the law of a certain country. The idea is that in the political system under which we live, each state has its own law and the *ratio* för applying choice of law rules is the desire af connecting a legal transaction with a foreign country and a foreign legal system. In fact, however, there are several states in which more than one system of private law exists.[191] This fact creates a new problem with regard to the construction of connecting factors.[192]

In what manner is this problem to be posed in respect of typical connecting factors such as place (and location, e.g. of property), domicile, nationality, and the will of the parties? If a contract has been concluded in the course of a telephone call between Gothenburg and New York and the question arises whether it was formally valid (e.g. because it concerns negotiable instruments the sale of which is subject to a form requirement in some American "blue sky law"),[193] a Swedish court will determine the *locus contractus* under Swedish rules. If that place is found to be New York, the following course of reasoning could theoretically be adopted: since New York is situated in the United States, and the law of the United States is thus applicable, it must be asked under what rules, according to the con-

[188] Engel, *op.cit.*, p. 43.
[189] Cf. Eek in *N.T.I.R.* 1955, pp. 70 ff.
[190] *Vide* Wortley in *Liber amicorum*, pp. 265 f.
[191] *Vide* above, p. 8.
[192] *Vide* on this point Gihl, *Principer*, pp. 402 ff.
[193] *Vide* above, p. 65.

flict law of the United States, the validity of the contract must be tried. In fact, however, this method is not adopted, as Gihl has pointed out.[194] The "local" connecting factors—the place of a contract, the location of property—are held to refer to the legal system of the place, not of the state. If we have found that the place is New York City, we apply the substantive rules in force in that city without paying regard to American conflict law or American inter-local law—if there is one. In a case like this, the conflict rule always leads to a result.

> Where the place of a contract is not within the territory of any country (on the high seas or in the air above the high seas, or in outer space) it seems reasonable to state that the event has always taken place on board some sort of craft or vessel. The matter is therefore considered as if the event had occurred within the country which has given the carrier its "nationality".[195] This may be called a subsidiary connection, for it is not necessary—in fact, it even tends to create errors—to use the fiction that a ship, plane or other aircraft or missile is part of the territory of its home state.[196] If the vessel belongs in a

194 Gihl, *Principer,* p. 406.

195 If a vessel or an aircraft is within the territory of a country, the law of that country is the *lex loci;* it is possible, however, that in case of mere passage or transit, a subsidiary connection with the law of the flag is reasonable. Cf. Grönfors in *T.f.R.* 1957, pp. 66 ff.; however, Grönfors' paper deals principally with the nationality of vessels from the point of view of criminal law. In international criminal law, an exception is made for naval vessels; crimes committed on board such ships in the waters of a foreign State are not supposed to fall within the jurisdiction of such state. (On the general rule, *vide* 1960 N.J.A. 479). It is doubtful whether this exception is well founded in private law relations. A sale concluded on the premises of a foreign embassy in Stockholm should probably be considered as made in Sweden and the same principle should be applied to a contract of sale concluded on board a foreign naval vessel in the port of Stockholm.

196 The statement of Hassler & Nial that "there is no *lex loci* for ships on the high seas" does not seem well-founded. It may lead to the application of the *lex fori* as a last resource. Cf. note 180 above; the example does not deal with the ship but with the lost cargo.—A particular question is what law governs transactions in respect of the ship itself, e.g. liens upon the ship. There is disagreement in conflict writing on the proper connecting factor for this purpose; the law of the flag and that of the ship's "domicile" have been suggested. *Vide* Nial, pp. 92 f. It is not impossible that with regard to events on board a ship on the high seas, or

state with more than one legal system, it seems necessary to choose the applicable substantive law by proceeding in approximately the same way as when a choice of law rule refers to the "law of the home country". This is likely to imply that the law of the home port or of the place of registration will be held applicable.[197]

If a Swedish conflict rule orders the application of the *lex domicilii,* we have already pointed out that the connecting section of the rule shall be interpreted on the basis of the Swedish notion of domicile (or "home"). The chosen domicile is a certain locality. If it is situated in a country with more than one legal system, the same proceeding is adopted as where the *lex loci* has been indicated: the substantive rules of the local law, i.e. of the town, province, etc., are applied.[198]

Chapter 7:1 (1) of the Act on international questions concerning marriage, etc., 1904, runs as follows:

"If the law of a foreign state shall be applied under the provisions of the present Act, and if such state is divided into districts each with its own special law, the question which of these laws is applicable shall be decided in accordance with the provisions of the foreign law under consideration."

Thus this principle referring explicitly to the conflict rules of the 1904 Act, which are based upon the principle of nationality ("under the provisions of the present Act"), is not extended to those cases where an application of the *lex loci* or *domicilii* has been prescribed. It is applicable only for the purpose of finding the *lex patriae* (law of the home country). This restriction is expressly stated in an otherwise identical provision—chapter 3:1 of the 1937 Act—which, according to its own wording, is applicable in cases where the "law of a foreign subject's home country" governs a suit. This rule means that the interlocal or interprovincial law of the foreign country (*vide* above,

property on board the ship, the law of the ship's domicile would be preferable as *lex loci,* but in general, courts do not seem to use this method.

197 A reference to the "law of the flag" has usually no concrete meaning when made in respect of a ship which flies the flag of the U.S.A. The reference must be more precise. When deciding this question, however, American courts have arrived at different solutions: in some cases the law of the place where the ship is registered has been applied, in others the law of the place where the shipowner has his residence. Cf. Ehrenzweig, *Conflict of Laws,* I, 1959, p. 26.

198 Cf. Gihl, p. 405, and 1939 *N.J.A.* 96.

pp. 8 f.) has the first claim to be applied. It is for the rules of that system to decide under what system of substantive law a person "belongs", where the nationality of that person constitutes the connecting factor of the Swedish choice of law rule. It is obvious, however, that difficulties may arise in actual practice. Suppose that we have to distribute the estate of a person who died in Sweden and had his residence there but was a Puritanian subject; the two provinces of which that country is composed have their own legal systems with completely different succession rules. The interprovincial law of Puritania lays down that questions of succession shall be decided under the law of the province where the *de cuius* was domiciled at his death. We can hardly consider this as a *renvoi* to Swedish law, and thus we have to find a subsidiary connection, e.g., with the deceased's last domicile in his home country, if that can be ascertained, or with the place of birth, in case the man was born in Puritania. If the foreign state has no interprovincial law—we refer to the United States—it follows from chapter 7:1 (2) of the 1904 Act that "where a person is domiciled in his home country the law of his place of domicile shall be applied". Thus domicile serves as a subsidiary connection. And finally, two more auxiliary provisions are added in the same enactment: "Where a person has no domicile in the state of which he is a subject, the law of the place where he had his last domicile in such state or, if he has never been domiciled within its territory, the law of its national capital shall be applied."

Where the will of the parties, as clearly expressed in a choice of law, is used as a connecting factor, it is likely to be most frequent that the choice of law clause has been drafted with the assistance of counsel. Such clauses therefore do not refer to "American law" but to the law of a certain state, if the reference is to the United States. If it occurs, however, that the parties do in fact refer to "American law" (the United States law), the judge will either have to ascertain what is here really meant or to make use of the "proper law" method in order to find the legal order within the United States where the "centre of gravity" of the matter may be held to lie, or finally to disregard the choice of law of the parties. In the latter case, the issue may be that "American law" is not found applicable at all.

Our discussion so far has dealt with cases where different laws are in force in different areas of the same state. Where special legal systems are applicable to different groups of persons within a state, it is usually the case that there is a special interpersonal law, which determines the sphere of application of these different systems. If the estate of a Greek citizen shall be distributed under Greek law and it appears that the rules applicable to intestate succession among the Moslem population of Greece are not identical to the law of the non-Moslem inhabitants, the principles of delimitation adopted in Greek law must be observed when choosing the applicable substantive rules.

§ 7. Foreign Law

The statutory material which a Swedish court will use when deciding an international (external) action consists of Swedish external substantive rules and choice of law rules. In addition to this, there is the foreign law indicated by the choice of law rule or rules applicable in the case. When they are considered *in abstracto,* their reference may take us anywhere in the world. In the individual case, however, the reference has become concrete, it points to a certain foreign legal system. In the next chapter of this book, which deals with the use made of the material, we shall deal with a number of question which arise when it follows from a provision in a choice of law rule that foreign substantive legal rules shall replace the rules of Swedish law. The judge has to pick out the applicable rules *within* the system of the indicated foreign law. Occasionally, he will be justified in declining to apply the foreign rule which, in principle, is pointed out for application, e.g. because it is held incompatible with the fundamental principles of the Swedish legal system *(ordre public)*. The adaptation of foreign rules to the Swedish legal system will also create considerable problems in actual practice.

What is Foreign Law?

Under this heading we shall deal with a few questions which do not concern the application of foreign law so much as the ascertainment in general of what shall be considered the applicable law or legal system; certain indications in addition to those given by choice of law rules are in fact necessary. These rules have been framed in consideration of the fact that, under the present international political system, many states with different laws exist in the world. A choice of law rule refers to the *law* or the *legal system* of a certain State. But what is meant by "law" and "legal system"? A Swedish judge is likely to use his own view upon the constitutive characteristics of the sources of law in order to find an answer to this question. In most cases, however, the problem is academic, since the structure of modern legal systems is largely identical.[199] Here, the principle is that rules actually applied by the authorities of the country to which the choice of law rule refers for the purpose of deciding actions between private parties shall also be enforced in the country into which they are imported and, in principle, all those facts shall be taken into consideration which would have some importance for the decision of a court in the foreign country.[200] It follows that even the question whether a foreign statute invoked by either party is compatible with the constitution of that country may be subject to the examination of the *forum*—but always in accordance with the law of the state from which the enactment thus put into question emanates.[201]

Occasionally, however, the question may arise what rules are efficiently enforced and recognized as "the law" in a foreign country indicated by a conflict rule. This may be the case in periods of revolution; different laws and decrees may struggle, as it were, for power, and within different areas of a state changing "governments" or fighting groups may alternate as rulers.[202] In these situations, the judge tries to find those rules which are backed by such authority and are upheld by such an organized administration of justice that they can be considered as effective and real foreign law. It may be that an actual splitting of a state

199 Similar problems arise in respect of recognition of foreign judgments. The question is what foreign decisions shall be considered as "judicial." Cf. Karlgren, pp. 177 f. This question assumes considerable importance in the application of conventions rules in this field. Cf. 1910 *N.J.A.* 292.

200 Cf., with regard to certain special cases, Wengler, "Fragen der Faktizität und Legitimität bei der Anwendung fremden Rechts," in *Festschrift Hans Lewald,* pp. 615 ff.

201 On this topic, cf. Karl H. Neumayer in *Rabels Z.* 1958, pp. 573 ff.

202 Cf. Batiffol, pp. 300 f.

into different areas of some stability where different legal rules are in force must be taken into consideration; *de facto* a system with several local laws within one state has come into existence. This problem is occasionally combined with the question of the *diplomatic recognition* of a new state or a revolutionary government.[203] At least under the principles adopted in Continental Europe and in Scandinavia, such recognition is usually granted when the government of the recognizing country has found the new political body effective.[204] By granting its recognition, therefore, the government may be said to have "done the job" for the courts; these may consider rules backed by the authority of the state or government thus recognized as legal rules, its laws as real laws. On the other hand, in those cases where a new state or revolutionary government has not been recognized by the government of the *forum* country, it is by no means obvious that the law applied in the new state or in the area commanded by the revolutionary government shall not be considered as real foreign law. Courts have to face the facts in respect of foreign laws; thus if, before Sweden recognized the Soviet Union, a Swedish court had declined to consider the Soviet laws actually operating within the territory of the Union as real law (and possibly replaced them by means of the fiction that the law of Czarist Russia, which had then been definitely set aside, was the legal system referred to in choice of law rules), this would have been repugnant to the well-established purpose and function of Swedish conflict law.[205]

Similar problems may arise in case of *annexation* and *occupation*. If a state is just trying to conquer another state, the law of which is, in principle, applicable, decrees by the conquering

[203] Cf. Hjerner, pp. 333 ff.

[204] Cp. concerning the attitude of United Kingdom Brierly, The Law of Nations, 6th ed. (by Waldock), 1963, pp. 144 ff.

[205] It should be noticed that if the court tries to find e.g. the law of the country in which a contract has been concluded, and arrives at the conclusion that the contract was made in Moscow and that Soviet law is effective there, there is no reason whatever to depart from the principle set out in the text above and apply only such rules of Soviet law as have been introduced *after* recognition. Cf. Eek, "Nya stater och Nya regimer," in *Skrifter åt minnet av C. A. Reuterskiöld,* Helsingfors 1945, pp. 63 ff., where certain holdings in the case 1931, *N.J.A.* 351 are criticized.

state will hardly be considered as the "law" of the land. But if the situation has been stabilized in favour of the conquering state, it is probable that whether the conquest has been recognized or not, the law effectively enforced shall be considered as the legal system to which choice of law rules refer. In case of *occupatio bellica,* the occupying power is bound under the principles of public international law to respect the private law of the occupied country. If this is not the case, the opinions of lawyers are divided on the question how the courts of other countries have to act where a reference is made to the law of the occupied country. Some argue that the legislation of the occupying power should not be considered as legal rules at all, others claim that the law actually enforced must be taken into account.[206] In this particular case, however, the law which would be applicable under general conflict principles may be excepted from actual application on the ground that it is repugnant to the law of nations.[207] In case of *succession of states* in any other way than annexation—cessions of provinces, splitting of one state into several, union of several states into one, etc.—the question now discussed about the actual "law" of the foreign country is hardly likely to arise, but occasionally courts will be faced by the problem which of several rival laws shall be given precedence.[208] This problem is similar to the one we are now going to deal with.[209]

206 *Vide* Niederer, p. 363, with reference to Sauser-Hall.

207 *Vide* below, pp. 211 f.

208 Succession of sovereignty may also raise questions about changes of otherwise permanent connecting factors (cf. above, p. 125). Lewald quotes an example *(op.cit.* at p. 38) concerning acquisition of title to real property by prescription in an Italian district near the Swiss border. In an adjustment of the border line the district was found to belong to Switzerland. The question of prescription—which is governed by the *lex rei sitae*—was decided by the Swiss courts in accordance with Italian law. Other examples are quoted by Graulich, *op.cit.*, at p. 33.

209 In cases of state succession governed by treaties rules are usually adopted for the solution of such concurrent claims of application; the function of such rules corresponds to that of transitional provisions in amendments of internal laws.

Changes in the Lex Causae

What is the effect of modifications in the legal system to which choice of law rules refer, if such changes have been introduced after the moment in which all the elements of the action at bar were already in existence? As an example of the sort of situations which we are now referring to, the following case may be mentioned. A former German citizen dies in Sweden after having been naturalized there. His estate is distributed by the rules of the Swedish Inheritance Code. However, under the Act on deceased persons' estates, 1937, the question whether property received *inter vivos* by a person entitled to succession from the *de cuius* should be deducted from the donee's portion of the estate as having been, as it were, inherited in advance is a matter for the law of the country "of which the *de cuius* was a subject at the time of the gift". Let us assume that the *de cuius* was still a German subject at the time of the gift. Thus German law has been indicated as the *lex causae* by means of the determination of the relevant time. But what is meant by German law: shall we apply German rules as they were at the time of the gift or as they stand when the action is tried?[210] Various proposals have been put forward in legal writing. Sometimes it is argued that the rule on the relevant time which, in the framework of the choice of law rule as a whole, serves to indicate the applicable local law, should be extended to serve also towards a solution of the intertemporal problem: the substantive rules of *lex causae* as it stood at the time of "the creation of the legal relationship" are applicable. In our example, this would mean that Swedish courts would apply German law as it was at the time of the gift. The prevailing opinion, however, is that the law of the foreign country should be applied in the shape which it has today as applied by the courts of the country where the *lex causae* is in force.[211] This means that the

[210] Makarov, in *Rabels* Z. 1957, p. 202, describes this later time as "der Zeitpunkt der Behandlung des Falles."

[211] Niederer (*op.cit.* at p. 361) points out a third possibility, viz. the intertemporal rules of the *lex fori*. However, the learned writer unreservedly embraces the opinion adopted in the text above. In an article in *Rabels Z.* 1958 ("Skizzen zur Lehre vom Statutenwechsel"), at pp. 535 ff., Wengler indicates six solutions, each with variations, as theoretically possible; he uses the term "change of statute" *(Statutenwechsel)* to denote the situation described in the text above, whereas "changes of statute" in our sense (*vide* p. 126 above) are defined as "Statutenwechsel im engeren Sinne . . . bei dem man besser von Anknüpfungs-

intertemporal rules (transitional rules) of the applicable foreign law be observed. In our example a Swedish court would thus have to apply German law as it stands at the time of the suit, particular attention being paid to such transitional provisions as may exist. Similarly, when the law of a certain country is applied as *lex rei sitae* (at the time of, e.g., transfer of title through confiscation), later amendments, through which the confiscation may have been deprived of effect, are observed.[212] The method now described would seem to be that most generally adopted in actual practice.[213] It is also the solution preferred by writers in most countries,[214] and in Sweden it may invoke the authority of precedents. In the so-called "gold clause case" (1937 *N.J.A.* 1), the Swedish Supreme Court, upon evaluating a number of connecting factors, held that the law of the state of New York was applicable. Thereupon, the Court was confronted by the question whether it ought to apply an enactment of the *lex causae*, the so-called Joint Resolution of 1933, which had been made after "the creation of the legal relationship" (i.e. the issuing of the bonds concerned in the action, 1924). It was not put into question that the law of New York as it stood at the time of the suit was applicable; the Supreme Court when determining the sphere of application of the 1933 enactment paid regard to the rules of the "retroactive" statute

wechsel sprechen sollte" (p. 537).—This intertemporal problem now being discussd has obviously nothing to do with the question dealt with earlier in the text, viz. what is foreign "law" and the importance of diplomatic recognition. Cf. Hjerner, pp. 339 f.

[212] Cf. Hjerner, p. 280, note 34.

[213] Nial (at p. 23) seems to take it for granted, since he points out that where the parties make a choice of law by referring to the substantive rules of a certain legal system, the parties "must be held subject to future modifications of that legal system which becomes *lex obligationis* through the choice of law of the parties—provided, obviously, that such modifications are made applicable to preexistant legal relations under the rules of the law concerned."

[214] *Vide* Batiffol, *op.cit.*, pp. 391 f.; Melchior, *op.cit.*, pp. 68 ff.; Roubier, *op.cit.*, pp. 569 f.; Gavalda, *op.cit.*, p. 300 ff. and authors referred to there. As for English law, F. A. Mann finds that it is permissible to make the following statement (31 *B.Y.I.L.* (1954), p. 247; cf. pp. 232 ff.): "If a change occurs in the municipal law of the country to which the English conflict rule refers, an English judge will, in principle, apply the transitional law of the *lex causae*, even if it is retrospective." Exceptions are made for such cases where the facts are suh that this principle would produce "inconvenience and wrong." On English law, *vide* also Erwin Spiro in 9 *I.C.L.Q.* (1960), pp. 357 ff.

itself and to the opinion of the United States Supreme Court on its constitutionality.[215]

The questions now discussed may be illustrated by the following examples which concern the application of chapter 1:1 of the law on international questions concerning deceased persons' estates, 1937; it is laid down in that provision that the estate shall be distributed in accordance with the succession rules of the country of which the deceased was a citizen at the time of his death.

A Spanish citizen dies in Spain in 1936, in the time of the Republic, and property left by him in Sweden is to be distributed in 1940, after the revolutionary Franco party has taken over power in Spain. The choice of law rule indicates Spanish law, and that legal system is applied as it stands (including transitional provisions) when the matter is being handled. A Spaniard dies in Paris, where he has fled and taken up his residence, in 1937, when the civil war is still going on. If no relevant facts are different, the solution of the choice of law problem will be the same as in the earlier example. If, in the later case, the Spaniard was deprived of his Spanish citizenship after his escape and died stateless domiciled in Paris, a subsidiary connection must take place (*vide* above, p. 133); French law is applied as it stands when the matter is being dealt with in Sweden, and such French transitional rules as may exist are duly taken into consideration.

An Alsatian dies at Strasbourg in 1915. He is a German citizen. The Swedish choice of law rule consequently indicates German law as the *lex causae*. The estate in Sweden is distributed in 1926, when Alsace has become French territory. But the location of the case to Germany refers to the time of death, and consequently German law as it stood in 1926 is applied.[216]

A person who was once a citizen of Latvia, becomes a Soviet citizen after his country has been annexed to the U.S.S.R. in 1940. He dies in December, 1940, in Riga. Property in Sweden is to be distributed in 1949. Soviet law as it is in 1949 is applicable (but *may* be rejected by application of the *ordre public*

[215] Cf. also 1937 N.J.A. 17.

[216] Cf. Makarov, *op.cit.*, p. 213.

mechanism). If the man had taken up a residence in Sweden at the time of his death, the result would be the same. On the other hand, if the man died in Latvia towards the end of 1941, when that country had been occupied by the German forces, it could possibly be argued that the legal situation of Latvia had been changed by the occupying power—whether in accordance with the law of nations or contrary to it—in such a way that the man had been deprived of his Russian citizenship and become stateless. If the *lex patriae* were replaced by the *lex domicilii,* the outcome would nevertheless be the same. For the law of the domicile would be that of Riga (or Latvia) and the law in force there at the time of the distribution in 1949, i.e. Soviet law, would be applicable, although it *might* be set aside in case of incompatibility with the law of nations or with Swedish *ordre public.* On the other hand, if the man died as a resident of Stockholm, Swedish law would be applicable. However, the assumption that the German occupation would have deprived the man of his Russian citizenship seems to be based on very weak grounds. The situation is different if the man died in Riga in 1941 and the distribution of the estate took place in Stockholm shortly afterwards, while the German occupation of Latvia still subsisted. In that case it could be argued that Soviet succession law did not operate effectively as *law* in Latvia and that the applicable legal system was that introduced (or reintroduced) by the occupying power and actually enforced (cf. above, p. 144).

If a Latvian subject died in Riga in 1936, the law of his home country, i.e. Latvian law, should be applied if his estate is distributed in Stockholm in 1949. In this case it may also be argued that the law of succession actually in force within the country indicated by the Swedish choice of law rule (Latvia) should be applied even though the constitution of that country has undergone such radical changes that it has ceased to exist as an independent state. On the other hand, it may also be possible to submit that since the nationality which is the localizing element of the choice of law rule no longer exists, because the home country of the *de cuius* has disappeared as a sovereign state, Latvian law as it stood at the time of the fall of that state (but not at the time of death) should be applied instead of Soviet law. At least, this is the solution suggested by Makarov for this special case (at pp. 215 ff.).

In this connection we shall, finally, devote a few words to the case 1937 *N.J.A.* 261, the problem of which presents certain similarities with the examples quoted above. The action concerned a claim against a Swede founded upon a contract which had been made in Moscow in 1917 between the defendant and a Russian citizen, one Swerintzeff, who had died in Leningrad in 1921. The latter's widow and children raised certain claims based upon the contract. The Swedish defendant argued that under Soviet succession law, the plaintiffs were not entitled to enforce rights which might have belonged to the deceased. There can be no hesitation about the applicability of Soviet law as the legal system of the deceased's home country, even though the 1937 Act on international questions concerning deceased persons' estates had not come into force when the decision of the Supreme Court in this case was rendered. The applicable Russian provisions were found in a decree of 27 April 1918—and thus issued before the death of the *de cuius,* although this fact was hardly material—and according to that enactment Swerintzeff's estate should become the public property of the Russian Socialist Federated Soviet Republic. The Swedish Supreme Court found that the plaintiffs were entitled to enforce the deceased's claim under the contract, since the 1918 decree "was not applicable with regard to property situated outside Russian territory". If this language was chosen in accordance with the pattern of certain cases dealing with foreign confiscations, there are grounds for the objection that, under Swedish conflict law, foreign statutes on succession *are* undoubtedly applicable with regard to property outside the country where these statutes are in force. The purpose of chapter 1:1 of the 1937 Act is in fact that we shall apply foreign succession law with regard to property situated within Sweden and left by a deceased foreign citizen. In another construction of the language of the Supreme Court, which seems less unsatisfactory, it would imply that *in accordance with its own tenor,* the Russian decree should not be applied in respect of property situated outside the Soviet Union (cf. above, pp. 65 f.). The final answer can be found only by studying Soviet law; in this connection it should be pointed out, however, that in a decision of 1925, where the German *Kammergericht* applied Soviet law "wie es der ausländische Richter anwenden würde", the Court did not find the Russian decree applicable to property outside the Soviet Union. Makarov (at p. 208) calls this assumption "eine irrige Annahme." However, the Swedish Supreme Court could have set aside the Russian rule as incompatible with the *ordre public* of the *forum*; an enactment which deprives the children of the *de cuius* of any claim of succession in favour of the state could *possibly* be considered "incompatible with the fundamental principles of the Swedish legal system".[217]

In the same decision, the Masters of the Supreme Court, in their proposals for a decision, obviously took for granted the applicability of Russian law as *lex causae* of the contract concluded in 1917, and found that Russian limitation rules, which had been introduced in 1923, should be applied. The underlying reasoning would seem to coincide with our opinion on the relevance of modifications in the legal system applicable in principle. It was held by the Masters, however, that the limitation rules could not claim "binding effect" with regard to legal obligations which had come into existence earlier than three years before they were introduced. The period of limitation was three years. Obviously, the Masters of the Supreme Court held the view that a claim which, at the coming into force of these rules, was still valid under earlier limitation provisions but was more than three years old could not be lost by limitation *simply by the entry into force of the statute.* This is possibly an illustration of those cases where the transitional rules of a new enactment (or the absence of such rules) are held incompatible with the *ordre public* of the *forum* country, and some consideration is accordingly given to earlier rules.[218] The Supreme Court did not consider the question of limitation, but, in principle, the

[217] It should be noticed that Mr. Justice Beckman classifies the decision under "*ordre public*" (pp. 41 f.). At p. 73 it is cited as an authority for the sweeping statement that "foreign law, by which the right of succession of private persons is abolished, is not applied with regard to property situated in Sweden."

[218] On the retroactive effect of new limitation rules, *vide* Hertzberg, *op.cit.*, pp. 205 f.

Court granted the plaintiffs' claim to recover money paid in advance under the disputed contract. It does not appear from the decision whether the Supreme Court held that it applied Russian or Swedish law in respect of the obligation.[219]

The method we have exemplified as the correct one has its *ratio* in the principle of the uniform solution referred to above (at pp. 107 f).[220] This fact is to some extent illustrated by the decision 1931 *N.J.A.* 403 (cf. 1929 *N.J.A.* 532). Two spouses had contracted marriage in 1892; at that time they were Swedish citizens. A question about the law applicable to the proprietary rights of the spouses was raised and decided in the sense that Swedish law (the law of the country of which the husband was a citizen at the solemnization of marriage) was applicable. The case was accordingly decided under section 14 of the Act on dissolution of the matrimonial community of property, 1898.[221] If the matter had been decided abroad, and the foreign court had applied the Act on the dissolution of matrimonial community of property, 1862, which was in force in Sweden at the celebration of the marriage, without observing later amendments in the law of Sweden, this would undoubtedly have been incompatible with the principle of the uniform solution.

The decision in 1931 *N.J.A.* 495 justifies a few more words on the present problem. In the heading of the report in the *N.J.A.*, the following question is posed (italics supplied): "Are the effects of marriage upon the proprietary rights of the spouses to be governed by English law *as it stood at the time of the solemnization of marriage?* Under that law there was no community of

[219] Cf. Hjerner, p. 585, note 2, and pp. 591 ff.

[220] Makarov, in *Rabels* Z. 1957, p. 205, states: "Für die Anwendung des jeweils geltenden Rechts spricht . . . das Prinzip der internationalen Entscheidungsharmonie. Denn der Staat, dessen Recht anwendbar ist, wird zweifellos jeweils sein geltendes Recht anwenden, inklusive der intertemporalrechtlichen Bestimmungen. Wenn wir diesem Beispiel folgen, entsteht keine Diskrepanz der Entscheidungen, der Fall wird im In- und Ausland einheitlich behandelt. Die Vorteile der internationalen Entscheidungsharmonie sind so allgemein anerkannt, dass man von diesem Grundsatz nicht abweichen sollte, soweit seiner Befolgung nicht das geschriebene Recht oder besondere Umstände entgegenstehen."

[221] The 1898 Act came into force on 1 Jan., 1899; only actions instituted before that day should be tried under the old law.

property between the spouses." In the decision of the Court of Appeal, which was not reversed by the Supreme Court, it is stated that at the time of contracting marriage the deceased husband was a British subject (Englishman) and that "on this ground, the effects of marriage upon the proprietary rights of the spouses should be governed by English law *as it stood at the time of the solemnization of marriage* (italics supplied)." The statutory provision underlying the statement of the Court of Appeal is chapter 1:2 of the Act on international questions concerning the legal effects of marriage, etc., 1912, where it is provided that the legal effects of matrimony with regard to the proprietary rights of the spouses shall be determined by "the law of the state of which the husband was a citizen when contracting marriage". The settling of the relevant time in the enactment is necessary to indicate the country from which the applicable substantive rules should be taken—*in casu* England—but it does not follow that the courts have to apply English law as it stood at the time of the marriage. Under the Swedish statute, it is not possible to change *lex causae* (cf. above, p. 127), but those words in the decision of the Court of Appeal and the heading of the report which have been put in italics say more than the statutory provision. The opinion of the Court of Appeal does not coincide with the principle which the present writer has described as the correct solution.

The facts of the case were as follows. For the purpose of assessing the estate duty to be paid on the estate of an Englishman domiciled (i.e. registered in the yearly census) in Sweden, the tax departement in the office of the Governor of Stockholm deducted the moiety of the net amount of the estate as being the widow's share and consequently free from estate duty. The comptroller of stamps and duties contended that the whole net value of the estate should have been subject to the estate duty since, under English law, no community of property existed between spouses who had married after 31 December 1882. The comptroller obviously held that English law was applicable to the mutual proprietary rights of the spouses. The widow objected that Swedish law should be applied for the purpose of deciding upon what grounds a public duty should be calculated. The Court of Appeal found that the deceased husband had been a British subject already at the solemnization of the marriage. The conclusion that English law was applicable is interesting in particular because this means that the choice of law rule in the 1912 Act was applied although the applicability of that statute in relation to England had not been ordered by special enactment (which, according to the language of the Act, is a condition of its being applied). From this point of view, the decision constitutes a precedent of some interest.[205] But the case did not imply any disputed question about the impact of *amendments* in the applicable legal system in the period following upon the contracting of marriage. In fact, English law in respect of the proprietary right of spouses had not been modified in the period 1883—1931, but so far as can be seen from the report no enquiry was made into this particular problem. It would seem, therefore, that the words italicized above in the decison of the Court of Appeal were put in, as it were, by accident rather than as a necessary element. At any rate, they are superfluous. This being so, the heading of the report is liable to lead the reader into error. Under the given circumstances, it would not seem possible to quote the holding of the Court of Appeal in support of the affirmation that Swedish courts do not adopt the principle of observing modifications in the *lex causae* introduced after the "creation of a legal relationship".

It could possibly be asked whether that principle should not be set aside in one particular case, viz. that dealt with in chapter 1:2 of the 1912 Act. There is, however, hardly any authority or other support for that opinion.[223] The general structure of

[222] Cf. Beckman, p. 66, and Malmar in *Sv.J.T.* 1937, p. 376.

[223] In the case 1909 *N.J.A.* 439, where the question was whether Swedish or Norwegian law should be applied, it is stated in the decision that questions concerning the effects of marriage upon the proprietary rights of the spouses should be governed "by the law of Norway as it stood at the time of the celebration of marriage." But no more than in the 1931 case did any question about the effects of a *modification* of Norwegian law arise. It does not seem to have been contended by any of the parties that amendments had been introduced. It is possible that the language just quoted was used because it was considered a general (both Swedish and Norwegian) *intertemporal* rule that amendments in the legislation about the legal effects of marriage are not applicable to spouses who have contracted marriage before the new rules entered into force.

the Act itself seems rather to speak against the assumption of such an exception. The Swedish *travaux préparatoires* show that there was disagreement concerning the correctness of the convention rule forbidding a change of *lex causae,* but nobody seems to have taken into consideration the possibility that the convention should make the proprietary questions permanently and invariably subject to the rules of the *lex causae* as it stood at the time of the solemnization of marriage.[224] The *travaux préparatoires* of the convention do not seem to deal with the problem of modifications in the *lex causae.*[225] In earlier Swedish writing it is essentially the change of "personal law" which is being discussed, and there seems to have been a strong opinion in favour of the principle that changes of *lex causae* should be allowed, at least where the new nationality acquired by the

[224] In *Royal Proposition* nr 58, 1912, the Minister of Justice stated (pp. 13 f.): "Whatever may be the actual standpoint of Swedish law, there are no reasons for any opposition against the adoption of the principle embodied in the convention"—i.e. the principle that a new citizenship does not imply a new *lex causae,* even if the new nationality is Swedish. The Council on Legislation stated (at p. 25 in the *Proposition*) that it was not "necessary, nor even adequate, to establish other rules applicable to foreign subjects in this respect (i.e. the proprietary rights of spouses) in Sweden than those rules which are in force in the home country of such persons."

[225] Also at the Hague conference, it was the change of personal law, i.e. the relevance of changes of nationality, but not modifications in the applicable law, which were discussed. In 1900, it was agreed that the draft convention should not contain that phrase which has the following tenor in chap. 1, sec. 2 of the Swedish 1912 Act: "Changes with regard to the nationality of either or both spouses during the marriage have no effect." This was held superfluous, since the immediately preceding sentence referred to "the law of the State of which the husband was a citizen at the solemnization of the marriage"; this provision, it was held, expressed "l'idée que le changement de nationalité des époux après le mariage laisse intact leur régime matrimonial" (*Actes* 1900, p. 226). But the explicit prohibition against changes of personal law in this respect was added in 1904, "pour exprimer ce qui dans le nouveau project *était implicitement admis* (italics supplied), savoir que le changement de nationalité des époux n'entraîne pas un changement de leur régime matrimonial" etc. (*Actes* 1904, pp. 179 f.). Thus, it is impossible to argue that the explicit prohibition against changes of *lex causae* in the convention and the 1912 Act justifies enquiries for any other restrictive meaning of the words "at the time of the solemnization of marriage" than the prohibition against changes of *lex causae.* What is meant is a repetition or an explanation *ex abundante cautela* of that rule.

spouses was Swedish.[226] In more recent conflict writing, neither the policy question of changes of "personal law", which has been solved in the 1912 Act, nor the problem about the importance of modifications in the *lex causae* seems to have been discussed in any detail.

There are certainly cases in which the applicable foreign transitional rules are such that it appears obviously incompatible with the fundamental principles of the Swedish legal system to apply the foreign rules. The natural solution is then to resort to the safety valve of *ordre public,* i.e. to return to *lex fori.* It has been discussed, however, whether in these cases it would not be enough to set aside the foreign transitional rules and apply the legal system concerned as it stood before the amendment.[227] The underlying reasoning would seem to be that the transitional rules of the *lex causae* should be replaced by the intertemporal provisions of the *lex fori* and that its rules require the application of the foreign law before the amendment.[228]

Foreign Law as Fact

In some cases, foreign law assumes importance as a fact to take into consideration. Thus foreign prohibitions against exporting or importing goods may be facts which prevent a delivery of such goods.[229] The legal importance of the obstacle is evaluated under the *lex causae,* but the finding of the contents of the foreign law establishing such prohibition may be just as difficult as if the purpose of the enquiry were the immediate application of such foreign law, although it should be pointed out that the duty of proving the foreign provisions in this case would seem to be incumbent upon the party invoking the obstacle. Several Swedish cases may be cited, in which foreign law has been of importance in various ways without actually serving as the legal basis

[226] Cf. Wikander, *Regleringen av äktenskapets legala förmögenhetsrättsliga verkningar,* 1913, pp. 33 ff.

[227] Batiffol, *op.cit.,* p. 392; Wolff, *Deutschlands,* p. 85.

[228] On these questions, *vide* further Gavalda, *op.cit.,* pp. 323 ff. Cf. above, p. 150. about the opinion of the Masters of the Supreme Court on the application of Soviet limitation rules in the case 1937 *N.J.A.* 261.

[229] Nial, pp. 151 f. *Vide* the comprehensive survey in Hjerner, *passim,* and particularly pp. 558 ff.

of the decision.[230] In this connection we shall discuss two cases which illustrate this fact in an interesting way.

The first case is reported in 1956 *N.J.A.* 343. A Gothenburg firm (A) had sold a consignment of food preserves to an English wholesaler (B), who in his turn sold the goods to another English merchant (C), whereupon it was found that the preserves were not in perfect condition. In relation to B, C did not observe the time limit for claims established in Swedish law, but B immediately upon receipt of the claim forwarded it to A. Under English law, C was entitled to recover damages from B in spite of his delay in complaining. After B had instituted in Sweden an action against A based on the condition of the goods, the latter argued that B had not complained within the period fixed in section 52 of the Swedish Sales of Goods Act, 1905. The Supreme Court, however, held that B's cause of action had not been forfeited, since the buyer of the goods from B had been entitled to recover damages from B under the law applicable to their mutual relations, i.e. English law. The Swedish vendor, it was held, must have realized that the merchandise was intended to be distributed by means of several successive sales. It was never contested that the proper law of the contract in the case was Swedish law.[231] Nor was the Swedish court called upon to decide any action between B and C; in that case, English law would undoubtedly have been applicable. The case simply implies that when deciding whether B had claimed too late, the Court took into consideration the fact that B would be held liable to pay damages to C or that B had not been in a position to count upon an "immediate" complaint from C (as provided in Swedish law) but had had to receive such complaint "within a reasonable time" as stipulated in the correspondinging English rules, which are more generous to the buyer in this respect. No statute other than the Swedish Sale of Goods Act, 1905, was applied, and there was no question about any other *lex obligatio-*

[230] In the case 1916 *N.J.A.* 297 a contract was held not to be binding (under Swedish rules) since it had been concluded under the influence of an error with regard to the contents of foreign law in certain respects (cf., on the point of Swedish law raised in the decision, 1910 *N.J.A.* 499.). *Vide* also 1954 *N.J.A.* 573 and the opinion of Sjögren, J., in 1911 *N.J.A.* 467.

[231] Cf. Karlgren, p. 108 (the footnote) and same author in *Sv.J.T.* 1961, pp. 651 f. No diverging solution is proposed by two other writers who have dealt with the case: Rodhe in *Sv.J.T.* 1961, pp. 272 f., and J. Hellner, *Köprätt*, 1961, p. 139. Beckman, however, at p. 54 seems to mean that two *leges causae* were put into operation.

nis. Nevertheless, English law was obviously of importance for the issue of the case.

The second decision in point is reported in 1939 *N.J.A.* 101. Anna Johansson died in Sweden in 1934 and was survived by her husband, Hindrik, and children of a previous marriage. When Anna's estate was to be distributed, the common property of the spouses was held to embrace property which Hindrik had come into under a will made in Massachusetts in 1932 by Hindrik's sister, Susanna Sundberg, an American citizen, who had died in Massachusetts on 8 December 1932. The will conferred Susanna's estate upon Hindrik "absolutely and in fee simple". Hindrik contended that the distribution of Anna's estate should be set aside in so far as the property which he had come into under the will had been included in the matrimonial community of property; it should be considered as Hindrik's private property. The dissolution of the matrimonial community took place under Swedish law; there was no connection with any foreign legal system. Swedish matrimonial rules were to determine whether the property was private because it had been received by the spouses through testamentary succession upon the condition that it should remain private. It did not appear, at least not clearly, from the will whether such a condition had in fact been laid down. Under chapter 3:1 of the Statute of Wills, 1930, wills "shall be construed in accordance with the presumable wishes of the testator". There is nothing in the decision which supports the assumption that this Swedish rule was *not* applied, nor did any of the parties produce any evidence about American rules on the construction of wills in general. Statements were made, on the other hand, on the rules of Massachusetts concerning matrimonial proprietary rights, on the probable intentions of Susanna Sundberg and on the hypothetical construction of her will by a court sitting in Massachusetts. In the decision, however, only the Swedish construction rule was used as *ratio decidendi:* Susanna Sundberg had intended to give Hindrik the property as private property. According to Malmar's comment in the *Sv. J.T.*, "regard was paid" to the law of Massachusetts in this decision.[232] In other words, in order to ascertain the wishes of the testator, which are decisive under Swedish rules on the construction of wills, the legal environment in which the testator lived was taken into consideration. When making her will,

232 Malmar in *Sv.J.T.* 1942, pp. 399 f.

it was assumed, she had wanted to give Hindrik her estate in such a way as not to confer any future rights upon his wife's children of a previous marriage, for this would have been the effect of the will in Massachusetts. In this case, foreign law is obviously relegated to a background position even more than in the preceding example.[233]

[233] Mr. Justice Karlgren (at pp. 140 f.) seems to understand this decision in the sense that American rules on the construction of wills were applied since it must be assumed that the testator had implicitly referred to these rules. Mr. Justice Beckman (at p. 74) states that the will "was construed in accordance with American law." It is not quite clear what the learned Justice means by his more general statement that the construction of wills is governed by the law generally applicable to questions of succession, "but that exceptions, particularly in favour of the *lex domicilii,* are often reasonable, since the wishes of the testator are decisive for the construction." When it is assumed that "the wishes of the testator are decisive," however, this implies in fact that the choice of law has already been effected and that Swedish law (*lex fori*) has been allowed to set aside the law applicable to succession. The latter legal system may very well contain a rule to the effect that in construing wills, no importance at all should be given to the testator's wishes; only the strict language of the will should be observed. What other "exceptions" are meant by Mr. Justice Beckman is not explained. It is possible that the statement just quoted only implies that in those cases where the *lex causae* is a law attributing decisive importance to the testator's wishes, attention may be paid to the "legal milieu" of the testator's domicile country when determining the actual contents of these wishes. In the present writer's opinion this is the only conclusion justified by the case now discussed.

Chapter III
How the Material is Used

§ 8. General Remarks. The Stages of an International Action

With some simplification it may be stated that an ordinary civil action implies four essential tasks for the judge. He has to pass a decision concerning a number of, as a rule, preliminary procedural questions (*forum, res judicata, lis pendens* objections, or objections to the effect that the judge has an interest in the outcome of the action and should therefore be replaced) which are of decisive importance *inter alia* for the general question whether the merits of th case shall be considered at all. The judge must undertake a more or less active enquiry into the facts of the case; at any rate he has to determine the value of the evidence produced in the action. Moreover, the facts thus ascertained must be confronted with such legal rules as have been invoked or are otherwise applicable. This comparison results in the judgment. Thus the "sequence" of stages in an ordinary action may be described as follows:

A. Procedural questio
B. Facts of the case
C. Legal rules
D. Decision.

When dealing with an international (external) action, however, we find complications at each of these stages. The material of private international law is used by the judge in order to master all these complications. This use of the material may also be characterized as the *solution of law conflicts;* "law conflict", in this context, means the intellectual dilemma of the judge when several systems of substantive rules raise, as it were, simultaneous claims to be applied.

Let us start with the procedural preliminary questions. In an international action, the problem whether the parties have capacity to sue or be sued must be solved in a particular way,[1] special rules on service

[1] Cf. above, pp. 69 f.

of process may have to be observed, the judge must decide whether a foreign plaintiff has a duty to offer bail under the statute dealing with that question,[2] the effect of a foreign judgment concerning the same action or of a suit going on abroad must be taken into consideration, etc. Above all, however, the question is raised whether the action shall be held to fall within the jurisdiction of Swedish courts.[3] In ordinary actions, the *forum* question may be the only procedural preliminary question which must be answered in each case (although the answer is usually given implicitly). In an international action, the jurisdiction problem is always raised and often turns out to be decisive for the issue. It appears from the reports that it assumes the importance of an essential question in international actions; in fact, it ranks beside the choice of law problem. It is only after the question of jurisdiction has been given an affirmative answer that the problem of the proper *forum* within Sweden is raised.

With regard to the next stage of the action, that of facts, it may be expected that the international action does not differ materially from the ordinary suit apart from the fact that the Act on taking of evidence in Swedish actions before foreign courts may be applied.[4] However, particular difficulties regularly arise when events which have occurred abroad are to be proved.[5] The incompleteness or insufficiency of the evidence makes its evaluation more difficult, and it does not seem unreasonable to fear that the decisions in international actions may therefore be of lower quality than those rendered in internal suits.

In the uncomplicated internal action, the legal rules are found in the Statute Book. Even in cases where the principal problem does not concern the facts but the meaning, construction and application of

[2] Cf. above, p. 69.

[3] Cf. above, pp. 72 ff.

[4] Cf. above, p. 68, note 26.

[5] It may well be asked, e.g., how a Swedish court should proceed when confronted by a Swedish woman's claim that a Afghan student be declared the father of her child and that the child be granted the special status—with certain advantages in comparison with the legal position of other illegitimate children—which Swedish law confers upon children whose parents were betrothed to each other before its birth, if this claim is based upon alleged sexual intercourse in San Francisco two years before the suit was instituted and if it appears that the Afghan student has returned to his home country, possibly long before the suit. Cf. 1957 *N.J.A.* 430.

legal rules, the necessary intellectual operations are performed in the judge's own legal *milieu.* In an international action, a series of decisions must be made before arriving at substantive rules; the application of these will be the next problem. First, the cause of action as such must be ranged within a legal category (characterized, classified) and confronted with such choice of law rules as may be applicable. Once a choice of law rule has thus been found applicable, its connecting section must be construed, and problems may well arise at this stage also. The whole of this intellectual operation may be called the "choice of law." Once it has been performed, an enquiry into the substantive rules of the *lex causae* is necessary, and it is only after its completion that the judge will at last have arrived at the stage corresponding to that of "legal rules" in an internal action. And yet these rules are by no means ready to be applied at this stage of the international case. The question may arise whether the judge shall accept a so-called *renvoi,* which refers to a new *lex causae.* There may also be reason to consider the problem whether the legal system indicated by the choice of law rule and thus applicable in principle shall be set aside as repugnant to *ordre public* or to the law of nations or as a rule of "public law". Further, absolute rules of the *lex fori* may claim to be applied instead of or alongside the *lex causae.* When, at last, all the applicable substantive rules have been singled out, they must be construed and applied correctly or, as it were, loyally with regard to the foreign *lex causae* country. This is a difficult task since the judge has to place himself, as it were, into a new legal environment, a new legal atmosphere.[6] Occasionally, special questions arise with regard to the adaptation of foreign law to the *lex fori.*

Schematically, the sequence of stages in an international action may be described as follows:

A. Jurisdiction
B. Procedural questions (attended by special complications)
C. Facts of the case
D. Legal rules
    1. Choice of law

[6] "The application of rules of foreign law is a cosmopolitan technique, born of a certain tolerance of foreign conceptions of justice," says Carswell in 8 *I.C.L.Q.* (1959), pp. 268 f.

2. Evidence about the contents of *lex causae*
3. *Ordre public*
4. Application of foreign rules
5. Absolute rules of the *lex fori.*

E. Decision.

The most important of the questions enumerated above will be dealt with in the present chapter. It must be kept in mind, of course, that not all of the possible complications exist in every case. The questions of jurisdiction, choice of law and the problems attending the application of foreign law are unavoidable, however. Obviously, the judge does not function like a machine, deciding each question in its turn according to the enumeration above, which is partly based upon the normal order of proceeding in an international action and corresponds to the order in which a conscientious judge usually accounts for his conclusions in the decision. It is quite natural that the judge may try out a complete preliminary solution before definitely making up his mind. In actual practice, the difficulty of choosing the right "pigeonhole" for the action in the world of legal concepts in order to arrive at a choice of law rule (the classification problem) may occasionally give rise to considerable hesitation over the choice of law. The question of jurisdiction may equally seem so doubtful that the judge may hesitate to make up his mind. Whether the *ordre public* of the forum is engaged or not is always a problematic question. If it appears that a certain solution of one of these problems would imply an undesirable decision of the matter as a whole, it may be tempting —and indeed quite justifiable—to return to some of the problems previously studied and to make a new evaluation of the particular element which results in a satisfactory solution of the dispute. Clear statutory rules and established precedents must be observed, and even where no such guidance is to be had, the decision must not be arbitrary. In many cases, however, the questions arising in international actions are of a new character and provide, as it were, illustrations of the legislative problems of private international law. The method of comparing the results of different imaginable solutions before the final decision in individual cases of this kind is likely to facilitate the finding of those solutions which embody the most reasonable principles in consideration of the tasks and function of private international law, and which are most likely to be permanently adopted.

Procedural Questions

We shall not discuss procedural questions in any detail in this connection. Both the theoretical and the practical problems of international procedure (and execution of judgments) call for thorough examination, but this falls outside the scope of the present study. On the other hand, certain problems which are also of fundamental importance for the use of the procedural "material" have been mentioned in the preceding chapter.[7] We have found that courts are increasingly prepared to make a clear distinction between the problems of international *jurisdiction* and of finding a *forum* in Sweden. They also seem to have abandoned an earlier inclination to combine the problems of jurisdiction and of choice of law.[8] As for those questions which arise because a matter has already been decided abroad—and thus constitutes a *res judicata*—or is being dealt in an action between the same parties, in a foreign country, we repeat our contention that, in principle, the "recognition" of a judgment implies that it is treated as equal to a decision by a Swedish court and must consequently be granted the effect of *res judicata*. Such other "effects" of foreign judgments as are illustrated by the decision 1935 *N.J.A.* 611 (where it was held that *in dubio* a foreign decision constituted in itself a cause of action in a Swedish suit) do not imply that the judgment is a bar to a new trial in Sweden. But judgments which, under the prevailing opinion, should be "recognized" in the Sweden as "constitutive" or bearing upon a person's status would appear to be obstacles to a Swedish action concerning the question answered by such judgment abroad.[9] Only, it is far from certain what judgments should be ranged within this category. The same effects are granted to other kinds of judgments, which may be enforced in Sweden under

[7] The statutory material in the field of international procedure is dealt with above, at pp. 29 ff.

[8] In 1957 *N.J.A.* 430, the City Court's decision on the question of jurisdiction raised in the action seems to echo the old view upon the connection between jurisdiction and choice of law ("Since even if Swedish law were applicable in the present case the alleged illicit intercourse did not take place in Sweden . . ."). It is possible, however, that the Court only wanted to state that the applicability of Swedish law might be one out of several more or less important "connecting factors" for the purpose of deciding the question of *jurisdiction*.

[9] Cf. the facts in 1956 *N.J.A.* 337.

special legislation, although the execution will often take place in a form different from the procedure normal when Swedish judgments are carried into effect. If a foreign court of justice has been seized with a matter, and the facts are such that the decision of such foreign court would be "recognized" in Sweden, it must be assumed that the objection of *lis pendens* may be successfully invoked against a simultaneous trial in Sweden (cf. sec. 7 of the Act on recognition and enforcement of Swiss judicial decisions, 1936).[10] It could possibly also be contended that the provision on *lis pendens* in chapter 13:6 of the Judicial Procedure Code should also be applicable where an action between the same parties is being tried abroad when the facts are such that, in a new trial in Sweden, the foreign judgment would be considered as evidence of a particular kind in accordance with the principle embraced in 1935 *N.J.A.* 611. If the action has been admitted to trial by the foreign court according to a clause of submission valid in the Swedish opinion, the objection of *lis pendens* must be entitled to success even if a new action in Sweden is necessary in order to obtain a Swedish levy of execution in accordance with the foreign judgment. As for arbitral awards, it is laid down in the 1929 Act on that topic that, in principle, the fact that a disputed question has been made the object of a foreign arbitration agreement is a bar to actions in the Swedish courts (secs. 3 and 4). As a general rule, foreign arbitral awards shall "be held valid within the Kingdom" (secs. 6 ff.).

§ 9. The Choice of Law

In the individual case, the judge is confronted by the particular situation that he has to pass a decision in an action which is characterized by the circumstance that the facts of the case embody foreign elements. In the last resort, therefore, he is searching for substantive rules upon which his decision can be founded. To find these rules, the judge must make *three different choices;* it can also be said that the choice of law proceeds in three successive stages. First, the judge must make a *choice of conflict rule.* For this purpose, he examines the facts of the case and tries to find the proper place in the legal system of the problem raised by these facts. The judge is likely to find that one or

[10] On these questions, *vide* Dennemark, pp. 11 ff.

possibly more choice of law rules claim attention as being perhaps intended to govern questions of the kind which he has to deal with. He confronts the facts with these rules and delimits their mutual claims of application. He refers the disputed question to one of them. The next task is the *choice of the applicable legal system,* the choice of law in the proper sense of the word. This operation is effected by means of applying the connecting section of the choice of law rule: it includes a construction of the connecting factor embodied in that rule.[11] If it is obvious that the action—which may concern e.g. the validity of a contract of sale concluded in Italy—should be decided in accordance with Italian law, those provisions of Italian law which are applicable *in concreto* must be picked out (the *choice of applicable rules in the* lex causae).

In these operations, the judge is bound by legal rules i.e. his successive decisions must be made upon the ground of these rules. The contents of the rules of private international law are therefore of importance for the technique developed for the purpose of the choice of law. Apart from this, however, there are no rules for this technique, which may vary from one country to another, and which is determined, in the last resort, by judicial tradition, the structure of legal rules in the *lex fori* in general, and the prevailing opinion about the purpose of private international law. What is important to remember, however, is that the judge's situation is different from that of legal theorists. The latter expound choice of law rules as provisions of a purely formal character, which refer, *in abstracto,* to an indefinite number of foreign legal systems. They give, as it were, a "static" description of these rules. Conversely, the judge is confronted by a concrete action where he has to make the static conflict rules work. His task is to make a choice between e.g. German, French, or Swedish law; in most cases the alternatives are *lex fori* and another legal system. The presence of certain more or less known laws claiming application gives the "conflict of competence" what might be called its individual colour. It also facilitates, at least in the majority of cases, a prior ascertainment of the issue of the case at bar by means of a preliminary investigation of the contents of that law which has a potential claim to be applied. This possibility of ascertaining the outcome of actions has undoubtedly been of some importance for the

[11] Cf. above, at pp. 127 ff.

development through successive decisions of a specific judicial technique in private international law cases in the course of which the courts have—to use the language of conflict theories—adopted certain opinions about essential "problems" in this field of law (e.g. classification, *renvoi,* the preliminary question, etc.).

The technique which Swedish courts may be *assumed* to use—the reports do not give much guidance on this topic—will now be illustrated by three examples. The two later illustrations concern particularly the choice of applicable rules in the *lex causae.*

The *first example* is chosen chiefly to illustrate the fact that a court will often have to study the actual contents of the foreign law which has a potential claim of applicability in the case.

> A Frenchman dies in Sweden, leaving property there. The deceased's wife and two children, all of them French citizens, are entitled to the estate. The spouses had made a joint will in favour of each other in Sweden and in observance of Swedish formal requirements. The children contest the validity of the will and the widow's claim to the property bequeathed upon her under that instrument; in support of their standpoint they refer to the fact that joint wills in the mutual favour of spouses are not allowed in France.

Under chapter 1:4 of the 1937 Act, a will shall be held *formally* valid if it has been made in accordance with the law of the place of making. It follows from chapter 1:5 of the same Act that the question of the *essential* validity of wills is answered by the law of the testator's home country. Which of these two choice of law rules shall the Swedish court apply? It has to interpret the terms "formal" and "essential" in the two referring sections and it has to confront the facts with the choice of law rules. The objection raised by the deceased's children against the will as such is part of the facts which must be studied in greater detail, and it is quite natural that the judge should study those provisions of the French civil code which are invoked. Let us suppose that he finds, in article 968 of the *code civil,* an enactment to the effect that a will signed by two persons, or rather, that two wills embodied "dans le même acte," shall not be considered to have been made in due form.[12] Although spouses are at liberty to make

[12] Article 968 has the following wording (amended in 1947): "Un testament ne pourra être fait dans le même acte par deux ou plusieurs personnes, soit

testamentary bequests in favour of each other, they are not allowed to combine their wills into one single document, a "joint" will in each other's favour, a *testament conjonctif*. It seems obvious, under these circumstances, that in the view of the Swedish court the children's objection is based upon the non-observance of French rules on topics which we cannot reasonably subsume under any other heading than that of *form*.[13] By application of chapter 1:4 of the 1937 Act, the Swedish court arrives at the conclusion that the will is formally valid, since the formal requirements of Swedish law have been complied with. The children's action is dismissed.[14] If the family had been Italian, however, and the meaning of the prohibition against joint wills in Italian law was that spouses should not be allowed to make testamentary bequest to each other at all, the outcome of the case would be different.[15]

Like the first example, our second illustration is not taken from the Swedish reports but is wholly fictitious.

> The Portuguese Castro, who is domiciled in Lisbon, has given the Swede Olsson, domiciled in Stockholm, the amount of five thousand escudos which Olsson has deposited in a Stockholm bank, where he has a savings account. The money is not subsequently touched. Two years later, Castro sues Olsson in the City Court of Stockholm and claims that Olsson should refund part of the amount since he, Castro, has met with financial misfortunes and is actually living in poverty. Olsson contends that he has received the money as compensation for supervising the care of a horse which Castro held in stables at the Ulriksdal race-

au profit d'un tiers, soit à titre de dispositions réciproque et mutuelle." Cf. Article 1097.

13 Cf. Wolff, *Deutschlands*, p. 230, and Batiffol, p. 728.

14 It should be noted that the outcome would be the same if the matter was tried by French courts. We suppose that the rule *locus regit actum* is upheld with regard to wills in French conflict law and that French courts consider the prohibition in Article 968 of the *Code civil* as a formal rule. Cf. Batiffol, pp. 727 f.

15 According to Wolff *(loc.cit.)*, the prohibition against joint wills in Italian law does not concern formal but essential validity, for its purpose should be to guarantee the testator's liberty to revoke his will, and testaments, therefore, must not contain anything which deprives the testator of this liberty in any way.

> course near Stockholm (although Olsson had forgotten to mention this income in his return to the inland revenue authorities). Castro admits that Olsson had looked after the horse occasionally but emphasizes that Olsson had never been asked to do this and that Castro's reason for giving the money to Olsson was that he hade liked Olsson and pitied him for his bad financial position. Moreover, Castro contends, the amount was in no way proportional to the insignificant "work" performed by Olsson. The evidence produced in the case gives no support whatever to the contention that a contract about Olsson's supervising the way in which the horse was taken care of had been made between the parties.

In this case, the Swedish judge who considers the question whether Portuguese law or the *lex fori* is applicable is not confronted by a choice between conflict rules if he adopts the "individualizing" method. Then there is only one conflict rule, and that a sweeping one. "The proper law of the obligation is the law of that country where the relations of the parties have their centre of gravity" is a statement found at p. 44 in Professor Nial's book *Internationell förmögenhetsrätt,* which the Swedish judge will most probably consult. But he has to determine where the centre of gravity is situated. He will find that it is contended by writers—supported by at least some judicial authority[16]—that the donor's national law is applicable to gifts *in dubio* whereas contracts of service should normally be governed by the law of the place where the work was performed. The latter opinion can also claim some support in judicial decisions.[17] One of the reasons invoked in favour of the former *in dubio* rule is that gifts are gratuitous transactions. After some reflections upon the concept "gifts with a purpose of remuneration" as occasionally discussed in Swedish law and upon the possibility of a special choice of law rule applicable in cases of doubt to this particular group of gifts, the judge arrives at the conclusion that, in Swedish legal terminology and systematics, the action concerns a gift *inter vivos.* If he has conciously adopted the sweeping conflict rule of the "individualizing" method, the judge will subsequently state either that *qua* gift *inter vivos,* the transaction has

16 Nial, pp. 60; 1934 *N.J.A.* 320.
17 Nial, pp. 62 ff.; 1911 *N.J.A.* 467. Cf. 1941 *N.J.A.* 350.

its centre of gravity in Portugal, or, if he assumes the existence of an independent or specialized choice of law rule applicable to gifts, that the action shall be decided under the law of the donor's home country, i.e. that of Portugal. This result has been obtained by ranging the facts of the action within a certain category (classification, characterization) which calls for the application of "gift" rules. When the decision is finally rendered, it seems permissible to state that in this situation the Swedish judge acts *as if* the action concerned a purely internal Portuguese matter, decided by a Portuguese court of justice.[18] In principle, he bases his decision upon all those rules of Portuguese rule which are applicable to the facts of the case. In other words, out of the Portuguese legal system, the relevant provisions are picked out for application. The judge does not "characterize" the foreign law in the sense of selecting for application only those rules in that legal system which deal with "gifts *inter vivos*" in Swedish legal systematics. Nor does he undertake any "secondary classification", i.e. single out for application only those rules of Portuguese law which concern "gifts" according to Portuguese legal terminology. Let us assume that he finds the following three rules, or fragments of rules, in Portuguese law (these rules as set out below are wholly fictitious).

1. The handing over of money from one person to another shall never be considered as a gift, if the slightest shadow of an earlier obligation between them can be found.
2. A person who has made a gift to another person is entitled to recover half the value of the gift, if he subsequently falls into penury, provided that the donee has not consumed it.
3. If one person has performed work for another without being asked, and such work has been of some utility for that other person, the latter is bound to grant a reasonable remuneration.

All these rules are invoked by Castro. Acording to the rules on "gifts" in Portuguese law, Castro has no valid cause of action against Olsson, for under rule No. 1, the case does not deal with a gift. Nevertheless, the judge applies rule No. 3, which refers to the very facts of the case.[19] It is for Portuguese rules to determine whether Olsson's

[18] This simile is obviously not justifiable in all connections, and particularly not where the *lex causae* is composed of substantive rules from several legal systems.

[19] A "secondary" classification in this case would result in a decision which, in actual fact, would not imply a loyal application of Portuguese rules. Castro's

supervision of the treatment of the horse had been of any "utility" for Castro, to assess the "reasonable remuneration", and to answer the question whether Castro is entitled to recover anything out of the money left to Olsson if the amount of 5000 escudos were to found more than reasonable remuneration and Olsson would consequently make an "unjustified profit", as the Swedish term has it, unless the money were paid back by him.

The assumption concerning the course of action of the Swedish judge is confirmed, at least partially, by the manner in which the decision of the court was obtained in 1930 *N.J.A.* 692, which may serve as our *example No. 3.* The action concerned a claim by a wife against her husband to recover unpaid alimony under a contract previously concluded by the spouses. The choice of a conflict rule and the determination of the applicable law did not cause much trouble. American law, more precisely the law of Massachusetts, was held applicable. The husband objected, *inter alia,* that the claim was prescribed. Both the District Court and the Court of Appeal took it for granted that the question of limitation should be governed by Swedish law. In the opinion of Bagge, J., which was adopted by the majority of the Supreme Court,[18] it is stated, *inter alia:*

"In consideration of the close connection which exists between the question whether the contract is valid and binding and the problem after what period of limitation the rights created by the contract can no longer be enforced, I find that the law of Massachusetts should also govern the latter question, regardless of the fact that the relevant provisions of that law must be regarded as procedural."

Under Massachusetts law, the claim could be enforced until twenty years had passed from the date when it became mature. The husband's defence was consequently not sustained. If Swedish law, which provides for a period of ten years, had been applied, the outcome would have been different.

action must be dismissed, since there was no support for it in the rules of Portuguese law on "gifts", and Castro's possible cause of action under rule No. 3 would not even be tried.

[20] There were no dissident opinions on this point in the Supreme Court. *Vide* Bagge *in Festskrift till Marks von Würtemberg,* 1931.

This case may be cited as an expression of the method illustrated in our second example: once the choice of law rule has indicated the applicable law and thus rendered the service that may be asked of it, the judge applies all those rules of the *lex causae* which are applicable to a case composed as the case at bar actually is. The quotation from Mr. Justice Bagge would seem to indicate, however, that certain rules in the *lex causae* may be set aside because they are considered as part of "public law" according to the systematics of the *lex fori.*[21]

> The question raised by this case is hardly a classification problem, if the latter term is taken to mean the ranging of facts within a certain legal category, the construction of the choice of law rule, and the confrontation of the facts and those choice of law rules the application of which is contemplated at least as a possibility.[22] In Swedish legal writing, however, the case is almost invariably described as an example of the problem of classification.[23] The explanation would seem to be that most writers assume that the Supreme Court *could* have undertaken a "secondary" classification and consequently selected only such provisions of American law as, according to American legal systematics, are private-law rules on the termination of obligations. In other words, the Supreme Court, when applying the American rule as a substitute for the Swedish private-law provision on limitation, which hade been set aside by the choice of law rule, rejected the doctrine of "secondary" classification.[24]

[21] Cf. below, pp. 205 ff.

[22] Some writers also use the term "classification" to denote the ranging of legal rules under such headings as "public" or "private" law, as rules belonging to "the law of succession" or as "formal" provisions.

[23] The late Professor Hult (in *Festskrift till Sundberg,* 1959, p. 243) calls this case "an excellent illustration" of certain classification problems, and holds that it implies the construction of a conflict rule to the effect that "procedural quesions are governed by the *lex fori.*" Limitation is not part of the field of procedural technique and therefore falls outside the sphere of application of the lastmentioned rule. What must be meant by these statements is that the rule on procedural questions does not imply any restriction to the reference to American law embodied in the choice of law rule which was originally chosen for the decision of the matter as a whole.

[24] With regard to similar German cases, Lewald states (*op.cit.* at pp. 78 ff.) that "la question de droit soulevée par le litige pourra, à mon avis, être formulée de la manière suivante: le débiteur peut-il, par suite de l'écoulement

The method for the choice of law which has now been described seems to be the one best fitted to meet the realities underlying legal problems.[25] It implies that the judge begins by analysing the factual elements—evidence, claims, arguments—and confronts them with the choice of law rules; the referring and connecting sections of these rules are construed with due regard to their international function. Where the judge finds that the choice of law rule contains a directive to apply the law of a foreign country, the decision is based upon the rules of that legal system in so far as they are applicable to the actual facts of the case; at this stage, "classification" is no longer necessary or called for. This method would seem also to function in cases where a claim presupposes the existence of a legal institution which has no counterpart in the Swedish legal system (dowry, morninggift, breach of promise, etc.). The judge examines the facts, and among them the rules of the foreign legal system; upon this basis, he will be able to formulate a choice of law rule which is wholly compatible with the fundamental principles of the *lex fori* and which can be used for the purpose of choosing the applicable law.

The method does not always work, however. If an action contains several disputed points and lies within a field of the law where specialized conflict rules are in force, the *third* choice of law, i.e. the choice of applicable rules in the *lex causae,* will be complicated. If a party contends, in a Swedish court, that a will is not valid both because it implies dispositions encroaching upon the portions reserved by law for the testator's children and because the testator has been fraudulently seduced into making the will, the first question has to decided under the law of the state of which the *de cuius* was a subject at the time of his death, e.g. Indonesian law, and the latter problem has to be solved under the law of the testator's home country at the time of

d'un certain délai, se soustraire à l'accomplissement de son obligation?" Since the question has to be answered in accordance with American law, no importance should be attached to the fact that, in American legal systematics, limitation rules are procedural. Otherwise, the result would be that a claim which was prescribed both under German and American law would be regarded as eternal: the *lex fori* has been set aside, and the limitation rules of the *lex causae* are disregarded. The German Reichgericht decided in this way in 1882, but not in 1934, when its decision followed the same principles as were adopted in 1930 *N.J.A.* 692.

[25] On the topics discussed in what follows, cf. Mr. Justice Karlgren in *SvJ.T.* 1954, pp. 497 ff.

the making of the will, e.g. Dutch law. If fraud (except for grave cases) does not invalidate a will under Dutch law, and if Indonesian law does not contain any rules on portions reserved for the testator's children, the will would be upheld in Sweden even if it would be void under Dutch law because of the encroachment upon the children's portions and equally invalid under Indonesian law because of the fraud. As the applicable Swedish rules have been drafted, none of these questions can be considered a mere "pertinent of the principal question" or as an incidental question which has to be decided under a principal "law of the will". Therefore, only those rules of Indonesian law should be selected which deal with the "contents" of wills (chap. 1, sec. 5 of the 1937 Act) and, from Dutch law, only those provisions should be taken which concern "fraud, error, duress or any other undue influence" (chap. 1, sec. 6 of the 1937 Act). The expressions quoted from the 1937 Act must be construed on the basis of Swedish legal systematics and terminology, although the international function of the rules should be kept in mind. This statement is true also of the classical cases concerning the relation between a spouse's succession claims and claims under matrimonial proprietary rules. Where a choice of law rule in the *lex fori* is applicable to questions of "succession," and another rule deals with the "matrimonial proprietary" rights of surviving spouses, and where the first rule refers to the law of X and the other one demands the application of Y law, it is necessary for the courts of Z to select only those rules which concern "succession" from X law and to pick out only those provisions in the law of Y which are applicable to "matrimonial property" claims. The law of Z, which establishes two choice of law rules which are to be applied successively for the purpose of distributing the assets in a deceased person's estate, obviously delimits the spheres of application of such rules on the basis of its own legal concepts or at any rate in such a manner that the meaning of the choice of law rules is invariably the same: even if "succession" in the choice of law rule does not mean altogether the same thing as "succession" in substantive rules, the sense of the term in the *choice of law rule* must not vary from one case to another. The fact that certain substantive rules are taken from X law and others from the law of Y may produce undesirable results, as demonstrated above (p. 116). It is a task for the legislator to draft choice of law rules in such a way that they do not produce these results.[26] The judge can hardly act otherwise than in the manner described here. Where alternative constructions are possible or where the judge "makes" the choice of law rule himself, however, it is not necessary for him to let specialization produce unreasonable results. The obvious dilemma of the legislature, on the other hand, is that certain policy considerations may be invoked in favour of specialized rules and therefore militate against the more dogmatic reasons which may be cited against them.

In international writing, an extensive and lively debate has been going on about the various problems of the choice of law, and different methods have been recommended as most suitable; it is sometimes asserted that they are logically necessary or follow from certain fundamental principles in the conflict of laws.[27] It is striking that it was never very difficult for the leading advocates of the various theories to demonstrate the unreasonable or shocking results which an adoption of the theories of the opposite school would produce in at least some illustrative case. This fact may possibly indicate that none of the proposed solutions is perfect. It must be kept in mind, however, that we are dealing with a practical legal problem. Courts are not, and

[26] In the classical case—which may not be very frequent in actual practice—of the widow who is left penniless as a result of the caprices of conflict rules, it is possible that the choice of law rule applicable to the economic effects of matrimony could be framed in such a way that questions arising at the death of either spouse shall be decided under the law of the deceased's home country. In most legal systems the rules on succession and the proprietary rights of surviving spouses make an organic unity. It must be examined, however, whether the slicing of the *matrimonial* rule which this solution would involve might produce undesirable results in other situations.

[27] A survey of the learned discussion as well as recommendations for the solution of the problem are given by Professor Malmström in *Det s. k. kvalifikationsproblemet inom internationell privaträtt,* 1938. In Sweden, a strict *lex fori* theory based upon the writing of the Italian scholar Roberto Ago has been expounded in several works by Professor Gihl. Mr. Justice Karlgren has taken an intermediate position. The late Professor Hult has levelled criticisms, particularly against Gihl. In Scandinavian literature outside Sweden, reference should further be made to Torben Svenné Schmidt, *Kvalifikationsproblemet i den innationale privatret,* Copenhagen 1954, and Borum, *Lovkonflikter,* 4th ed.; according to the preface of the latter work, the chapter on classification is "through and through inspired" by an unpublished work by Professor Allan Philip, which was rewarded with the gold medal of the Copenhagen Faculty of Law.

are not intended to be, electronic brains which automatically deliver the answers to questions put to them. What has been said above on the "technology" of the choice of law does not purport to be anything else, or more, than a schema, from which exceptions may be called for by the facts of the case. "States and courts have to carry out the rule of reasonableness."[28]

Renvoi

We have used the expression "third choice of law" to denote the selection of rules applicable *in casu from* the legal system indicated as *lex causae* by a choice of law rule. Let us take an example. A Swedish engineer, domiciled in Stockholm, has performed a certain job in Spain where he has been called in as an expert by a Spanish firm; subsequently, the firm institutes an action aginst him in Stockholm in order to recover damages for negligence in performing the work. The Swedish court arrives at the conclusion that Spanish law (the law of the place where the work was performed) is applicable. When studying the various rules of Spanish law, the court finds that there is among them a clear and unambiguous choice of law rule to the effect that in cases like that at bar, the law of the employee's domicile governs the action. If the action had been brought in Spain, Swedish law would have been applied since that is the system of substantive provisions referred to by the Spanish choice of law rule. In this case, it may be stated that the Spanish rule contains a reference back or remission to Swedish law *(renvoi)*; if the Swedish engineer were domiciled in Paris, the Spanish rule would imply a further reference or transmission.[29] The question is whether we should not after all consider the third choice of law to be finally made and refuse to accept the remission to Swedish law. The problem may also be stated as follows: Does the reference to foreign law embodied in a Swedish choice of law rule embrace only the substantive rules of the legal system thus indicated or does the provision also imply the applicability of the private international law of the foreign country concerned? If the latter solution

[28] Nussbaum, pp. 93 f.

[29] The terms "remission" and "transmission" are suggested by Cheshire, *op. cit.*, at p. 65. They hardly seem to have been generally accepted, but since they are short, convenient and clear expressions of what is meant they will be used in the following pages.

is correct, it is obvious that both remission and transmission must be accepted.

Like many other classical and famous questions in conflict writing, this problem is really one of policy. It concerns the *meaning* of conflict rules, which is essentially established by construction and not through general considerations. However, conflict rules are usually silent on this topic, and in the various legal systems it has therefore become the task of courts to determine whether conflict rules shall be supposed to refer only to the substantive provisions or also to the private international law rules of the *lex causae*. This question has been answered differently in different countries. Ever since Sir Herbert Jenner, delivering his opinion in *Collier* v. *Rivaz*[30] in 1841 and the French courts, deciding in the *Forgo* case[31] in the eighteen-seventies, adopted the *renvoi* principle, writers on the conflict of laws have devoted much labour to consideration of this topic, and violent battles have been fought between the partisans and the enemies of *renvoi*. In this connection, however, we have no reason to discuss this problem in any detail, since it is generally held that the Swedish Supreme Court *in pleno* definitely rejected the doctrine of *renvoi* in 1939 *N.J.A.* 96.[32] Incidentally, the question has been treated rather extensively in Swedish conflict literature.[33] It will only be pointed out that the essential policy consideration in favour of *renvoi* is that a decision under foreign law is not "loyal" if its conflict rules are wholly disregarded, and that the outcome of the action may not be the same as if it had been tried by a court in the country from which the applicable law was taken. Against this point of view it is urged that, when framing its conflict rules, each country had expressed an evaluation. It has been held, e.g., that the distribution of the estate of an alien should take

30 *Collier* v. *Rivaz* (1841), 2 Curt. 853.

31 10 *Clunet* (1883), p. 64.

32 Cf. 1919 *N.J.A.* 546, where a remission was accepted. Mr. Justice Beckman states, at p. 44, that the decision of the Supreme Court *in pleno* from 1939 means that "the application of the doctrine of *renvoi* as a general principle has been banished from Swedish law."

33 Particularly by Ekström, *op.cit.*, pp. 164—208, and Gihl, *Principer*, pp. 411—475. *Vide* further Karlgren, pp. 65 ff., Undén in *Sv.J.T.* 1922, pp. 246 ff., Malmar in *Festskrift till Marks von Würtemberg*, 1931, pp. 410 ff. Statements in favour of *renvoi* are found in Reuterskiöld, pp. 36 ff., Ramel, *op.cit.*, pp. 55 ff., Michaeli, *op. cit.*, pp. 10 ff., Hassler, *Internationella adoptionsförhållanden*, p. 11 and p. 45.

place in accordance with the succession rules of the country of which he was a national. This means that the lawmaker has rejected the idea that the succession rules of e.g. the deceased's domicile had a stronger claim to be applied, and, by this choice between two solutions, he has solved the conflict question. Once this is the case, the judge should not try to find an answer to the same question abroad. If he does, he incurs the risk of offending against that evaluation, or policy, which is expressed in those rules about the sources of law which we call choice of law rules.[34] The claim for "loyal" application therefore refers to *substantive rules* of foreign law, and the saying that the court should decide the action as if it were sitting in the country of the *lex causae* must be modified so as to refer only to a court in the *lex causae* state trying an *internal* action. To these arguments should be added the often expounded and sometimes possibly exaggerated practical difficulties created by *renvoi:* it has been held a logical necessity that a remission to Swedish law from, e.g., English law should also refer to the *conflict rules* of the Swedish legal system which, in their turn, would kick the ball back to the law of England. It has been stated that *renvoi* ends in a *circulus vitiosus,* that its advocates devote themselves to *"l'application du lawntennis au droit international"* or sit in a "logical cabinet of mirrors."

However, some Swedish statutes provide that consideration be given foreign rules of private international law. For example, in chapter 1:2 of the Act on international questions concerning marriage, etc., 1904, it is laid down that questions concerning an alien's capacity to contract marriage shall be tried under the law of his home country, i.e. the state of which he is a national. It is added that if that law admits the application of some other legal system, it is permitted to decide the question under that other law. The right to marry of an Englishman domiciled in Copenhagen is thus primarily examined under English rules on capacity to enter into marriage, but since it follows from English conflict principles that this question should be resolved by Danish law, the Englishman is allowed to invoke Danish rules if he so prefers.[35] This does not mean, however, that the rules of Danish priva-

[34] Cheshire expressly states (*op.cit.* at pp. 68 f.) that the acceptance in England of a remission from Italian law would mean that English private international law "is jettisoned because it does not meet with the approval of the lawmaker in Italy".
[35] Cf. below, p. 237.

te international law be taken into consideration. Under section 79:2 of the Bills of Exchange Act, 1932, the capacity of an alien to undertake an obligation by issuing or accepting a bill of exchange shall be governed by the law of his home country. "If it is laid down in that law that any other legal system shall be applied, that provision shall be observed." (Cf. sec. 58 of the Cheques Act, 1932.) Nor is it impossible that, in one form or another, the doctrine of *renvoi* may influence Swedish legislation and judicial practice in the future.[36] The Hague Conference in 1951 discussed the possibility of making a specialized use of a *renvoi* mechanism in order to resolve the opposition between the principles of nationality and domicile.[37]

The So-Called Preliminary Question

> In later years a new opportunity for intellectual *tours de force,* in addition to the problem of classification, has recently been created through the introduction and discussion of the so-called *preliminary* or *incidental* questions (German: *die Vorfrage).* In Swedish writing it has been discussed in connection with the problem what is actually meant by "application" of legal rules —largely a question of terminology but undoubtedly one of great theoretical interest.[38] It has been claimed that the theoretical analysis admitted certain conclusions about the correct solution of the problems raised not only by the so-called "preliminary question" but also, e.g., by *ordre public.*
>
> As for preliminary questions in general—for internal-law purposes, the term "prejudicial question" seems more adequate —it should be remembered that in the course of applying a

[36] In *Festskrift till Herlitz,* 1955, Nial states (at p. 239) that it may occur that a court which consults the law of a company's country of registration as its "personal law" in order to find an answer to certain questions concerning the company will discover that under the legal system thus referred to "the company is held to be governed by the law of a third state, in which the board of the company has its seat". In such cases, it is stated, Swedish courts should hardly consider the law of the country of registration as the company's personal law. This would seem to be tantamount to advice to accept transmission.

[37] *Vide* Borum in *Liber amicorum,* pp. 16 ff.

[38] This discussion was initiated by Professor Gihl in some papers (comprised in Gihl, *Studier,* pp. 251 ff.) It was carried on by Karlgren (*T.f.R.* 1951 and 1952), Hjerner (*T.f.R.* 1953) and Alf Ross (*T.f.R.* 1954 and 1955). A reply by Gihl is printed in *Studier,* pp. 259 ff.

Swedish rule, courts often have to go back to *other* Swedish rules even though immediate application of the latter rules is not intended. If A brings an action against B with a claim for recovery of damages for injuries to a mower which, according to A, belongs to him, the prejudicial or preliminary question whether A really has a title to the machine may be raised.[39] It must be answered before the court passes on to the problem whether B's act creates a liability in tort. Rules on the acquisition of title are used for answering the preliminary question and are cited in the decision as part of the *ratio,* but the effect of *res judicata* does not embrace more than the actual decision of the case at bar. Such references to other rules are frequent and generally do not cause courts any trouble.

In the conflict of laws, the discussion about the "preliminary question" generally concerns the specific situation arising when an action has to be decided under *foreign* law and when the applicable foreign rule in its turn refers to a state of things or a relationship which is described in legal terms. A frequently used illustration is the determination by a court of child's legitimacy.[40] If the *lex causae* recognizes the legitimacy of children born "of a valid marriage" it is for the court to decide the "preliminary" or "incidental" question whether the marriage is valid. This has become a problem in private international law; the question has been raised whether the conflict rules of that legal system to which the otherwise applicable rules on legitimacy belong (*lex causae* in the principal question) or the conflict rules of the *lex fori* shall be resorted to for the purpose of choosing the substantive provisions under which the validity of the marriage shall be tried.[41] Sometimes, the problem may arise in several stages. At the distribution in Sweden of a Frenchman's estate, a son of the deceased brother of the *de cuius* may

39 Cf. Karlgren in *T.f.R.* 1951, pp. 459 f.

40 *Vide* Hult, pp. 61 ff.

41 These two opinions are fairly evenly represented among theorists. However, those who recommend the solution of the preliminary question under the conflict rules of *lex causae* tend to admit exceptions in special cases. *Vide,* e.g., Wolff, *Private International Law,* 2nd ed., 1950, pp. 206 ff., and Lewald, *op.cit.,* p. 63. The judicial habits of various countries in this respect are not wholly clear. According to Cheshire, *op.cit.,* p. 85, English courts apply the conflict rules of the *lex fori.*

claim a portion. The distribution has to take place under French succession rules. The brother was a United States citizen, however, and so is his son. It is contended in the action that the son has no right to come into a portion of the estate, because he is illegitimate. Shall the preliminary question of legitimacy be answered by the law indicated by French conflict rules or by the legal system which is competent under Swedish private international law? Now if the judge has arrived at the conclusion that the law of, e.g., Louisiana should determine the question of legitimacy, it may be that under this law, it has to be examined whether the son was born in a valid marriage or not. The matrimony between the parents was solemnized in Mexico. Shall the question whether this ceremony created a valid marriage be answered by means of the substantive rules indicated by the *lex fori* (Swedish conflict rules), by the *lex causae* of the question of succession (the essential question), or by the law of Louisiana, which has a decisive influence upon the incidental question first raised?

At bottom, this problem, like that of *renvoi,* is one of policy.[42] Several solutions are possible, and the legislature or judge framing conflict rules has to make a choice. Neither solution is in itself "correct" from the point of view of theories or principles. The reasons militating against specialized choice of law rules[43] would seem to support the solution that, *after* having determined the *lex causae* of the essential question,[44] the judge should consult the conflict rules of that legal system for the purpose of answering prejudicial questions. This suggestion is also supported by the fact that even if those rules which are applied for answering the question of the validity of a marriage as a preliminary question in a succession or legitimacy action are not immediately invoked as a basis for the decision of the court, it is nevertheless true that they are of decisive importance for the issue. The actual contents of the applicable succession or legitimacy rule are determined by the solution of the preliminary question, and the rule thus consulted for a prejudicial purpose

42 Cf. the treatment of this problem by Raape, at pp. 113 ff.

43 Cf. above, pp. 116 f.

44 In fact, the "preliminary question" is not raised until *after* the choice of law. Cf. Nussbaum, p. 105.

could easily be part of the legitimacy rule.[45] In favour of an application of the conflict rules of the *lex fori,* the same reasons as are used against *renvoi* are occasionally put forward. The essential objection to *renvoi* from a policy point of view is that the conflict rule of the *forum* implies an evaluation in respect of the question what substantive rules shall be applied for the purpose of deciding certain actions, and that this evaluation shall not be set aside in favour of the conflict evaluations prevailing in the home country of the applicable substantive rules; in the opinion of the *forum* country, these evaluations may appear both unjust and unpractical. Now, are these considerations valid also as a reason against using the conflict rules of the *lex causae* for answering the preliminary question? It may be stated, in support of a negative answer, that we are not at all dealing with the same sort of situation.[46] When the preliminary question is raised, the choice of law has already been made, and we have to construe that law which has already been found applicable.[47] The question is not, as in the case of *renvoi,* whether the conflict rule of the *lex fori* shall be replaced by another conflict rule, taken from foreign law, for the purpose of deciding the same question. The situation is rather that a *new* problem of private international law is raised within the framework of the *lex causae,* in the course of its loyal application.[48] This is an essential difference: the conflict evaluations of the *lex fori* are fading at a considerable distance. It should be pointed out, however, that in countries where *renvoi* (remission and transmission) are accepted, this fact influences the approach to the problem of the incidental question. The reason why *renvoi* is accepted is the desire that an action should be decided in the *forum* country in the same way as in the country of the *lex causae,* and it would be contrary to that wish to isolate preliminary questions from the essential problem and to answer them under a law indicated by the conflict rules of the *lex fori* even if that law is another than the *lex causae* itself or another than the legal system poin-

45 Cf. Ross in *T.f.R.* 1954, particularly pp. 253 ff., and Hjerner, *T.f.R.* 1953, p. 46; also Gihl, *Studier,* pp. 313 f.

46 Cf. Melchior, p. 247.

47 Wolff, *Private,* p. 206.

46 Lewald, p. 65.

ted out by the conflict rules of the *lex causae*.[49]

Although a summing up of all reasons for and against leads to the conclusion that it appears most satisfactory to apply the conflict rules of the *lex causae* to prejudicial questions, it must nevertheless be taken into consideration that the conflict provisions of a legal system may be framed in such a way that it must be held impossible or prohibited to decide certain so-called preliminary questions by application of *lex causae*. In the Spanish child example (above, at pp. 118 f.) the question of the child's capacity to come into property by succession is an incidental question in relation to the problem which the court has to give a definite solution, viz. how the estate shall be distributed. It seems obvious that under the 1937 Act on international questions concerning deceased persons' estate, this preliminary question should be answered by an application of the conflict rules of the law indicated in chapter 1:9,[50] and not under the legal system to which the private international law of the *lex causae* refers.[51] However, occasional exceptions from this principle may perhaps be defensible even where there is a written conflict rule. Thus Professor Hult held that when answering the preliminary question whether a marriage is valid in an action concerning legitimacy, the conflict rules of the 1904 Act are unconditionally applicable only if their application results in the recognition of the validity of the marriage.[52]

49 Melchior, *loc. cit.*

50 *Vide* above, p. 118.

51 Cf. *N.J.A.* II 1938, pp. 217 f. If this is the incontestable meaning of the legal provision, there is obviously nothing to do about it. In our example, the general application of Dutch law would also produce satisfactory results, however, provided that the applicability of Dutch conflict rules was equally recognized and that there was among these rules a provision of the same kind as chap. 1, sec. 9, of the 1937 Act. It must be assumed, however, that in this case, the special rule of Swedish conflict law was introduced because it was found important to single out the capacity questions; this would seem to imply that the framer of the rule did not trust foreign rules to produce the desirable result.

52 Hult, *loc.cit.* The child would thus be legitimate if the marriage was found valid under the rules referred to by the 1904 Act although it was null under the matrimonial law of the *lex causae,* conflict rules included. Any other solution would imply an "intolerable contradiction". But would it not be possible to state that although the spouses are married in the sense that all consequences of

It should, finally, be pointed out that foreign law may have a claim to prejudicial consideration in several cases where a court renders a decision on the basis of *Swedish* law. Thus when the estate of a deceased Swedish citizen is to be distributed under Swedish law, it may occur that, e.g., questions about a presumptive foreign heir's legal relations with the *de cuius* shall be answered as incidental questions under foreign law.[54] Situations of this kind may also occur outside the sphere of activity of courts of justice. Thus the granting of social benefits may be conditional upon a person's citizenship in a certain country with which Sweden has concluded an agreement on the granting of such benefits.[55] The competent Swedish authority then has to determine whether a certain person is or is not a citizen of the state concerned. If an authoritative and trustworthy answer cannot be obtained from the foreign country itself, it may become necessary to study its nationality legislation. Similarly, a Swedish authority may have to determine whether a person is married or not. If the question is raised in the handling of an administrative case, e.g. a matter of social benefits, there is no *lex causae* to refer to. The decision must be founded upon Swedish private international law. If the person concerned has been united in marriage with another person, who is still alive, through a valid ceremony (chap. 1, se. 6, of the 1904 Act), and if the marriage has not been declared void or been otherwise dissolved by a decree entitled to recognition in Sweden, such person shall be considered to be married.

However, if an authority has arrived at this conclusion and granted the person a social benefit due to married people, the personal status of the individual concerned has not been determined in such a way as to be respected if questions about it are raised in any other connection.[56]

matrimony must be drawn with regard to their *mutual* relations, which could become relevant in Sweden, the marriage is nevertheless not such that any succession or legitimacy claims may be founded upon it in the home country, a state of law to be respected also in Sweden?

54 Cf. the example below, at p. 200, note 96.

55 Cf. Eek, pp. 58 f. and 165 ff.

56 Occasionally, certain benefits are subject to conditions of reciprocity. If a court or any other authority entrusted with the administration of the law has to determine whether the condition of reciprocity is fulfilled or not, this preju-

§ 10. The Applicable Law (*Lex Causae*)

In many international civil actions, the immediate object of controversy is the choice of law; the parties cannot agree on the question whether English or Swedish rules of sale shall be applied, but they both know what are the substantive contents of the competing legal systems. If Swedish law is applicable, the plaintiff's claim for recovery of damages because of deficiencies in the goods he has bought will fail, because he has not claimed "immediately"; should English law be applied, his plea would succeed, since it is obvious that he has claimed "within a reasonable time". The contents of foreign law in a case like this are not difficult to ascertain, and to some extent the whole action is due to the knowledge that this law has different rules from those of Swedish law. In other cases, it may be clear enough that the choice of law is limited in the sense that, e.g., only Swedish or English law may come into consideration, but it is still uncertain what the one or the other solution would mean for the final issue. The question what law is applicable is only one among several uncertain elements in the action. There are situations where there is agreement between the parties concerning the *lex causae;* the court, nevertheless, has to decide this question independently of the opinion of the parties and—at least in principle—without having made any preliminary enquiries into the contents of that foreign law which may possibly be applicable. There are also cases where the parties hold that they know the rules of the applicable law and

dicial question necessitates enquiries into foreign law. Chap. 15, sec. 2, of the Inheritance Code, 1734, contained a provision which originally had the following tenor: "If a foreign heir lives in a place where Swedish subjects are entitled to acquire property by succession, then such heir is entitled to the same right in Sweden." The investigation which the application of this rule demanded in each particular case was very difficult (*vide,* on this topic, Flintberg, *Lagfarenhetsbibliotek,* vol. 2, 1797, pp. 288 ff.). It is therefore more satisfactory if an enactment binding upon the court states where the condition of reciprocity has been fulfilled (cf. § 223 a in the Danish Judicial Procedure Code on the recognition of foreign judgments). The principle of reciprocity may also be replaced by a principle of retorsion, as is the case in the new Swedish Inheritance Code, 1958. Cf. p. 67 above.

consider this question to fall outside the dispute. Finally, it may occur that through its choice of law, which is determined by a choice of law rule, the court has undertaken to apply substantive rules from a foreign legal system which is wholly unknown to the court. Thus in a number of situations the outcome of the choice of law necessitates an enquiry about the provisions of the foreign legal system.[57] The *lex causae* appears an "unknown quantity", and it is thus a precondition for a decision founded upon loyal application of the indicated foreign law that an enquiry into its rule be undertaken.

In the following pages we will discuss the problems which arise in actions in the Swedish courts. However, for Swedish parties who have to conduct litigation in foreign courts it is most important, from a practical point of view, to realize that the international procedural rules of various countries differ considerably with regard to the enquiry into foreign law and questions arising in that connection. Even in cases where it is evident that an action in a foreign court will be governed by Swedish law—e.g. where there is an explicit choice of law by the parties which is known to be accepted in the *forum* country, or the action concerns personal relations between Swedish parties and is brought in a country which has adopted the principle of nationality—it may be that the court has more severe demands than those put by Swedish courts with regard to the enquiry about the contents of Swedish law. Occasionally, formal requirements—the proving in certain forms of, e.g., the fact that the text of the annual Statute Book or the official series of statutory instruments constitute the law of Sweden—may be burdensome, etc.

In English law and—with variations in details—in American law, the main rule is that foreign law is applied only if it is claimed by either party; if foreign law is to apply it is for the interested party to prove its contents. The normal, although not the only, evidence about the contents of foreign law consists of statements by witnesses who possess expert knowledge of the foreign law, acquired by practical experience. Moreover, since this is formally a question of fact, the court has to assess the

[57] It should be observed that the so-called "third choice of law," which we have discussed above, is made only after the rules of the applicable foreign law have become at least partly known.

value as evidence of the statements of expert witnesses. There are also other countries where a party may sometimes carry the burden of proof with regard to the contents of the applicable foreign law and incurs the risk of failing in his action if that duty cannot be fulfilled. The rules about the duty of the Bench to make use of such knowledge of the foreign law as it actually has or to take measures for ascertaining the contents of the foreign law vary considerably. Thus, in each individual case when an action is to be brought abroad and rules other than those of the foreign *forum* country may have a claim to be applied, there are good reasons for ascertaining what demands courts make upon the parties in this respect.

Enquiry into the Rules of the Lex Causae

The Swedish judge must apply conflict rules *ex officio* (p. 94 above). This also implies that the foreign legal system which is indicated by a choice of law rule shall be applied without being claimed by the parties.[58] The principle of application *ex officio* of the *lex causae* further implies that, even if the parties have come to an agreement (owing, perhaps, to mutual misunderstanding) on the contents of the *lex causae,* this does not exempt the judge from basing his decision upon the applicable foreign law as it actually is.[59]

In internal law, the maxim *jura novit curia* is adopted; in principle, the court has a duty to know the law, and it is consequently stated in chapter 35:2 of the Swedish Judicial Procedure Code that no evidence is required as to the contents of legal rules. Obviously, it is not reasonable to impose the same duty upon the judge with regard to foreign law. When he actually knows the contents of a foreign legal

[58] Cf. Karlgren, pp. 74 f.; Kallenberg, *Svensk civilprocessrätt,* vol. II (1927), pp. 99 ff.; Reuterskiöld, p. 34. On older views, *vide* Ekström, *op.cit.,* p. 64. However, the conflict rule may occasionally be framed in such a way that the applicability of foreign law depends upon its application being claimed by either party. *Vide,* e.g., the legislation on deceased persons' estate, etc. in inter-Nordic relations, 1935.

[59] Wolff, *op.cit.,* p. 218, gives an example from a German court where both parties contended that the applicable Belgian law was identical with the law of France. The judge made an enquiry and found that, through special legislation, Belgian law had come to differ from the French *Code civil.*

system, he has to base his decision upon it. If he does not possess such knowledge, the principle would seem to be that he should make all reasonable efforts in order to acquire it.[60] In the choice of sources, he is free.[61] He may consult collections of statutes, law reports, and legal writing; he may look for guidance in statements by courts or other authorities in the state of the *lex causae*. There are some Swedish reports which illustrate this research activity. The usual solution is that information is obtained from the Legal Department of the Ministry for Foreign Affairs,[62] which in its turn is in a position to secure such information about foreign law from its consulates and embassies.[63] Where Swedish choice of law rules have been introduced as a consequence of conventions with foreign states, in which Sweden has undertaken to apply the substantive law of another signatory state in certain cases, this obligation under the law of nations adds additional strength to the demand upon the courts that they (assisted by other competent public authorities) undertake energetic research into the *lex causae*. At the same time, a convention obviously implies a duty for other signatory states to facilitate that research. It is laid down in the provisions in chapter 7:4 (2) of the 1904 Act on international matrimonial questions, etc., and in section 3 of the Act on international questions concerning the legal effects of marriage, 1912, that where the rules of foreign law are not already known to the court, the latter is bound to try to find information about it according to the methods prescribed by the King in Council; these rules would seem to have been introduced in order to fulfil the conventional ogligations of Sweden.[64] However, the King in Council has not issued any regulations on the finding of foreign law by the courts of justice.

[60] Cf., with regard to Danish law, Borum, pp. 66 ff. *Vide* also concerning Norway Alten, *Tvistemålsloven,* 3d ed., Oslo 1954, p. 213.

[61] Cf. Skeie, *Den norske civilprosess,* I, 2nd ed., Oslo 1939, p. 435.

[62] On the tasks of the Legal Department, *vide* Hellners in *T.S.A.* 1964, pp. 101 ff.

[63] Occasionally, courts ask for other kinds of information from the Ministry for Foreign Affairs. In the case 1921 *N.J.A.* 474, a question was put about the relations between Sweden and the "Russian Soviet Republic". In 1957 *N.J.A.* 195 the question was put, through the intermediary of the Ministry, to the Chinese Embassy whether it claimed immunity, etc.

[64] Already at the introduction of the 1904 Act it was foreseen that a special international convention would need to be concluded about reciprocal intergovernmental assistance for the purpose of finding out the rules of foreign law.

It is only natural that a court may fail in its efforts to obtain information about the rules of the applicable foreign law. It is also natural that the parties, or one of them, may spontaneously try to make the necessary research. It must further be considered a duty for the judge, who has to take the applicability of foreign law into consideration *ex officio,* to draw the attention of the parties to the fact that foreign law should be used and, if he has some knowledge of the applicable foreign law, also to inform the parties about it. Thus the parties are given the opportunity of producing such evidence (also about facts) as is required for the application of the *lex causae.*[65] However, the court is also entitled to order the parties to collaborate in the enquiry into the rules of foreign law. Under chapter 35:2 of the Judicial Procedure Code, the court may order a party to produce evidence as to the rules of the foreign legal system which is to be applied, provided that the court is ignorant of these rules. Since foreign law shall not be considered as a fact which the parties are at liberty to invoke or to leave aside, however, and since its applicability does not presuppose a claim from any of the parties, the rule in chapter 35:2 would not seem to mean that the duty of producing evidence is incumbent upon that party who may be assumed to have a particular interest in the application of foreign law, nor that it is prejudicial for the party if he fails to produce the required evidence.[66] In principle, both parties should be instructed to produce evidence, and it is by no means an impossible idea that the court should first enjoin the task upon one of the parties if that party may be assumed to be able to fulfil it with less difficulty than the other, e.g., where the former is a national of the

(*Vide Actes de la troisième conférence de la Haye,* 1900, pp. 60 f., 190 ff. and 246; cf. also below, p. 189, note 76.) The original bill only contained a provision to the effect that the King in Council should issue regulations on how to find foreign law. After the opinion of the Supreme Court on the bill had been taken, however, the enactment was redrafted in such a manner that it became perfectly clear that the courts would be bound to make use of the methods which the King in Council might indicate. *Vide Royal Proposition* No. 21, 1904, pp. 34 f.

65 *Vide* Kallenberg, *op.cit.* pp. 100 f.

66 According to the Royal Commission for the Reform of Procedural Law, which prepared the present Judicial Procedure Code, 1942, such an order does not necessarily mean that the court has made up its mind with regard to the question whether failure to produce evidence by a party shall imply that the pleas of that party will not be successful. *S.O.U.* 1938 No. 44, p. 380.

foreign country concerned or carries on extensive international business.[67] Rules similar to chapter 35:2, of the Judicial Procedure Code are found in the Bills of Exchange Act, 1932, (sec. 87), the Cheques Act, 1932, (sec. 65), and the Act on foreign arbitration agreements and arbitral awards, 1929 (sec. 13). The enactments on family law contain provisions which are to some extent framed upon a different pattern. The rule in the 1912 Act has the same structure as the rule in the Judicial Procedure Code.[68] As for chapter 7:4 of the 1904 Act on the other hand, it would rather seem to imply that a party who has petitioned for annulment, separation or divorce has to prove the rules of the foreign legal system applicable under the 1904 Act. In the Inter-Nordic Act on deceased person's estates, 1935, it is laid down that anyone claiming the application of the law of his home country shall prove, whenever it is necessary, that the facts of the case are such as to admit the application of that legal system, and shall also prove the rules of that law. Since Scandinavian law is concerned, the duty to prove the rules of the legal system in the party's home country is not likely to be very burdensome. The *travaux préparatoires* also seem to show that the enquiry which the drafters of the law have not wanted to lay upon the authorities having to deal with the distribution of deceased persons' estates primarily concerns those facts—the nationality and domicile or residence of the deceased—which constitute such connecting factors as render the application of the national law possible instead of the *lex domicilii*.[69] The duty of investigation under section 7 of the 1935 Act is made less burdensome through a special provision in the protocol to the Inter-Nordic Convention on the distribution of deceased persons' estates, according to which the authorities of the deceased person's home country must assist any one who has to produce evidence about the rules of the national law of the deceased.[70]

67 Cf. *Royal Proposition* No. 58, 1912, pp. 41 f.

68 Cf., however, sec. 70, second para., of the Execution Act, 1877, as amended in 1912 (below at p. 192, note 80).

69 *Vide* 1935 *N.J.A.* II, pp. 364 f. and 375 f.

70 It is stated in the protocol: "It is agreed between the Signatory States that demands for information about the law of any of the Signatory States shall be handed over from the Ministry for Foreign Affairs or of Justice in the country from which such demand is made; the question shall be put, where Danish, Finish, Icelandic or Norwegian law is concerned, to the Ministry of Justice, and where Swedish law is concerned, to the Legal Department of the Ministry for

It is possible that the provisions in this protocol may be held to describe what is considered a good custom between the Scandinavian states also outside the strict sphere of application of the Convention on deceased person's estates.[71] However, the international problem remains unsolved. Attempts have been made to create a system of mutual "legal assistance" between states in this respect, but no results of importance have been achieved. In some countries there are institutions which, upon demand, deliver opinions, and certain states have official institutes for comparative law.[72] What is needed, however, is a systematic creation of navigable channels between the authorities of the different countries, and, within this framework, to issue rules for the giving of reliable, complete and authoritative information of the rules of law in the country concerned.[73]

The Rules of the Lex Causae not proved

"It is in the nature of things," Professor Kallenberg stated, "that the court is free (not bound by legal rules) in its trial of the question whether the rules of foreign law have been proved with certainty."[74] It may occur that the court does not succeed at all in finding out the impact of the relevant rules of the foreign legal system. In other cases, the evidence may be incomplete or unreliable. Thus, if Kallenberg's claim for *certainty* about the contents of foreign law is upheld, it may undoubtedly occur that the court is confronted by a situation where it has no rules to apply. How is this dilemma to be solved?

A case from the Court of Appeal for Western Sweden (1950 *Sv. J.T.* 958) concerned the validity of the revocation of a will. The

Foreign Affairs. Such information shall always be given in so far as there are explicit statutory rules; in other cases, it shall be given to the extent admitted by the circumstances."

71 Cf. Borum, p. 72.

72 *Vide* Riezler, *op.cit.*, pp. 495 f.

73 The statement of the Swedish delegates at the Hague conference in 1904 is still true: "Au cours des travaux législatifs qui ont été nécessaires pour préparer l'adoption par la Suède des conventions de l'an 1902, nous avons eu l'occasion de nous convaincre de plus de l'importance extrême d'une entente internationale sur les certificats de législation (certificats de coutume). C'est pourquoi nous regretterions beaucoup que cette question ne fût pas l'objet des délibérations de la prochaine conférence et qu'elle n'y trouvât pas une solution favorable." *Actes* 1904, p. 333.

74 Kallenberg, *op.cit.*, p. 98.

court of first instance seems not to have observed that foreign law was applicable. The Court of Appeal, however, found that under chapter 1:6 of the 1937 Act on international legal questions concerning deceased persons' estates, the action was governed by the law of the state of New York and ordered the plaintiffs—who contended that the testator had acted under the influence of mental alienation when revoking the will—to produce evidence about the rules of the applicable foreign law. The plaintiffs thereupon submitted to the Court what is called in the case report "a letter from the Legal Departement of the Ministry for Foreign Affairs, in which information taken from available textbooks about certain legal rules on wills in New York State was furnished". The Court unanimously held that the contents of foreign law had not been satisfactorily proved "but as far as the evidence goes, it cannot be held that it differs essentially from Swedish law on the relevant point". The action failed under the substantive rules of the Swedish Statute of Wills.

This decision seems to be the only case available in Swedish reports, where a court has answered the question what to do if the contents of the *lex causae* have not been proved at all or at least have not been sufficiently proved.[75] This case cannot be considered a precedent, and it is certainly not beyond criticism.[76] Nor can any solutions of a general character be found in Swedish legislation or in the *travaux préparatoires* of statutes. In chapter 7:4 of the Act on international matrimonial questions, etc., 1904, there is, however, a special rule: "If a person who has brought an action of annulment or entered a petition for a divorce decree or for separation cannot prove the contents of the foreign law which, under the provisions of this statute, is applicable in the case, his action shall not be sustained." The *exposé de motifs* of this enactment also makes it clear beyond any doubt in respect of the kinds of litigation concerned "that if a party who claims annulment, divorce or separation cannot prove that the applicable law grants this relief on the grounds invoked by the party, the action shall not be sustained".[77] Does this mean that the action must fail

[75] Cf. however, the City Court in 1951 *N.J.A.* 753. It is possible that in other cases the problem has been avoided by means of various conflict constructions or by the failure of courts to discover that foreign law was applicable.

[76] *Vide* Eek in *T.f.R.* 1955, pp. 144 f.

[77] *Royal Proposition* No. 21, 1904, pp. 34 f. and 57 f. (opinion of the Supreme Court).

upon its merits and that the party should therefore be barred from returning with the same claim on the same grounds (e.g. the same case of adultery) even though he has now produced evidence which proves that in the *lex causae* a divorce decree is granted for adultery? The language of Professor Kallenberg seems to show that this is the opinion of the learned writer.[78] It may be objected against this view, however, that the refusal of the court to sustain the plaintiff's plea is not founded upon Swedish substantive rules or, in fact, Swedish rules on evidence but exclusively on the special provision in the 1904 Act. Apart from this enactment, the only certain statement about the position of Swedish law is that it recognizes the substantive applicability of the unknown *lex causae*. On the other hand, the action has not been dismissed under any substantive rule of that unknown foreign law. In other words, the decision of the court does not fulfil the conditions for a judgment by which the action is brought to an end, viz. becomes a *res judicata* in the sense of chapter 17:11 of the Judicial Procedure Code. The *ratio* of the rule in the 1904 Act is to be found in the deference due to the unknown *lex causae* and to the Swedish conflict rule. It would seem to follow that the refusal to sustain the action only means that it cannot succeed *at present* and that, consequently, the plaintiff is entitled to institute a new action when he has produced evidence about the contents of the foreign law.[79] If this construction is correct, however, we are still not in a position to draw any definite conclusions about a general rule of Swedish law. It appears clearly from the *travaux préparatoires (loc.cit.)* that the rule in chapter 7:4 of the 1904 Act is intended to be a special provision.[80]

[78] Kallenberg, *op.cit.*, p. 100.

[79] This construction would not seem to be incompatible with the *ratio* of the principles underlying the *res judicata* rules of procedural law. Cf. Olivecrona, *Domen i tvistemål*, 1943, pp. 198 ff., and *Rätt och dom*, 1960, pp. 280 ff.

[80] Sec. 70, second para., of the Execution Act, 1877, as amended by an enactment of 1 June 1912, had the following tenor (which was deleted under a new amendment in 1936) : "If the mutual proprietary rights of spouses are governed by foreign law, and if either spouse wants to exempt certain property from seizure in the common property or the property of the other spouse on the ground that such property shall not be used for the payment of such debts under the foreign law, then such spouse has to prove forthwith such circumstances, or the property shall be subject to the rule in the first para. of this section." It is not explicitly stated that the "circumstances" which shall be proved are the contents of foreign law. Even if that is the case, however, the rule does not imply that a party has to prove foreign law or otherwise fail. If a

Outside its sphere of application, it is stated, "it is a most controversial question in international legal science what will be the ultimate effect of the impossibility of obtaining evidence about foreign law". In Swedish legal writing, Kallenberg *(loc.cit.)* has put forward the idea that Swedish law *(lex fori)* should be applied when the normally applicable foreign legal rules are unknown.[81] However, the *lex fori* theory as well as any other theory cannot claim any support in statutory provisions, and no guidance can be found in legislative material or precedents.

In the international discussion the following possible solutions of cases where there is not sufficient evidence about the contents of foreign law have been discussed: (a) non-cognizability of the action; (b) dismissal upon trial of the merits of the action; (c) application of the substantive rules of the *lex fori;* and (d) application of the substantive rules of a *lex probabilis ("das wahrscheinlich geltende Recht").*

As we have already pointed out, a dismissal of the plaintiff's action with the effect of *res judicata* does not seem to be desirable. This solution would mean that his cause of action is lost even if it is well founded under the *lex causae* indicated by the choice of law of the *forum* or, indeed, under the *lex fori* itself. A judicial statement to the effect that a claim has no substantive grounds, which is made because the court does not know whether the claim is founded or not, implies, as Riezler justly says, a denial of justice *(Justizverweigerung).*[82] The comparative method, which implies that the "gap in the foreign legal system"[83] shall be filled through examination of the rules of connected systems with special regard to historical affinities and general principles of law, is not to be recommended either. A loyal application of the real *lex causae* will rarely, if ever, be attained by searching for the *probably* applicable law. Nor is it desirable to make the unrealistic as-

spouse could prove at the seizure that foreign law was applicable and exempted certain property, the interests of that spouse were protected already at this early stage.

81 *Vide* also the statement of Professor Hult at p. 47 (athough it is made only incidentally).—Kallenberg puts the question whether an action should not be dismissed in cases "which may be analogous" with those dealt with in the provision in chap. 7, sec. 4, of the 1904 Act. *Contra,* Michaeli, *op.cit.,* pp. 62 f.

82 Riezler, *op.cit.,* p. 497.

83 Cf. B. Palmgren in *Tidskrift utg. av Juridiska Föreningen i Finland,* 1937, pp. 34 ff.

sumption that the *lex fori* should be applied on the basis of the probability of identity or affinity between *lex fori* and *lex causae*.[84] As a rule, where the contents of foreign law cannot be ascertained in actual practice, this is due to the fact that it is remote from the *lex fori* either locally, temporally or in respect of leading principles, and there would seem rather to be a probability *against* identy between them. The recourse to the *lex fori* therefore constitutes a pure emergency solution, a *Verlegenheitsausweg* as Riezler calls it.[85] This solution is not satisfactory, however, for it implies the application of a substantive rule which is *not* applicable under the choice of law rule of the *lex fori*.

A refusal to take cognizance of the action is the last remaining way out of this practical problem. In many cases, this solution seems the most attractive one. By declining to try the merits of the action, the courts avoids any clashes with the principle claiming that the anonymous *lex causae* be given an opportunity of being applied. The parties retain the possibility of coming back when satisfactory evidence about the rules of applicable foreign law has been produced and the action has thus become mature for a decision by a Swedish court. In actual practice, a refusal to try the action may imply a reference to the courts of the *lex causae* state, which must be assumed to know their own *lex fori*.[86] The method of refusing to take cognizance has its limits,

[84] The decision of the Court of Appeal in the case 1950 *Sv.J.T.*, p. 958 would seem to come nearest to this solution.

[85] At p. 497.

[86] Some support for this solution may be found in Karlgren, p. 75 (the footnote) and Matz, *Om underdomarens processledning i svensk ordinär civilprocessrätt*, 1919, p. 114. The principle of non-cognizance is embraced by Borum (p. 73) and the Norwegian writer Gjelsvik *(Laerebok i Millomfolkeleg Privatrett*, I, 2nd ed., Oslo 1938, pp. 70 f). Hurwitz, a Danish scholar, (*Tvistemaal*, Copenhagen 1941, p. 130) recommends a refusal to hear the action in those cases where the lack of evidence concerns "easily available information, particularly about the rules of neighbouring countries in uncomplicated fields of law". As an argument against a refusal to try the case it has been stated by Kallenberg and others (cf. Eek in *T.f.R.* 1955, pp. 140 ff.) that such a course of action would mean a denial of justice and be incompatible with the fundamental duty of the courts to protect existing rights and to answer legal questions. An action, it has been argued, cannot be concluded with a *non liquet*. We may also refer to Art. 4. of the French *Code civil:* "Le juge qui refusera de juger, sous prétexte du silence, de l'obscurité on de l'insuffisance de la loi, pourra être poursuivi comme coupable de déni de justice." This may be quite true from a strictly national point of view; the courts have to guarantee the

however. Certain cases may be of such a character that a trial of the merits of a question is unavoidable. It may concern guardianship or the right to dispose of a consignment of goods subject to rapid deterioration. Possibly, cases may also arrise in which an enquiry into the contents of foreign law encounters insurmountable difficulties, e.g. because of a war cutting off intercourse with the *lex causae* country.[87] In these cases, the question how the decision shall be found arrises again. It is necessary to look for another rule than that indicated by the principle embodied in the applicable choice of law rule. This choice seems to fall upon the *lex fori* as an unavoidable emergency solution. The real implication of such a decision is that the court sets the conflict rule aside in the same way as when bringing the mechanism of *ordre public* into function. The impossibility of applying the indicated foreign law and the necessity to decide the action give rise to a "general clause" which modifies the choice of law rule and which is not of a procedural character but belongs to conflict law.

The opinion expressed above can be summarized as follows: Where the rules of the *lex causae* are unknown or insufficently proved, the general principle is that the court shall refuse to try the merits of the case (in certain cases, "refuse to sustain" the action). Where special considerations based upon the necessity to protect rights or interests placed in a precarious situation call for a trial of the merits of the action, the court should set aside the choice of law rule and render its decision in accordance with the substantive provisions of the *lex fori*.

public peace of the land by putting an end to such litigation as is brought before them This does not mean, however, that Swedish courts are bound to hear and decide actions which have no close connection with Sweden or that they ought to do so. There are situations where no jurisdiction is put at the disposal of the parties; it is equally justified to refuse to try the merits of an action which falls under Swedish jurisdiction but in which the decision prescribed by the law of Sweden cannot be rendered because of complications related to its connection with a foreign country.

[87] If the *lex causae* has not been proved and the parties claim that the *lex fori* be applied and the action is of the nature where a reference to Swedish law by the parties would have been accepted by the court, the decision should be based upon Swedish law. But the freedom of parties to dispose of the applicable law would not seem to go beyond this limit (cf. Borum, p. 67; Kallenberg, *op.cit.*, pp. 98 f.). However, the parties must always be at liberty to prove that an immediate decision (under the *lex fori*) is necessary for the protection of rights or interests brought in a precarious situation.

§ 11. Refusal to Apply the *Lex Causae*

The choice of law rule has been framed on the basis of general policy considerations and evaluations according to which, in civil actions of a particular character, a certain connecting factor should, in principle, indicate the legal system from which the applicable substantive rules are to be taken. These policy considerations are founded upon the assumption that although the rules of different legal systems vary, these systems are nevertheless largely based on what may be called in our period of civilization "general principles of law recognized by civilized nations" (Art. 38 of the Statute of the International Court of Justice, which is almost universally adhered to in our days). On the strength of these considerations the legislature has allowed the choice of law rule to refer to foreign law *in abstracto*—to make *"ein Sprung ins Dunkle"*[88]—i.e. to make a reference which in a forthcoming case may raise the question of applying substantive rules from any one of the various national legal systems of the world.[89] Under these circumstances it is understandable that it may occur *in individual cases* that the practical result which would follow from an acceptance of the directions embodied in the choice of law rule will appear unsatisfactory, unjust, unreasonable or even shocking when confronted with the general policies and evaluations of the *forum* country. In some cases such a result can be avoided—as we have emphasized repeatedly—by means of considerations which influence the construction of the choice of law rule. This rule may be, as it were, corrected. However, the judge is not always likely to be free or prepared to obtain a satisfactory result *in casu* by means of an interpretation of the choice of law rule whereby that rule would assume a modified character. It is not admissible, at any rate, that the judge correct the choice of law rule *against* the evaluations prevailing in the *forum* country. Now there are other methods in the conflict of laws which are intended both to avoid inacceptable results of an application of choice of law rules which is correct in itself, and, at the same time, to leave the character and validity of the choice of law rule unaffected for future actions.

88 Raape, p. 87.

89 Cf. Nussbaum, *op. cit.*, p. 110: "Conflict rules constitute a one-sided commitment towards an indefinite number of foreign countries and towards the most varied and unforeseeable foreign policies."

First, it should be pointed out that the legislature may avoid certain non-desirable results by conferring an absolute character on some municipal provisions which are thus applicable without exceptions at the same time as the foreign law indicated by the choice of law rule, and the application of these provisions occasionally results in the rules of the *lex causae* becoming inoperative. This does not mean, however, that foreign law is set aside *in casu* because of its character. We have to do with general rules of an absolute character. These do not imply that the choice of law rule of the *lex fori* originally resorted to is rejected, even in the individual case.[90] This solution is therefore more properly dealt with in another context (below, at pp. 224 ff.). When a court makes use of the *mechanism of ordre public (Vorbehaltsklausel),* on the other hand, the purpose is in fact to set aside a conflict rule in the *lex fori* because those foreign rules which are indicated as applicable *in casu* would lead to an unacceptable result.[91] Finally, there are cases where the rules of the *lex causae* do not seem incompatible in themselves with the *ordre public* of the *forum* but their application would nevertheless appear undesirable in the *forum* country. In Anglo-American writing, it is sometimes stated that the application of a certain law would be repugnant to the "public policy" of the *forum,* e.g., because the foreign enactment has the character of "penal law" or is incompatible with the law of nations. It would seem, therefore, that the notion of public policy in common law jurisdictions has a wider sense than the Continental *ordre public* strictly applied.

A. THE MECHANISM OF ORDRE PUBLIC

The Swedish legislation on conflict questions has foreseen the possibility of situations where an application of the substantive rules indicated by a choice of law rule is not desirable. An illustration of the in-

90 Such absolute legislation is occasionally referred to in conflict writing as *lois d'ordre public.* They are sometimes subsumed under the concept *ordre public international* as distinguished from *ordre public interne,* which would embrace such rules in the *lex fori* as are binding (compulsory) in the sense that they cannot be set aside by the parties by means of a contract as long as the legal relations between them shall be governed by the *lex fori.* Gihl (*Lois,* p. 215) expresses the following opinion on the notion *lois d'ordre public:* "Cette conception commence à se faire rare, et on réserve généralement à l'ordre public la fonction d'une sorte de filtre excluant des lois étrangères nuisibles."

91 Cf. note 93 below.

structions to the judge given by the legislature in this respect may be found in chapter 1:12 of the Act on international legal questions concerning deceased persons' estates, 1937: "Provisions of foreign law which are obviously incompatible with the fundamental principles of the law of the Kingdom shall not be applicable in Sweden."[92] In the Act, this provision follows upon a series of choice of law rules; it is intended to admit exceptions from these provisions. If the national law of the deceased contains, e.g., a rule to the effect that "non-Aryan" children have no right of succession, this rule is likely to be considered "incompatible with the fundamental principles of the law of the Kingdom" and is therefore inapplicable. The racial discrimination which would follow from an application of the foreign rule on succession does not appear acceptable. The rule is therefore set aside *(rejected)* as repugnant to *ordre public.* The court makes use, we might also say, of the *mechanism of ordre public* in order to discard the objectionable foreign rule.[93] It is an established opinion that the mechanism of *ordre public* may also be used by the judge in the absence of explicit statutory rules.[94] Occasionally, however, it may

[92] In external procedural law, the mechanism of *ordre public* is resorted to in order to avoid recognition of a foreign judgment which ought to be recognized under the normal rules on this topic.

[93] In the interest of lucidity, the term *ordre public* should be reserved for this "mechanism". It would not seem to have any purpose to give the name of "*ordre public rule*", e.g., to the provision in chap. 1, sec. 2, second para., of hte 1904 Act, where it is laid down that a foreign subject who is married is not in any case allowed to celebrate a new marriage before Swedish authorities. It is true that the *ratio* of the enactment is to be found in points of view similar to those which are embodied in the *ordre public* principle, but on the other hand, the enactment is part of codified private international law, and its application does not imply the setting aside *in casu* of any Swedish rule of law (the choice of law rule indicating the *lex causae*). Nor is there any reasonable ground for the statement that a certain *choice of law rule* (e.g. on the application of the *lex fori* or the law of the child's domicile in all actions concerning illegitimacy instituted in Swedish courts) embodies the principle of "*orde public*".—On this concept, *vide* further Gihl, *Principer,* pp. 476 ff., and Hjerner, pp. 465 ff.

[94] In the decision 1942 *N.J.A.* 65, it is true that *ordre public* was not formally invoked, but the Supreme Court recalled the principle, that foreign law should be set aside if it is incompatible with "fundamental general principles of the legal system of this country". When the 1904 Act on internationa questions concerning matrimony, etc. was introduced, it was probably taken for granted

be a difficult problem of construction to determine whether a statute which contains choice of law rules but no provisions of the same kind as the rule in the 1937 Act, actually implies a prohibition against recourse to the mechanism of *ordre public.* This is not necessarily the case. When solving this problem it is of great importance to know whether the choice of law rule is based upon an international agreement or not. If that is the case, and if it appears from the agreement that the signatory states are not entitled to make other exceptions from the choice of law rules agreed upon than those set out in the treaty, it would seem that the Swedish statute cannot be assumed to allow courts to make further exceptions on the ground of *ordre public.*[95]

According to the definition of *ordre public* in Swedish statutory language, "provisions" of foreign law are occasionally not "applicable" in Sweden. The non-applicability of a foreign rule must not be understood in such a narrow sense, however, that the mechanism of *ordre public* should not be resorted to where the objectionable rule assumes importance only for the purpose of answering a so-called preliminary question. An illustration:

Z, who is an illegitimate child of German nationality, has instituted an action in a Swedish court against the Swedish subject A. The father of Z, B, who used to pay maintenance to the child, was killed in Germany in a highway accident for which A is held liable. German law should be applied as *lex loci delicti commissi* in order to determine the existence of a liability in tort, its extent, etc. If it is laid down in a German rule, upon which the decision has to be founded, that damages shall be assessed on the basis of the father's legal duty to pay main-

that exceptions from the rules of the Act could be made on the strength of the *ordre public* mechanism. The Minister of Justice stated when submitting the Bill: "Since this legislation has a general scope, it seems unavoidable that exceptions will have to be made, particularly in relation to non-Christian states. However, such exceptions should be admitted only when they appear strictly necessary." (1905 *N.J.A.* II, No. 5, p. 9). It should be observed that the statement does not concern the public international law problem of the permissibility of exceptions in relation to the other (Christian) signatory powers.

95 *Vide* Eek in *Sv.J.T.* 1959, pp. 561 ff. The cited article has also been published in *Internationalrechtliche und staatsrechtliche Abhandlungen. Festschrift für Walter Schätzel zu seinem 70. Geburtstag,* Düsseldorff, 1960, pp. 117 ff., and in XVI *Diritto internazionale,* 1962, pp. 3 ff.

tenance to the child, the latter question is "preliminary". If the answer is that an illegitimate child has no right to claim maintenance from its father under German law, this may possible seem so objectionable that a Swedish court may find itself bound to reject the perfectly respectable rule that the damages to be paid for unintentional manslaughter shall be fixed at an amount corresponding to that which the deceased had a legal duty to pay to his family. The problem may appear more clearly if the facts of the example are modified: the deceased and his son were Chinese nationals, the son was born in wedlock, and it is laid down in Chinese law that parents are not bound to support legitimate children beyond the age of five.[96] If the lia-

[96] An extensive discussion has been carried on in the review *T.f.R.* about *ordre public* and the so-called preliminary question *(vide* above, p. 178, note 38). Gihl, who initiated the debate , put the question why a Swedish court is not unlikely to grant a child of a polygamous marriage a right of succession, although the matrimony as such is not recognized. His answer was that the foreign rule invoked to solve the preliminary problem (a rule to the effect that a man may have four wives) was not "applied" and that there was therefore no ground to reject it. At the end of the ensuing discussion, however, Gihl arrived at a less formal explanation which implied, *inter alia,* that certain legal effects of a polygamous marriage are accepted, e.g. the right of succession of children born of such a union, whereas other consequences are not drawn by the Swedish courts. The problem is thus one of policy; undoubtedly, there may be reasons for rejecting an "innocent" rule if the application of that very rule would involve a recognition of an undesirable legal effect of an objectionable rule.

In his final reply to Gihl (*T.f.R.* 1955, pp. 496 ff.), Professor Ross once more emphasized his view that in the example dealing with the right of succession there are not two rules, one belonging to the law of succession and the other to matrimonial law, but that "logically there are only fragments of one single rule which connects certain facts (those which are said to create marriage) and certain legal effects (one of them being a status modification, another the right of succession)". It would be of great interest to have this idea tried systematically in the conflict of laws; it would probably imply a new aspect upon the questions of specialization of choice of law rules, *renvoi* and "prejudicial application of foreign law".

If we have to distribute a deceased person's estate according to *Swedish* law and, among the persons claiming to have a right of succession, there are the deceased's children born in various foreign polygamous unions, the legal rule connecting certain facts with certain legal effects obviously consists of a Swedish fragment from the law of inheritance and a wholly undetermined number of fragments from matrimonial law, embracing all conditions for the creation of a "valid marriage" of the whole world.

bility rule was part of the *lex fori* it is also imaginable that it must be modified, "adapted", if the answer given by foreign law to a preliminary question is founded upon an objectionable foreign rule of law. In such a case, however, it is not proper to state that the mechanism of *ordre public* is used against the substantive rules of the *forum* country. Yet statements to that effect may be found in conflict writing. Professor Niederer illustrates this siutation with the following example: a testamentary executor in state A claims that a Swiss bank delivers money which a citizen of A, who died in Switzerland, has deposited with the bank. The heirs of the deceased, who have all left country A, are opposed to this claim, but under Swiss law the executor's action shall succeed. "Nach schweizerischem Recht steht die Verwaltung des Nachlasses dem Willenvollstrecker zu." The question now raised by the learned writer is whether the Swiss judge should not dismiss the executor's action, in spite of the Swiss rule, if the money is obviously liable to be confiscated in country A.[97] "Der Vorbehalt des ordre public hat nicht die Aufgabe, fremdes Recht als solches auszuschalten, sondern er soll ausschließlich ungerechte Ergebnisse im einzelnen Falle verhindern."[98] The attention devoted to this kind of "preliminary" or "prejudicial" questions—the terms should be put between double quotation marks—should not be pushed too far. At any rate, there must be some support for a suspicion about what is going to happen in country A, its presumed measures must really be incompatible with the *ordre public* of the *forum* country, and finally, it would seem, they must also have some "effect" within that country or be connected with it in some essential respect.[99]

[97] Niederer, p. 294. It may well be asked whether in this example it does not also follow from Swiss private international law that the capacity of the executor is governed by the law of state. A. It is possible that if the foregin rule on the executor's capacity did not leave him any other choice than to obey the directions of confiscating authorities, that foreign capacity rule could be rejected, instead of the Swiss provision concerning a competent executor's right of administration.

[98] Niederer, p. 295.

[99] It is stated by Professor Hjerner (at pp. 254 f.) that American courts have refused to deliver deceased person's estates to countries where the estate would be wholly or partially lost to the heirs because of confiscation, high estate duties

It follows from the statutory definition that the mechanism of *ordre public* should be resorted to only where a foreign rule is "obviously incompatible with the fundamental principles of the legal system of the Kingdom". It is for the judge in each individual action to try whether it is a case of "obvious incompatibility" or not. He has to make an evaluation which must not be wholly subjective but which leaves the judge some liberty within the framework of the opinions about law and justice prevailing at the time in the *forum* country. It would seem natural that some regard be paid not only to the character of the foreign "rule" but also to other facts, e.g. the strength of the ties connecting the action with the *forum*. It is not required that a certain outcome of an action shall appear to be a regular "attack" upon the Swedish legal system or Swedish interests, but if no such interests can be found in the case it may be reasonable to apply even a rule which, under other circumstances, would be rejected.[100] The incompatibility of the rule—or rather of its application *in casu*—with the fundamental principles of the Swedish legal system must at any rate be obvious.

Swedish courts do not seem inclined—in fact, they may have too little inclination[101]—to have recourse to the safety valve of *ordre public*. There are hardly any precedents in this field.[102] A similar

or unfavourable official rates of exchange. On "Soviet Heirs in American Courts," see further Harold J. Berman in 62 *Columbia Law Review* (1962), pp. 257 ff.

100 Cf. Karlgren, pp. 47 f.; Lewald, pp. 125 ff., Raape, pp. 90 ff.

101 Cf. the outcome of the case 1962 *N.J.A.* 123, mentioned above p. 72. It is to be noticed that in that case the courts decided not to admit the action; it was not rejected. This could be an indimcation that at a time when not only the mother's husband but also the mother and the child had become Swedish citizens an action could be tried as purely Swedish and so not calling for any choice of law considerations. Cf., however, 1963 *N.J.A.* 489.

102 Notice the decision 1942 *N.J.A.* 65, mentioned above. In 1934 *N.J.A.* 491, the question turned upon the construction of the expression "moral principles" in sec. 7 of the Act on foreign arbitration agreements and arbitral awards, 1929, In 1930 *N.J.A.* 692 it may possible be taken from an expression used by the Supreme Court that in the view of the Supreme Court there was no reason to make use of the *ordre public* mechanism in a case where a modification of the amount of alimony agreed upon by two divorced spouses had been claimed by one of them and where the *lex causae* had no rules about such modifications. If the mechanism of *ordre public* had been put into function in this case, it must be assumed that it would have been directed against that rule of the *lex*

reluctance to make use of this mechanism is said to characterize the decisions of Danish, Norwegian and also English courts.[103] On the practice of French courts, on the other hand, Professor Batiffol has stated that "d'une manière générale on peut estimer que la jurisprudence française a tendance à abuser de la notion d'ordre public."[104]

The foreign provision indicated by the choice of law rule is rejected because it is found objectionable or, to put it in a more realistic way, because any attempt to graft it upon the legal system of the *forum* country would produce results which are excluded by general considerations of legislative policy.[105] The purpose of the mechanism of

causae which implied that contracts on alimony remain valid even though the facts upon which they were once founded have changed radically. Certain writers find an application of *ordre public* principles in some of those rather numerous cases where Swedish courts have dealt with foreign compulsory administration, confiscation, etc. This construction is occasionally possible, but it would not seem permissible to interpret the whole series of decisions concerning foreign "public law" rules in this manner. Cf. below, pp. 205 ff.

103 According to Professor Borum (at pp. 74 ff.), *ordre public* is invoked by the Danish courts only "in obviously extreme cases". The Norwegian writer Hambro (at p. 354) points out that "as might be expected", there are few Norwegian decisions dealing with *ordre public.* In the Anglo-Saxon countries, the warning pronounced by Burrough, J., against public policy as an "unruly horse" in an old English decision (*Richardson* v. *Mellish,* (1924), 2 Ding. 229, 252; 130 Eng. Rep. 294;) seems to have exercised a considerable influence: "Once you get a stride of it, you never know where it will carry you." *Vide* Nussbaum, *op.cit.,* pp. 112 ff. It is objected by another writer, Lederman, in *Law and Contemporary Problems,* 1956, p. 596: "It is not the ultimate or extraordinary public policy here that is an unruly horse; rather, the unruly horse is the uncertainty of substantive results implicit in our indicative rules, because they require us prima facie to adopt the laws of a foreign country at the material time, whatever their effect may be. The public policy reservation on the operation of these rules, then, is not the unruly horse, but the checkrein on the beast."

104 Batiffol, p. 419.

105 Cf. Paul Lagarde, *Recherches sur l'ordre public en droit international privé,* Paris 1959, pp. 238 f.: "La disposition étrangère n'est pas écartée parce quelle est contraire à un principe fondamental du droit du for. Elle est écartée parce qu'intégrée dans le droit du for, eller ne peut se combiner de façon cohérente avec les diverses dispositions de celui-ci avec lesquelles elle se trouve en relation. Si l'ordre public n'intervenait pas, la solution du litige serait insensée, puisque la disposition étrangère et les dispositions du for n'ont de sens que par leur combinaison, et que cette combinaison est par hypothèse impossible. L'ordre public intervient justement pour redonner sens et vie à l'ensemble, en procédant aux ajustements nécessaires."

ordre public is thus not to bring about an application of the *lex fori.* Nevertheless, the rejection of the *lex causae* rule often leads to its replacement by a provision taken from the *lex fori.* Occasionally it is stated that the *ordre public* mechanism has a purely negative function, e.g. where a court declines to apply a foreign rule on racial discrimination. In this case, however, the principle of equality adopted by the *lex fori* is substituted for the discriminating foreign rule. In other cases, this substituting function of the *lex fori* is more obvious. If a foreign rule to the effect that a certain kind of obligation is not subject to be lost by prescription is held incompatible with *ordre public,* the general limitation rules of the *forum* are applied in its place. It has occasionally been argued, particularly in German legal writing but also by German courts, that instead of applying the *lex fori,* the correct solution would be to try to replace the objectionable provision by another rule of the *lex causae (Ersatznorm).* Thus instead of the foreign rule under which no prescription will take place, the court would apply, e.g., the most liberal limitation rule known in the *lex causae* for any kind of obligation.[106] But the result would then be incompatible both with *lex fori* and *lex causae.* This suggestion, therefore, should not be adopted.[107] On the other hand, it is important to show deference to the choice of law rule of the court's own law—which is put out of function *in casu* by the mechanism of *ordre public* —and therefore only to reject those elements of the foreign law applicable in principle which must necessarily be excluded. If a Swedish court has to distribute the estate of a person who died a national of a country in which first cousins have a right of succession but "non-Aryans" take only half the portion due to "Aryans" and if we further assume that the deceased left as sole heirs a number of cousins of both kinds, the Swedish court should certainly reject the rule based upon racial discrimination, but it should not fall back entirely upon the *lex fori* which, *in casu,* would produce the result that none of the cousins would be entitled to a portion of the estate, which would come under the custody of a Swedish public fund for property left by persons deceased without successors.[108] It must be the task of courts in

106 Cf. Niederer, p. 292.

107 *Vide* Lagarde, *op.cit.,* pp. 201 ff.

108 In France the courts used to hold that since German rules on the proving of paternity in illegitimate filiation cases were repugnant to French *ordre public,* the German rules should be completely rejected and replaced by French

each individual case to eliminate only those rules of the *lex causae* which cannot be adopted, as being repugnant to *ordre public,* and also such rules as are inseparably connected with the rule or rules thus set aside, even if they are not in themselves incompatible with the *ordre public* of the *forum* country.

B. "PUBLIC" LAW

We have already pointed out above (at pp. 78 f.) that Swedish courts do not take cognizance of claims founded upon foreign public law, e.g. fiscal legislation. This principle, which is adopted by other countries also, has often been explained by statements to the effect that the task of enforcing such foreign legislation as immediately serves the interests of the foreign state from which these laws emanate "is no concern of the courts of other countries"[109] or does not "interest"[110] them. Since e.g. fiscal enactments, requisition laws and currency or clearing legislation are nowadays universally adopted, the explanation of this behaviour on the part of courts can hardly be that such legislation is repugnant to *ordre public* or "odious" (although that may be the case in some special situation). The explanation would seem to be found in considerations of general policy rather than of legislative policy. Just as it is a custom that foreign states cannot be cited against their will in civil actions and are not subject to execution measures (immunity rules), so national courts also avoid acting as judges over foreign public administration by trying claims under such circumstances that the success or failure of the action presupposes an evaluation of the "public" law of a foreign state. The meaning of the term "public" is fluid as is also that of other expressions which are occasionally used in its place for the purpose of delimiting the con-

law e.g. in a case concerning paternity and alimony. This meant, in the issue, that even where paternity had been proved under those French provisions which replaced the law of German the *alimony rules* of German law were set aside even though they were applicable in principle and not incompatible with French policy. Nowadays (after the *Fayeulle* decision in 1943), however, French law has adopted the standpoint advocated in the text above. *Vide* Lagarde, *op.cit.*, pp. 212.

109 Nial, p. 117.

110 Gihl, *Lois,* pp. 247 f.

cept more narrowly, e.g. "political laws" or "laws in the exclusive interest of the state". Many enactments which would traditionally be considered as "public" would in fact hardly seem to be of such a nature that claims based upon them should be dismissed without trial, and the identical development of economic and social policy in most countries as well as the increasingly intensified international intercourse in the field of "welfare policy" are likely to make municipal courts successively more "interested" in claims which in the view of an earlier period would be considered "political" if not "fiscal".

If an action of this kind is admitted to trial—let us assume that the plaintiff is a body authorized by a foreign state to run a compulsory health insurance scheme and the claim concerns recovery of dues for such insurance under the statute creating liability to pay these dues—the general principle is that a choice of law must be undertaken. In general, however, it would not seem possible to do anything other than to apply that foreign rule upon which the claim is founded. In some cases, a choice of law rule may refer unmistakably to foreign public law (cf. above, p. 102). It is possible, however, that the choice of law will result in the applicability of Swedish law. It may occur that the court wishes to make a trial of the claim possible but to try it only from a limited point of view, namely whether it can be successful under Swedish substantive rules, which, in a case of this kind, would mean rules of private law.[111] Swedish *public* legislation would obviously not often be able to furnish a ground for the success of the claim. However, the questions of jurisdiction and choice of law fall outside the topic dealt with in the present section, which is devoted to the problem whether certain elements of the foreign legal system found applicable in principle shall be rejected because they are considered as "public-law" rules.

The question whether foreign law shall be set aside because it is of "public-law" character arises after the choice of law has been per-

[111] In the decision of the Stockholm City Court, 30 June 1958, in the action between the State of Bulgaria and the merchant Takvorian (referred to above, p. 88, note 47), a claim that the court should order that an amount of money belonging to Takvorian and deposited with the office of the High Governor of

formed.[112] It now appears that the applicable foreign law *(lex causae)* contains rules which provide for the invalidity of gold clauses, prohibitions against sale, currency restrictions, etc. A question whether an enactment in the *lex causae* invoked by either party is compatible with the constitution of the country from which it emanates may in fact confront a foreign court with the necessity of envisaging an application of foreign constitutional law—at least at one stage of the action.[113] The uncompromising formula that foreign "public law" shall never be applied has no sense; this rule must at any rate be qualified by the further statement that those laws of this character which are in fact applied do not belong to the field of "public" law.[114] As Gihl has stated in his works on this topic, it is equally incorrect—and most confusing both for the courts and for others—to state that "public" law has only a "territorial" validity and therefore "cannot" be applied outside the country where it was enacted. The territorial applicability of a law can only be determined by that law itself.[115] Theoretically, there is nothing to prevent Swedish courts from applying, e.g., Hungarian confiscation laws; the legislature passing such enactments usually gives them the widest possible applicability. The mechanism of *ordre public* in the technical sense can but rarely be used against foreign law of this character, since that mechanism is

Stockholm should be transferred to the Swedish-Bulgarian clearing account, where it should be put to the credit of the Bulgarian National Bank, was admitted to trial. In the decision, there is no discussion of the question of the applicable law, but the action of the Bulgarian State was dismssed; the court seems to have arrived at this result by application of Swedish law (thus it is stated that the Bulgarian State "was not entitled to represent Takvorian"). Bulgarian law (private or public) therefore was not taken into consideration. This seems quite reasonable, however, since the disputed money was located in Sweden and had been paid by a Swedish corporate body which owed it to Takvorian, who in his turn was a French citizen.

112 In Swedish legal writing these questions are treated by Karlgren, pp. 51 ff., Nial, pp. 117 ff., Hjerner in *Främmande valutalag* and in *Scandinavian Studies in Law,* 1958, pp. 175 ff., and by Gihl in *Lois,* and *Studier,* pp. 332 ff. and 357 ff. *Vide,* for further references, the bibliographies of these works.

113 Notice the opinion of Ekberg, J., in the "gold clause case," 1937 *N.J.A.* 1, where it is assumed that the Supreme Court of the U.S.A. would not have considered the Joint Resolution of Congress declaring gold clauses invalid as being an unconstitutional statute if the Court had been given an opportunity to try that question.

114 *Vide* Gihl, *Studier,* pp. 372 f., on the American Joint Resolution.

115 Cf. above, pp. 63 ff.

intended for use against foreign rules incompatible with the legal system of the *forum* country. Most legal systems, however, comprise certain rules which are natural and by no means odious elements—but which, on the other hand, are considered as "public" law and contain restrictions on, e.g., the freedom of contract or the liberty of owners to dispose of their property, allow expropriation or nationalization of certain branches of industry, introduce currency regulations, prescribe a moratorium, etc. What remains, indeed, of the principle that foreign "public" law is not applicable is that *in certain cases* courts decline to apply foreign rules even though they belong to the legal system pointed out as *lex causae*. What is the nature of the rules thus rejected? It may perhaps be stated that these rules are such as appear, in the view of courts, intended to serve *immediately* the interests of the *lex causae* state. Thus foreign legislation on gold clauses is applied, but not, for example, foreign rules to the effect that a special tax or public due shall be collected for the Treasury by the debtor (by means of keeping part of the money due) when refunding loans in the form of bonds which the law of the state issuing such rules is considered applicable as *lex obligationis* under the choice of law rules of the *forum* country. Possibly, however, the attitude actually adopted by the courts of most countries is better described by Niederer in the following statement: "Der Richter hat . . . das fremde öffentliche Recht in beschränktem Umfange zu beachten—dann, wenn es der international-privatrechtlich zuständigen Rechtsordnung angehört und mittelbar oder unmittelbar im Dienste des privaten Rechtsverkehrs steht, —und ferner dann, wenn der Territorialstaat in die auf seinem Staatsgebiet liegenden Vermögenswerte eingreift."[116] In both cases, however, it is imaginable, that the mechanism of *ordre public* will be resorted to, in accordance with the implicit conditions for its operation, to reject for foreign law thus found applicable. In Swedish conflict theory (Professor Nial and, more particularly, Professor Hjerner) this question has been dealt with by means of an analysis of the various groups of typical rules of this kind and of certain typical situations which necessitate a decision in actual practice. It would seem desirable that the judge proceed in the same manner in civil actions which he has to decide. The result, then, would be that in certain cases, the judge may have reasons not to apply rules of the *lex causae* which, very

[116] Niederer, at p. 89. Cf. Nial, pp. 118 ff.

roughly, may be described as "public-law" rules. In such cases there is no question of the rejected rules being replaced by provisions from the *lex fori.* The public-law rules of that legal system are applied where they are of a compulsory character, but otherwise the action is decided under the *lex causae* as if the rejected rules did not exist; if this is technically impossible, we have found a reason for accepting these rules after all.

Confiscations

Questions about foreign confiscatory legislation and confiscations have occupied a particularly large space in legal discussions both in Sweden and abroad. The reason for this is to be found in the social changes which have taken place in almost all parts of the world in the course of this century and brought about, *inter alia,* a total or partial nationalization of many branches of the economy which earlier were in the hands of private enterprises. The flight of numerous individuals from countries where social changes have assumed a revolutionary or particularly brutal character has also created special legal problems in those countries where refugees have settled with their property and their claims.

When dealing with questions about confiscations, it is usual to recall the fact that immunity rules exclude actions against the confiscating state; thus vindication claims concerning works of art which have been confiscated in a country and now adorn the walls of its Stockholm embassy are not admitted. Furthermore, if the confiscating state claims delivery of property in Sweden which falls under the confiscatory legislation but has not come into the possession of the confiscating authorities, and if these claims are put forward in an action brought in Sweden, the courts will not admit them to trial. Those cases which give rise to problems in the practice of courts are of a different character. They concern, e.g., the claims of former owners against those who have acquired property once taken by the foreign state by virtue of the confiscation legislation and thereupon assigned, in that state or abroad, to a third party; they may also concern claims by the confiscating state to recover property which has been taken back ("stolen") by the former owner after confiscation measures and brought into the *forum* country. In general, it should be possible to find a solution in such cases by application, as a general principle, of the *lex rei sitae* (the law of the place where the property was situated at the time of the disputed transfer of the goods), perhaps with the supplementary application of the *ordre public* mechanism.[117] To restore all property to the former owners without exceptions, even where the confiscating authority has once taken possession of such property in its home country, would mean an extension of the *ordre public* principle incompatible with reasonable demands for security in international intercourse even in a world which is divided into different ideological camps.[118] On the other hand, it does not seem unreasonable not to admit (or dismiss) upon humanitarian grounds a confiscating state's vindication claims against a refugee who has managed to recover his property after it had been confiscated abroad and taken it to Sweden in connection with his flight.[119]

In his conflict works, Professor Hjerner has developed a special "individualizing method" for fighting foreign confiscations. He holds that ordinary choice of law rules are not appropriate in these cases and therefore wishes to replace them by a number of principles by means of which he tries to explain the methods really used by courts in a rational way. This method has its merits, not least for the purpose of discovering "latent" confiscatory measures in the form of, e.g., claims by companies, which are formally private but are in fact controlled by states, with regard to property situated abroad and belonging to companies which have been dissolved. Nevertheless, Hjerner's method must in the first place be evaluated on the basis of legislative policy. The policy question which has to be answered is *how* odious confiscations should be considered and to what extent it is a

117 Cf. Gihl, *Studier,* pp. 364 ff., Nial, pp. 130 ff. Unconditional approval would seem due to Hjerner's statement (*Scandinavian Studies in Law,* 1958, p. 205) that the mechanism of *ordre public* may very well be resorted to with regard to so-called incidental questions also.

118 Cf. 1941 *N.J.A.* 424, IV.

119 *Vide* on this topic Schmidt in *Sv.J.T.* 1944, pp. 609 ff. Cf. Wengler's *Vorbehaltsklausel der Humanität,* which is particularly intended to solve certain questions concerning what legal system shall be considered as the applicable "law", *Festschrift Hans Lewald,* pp. 629 ff.

Swedish interest to counteract the enforcement of foreign legislation which contains more or less drastic derogations from those ideas about the sanctity of private property which are still among the essential ideological foundations of our legal system.

C. SPECIAL SITUATIONS

Legislation Incompatible with the Law of Nations

Cases may occur where the applicable foreign law is incompatible with public international law. Thus it may have the character of private law introduced by an occupying power in the occupied area in violation of the law of nations on *occupatio bellica*. There is no agreement on the solution of the problem whether such incompatibility with international law must have the effect that a third country always rejects the enactments indicated by choice of law rules in these cases.[120] What this problem really concerns, however, is the question (already dealt with above, at pp. 141 ff.) what is meant by the term "foreign law". Other cases where incompatibility with the law of nations is discussed usually concern confiscations. If a state has seized property siutated in its territory but belonging to foreigners without compensation, its measures have been considered contrary to international law and former owners have raised claims of recovery in the municipal courts of countries where the confiscated property has been brought after having been sold to third parties. If it is assumed that the law of the confiscating state was also the *lex sitae* at the sale to the third party and thus normally governs the validity of buyer's title, should these generally applicable rules, under which the title is valid, be set aside as "repugnant to the law of nations" and possibly be replaced by rules from the *lex fori?* In *some* situations, it would seem, the mechanism of *ordre public* may be resorted to, whereas in other cases there seem to be good reasons for recommending that municipal courts trying private actions not pass any decisions upon disputed questions which really concern the

[120] *Vide* Niederer, p. 363.

mutual relations not of private parties but of states.[121] Nor does it seem possible to arrive at a solution by "applying" rules of public international law which merely imply that the confiscation gives a claim of recovery to the state of which the foreigner hit by the measure is a national.[122] Generally speaking, it would seem to be only in execptional cases that a municipal court will be in a position to reject a foreign legal rule which is applicable in principle on the ground of incompatibility with the law of nations as a special reason for rejection. As an example, we may mention cases where the applicable foreign law would be incompatible with a convention between the *lex causae* and the *forum* countries.[123]

Fraudulent Evasion of Legal Rules (Fraus Legis)

The law has a purpose; it is intended to create a certain regulation of those social facts to which it is made applicable. Legislative technique is but imperfect, however, and the legislation of states often makes it possible for the citizens to take certain mea-

[121] The Bremen Court of Appeal *(Oberlandesgericht)* which, in 1959, dismissed the actions of Dutch companies which claimed the seizure of certain consignments of tobacco brought to Germany from Indonesia, stated.: "It is also doubtful whether it is suitable to practically enter into an economic blockade by non-recognition in the field of civil law of foreign expropjriation acts. Such an action, moreover, cannot be carried through flawlessly and will result in uneasiness in the international economic life. A further development of international law as far as a greater guarantee for foreign private property is concerned for practical purposes should rather be promoted by further extending international organization or by international treaties"; quoted from *The Bremen Tobacco Case,* publ. by the Indonesian Embassy at Bonn. As for the Dutch view of Indonesian expropriation measures, vide *Ne.T.I.R.* 1958, pp. 227 ff. Further on the Bremen decision in 54 *A.J.I.L.* (1960), pp. 305 ff. (Domke) and pp. 801 ff. (Baade).

[122] On the decisions at Aden and Venice in 1953 in actions between the Anglo-Iranian Oil Company and buyers of oil from the Iranian State, *vide Gihl* in *Liber amicorum,* pp. 56 ff. Cf. also Hambro, pp. 292 ff.

[123] Wolff, *op.cit.,* pp. 214 f. If, on the other hand, the *lex causae* would be incompatible with a treaty between the *lex causae* country and another state, the question of loyal application of the *lex causae* is raised. The judge of the *forum* country has to examine whether this incompatibility would cause the courts of the *lex causae* state not to apply the legal provision. Cf. also Batiffol, pp. 392 f.

sures by which they commit no infringement against the law but nevertheless obtain a result which does not fall within the purpose of the law or is even incompatible with that purpose. Such a course of action is called "evasion" of the law (German = *Gesetzesumgehung,* French = *fraude à la loi*),[124] and it is often stated that courts of justice have the task of preventing it in various ways; in the field of fiscal law, they are confronted by problems which are really difficult and interesting. In the conflict of laws, the question turns upon the potential existence of "fraudulent connecting factors" (*fraudulose Anknüpfungen;* Wolff). There is considerable disagreement, however, whether the conflict of laws has really any place for *fraus legis* in the sense that a judge who finds that a certain course of action has been chosen in order to obtain the applicability of certain substantive rules should refuse to apply the latter and thus put out of function the choice of law rule in the *lex fori* which orders their application.[125]

Certain problems of this kind are solved simply by framing the choice of law rule in such a way as to make arrangements concerning connecting factors impossible. This technique implies, in Continental conflict terminology, that "changes of statute" are not allowed (*vide* above, p. 126 f.) Thus, under the Swedish Act on international questions concerning the legal effects of marriage, 1912, the effects of matrimony on the proprietary rights of the spouses are governed by the law of the country of which the husband was a national at the time when marriage was solemnized; the law thus applicable cannot be evaded through a change of nationality (the *lex causae*—or "statute"—remains the same). Similarly, choice of law rules may be drafted in such a way that a pregnant woman cannot secure the applicability, in her action against the child's father, of a law which is more favourable to herself and the child merely by changing her domicile before the delivery.[126]

124 See Helmers *Kringgående av skattelag,* Stockholm 1956, pp. 23 ff. *Vide* also Schmitthoff in *Law and Contemporary Problems,* 1956, p. 441.

125 Cf. the negative attitude of Niederer, p. 336; Hambro, p. 304; Nussbaum, p. 130. In France *fraude à la loi française* is regularly fought by the courts; *vide* Batiffol, pp. 429 ff.

126 Cf. the example from Lewald above, at p. 126, note 158.

Changes of the *lex causae* are also prevented by rules on the cumulative application of more than one legal system; an example is chapter 3:2 (2) of the Act on international questions concerning marriage, etc., 1904, where it is laid down that facts which occurred while two spouses were subjects of one state may not be invoked as grounds for divorce after they have become nationals of another state, unless such facts constitute grounds for divorce in the latter also.

In those cases where the parties do not try to "evade" a law in the proper sense but rather undertake a *simulated* choice of law, the courts have to exercise their controlling activity in connection with the interpretation of conflict rules. If the *lex domicilii* is applicable, it must be proved that an alleged new domicile is really *bona fide,* e.g. that the *animus manendi* required for the establishment of a domicile is really present. If a contract is signed in Oslo but London is set out as the place of the contract, this fictitious localization shall not be accepted for the purpose of, e.g., deciding whether the formal requirements of the *lex loci* have been complied with. But if a Frenchman who lives at Évian les Bains crosses Lake Leman to Geneva and there makes a promise about a gift in the form prescribed by Swiss law, and if the trip is undertaken in order to avoid paying the fee of a *notaire,* whose services must be used under French law if a promise about a gift is made in France, we have no longer to do with simulation but with a case of "evasion". Is this evasion a *fraus legis?* Shall a Swedish (or even a French) court consider the promise to be a nullity because the voyage was made with the sole purpose of avoiding compliance with a French formal rule? Wolff points out that the *ratio* of the French provision is certainly not to feed the *notaires* of the country.[127] Nussbaum emphasizes, in a general fashion, that "the individual should not be blamed for exercising a choice which the conflict norm opens to him; rather, it is felt that the lawmaker should qualify the rule where it leads to undesirable exploitation."[128]

127 Wolff, *op.cit.,* pp. 143 f.

128 Nussbaum, p. 130. *Vide* also Niederer, p. 332.

The reason why questions of *fraus legis* are raised would seem to be that there are in fact a very great number of methods for avoiding real conflicts of laws and that among the numerous useful and entirely honest methods of this kind there may occur one or two which have a "fraudulent" aspect. In property and contract, the methods now referred to are, e.g., choice of law by the parties. In company law the country of registration and/or the seat of the board are of decisive importance as connecting factors in many respects, and it has therefore become common to locate companies in certain countries, the law of which seems attractive to the founders; among these states is Liechtenstein, where, according to Wolff, "the number of legal persons is possibly greater than that of natural persons".[129] With regard to ships, a suitable "law of the flag" is selected by registration in, e.g., Panama or Liberia (so-called flag of convenience).[130] As for matrimonial law, it is a frequent and mostly a successful practice to marry in a country where the national incapacities of nuputurients are disregarded. The symbol of this method is the blacksmith of Gretna Green in Southern Scotland who united —with full effect in England—young runaway couples who could not contract marriage in England because their guardians did not consent.[131] It follows from chapter 1:6 of the 1904 Act that in Sweden marriage ceremonies performed in compliance with the *lex loci celebrationis* are held to create valid unions (with reservation for certain possibilities of annulment) and it is therefore possible even to marry abroad by proxy.[132] As for divorce decrees obtained in a foreign country, e.g. by means of taking up a domicile there, the Swedish Act of 1904 contains a number of rules against the validity of such decrees.

129 Wolfff, *op.cit.*, p. 140, note 2. *Vide* also Mason in *J.B.L.*, 1961, pp. 148 ff. on "Bahamas Companies" and Philips, *Studier i den internationale selskapsrets teori,* Copenhagen 1961, pp. 153 ff.

130 On these problems, vide McDougal *et al.* in 54 *A.J.I.L.*, (1960), pp. 25 ff.

131 In the 18th century, it is told, Swedes crossed the border to Norway to be married there; the sole purpose was to avoid Swedish rules on incapacity to marry. In Sweden, this "fraudulent purpose" was not considered to deprive the marriage of its validity. *Vide* Joh. Hellner, "Om giltigheten av utomlands ingångna äktenskap", in *Förhandlingar å det åttonde nordiska juristmötet,* 1896, pp. 37 f. and appendix II, pp. 17 f.

132 1954 *R.Å.* No. 33. See below p. 239, note 14.

Nevertheless, successful arrangements are far from impossible and there are many examples of "divorce markets" which have been used by nationals of foreign countries to circumvent the divorce rules of their own countries.[133] Occasionally, the result obtained seems objectionable, as where a German becomes a British subject or a Scot takes domicile in England merely in order to deprive his children of their legal portion of the parent's estate.[134] These cases are rare, however, and usually of an extreme character; it should be possible to meet them either by means of rules against simulation (particularly in cases of artificial domicile) or by recourse to the *ordre public* mechanism. In some cases, rules against abuse of rights in the *lex causae* may also produce the desired results. In the majority of other cases, however, it would seem reasonable to accept the thought expressed in a quotation from Professor Nussbaum (above, p. 214), viz. that the individual should be allowed to make those arrangements to which the law opens a possibility. In the fields of company law and maritime law, arrangements are often dictated by a desire to evade fiscal law or social welfare legislation (safety rules about ships, working hours, etc.). In these cases, special remedies against evasion should be looked for and found, particularly in the form of treaties. The problem raised by these cases hardly concerns the rejection of foreign rules which would otherwise be applicable in principle (i.e under a choice of law rule in the *lex fori*).

If it is concluded that a special *fraus legis* mechanism is not necessary, or even desirable, in the conflict of laws, this is also due to the difficulty of defining and proving that "fraudulent" intention which is supposed to be characteristic of unpermissible evasion of a legal system. It is also uncertain what rules would be put instead of the rejected ones if a *fraus legis* principle were adopted. What law has been evaded? Shall a new domicile, chosen in order to avoid an obstacle to marriage or divorce, also be held inoperative if there should arise some other

133 Klausenburg in Hungary (*vide* Fuchs, *Die sogenannten siebenbürgischen Ehen,* 1889); Fiume in the period 1920—1924; Riga in the nineteen-twenties and -thirties (*vide Sv.J.T.* 1934, pp. 610 f.); Reno, Nevada, U.S.A.; certain Mexican States, where so-called mail order divorces can be granted, etc.

134 *Vide* Wolff, *op.cit.,* p. 141, and Raape, p. 92.

legal question which should likewise normally be decided under the *lex domicilii* of the person concerned? There is one field, however, where these questions do not seem to create insurmountable difficulties and where the idea of evasion could have some importance. In contract and property, the will of the parties is given decisive importance as a connecting factor. If, in the interests of international intercourse, courts were to adopt the principle that a choice of law by the parties shall be accepted so long as it is not "utterly senseless or frivolous",[135] and consequently reject the opposite view, viz. that a choice of law by the parties shall not be accepted unless the positive condition of "a substantial connection" with the chosen law is fulfilled,[136] it would be necessary to make use of a kind of *fraus legis* mechanism as a "safety valve" for those exceptional cases where the choice of law the parties is really "senseless or frivolous".[137] In these cases, the law indicated by the individualizing method would be substitued for the law chosen by the parties.

§ 12. The Decision

After the question of the applicable law has been decided, the rules of the *lex causae* have been proved and it has been found that *ordre public* or other reasons are not opposed to the application of that law (or the applicable law has been to some extent adapted to the *forum* law by use of, e.g., the mechanism of *ordre public*), the judge has to reach his final decision of the action. He must confront the facts of the case with rules taken from the legal system found applicable. A certain legal system, i.e. a complete set of rules, has been found applicable in principle. When the judge proceeds to a decision, he examines the applicability *in concreto* of the various rules of the foreign legal system.

In this connection, certain new problems dealing with the "adaptation" of the *lex causae* to the law of the *forum* may arise. It is no longer a question of actually excluding certain rules of the *lex causae*

135 Cf. Hambro, p. 313; Hjejle, *Frivillig Voldgift*, Copenhagen 1937, pp. 187 ff.; Eek in *Sv.J.T.* 1959, p. 346.

136 On this topic, *vide* Nial, *passim* and particularly, p. 19; Borum, *passim* and particularly p. 146; Karlgren, *passim* and particularly p. 95.

137 Cf. Schmitthoff, p. 115 f., and below, pp. 280 ff.

from application. In some cases, the judge has to apply compulsory rules of the *lex fori* along with the provisions of the *lex causae*. In other cases, the very fact that the judge has been placed in a foreign legal environment creates special problems of construction. This fact has been described by Wolff in the following expressive manner: "Es ergibt sich, daß die rechtliche Kennzeichnung der Lebensverhältnisse das *internationale Privatrecht* nicht vor so schwierige Fragen stellt, wie oft behauptet wird, daß aber das Ineinandergreifen der *materiellen* Rechtsordnungen verschiedener Gebiete für die Auslegung *dieser* Rechtsordnungen zahlreiche Einzelprobleme entstehen läßt, die noch nicht beit Tatbeständen rein inländischen Lebens, sondern erst bei Tatbeständen mit Auslandsberührung sichtbar werden, wie die ultravioletten Strahlen erst im Hochgebirge bemerkbar sind."[138]

A. APPLICATION OF FOREIGN LAW

Where Swedish courts have to apply foreign rules by virtue of a Swedish conflict provision, it must obviously be demanded that *such application shall be loyal.* This requirement may be described by the not very precise saying that the action must be decided as if it were being dealt with by a court in the *lex causae* country.[139] The foreign, "imported" rules must be treated as equal to Swedish rules of law. The principle now expressed seems to be advanced by a majority of conflict writers. Its ground is not to be found in any particular duty to respect the foreign legislature. After all, it is a Swedish norm which lays down that the most practical and just solution of the action is in fact obtained by application of the foreign substantive rules, and it follows that the judge should adopt the same attitude to these rules as if they were municipal Swedish rules claiming application. It ought to be unnecessary to emphasize this, but there is in fact an ascertainable tendency in the courts of all countries, when obliged to apply foreign law (perhaps much against their will), to consider these rules as being less respectable than those of the *forum* and in need, as it were, of being controlled and improved.

It follows from the principle of loyal application that regard must be paid not only to statutory rules but also to judicial decisions under

[138] Wolff, *Deutschlands,* p. 60. Cf. Raape, pp. 100 ff.

[139] Cf. Borum, p. 69; Nussbaum, pp. 257 f.; Raape, p. 120. *Contra* Pillet, *Traité pratique de droit international privé,* vol. I, Paris 1923, pp. 152 f.

the *lex causae*. It is the whole of the foreign law which is put into function; undoubtedly, it will cause considerable difficulties for, e.g., Swedish courts to apply the Common Law of England, possibly in combination with English statutory law, but this is a situation which must be met. It is true that enactments with an international origin, e.g. in the field of maritime law, shall be construed "in an international spirit" (cf. above, pp. 45 ff.), but in so far as the text contains elements of a foreign *lex causae,* it is nectssary to pay some regard to the question what is the place in the foreign legal system of the enactment concerned. It is frequent in conflict writing to warn against, e.g., attempts to find guidance in French precedents and textbooks for the purpose of construing a provision of the Belgian *Code civil* which has the same wording as a rule in the French *Code civil.* A development of customary law may have created a difference between the two rules as actually applied. The same caution is required where for instance the Turkish civil law, which was taken over from Switzerland, is to be applied; elements of construction taken from Swiss law cannot be used with any certainty. The obvious necessity of paying regard to foreign law as it is actually applied in its own country must also influence the methods of construction in the *forum* country. Raape warns against literalism in respect of foreign law: "Der Buchstabe ist hier tödlicher als sonst."[140] On the other hand, Scandinavian or Continental methods of construction, which are characterized by the considerable importance attached to the function of legal rules and to the *ratio legis* (as expressed in the legislative material) are largely impossible to use in respect of English law, for example, where literal constructions of single words and grammatical analysis of phrases still prevail and where it is not held permissible to ascertain the purpose of an enactment by means of any fact not embodied in the statute as such.[141]

It is impossible to describe systematically those questions of "adaptation" which may arise. They concern practical problems and thus emerge in endless variations. In conflict writing, such situations are usually illustrated by means of references to actually decided cases. We shall give a few examples furnished by Lewald, who has taken a

[140] Raape, p. 101.

[141] *Vide* e.g. O. Hood Phillips, *A First Book of English Law,* second ed., London 1953, pp. 91 ff.

particular interest in "l'adaptation de la loi compétente à la situation individuelle de l'espèce". One example is taken from a decision delivered in 1932 by a court in Venice. A Swiss widow had married an Italian and thereby acquired Italian nationality. The problem arose how Italian law would answer the question whether the widow still had a right to administer the fortune of her children (of the first marriage), who were Swiss citizens. Under Italian law, the condition for this was a decision to that effect made by a family council before the new marriage was contracted. Before the marriage, however, Italian law had not been applicable. On the other hand, whereas the legal institution of family councils is unknown to Swiss law, the question whether the right of administration is lost by a new marriage may be raised as a special action. In this dilemma, the Italian court decided to let Swiss law govern the whole matter (in spite of the contrary provisions in both Italian and Swiss law). Lewald points out, however, that it would have been enough to adapt the Italian rule in consideration of the international character of the action, i.e. allow an exception from the otherwise rigorous principle that the righ of administration was lost unless a family council had been held before the new marriage was contracted.[142] Had that solution been adopted, it would have meant an adaptation of the rules of the *lex fori*. Another example illustrates a case where the *lex causae* was foreign law and a certain adaptation of its rules appeared necessary. In 1936, the German Reichsgericht decided an action where an Italian husband claimed that his wife, who also was Italian, should resume matrimonial life with him. Italian law was applicable; under its provisions, the wife could refuse to live with her husband only by securing a separation decree. Under German conflict rules, on the other hand, judicial separation cannot be granted to spouses in whose national law only separation, but not divorce, is known. The applicable Italian law was "adapted" in such a way that it was held sufficient that the wife could prove *grounds* for separation in accordance with Italian law in order to avoid the obligation to resume married life together with her husband.[143] From Swedish conflict law, the rule in chapter 3:2 of the 1904 Act may be selected as an example. Under the language of the provision, it is a condition for the right of foreign spouses to obtain a

[142] Lewald, pp. 140 ff.
[143] Lewald, pp. 145 f.

decree of separation in Sweden that the institute of separation be known in their national law. It would seem reasonable, however, not to refuse a decree of separation where divorce is possible according to the national law of the spouses.[144] Such "adaptation" would imply a less drastic and more elegant modification of the conflict system than that chosen by the Swedish Supreme Court which, in a case of that kind, decided to apply the *lex fori.*[145]

It appears from these examples that "adaptation" shall not be understood as exceptions from the principle that foreign law shall be applied loyally. Adaptation is undertaken in order to obtain reasonable results in concrete cases, which do *not* imply any attacks upon the fundamental principles of the *lex causae*. The avoidance of such attacks as well as of judgments which assume importance beyond the individual case in a manner that may be incompatible with the claim of foreign law to applicability in its own sphere would seem to be the guiding principle which courts have to observe.

The decision 1947 *Sv.J.T.* 22 (discussed above, at p. 52 ff) could be cited as an illustration of a case where adaptation is not loyal. Here, the court made an "assumption", which was hardly well founded, about the recognition by Greek authorities of a Swedish adoption decree which, in fact, modified the status of a Greek subject. There are other examples from Swedish courts, however. Thus the facts of the case 1957 *N.J.A.* 135 would seem to provide a good illustration of the problem of "l'adaptation de la loi compétente à la situation individuelle de l'espèce." A Norwegian married woman, A.M., moved to Sweden in 1951, began to live with a Swede in 1952, was granted a Norwegian decree of separation in respect of her marriage with a Norwegian in 1953, gave life to a child later in the same year, and was finally divorced by a Norwegian decree in 1954. A.M. thereupon instituted an action against the Swedish man with the claim that he be declared the father of her child. The man admitted that he was the father. The Norwegian husband testified that he had not lived with A.M. since 1951 and that he had

144 Westring, *Den nya giftermålsbalken,* 1920, p. 383; Eek in *Sv.J.T.* 1957, p. 535. Cf. however, 1928 *Sv.J.T.* 1; 1958 *Sv.J.T.*, p. 1 and Undén, pp. 86 f.
145 1949 *N.J.A.* 82. Cf Eek in *Scandinavian Studies in Law,* p. 48 (as compared with pp. 34 f.).

not had sexual intercourse with her at such times that he could be the father of the child. Convincing evidence was produced against the paternity of the Norwegian, whereas it seemed proved with such certainty as can be obtained in such cases that the Swede was the child's father. The latter and A.M. stated in court that they were engaged to be married, and the purpose of the action was obviously to create normal family relations. However, the child was born before its mother had obtained a decree of divorce from her Norwegian husband. The paternity suit against the Swedish citizen was governed by Swedish law, but under the rules of that law such suits are not allowed to succeed until the child has been declared illegitimate, and children born in wedlock are presumed legitimate in the absence of a judicial decision to the contrary (the *pater est* presumption). The court of first instance therefore dismissed A.M.'s action, and the same solution was adopted by the Court of Appeal. The question whether the child was legitimate or not should be governed by Norwegian law, however. The Supreme Court found that under Norwegian precedents a husband's paternity in relation to his wife's children could be held excluded if another man was proved to be the child's father in a paternity suit against the latter. In other words, unlike Swedish law, the Norwegian rules did not require a special action against the mother's husband in order to rebut the presumption "*pater est quem nuptiae demonstrant*". It could therefore be argued that in the case at bar the presumed legitimacy of the child was no obstacle to a trial of the action against another man; if that action was successful, it would follow from Norwegian rules that the husband's paternity was automatically excluded. The Supreme Court, however, held that it was uncertain whether Norwegian courts would grant that effect to a Swedish judgment establishing illegitimate filiation.[146] Even if it were quite ob-

[146] In this connection, we need not discuss the principal argument put forward in the *ratio decidendi* of the majority of the Supreme Court, viz. that it must at any rate be held "incompatible with fundamental Swedish rules on parental relations to let the question whether a child is legitimate or not ... depend upon the issue of a filiation suit based upon principles completely different from those embodied in chap. 2 of the Parents and Children Code or enactments corresponding to them." Cf. below, p. 229 f.

vious that a Swedish judgment was not entitled to such effect in Norway, this was a case where *it was possible* to "adapt" Norwegian law in such manner that its distinction between Swedish and Norwegian decisions were disregarded.[147] It might be argued against such a solution that it involves a risk of, e.g., claims based upon legitimate filiation which could later be raised against the Norwegian man. However, this risk could be countered by an action instituted by the man in Norway. A further argument against the need for adaptation could also be the actual possibility for the mother to obtain a decision to the effect that the child was illegitimate—either in Norway or in Sweden. If there were no such possibility, the facts of the case would seem to provide good reasons for an "adaptation" of the kind referred to above; this would also seem to have been the opinion of the Master in charge of the case in the Supreme Court.

Another example, which is fictious but concerns Swedish rules, may be cited. A Spaniard contracts a civil marriage with a Norwegian woman in Norway, and the couple takes up a domicile in Sweden. A few years later, events occur which constitute valid grounds for divorce under Swedish law, and one of the spouses files a petition for a divorce decree. It is required by Swedish law that divorce be possible under Spanish rules also. Spanish law, however, does not know divorce. In normal cases, the Spanish rules must be respected; this, after all, is the purpose of the conflict rules. If it should turn out, however, that in the view of Spanish law, the Norwegian civil marriage ceremony never created a valid marriage, it seems reasonable to accept an "adaptation" to the effect that the Swedish courts granted a divorce on the ground that no marriage can be held to exist under Spanish law. The rationale of the choice of law rule, which refers to the husband's national law, *in casu* the law of Spain, is a desire to avoid a *matrimonium claudicans.* To pass a judgment based upon literal construction in a case like that described in our example would be completely opposed to this rationale and produce the result that a union which is already a

[147] It is curious that the argument of the Supreme Court referred to the effect in Norway of *any* Swedish decision in a filiation suit. For the purpose of the individual case, it should be decisive whether the future judgment of *the case at bar* was likely to have such effect in Norway or not.

matrimonium claudicans would be conserved, perhaps for ever.[148]

If the action of a Lebanese merchant in Sweden is dismissed because he has not observed a period of limitation prescribed by the Swedish Sale of Goods Act but unknown in the law of Lebanon, the issue of the action is likely to produce both indignation and astonishment on the part of the Lebanese. The opposite party, a Swede, would react in the same way if a Swedish court applied rules of Lebanese law, the existence and possible applicability of which the Swede had never foreseen. The disappointment which the losing party must always be presumed to feel is undoubtedly strengthened where his plea is rejected under foreign rules operating outside their original legal *milieu*. The collision between opposed legal attitudes and systems of rules has always to some extent the effect of a shock. It is not unusual that even judges react against the "grotesque" results of the application of foreign law. It therefore seems appropriate to remember that these results must be accepted as soon as it has been decided, in the interest of international intercourse, to make use of choice of law rules.

Upon the whole, these rules and the method of deciding international actions which is described above and which has been created through cooperation between theory and practice and gained a certain customary stability would seem to realize acceptably the purpose of private international law, viz. to obtain reasonable and equitable solutions of litigation connected with more than one country.

B. ABSOLUTE RULES IN THE LEX FORI

In certain cases, rules of the *lex fori* must be unexceptionally applicable according to the view prevailing in the *forum* country. These rules may be called "absolute". They should be distinguished from those rules of internal private law which are called compulsory and which cannot be set aside by contract. The latter kind of rules usually intervene only when a statute is applied in which they are embodied,

148 Cf. the jurisdiction rule in chap. 3, sec. 1 *(in fine)* of the 1904 Act where it is laid down that Swedish courts shall not try foreign matrimonial causes if the *lex causae* reserves the trial of such actions for its own authorities, unless it follows from the rules of the *lex causae* that no valid marriage has been contracted between the parties.

and it is therefore possible for the parties to avoid them by means of a choice of foreign law.[149] On the other hand, where foreign law is applicable, its compulsory rules must be enforced. Certain specially qualified rules of the *lex fori*—the absolute rules—are endowed with such strength, however, that they have to be applied independently of the will of private individuals. Sometimes, such rules may be framed as "unilateral" choice of law rules; it is prescribed, e.g., that the local law is applicable to all contracts of insurance made within a country. This excludes the applicability of foreign law. It is also possible that the system created by conflict rules is merely being modified.[150] In general, however, absolute rules are not considered in connection with conflict provisions. They simply claim to be applied along with the *lex causae* in the same way as they have a claim to applicability along with other kinds of rules of the *lex fori* in an action without international elements. Nevertheless, they imply certain modifications of the actual effects of the applicable law and sometimes, as we shall demonstrate below, deprive it of any effect.

Some absolute rules are introduced specifically for the purpose of meeting international cases and are therefore easy to recognize. Examples of this kind of rules are found in the Swedish Maritime Code, 1891 (e.g. sec. 5), enactments on quarantine, import prohibitions, currency legislation, etc.[151] When a Swedish court—applying foreign law—enjoins a person to effect a payment to which Swedish currency rules are applicable, the court refers to this fact by stating in its deci-

[149] It appears from Professor Nial's course of reasoning (e.g. at pp. 22 f.) that this is also his opinion. However, Nial seems to hold (at p. 55) that such rules as are found in sec. 37 of the Swedish Contracts Act, 1915, or sec. 8 of the Promissory Notes Act, 1936—both contain rules against the enforcement of inequitable clauses in contracts or promissory notes—could be applied "to protect the buyer, where the sale is otherwise governed by foreign law"; the statement refers to conditional sales to which the Swedish Conditional Sales Act is not applicable. In our view, those rules of private law which are usually called "compulsory" or impossible to contract out from, should not be applied "to protect the buyer", where it follows from Swedish choice of law rules that a foreign legal system is the *lex causae*. It is only where the rules of the applicable law are such as to be repugnant to Swedish *ordre public* that they should be set aside and Swedish rules be substituted for them *in the individual case*. This is possibly what Nial has intended to say. Cf. below, på 228, note 160.

[150] Above, at pp. 60 ff.

[151] Cf. above, p. 68.

sion that the currency legislation shall be complied with at the performance of payment.[152] This may obviously result in an issue of the case which is less satisfactory than the successful party had counted upon. A Swedish import prohibition may also produce the result that, e.g., a foreign exporter does not obtain the judgment which he would have been entitled to if only the *lex causae* had been applied. The obligation of the opposite party is modified.[153]

It is more difficult to discover those rules of the *lex fori* which are sometimes—not very properly—called "*ordre public* laws". It is incontestable that every legal system contains laws of this kind. On the other hand, it is extremely difficult to distinguish them from others. In the theory of private international law, there are Pillet's attempts to distinguish laws intended to protect the individual and laws with the purpose of protecting society.[154] The last category *(lois de garantie sociale ou d'ordre public)*, Pillet states, should always be applied by the courts of the *forum*. In Swedish conflict writing, Professor Hult has put forward critical remarks on the possibility of carrying out this distinction in actual practice.[155] Absolute rules are usually found in various kinds of enactments protecting certain interests. The rights of guardians with regard to the care of the infant's personal interests are governed by *lex causae,* but the guardian has to suffer such actual encroachments upon his right of control as are caused, e.g., by rules on vaccination in the *lex fori* or rules on so-called "protective education" and other similar measures which demand that the infant be taken care of by public authorities. A good illustration is furnished by the so-called *Boll case*.[156] The question which the Netherlands submitted to the International Court of Justice in that case was whether the measures of taking into care a Dutch girl, Boll, under a section in the Swedish Children's Welfare Act, 1924, dealing with neglected children, and of conferring upon her Swedish grandparents the actual custody of the girl were compatible with Sweden's obligation under the Hague Convention on guardianship for infants, 1902, to grant the

152 Cf. Nial, pp. 144; also 1941 *N.J.A.* 424 and 1936 *N.J.A.* 586.

153 Cf. Hjerner, pp. 597 f.; Jan Hellner, *Om obehörig vinst särskilt utanför kontraktsförhållanden,* Uppsala 1950, pp. 397 f.

154 Pillet, *op.cit.,* pp. 109 ff.

155 Hult, pp. 10 ff.

156 *I.C.J. Reports,* p. 55.—Cf. *R.A.* 1954, note S. 127, and 1956, note S. 30; also 1955 *N.J.A.* 377.

guardian appointed in the girl's home country a right to dispose of the infant's person. The case dealt with the nature of a treaty obligation. The Court, however, based its decision on an examination of the Swedish Children's Welfare Act and the provision of the Act invoked *in casu*. Was this Act a *"loi de garantie sociale ou d'ordre public"*? Were its rules "absolute" and could they be put in operation regardless of the 1902 Hague Convention?[157] Questions of this kind recur in many connections and with regard to various kinds of legislation, not least in those fields where the traditional distinction between private and public law has been obliterated, for example in respect of legislation on working hours, paid holidays, workers' protection, etc. The Swedish Workers' Protection Act, 1949, would seem to be of an absolute character within its sphere of application. But what about the Domestic Servants' Act, 1944, with its provisions on the form and contents of contracts relating to domestic work? The Act does not contain any rules on its own sphere of application. It is possible that it governs only work performed in Sweden, but this construction is by no means self-evident.[158] It may easily occur that the work is performed within Sweden but a foreign law governs the contract, e.g. because the case deals with a Swiss domestic servant's work for a Swiss family domiciled in Stockholm under a contract in which the parties have referred to Swiss law as *lex contractus*. If, on the other hand, the question is raised in respect of work performed for a Swedish family outside Sweden, it may follow from ordinary choice of law rules that the law of the place where the work is performed should be considered the *lex causae*.[159] Suppose that Swedish courts are seized of an action concerning, e.g., compensation for overtime work in any of these cases: should the provisions of the Swedish Domestic Servants' Act be cumulated with the *lex causae* as absolute Swedish rules? Or should

157 *Vide* further Eek in *Sv.J.T.* 1959, p. 561 ff., same author in *Internationalrechtliche und Staatrechtliche Abhandlungen (Festschrift Schätzel)*, 1960, pp. 117 ff. and in *Diritto Internazionale* 1962, pp. 3 ff. Also Lipstein in 8 *I.C.L.Q.* (1959), pp. 506 ff., Batiffol and Francescakis in *Revue critique de droit international privé* 1959, pp. 259 ff., and Kollewijn in *Ne.T.I.R.* 1959, pp. 311 ff.

158 Cf above, p. 64.

159 It should be observed, however, that according to Gamillscheg, *Internationales Arbeitsrecht*, 1959, p. 176, it is held by the majority of conflict writers that the employer's national law shall be applied to "domestic employees".

these Swedish provisions be allowed to disappear from the judicial horizon once a Swedish choice of law rule has pointed out a foreign law as being the *lex causae?* Or should, perhaps an intermediate solution be adopted: the Swedish Act is applicable, as a subsidiary source of law, only in those cases where Swedish public interests are considered to be engaged with particular intensity, viz. where the work is performed in Sweden, the contract was made here, or the servant (and/or employer) is a Swedish citizen? The problem may perhaps be solved in actual practice by giving the Act as such a limited field of application, comprising e.g. only work which is performed in Sweden, and by construing it as an absolute law in the sense that a choice of law by the parties is inoperative in so far as the Swedish Act lays down rules different from or more far-reaching than those of the *lex causae*. The adoption of such a solution by the courts, however, might have the consequence that absolute laws would be given a scope which would be held unreasonably wide if we hold to the principle that the function of the conflict of laws is to bring about the most purposive and equitable issue in litigation arising in international relations. A solution within the framework of conflict rules therefore appears more attractive. It could imply that the Act is not applied where the *lex causae* is a foreign legal system. *In dubio* the place where the work is performed is considered as the connecting factor of the choice of law rule, although the "proper law" method has a sufficient scope to exclude the application of foreign law in cases where the connection with Sweden is particularly strong, e.g. because the parties are Swedish citizens or domiciled in Sweden though the work has been performer abroad. Upon the whole, it seems most attractive to adopt this method in respect of statutes or single provisions which are not strongly marked by their absolute character, that is concern public order and safety in a direct way. Other illustrations may be found in the Vacations Act, 1945, and the legislation on conditional sales.[160]

[160] When determining the applicable law by the "individualizing" method in actions concerning conditional sales, not only such facts as the nationality or domicile of the parties, but also the location of the goods at the time of the contract or the place where the goods are situated at the institution of the action assume considerable importance. However, Nial (ap p. 55) seems to consider the Swedish Conditional Sales Act, 1915, as absolute; thus he states that its rules for the protection of buyers "are likely to be applied by Swedish courts

However, it is not only provisions or principles of law characterized, in the customary terminology, as more or less "public", which may appear absolute in the conflict of laws. There is also a tendency, particularly visible in the law of parents and children, to let the *lex fori* intervene along with, or as a corective of, the foreign law applicable in principle. In some cases this effect has been obtained by considering the *lex fori* (possibly in its additional quality of being the child's *lex domicilii*) as the applicable law, i.e. by adopting a solution within the framework of conflict rules.[161] But in other cases decisions may be found where rules of Swedish law seem to have been given an absolute applicability. Thus in 1957 *N.J.A.* 135 the majority of the Supreme Court invoked "fundamental principles of the Swedish law of parents and children" among the reasons for refusing to apply Norwegian law as pleaded by one of the parties.[162] When answering questions of guardianship, the general principle would seem to be that the law of the family is applicable.[163] The problem whether the Finnish mother of a Finnish child resident in

even if the sale is governed by a foreign *lex causae,* at last if the goods are situated in Sweden". The precise time at which the goods should be located within the Kingdom is not indicated, but Nial seems to refer to the time when the action is brought. Karlgren (p. 103, note 8) states that "it may follow from considerations of *ordre public* that the compulsory rules of Swedish law on conditional sales, even those which deal with the obligations of the parties, are always observed by Swedish courts, if the goods are situated whithin the Kingdom". The relevant time is not set out by this author, either. A principle of such generality as that formulated by Karlgren cannot be founded upon *ordre public,* however, at least not if that term is taken in the sense adopted in general forensic language and also in this book (above, at p. 197). It is rather a question of giving the protection rules of the Conditional Sales Act an absolute character.—As for the Swedish "social legislation for the welfare of workmen", Nial (at pp. 64 f.) seems to consider these rules as absolute, i.e. applicable also where the *lex causae* is foreign law, but finds no obstacle against applying similar foreign legislation in Sweden. In that case, how is the "conflict" between e.g. Italian and Swedish rules on compensation in money for vacations to be solved when the Italian rules call for application as being part of the *lex causae* and the Swedish provisions because the court sits in Sweden?

161 *Vide* the decision 1956 *N.J.A.* 337, in particular the opinion of Karlgren, J.: also 1946 *N.J.A.* 310, 1952 *N.J.A.* note C 749 and 1957 *Sv.J.T.,* p. 54. The two latter cases deal specifically with refugees, however.

162 Cf. above, pp. 218 ff. Karlgren finds "*ordre public* considerations" in this case (in *Sv.J.T.* 1961, pp. 649 f.).

163 Cf. 1956 *N.J.A.* 337.

Sweden is entitled to demand the transfer of the child to Finland should thus be solved under Finnish law. In cases of this kind, however,—which constitute an important category, for in the years 1939-45 thousands of Finnish children found a second home in Swedish families and often stayed on after the end of the war—the Supreme Court seems to have set aside the *lex causae* in favour of absolute rules of the *lex fori,* under which even a lawful guardian's right to take care of a child cannot be enforced if there are reasons for fearing that its enforcement would endanger the child's mental health.[164] What is characteristic in these connections is that the decisive question has become whether the enforcement of the guardian's wishes against the child's desire with the help of public powers shall be allowed. It may obviously be said that this question should be answered unequivocally under the *lex fori.* However, it is important to make clear why this should be so and to what extent principles of private law, particularly in the law of parents and children, should be considered "absolute".[165]

164 *Vide* 1953 *N.J.A.* 262 and 1951 *N.J.A.* 177; cf. 1954 *N.J.A.* 13 (the "Monica case"). Cf. also Malmström, *Föräldrarätt,* 1956, pp. 129 ff.

165 Against certain Swedish measures, Finnish parties seem to have invoked the Inter-Nordic convention on *inter alia* guardianship. *Vide* Backström in *J.F.F.T.* 1949, pp. 291 ff.

Chapter IV
The Swedish Conflict Rules — A Resumé

§ 13. The Personal Law

In the Swedish conflict of laws "the personal law" (*personalstatutet*) is said to be the *lex patriae* of the *propositus*. This statement is generally qualified by an explanation that matters relating to personal status are to be settled by the application of the law of the country to which the *propositus* "belongs" as a citizen. However, it must be recalled that any discussion concerning the personal law must separate two distinctly different questions. One question concerns the scope of the personal law: which matters are to be settled by the application of the personal law? The other question concerns the choice of the personal law: within a given legal order, which law is the personal law.[1]

A. THE CHOICE OF LAW

The Swedish legislation based on the Hague conventions and still in force embodies the "principle of nationality". This means that the personal law of an individual is the law of the country of which he is a citizen. In statutes the country referred to as his home country (*hemland*) is the one to which he is declared to "belong".[2] As already mentioned above (pp. 132 f.), the word "belong" as indicating citizenship has been interpreted in the case of stateless persons

[1] In contemporary law no conformity exists as to the scope of the personal law and therefore the usefulness of the whole concept may be questioned. In any case, the legislator should not, as so often the text-book writer finds necessary to do, set out first to define the personal law and then to delimit its scope. His job is to study which law is the most suitable to apply in a series of questions relating to divorce, guardianship, inheritance, alimony, adoption, etc. He may suggest that concerning some relationships the *lex patriae* should apply and in others the *lex domicilii*, and there are, of course, other possible connecting factors to consider as well as combinations of various kinds. What is important to remember, however, is that from the point of view of legal policy it might be reasonable to claim "that uniform regulation of matters of status is justified, at least with respect to the basic facts of personal life" (Rabel, *The Conflict of Laws*, I, p. 117).

[2] Concerning the Nordic conventions see above pp. 34 ff. and below p. 236.

as referring to their country of domicile or residence. It was also mentioned that for reasons of legal technique, the Act of 1904 (ch. 7, sec. 1) includes a rule by which, in cases concerning divorce or separation, the effectively applied personal law of the spouses or of one of them, for instance the Swedish wife of a foreigner, may be another law than the *lex patriae.*

In the case of stateless persons the *lex domicilii* was chosen only because no *lex partiae* existed, and this choice of law can hardly be said to indicate an inclination on the part of the Swedish legislator and the courts towards a switch to the principle of domicile as the basis for the choice of the personal law. The cases are slightly different which relate to persons (refugees) who have not lost their foreign nationality and therefore, according to the Swedish statutes, "belong" to a foreign country. The courts have tried in various ways to "re-define" nationality as a connecting factor in order to avoid undesired results of the application of the Swedish statutes and the foreign law selected in accordance with them. In one case[3] a former Estonian citizen who had acquired Soviet citizenship was regarded as "quasi-stateless" as he did not "enjoy the protection" of his home country. In a later case[4] the Supreme Court said that "the arguments leading up to the idea that stateless persons ought to be subject to the law of their domicile must on important points be considered applicable also to foreigners who . . . have no real connection with their native country". Here, "real connection" was contrasted with what was called in an earlier part of the decision a citizenship "of a purely formal nature". In some later cases, however,[5] the *lex domicilii* was not applied to refugees who held the nationality of the country from which they had escaped, as "such circumstances" were said not to be present in the case as would motivate a deviation from the principle of nationality. It seems possible to solve the judicial problems raised by "quasi-statelessness" in accordance with elementary principles of justice without violating the statutory rules in force.[6] Moreover, the court decisions leave open the question what "circumstances" might lead to the conclusion that the personal law

[3] 1948 *N.J.A.* 805.

[4] 1949 *N.J.A.* 82.

[5] 1951 *N.J.A.* C 733; 1955 *N.J.A.*, 571; 1956 *N.J.A.* 601.

[6] See Eek, *Scandinavian Studies in Law,* 1959 pp. 23 ff. Cp., further, pp. 248 f. below.

of an individual who has foreign citizenship is his *lex domicilii.* But nevertheless the cases mentioned indicate a trend from the principle of nationality towards the principle of domicile.

B. THE SCOPE OF THE PERSONAL LAW

The scope of the personal law can not be explained by any overall definition. Status in a narrow sense (name, legitimacy, general capacity to have rights and duties, cf. above pp. 68 ff.) is clearly to be governed by the *lex patriae* as the personal law. Its scope, however, can be established only by an analysis of the various choice of law rules in force. For instance, a person cannot marry in Sweden if his personal law contains a prohibition against his marrying; he cannot obtain a divorce in Sweden for a cause not recognized as a cause for divorce by his personal law; a third-country divorce contrary to this requirement will not be recognized in Sweden; questions concerning the matrimonial property are governed by the personal law of the husband at the time of the marriage; an alien can adopt or be adopted only if a Swedish decree of adoption would be recognized by his personal law; a deceased person's property will be distributed in accordance with the law of inheritance in the country of which he is a citizen at the time of his death, etc.

Recent cases show an inclination on the part of the courts to substitute domicile for nationality as a connecting factor when this can be done without violating statutory provisions. This tendency can also be described as a gradual limiting of the scope of the personal law. As an example may be mentioned the case *Désirée* v. *Witold Szwabowics.*[7] The Supreme Court had to decide the question whether Polish or Swedish law should apply in a dispute concerning custodianship of a child who held Polish citizenship and was born in a marriage between spouses, the parties to the dispute, who were also Polish citizens. The Court held that in principle disputes concerning custodianship should be settled by applying the "personal law" of the family and that the "personal law" should be determined by the family's nationality. The Court stated that the principles outlined would point to Polish law as being applicable. However, Désirée, who was a former Latvian citizien, had married Witold in Germany and had only thereby acquired Polish citizen-

[7] 1956 *N.J.A.* 337.

ship. She had never been domiciled in Poland. Witold had during the past ten years been a resident of Germany as, in view of the political situation in Poland, he did not wish to return to that country. The mother and the child had been living together in Sweden since 1947 and the mother (who at the time of the decision had married a Swede and become naturalized in Sweden) evidently had the intention to remain in Sweden. The Court held as follows: "The general principle cannot reasonably be applied in such a special case as the present one, where the fact that forms the basis of the principle, that is, the common nationality of the family, presents itself as predominantly formal." Swedish law was applied. This, it appears, is a typical judicial approach to the choice of law problem involved. It might be said that nationality was "re-defined", while the scope of the personal law was left untouched. Mr. Justice Karlgren, who did not agree with the majority of the court in the *ratio decidendi,* stated, however, in a separate opinion that even when foreign law applies in cases concerning custodianship "as it is the personal statute of both the parents and the child", there are reasons why Swedish courts should not go against the fundamental rule of Swedish law that the welfare of the child shall be the first consideration when the custodian is being chosen. Legal writers on conflict of laws may interpret this statement in a number of ways, but it seems permissible to say that decisions following this line of thought would limit the scope of the "personal law"; the "personal law" is in principle applicable but it does not apply to all questions relating to custodianship, as one of the main questions involved is decided by the application of the *lex fori* (or the *lex domicilii* of the child). But the case, regardless of how it is to be interpreted, is evidence of a widespread feeling amongst lawyers that the domicile principle is often more suited to modern conditions than the nationality principle.[8]

[8] Swedish internal law does not make any distinction between "domicile" and "residence." Legal texts use the term *hemvist,* which refers to the place (or home) where a person permanently lives, In Swedish conflict of laws (statutory texts, cases and legal writing) the term *hemvist* is likewise used, although the term domicile may be found here and there in Swedish legal writing. It is sometimes assumed that the presence of *hemvist* or residence in Sweden in the municipal-law sense does not necessarily involve domicile, which would require, in addition, an intention to remain in Sweden. On the other hand, *hemvist* in itself

Some limitation of the scope, in the traditional sense, of the personal law (the *lex patriae)* can also be noted in Swedish legislation. Examples will be found below. Here it may be mentioned that, under the Act of 1937 concerning international questions with regard to deceased persons' estates, the administration of an estate is to be governed by the Swedish law if the deceased had domicile in Sweden even though the distribution of the estate (the succession) is to be governed by his *lex patriae.*

C. DURATION OF PERSONALITY

There are differences between domestic laws with respect to the time when personality begins—i.e. whether on completion of birth or of a specific period of time thereafter—and to the status of a child *en ventre sa mère.* With respect to the end of personality the presumption of death in the case of absentees raises legal questions.

Chapter 25 of the Inheritance Code contains provisions concerning the declaration of death of absentees. Swedish courts have jurisdiction in all cases concerning Swedish citizens. As to foreigners, the Statute has nothing to say, but the general opinion is that Swedish courts would assume jurisdiction if the absentee had his last known domicile in Sweden and probably also in cases where assets were left in Sweden or where, for other practical reasons, a Swedish decision is needed.[9]

What law should apply? The principle of nationality would require that in the case of a person with a foreign nationality his *lex patriae* should apply, for instance with respect to the duration of absence or the date at which the death should be deemed to have occurred. The choice of law question does not, however, seem to have been settled in Sweden.

As to recognition, to fulfil "the national test" the foreign authority

imports a quality of permanence, distinguishing it from mere sojourn or stay. The question of the meaning or, rather, the employment of the various terms is not important for the discussion in this résumé, where the terms "residence" and "domicile" are used alternatively and merely denote the fact that a person is living permanently in Sweden. Cf. above p. 129 f.

9 Guldberg & Bergendal, *Kommentar till ärvdabalken,* II., Stockholm 1962, p. 333; Michaeli in *Sv.J.T.* 1946, pp. 456 ff.

must have been entitled to entertain jurisdiction under the rules which pertain in Sweden. A foreign decision in the country to which the absentee belonged as a citizen will be recognized.[10] In principle, recognition should also be given to a decision from the country of the last domicile. A further requirement of "the national test" is that the foreign authority had applied the *lex patriae* of the absentee.

§ 14. Family Law. Inheritance

We have already explained (above pp. 34 ff.) that in the area of family law there are two systems of rules in Swedish conflict law, one set of Nordic rules and one set of general rules.

Technically the Nordic rules are exceptions from the general rules, but the Nordic rules are complete enough to form a separate system of law. This résumé will deal only with the general rules. As to the Nordic rules a comprehensive exposé by Allan Philip is found in *Recueil des Cours,* 1958, under the title "The Scandinavian Conventions on Private International Law".

It must be recalled, however, that in these conventions Sweden has to a considerable extent left the principle of nationality and adopted, although with some qualifications and modifications, the principle of domicile, which has long prevailed in both Danish and Norwegian law.

We shall find below that the system of general rules has been gradually remodeled. Some rules apply only in relation to countries which are signatories to the Hague conventions. To-day, when Sweden is no longer bound by the Hague conventions, a thorough revision of the general rules is under consideration.[11]

A. THE CONCLUSION OF A MARRIAGE

The private international law rules concerning the conclusion of a marriage (jurisdiction, choice of law and recognition) will be found in the Act of 1904 and supplementary acts (see above p. 27). The rules are based on the Hague Convention of 1902 to regulate the Conflicts of Laws in regard to Marriage.

[10] *Vide* Rosén in *Sv.J.T.* 1959, pp .43 ff.
[11] Cf. Eek in *Sv.J.T.* 1962, pp. 751 ff.

A marriage can be celebrated in Sweden or outside Sweden and different rules apply to these different situations. But it should also be recalled that a distinction must be made between Swedish marriages, viz. marriages performed in accordance with Swedish municipal law and by an authorized Swedish agent, and foreign marriages. A further distinction must be made between cases where both parties are Swedes and where one or both of them are citizens of a foreign country.

Swedish Marriages

A Swedish marriage which is celebrated in Sweden between Swedish parties does not create any problems of concern to us. Some specific rules apply, however, to Swedish marriages celebrated abroad. Such a marriage is not possible if both parties are foreigners. Both parties or one of them must be Swedish. The jurisdiction is, in other words, limited with respect to the parties.

Within Sweden, on the other hand, there are no jurisdictional limitations with respect to marriages between foreign parties. The formalities of such marriages follow Swedish municipal law. Under the Act of 1904 (ch. 1, sec. 2) the capacity of a foreigner to marry is governed, as a rule, by his *lex patriae*. There are two exceptions to this rule. If according to his *lex patriae* this capacity of a person to marry is governed by another law, for instance the *lex domicilii*, the party may request its application. The second exception is found in the Act of 1904 (chap. 7:4 a). If a foreigner has been domiciled in Sweden at last two years, his capacity to marry shall, at the request of the betrothed coupled, be decided by Swedish law alone.

While as a general rule the existence of obstacles to marriage shall be decided by the application of the *lex patriae*, the Act of 1904 provides for its cumulation with Swedish law. In no case may a foreigner conclude a Swedish marriage if he is already married; in addition, incestuous marriages are prohibited. No other Swedish prohibitions need be observed, nor is it possible to reject foreign prohibitions as contrary to Swedish *ordre public*. The rule that a person can not conclude a Swedish marriage if he is already married relates to the rules concerning the recognition of a foreign divorce decree (see below pp. 246 ff.). If a foreign divorce decree is not to be recognized in Sweden, the person so "divorced," is still bound by the prohibition against a new marriage.[12] This seems to apply even if the divorce is recognized in the country to which the person belongs as a citizen.

According to the Marriage Code (ch. 4, sec. 5) a marriage ceremony in Sweden is a nullity, i.e. void *ab initio,* only if the person who performed the ceremony was not authorized by law to do so ("the proper officer"), if the parties were not both present at the ceremony and consented to the marriage or they were not declared husband and wife. A Swedish marriage, therefore, is not void *ab initio* because it is bigamous or contravenes an absolute prohibition in the applicable law. Proceedings for the annulment of the marriage must or can be initiated.

Foreign Marriages

As indicated above a foreign marriage can take place in Sweden. The Act of 1904 (ch. 1, sec. 5), includes a provision by which the King in Council may permit foreign diplomatic or consular officers to marry parties who are not Swedish citizens. Such a ceremony performed in accordance with the legal formalities governing the officer shall be regarded as valid. Under the same article the King in Council may permit ministers of foreign churches to conduct marriage ceremonies in Sweden. Only one of the parties need have the nationality of the country to which the foreign church belongs. The formalities of the law of that country shall be followed. However, the King in Council, when issuing the permit, may establish further conditions.

Normally a foreign marriage takes place abroad. Special rules are laid down for the recognition of foreign marriages where the ceremony was conducted by a foreign diplomatic or consular agent (the Act of 1904 ch. 1, sec. 7). For all other foreign marriages outside Sweden the Act of 1904 (ch. 1, sec. 6) states that a marriage solemnized abroad according to the formalities of marriage prescribed by the *lex loci celebrationis,* shall be regarded in Sweden as having been concluded *"i behörig form;"* i.e. as being "valid as to form." This means that the foreign ceremony is put on the same footing as a

[12] Cf. below pp. 248 concerning the case where one of the spouses in the first marriage dissolved abroad by a decree not recognizable in Sweden, has married anew.

Swedish marriage ceremony[13]. At their request the parties must be recorded in Sweden as married.[14] If, however, the conclusion of the marriage was contrary to rules relating to the essentials of marriage, it can be dissolved by annulment (below pp. 241 ff.). The rule now referred to applies also to Swedish citizens. It is said in the Act of 1904 (ch. 1, sec. 1) that a Swedish citizen may not enter upon a marriage abroad if Swedish law prohibits the marriage. But this does not prevent a foreign authority from performing a marriage ceremony creating a matrimonal union which, according to the 1904 Act, must be regarded as valid in Sweden until dissolved. It should be added that amongst the various prohibitions against marriages which can be found in Swedish municipal law (the Marriage Coae, chapter 2), only one is absolute. If a marriage ceremony was performed which contravened the prohibition against incestuous marriages,

[13] The Act of 1904 ch. 1, sec. 4, requires that a Swede who wants to marry abroad shall observe the Swedish rules concerning publication of bans. This does not mean, however, that the non-observance of these rules invalidates a marriage abroad if the formal requirements of the *lex loci celebrationis* were followed. The Swedish law on this point seems to have been misunderstod by Rabel, *op.cit.*, pp. 234 and 245. Domestic formalities are not exclusive.

[14] The following decision of the Supreme Court of Administrative Justice should be noted (1954 *R.A.* ref. No. 33). An Italian, R, living in Sweden and married to an Italian wife, was divorced from this wife by a decision of a court in Bravos, Chihuahua in Mexico. The following day R and a Swedish woman, C, unmarried and living in Sweden, were married by proxy in Juarez in Chihuahua in accordance with the formalities required by Mexican law. Thereafter C requested the vicar of the parish in Stockholm where she lived to record her marriage to R. The vicar refused and his decision was upheld by the Chapter of the Diocese of Stockholm. The Supreme Administrative Court of Justice decided to refer the matter back to the vicar who, therefore, became obliged to record R and C as married. The Court said that the question whether the marriage should be regarded as void because R and C at the time of the marriage ceremony had been in Sweden and had been represented by proxy, in spite of the fact that the formal requirements of Mexican law had been followed, had not been raised by anybody whose rights were involved and that such a question could not be resolved by administrative procedure.—In other words, the marriage was performed in accordance with the formalities required by Mexican law and was therefore to be regarded as valid in Sweden. It should be noted that in an ordinary court of law a person whose rights were involved, e.g. R's Italian wife, could have brought an action aiming at establishing the continued validity of R's first marriage or at annulment of the second marriage. The public prosecutor might also initiate proceedings to that effect. But until the marriage hade been nullified in one way or another by a court decision, it remained valid.

the public prosecutor must take action for annulment. This he must do also in the case of a bigamous marriage, but if the first marriage is dissolved before he takes action a decree of annulment can not be granted.

When considering whether the foreign formalities of the marriage have been observed, the *lex loci celebrationis* must be consulted. If, according to that law, some rules relating to the ceremony have not been followed but this omission does not make the marriage invalid in the country where the ceremony took place, the marriage is also valid in Sweden. Swedish law does not include any statutory provisions under which the forms locally required must be in accordance with those of "a Christian country" or otherwise with what is required in Sweden as a minimum of form. Even marriage ceremonies conducted in a primitive society but in accordance with its formal rules may create marriages valid in Sweden[15].

If the foreign formalities have not been observed and, therefore, a marriage does not exist according to the *lex loci celebrationis,* the Act of 1904 (ch. 1, sec. 9) provides that the marriage will still be regarded as valid *(gillt)* in Sweden if it is regarded as formally valid in the country to which the parties belong as citizens, or, if they belong to different countries, in both countries. This rule applies only to foreign citizens.

B. NULLITY. ANNULMENT

Nullity

A Swedish marriage is void *ab initio,* a nullity, only if it was not performed by a proper officer or the parties were not both present at the ceremony and consented to the marriage or if the officer did not declare the parties husband and wife (above p. 238). A foreign marriage is a nullity if the formal requirements of the *lex loci celebrationis* were violated and, as a result, according to that law a valid marriage did not come into being.

[15] Cf. Undén, pp. 30 ff. A handbook prepared for the Swedish clergymen by the Ministry for Foreign Affairs includes a statement that in some countries common law-marriages may come into being *solo consensu.* The handbook adds: "If two Swedes in such a country after an agreement live together as husband and wife, they are also according to Swedish law to be regarded as legally married."

Nullity means that the parties are not married. Any public authority can be put in the position of taking note of this fact, for instance tax or immigration authorities. Although nullity does not depend on a court decision, either party can, however, under the Marriage Code, chapter 5, section 2, apply to a court for a declaratory judgement settling a dispute between a man and a woman concerning the question whether or not they are married to one another.

There are no statutory rules regulating jurisdiction in this kind of dispute, further there is no case-law and writers disagree. It is however obviously of public interest that an authoritative court decision can be obtained in order to solve dubious questions concerning the existence or non-existence of a marriage connected with Sweden. Therefore, it seems reasonable that jurisdiction should not be refused when the person who seeks a decision is a Swedish citizen or is domiciled in Sweden. Public interest also demands that jurisdiction be assumed when it is claimed that a marriage was or was not brought into being by a ceremony supposed to follow the procedure which creates a Swedish marriage.

A foreign decree stating that a marriage is valid or void *ab initio,* could probably not be "recognized" in Sweden. The question is whether the original act purporting to create a marriage is to be recognized in Sweden according to the rules of Swedish private international law, and this question can not be answered abroad. But as nullity is related to the observance or non-observance of formal requirements alone, a declaration made by a public authority in the foreign country where the ceremony took place is conclusive evidence in Sweden.

Annulment

Although a marriage is valid as to form, it may be annulled if any of the substantial requirements for marriage is missing. The marriage is dissolved on grounds which existed at the moment of solemnization and which should at that time have been recognized as obstacles to it. The Act of 1904 contains a few provisions concerning annulment in conflict cases. These provisions apply directly only to marriages between "foreign citizens", but their application is not restricted to foreign marriages.

Jurisdiction. No statutory rules exist governing jurisdiction. It is

9 — 637386. Eek

generally assumed that the rules concerning jurisdiction in divorce cases (see below 245) can be applied by analogy. When the defendant party is domiciled in Sweden, jurisdiction would, therefore, always be entertained.[16] For reasons of public policy Swedish courts may also take jurisdiction whenever a Swedish marriage is concerned. In the special case where the wife had Swedish nationality before her marriage, jurisdiction might also be entertained.

The Act does not concern itself directly with marriages where one of the parties is a Swedish citizen. In such cases however, the rules providing for jurisdiction where both spouses are foreigners will certainly be followed. In addition the rule in the Act (ch. 7, sec. 2, subsec. 2, below pp. 245 f.) would probably be applied by analogy.

Applicable law. The Act of 1904 is based on a policy in favour of marriage. A marriage between two foreigners will, in principle, not be annulled in Sweden, unless it is voidable under Swedish law as well as under the *lex patriae* of the spouses or the *lex patriae* of one of them. However, in respect of some countries[17] the general rule does not apply; the marriage can be annulled in Sweden if one or both of the spouses belong to such a country and the marriage is voidable under its law. The policy in favour of marriages goes further, however; thus even in the case of the "favoured" countries, the marriage will not be annulled if the ground on which the marriage is voidable according to the foreign law is a prohibition in that law against a new marriage after a divorce, against marriages between persons of different religion or against a marriage contrary to a promise to stay unmarried (priests, nuns). Moreover, if one of the spouses was entitled under his *lex patriae* to request the application of another law for deciding his capacity to enter upon the marriage, this second law shall be consulted only if under its rules the contracted marriage is not voidable. If it is voidable under the second law but not voidable under the *lex patriae,* annulment is not permitted. In a case where a marriage

[16] In a case (1946 *N.J.A.* 479) concerning refugees who had not acquired domicile in Sweden, jurisdiction was assumed due to the circumstances under which the spouses lived in Sweden. The absence of a rule in the Act forbidding jurisdiction made it possible to follow the demands of reasonableness and, perhaps also of the Law of Nations; no other court in the world than a Swedish court was available to the parties.

[17] Austria-Hungary, Belgium, Denmark, France, Germany, Italy, Luxembourg, Netherlands, Norway, Poland, Portugal, Rumania, Russia, Switzerland, Spain, United Kingdom.

was celebrated in Sweden in accordance with the Act of 1904 chapter 7:4a annulment is possible only if the marriage is voidable under Swedish law, regardless of the nationality of the spouses.

The Act does not provide for the situation where one of the spouses is a Swedish citizen. It might be argued that the policy in favour of the marriage would motivate a rule according to which such a marriage could be annulled only if voidable under Swedish as well as under that of the foreign party. But it is possible that a national of one of the "favoured" countries might obtain an annulment where a ground could be found only in his *lex patriae*.[18]

Recognition of foreign annulments. The Act of 1904 is silent on this matter. There are provisions, however, concerning the recognition of foreign divorce decrees (below pp. 246 ff.), and it has been argued by writers that they could be applied by analogy. It would follow that a foreign annulment of a marriage would be recognized in Sweden where both parties were of the same nationality as the authority which issued the annulment decree. As to other foreign annulments the law is not clear. As previously mentioned, it is the prevailing opinion of writers that recognition of foreign judgements relating to personal status is subject to what we have called "the national test." It should be added here that this test is also required by the Act concerning the recognition of Swiss judgments (above p. 31). The Act provides that a Swiss decision in cases relating to personal status, family law or inheritance shall not be recognized in Sweden if it is "based upon a law whose provisions on the relevant subject are contrary to the law which ought to have been applied according to Swedish private international law." In addition, the Swiss court must have been entitled to exercise jurisdiction which would be the case "if under identical circumstances a Swedish court would have had jurisdictional competence." The national test is difficult to apply to foreign annulments both because of the uncertainly existing with respect to the scope of Swedish jurisdiction in annulment cases and because of the construction of the Swedish choice of law rules, based as they are on the policy in favour of marriage.[19]

18 This seems to be the opinion of Undén, pp. 55 f.

19 As will be seen below the national test is difficult to apply in other matters also. It would seem to be reasonable only if it became an *international test,* that is if universal rules concerning jurisdiction and choice of law existed. The test, then, would exclude from recognition decisions which deviated from the uni-

C. DIVORCE

The relevant provisions in the Act of 1904 still reflect the principles contained in the Hague Convention of 1902 to regulate the Conflict of Laws and Jurisdictions in regard to Divorce and Separation, although some amendments have been introduced since Sweden left the Convention. The Act, like the Convention, applies on the whole the same rules to divorce and separation.[20] We shall, therefore, limit our discussion to divorce. However, it should be pointed out that some special problems exist with respect to the recognition of a foreign separation decree, or of its effects.

The questions relating to divorce concern (I) Swedish jurisdiction in divorce proceedings, (II) the applicable law in such proceedings between "foreign citizens" and (III) the recognition of foreign divorce decrees regardless of the nationality of the spouses. With respect to the rules relating to divorce and separation the Act of 1904 redefines nationality and contains special provisions concerning domicile. The result of the transformation rule concerning nationality (above pp. 133 f.) is that in some cases a foreign citizen may be regarded as a Swede and in others, a Swedish citizen as a foreigner. The Act of 1904 applies only where the spouses were at the time of the beginning of the litigation to be regarded as belonging to a foreign

versally applied principles. The scope of recognition of foreign decisions concerning personal status could very well be widened. Recognition does not create a new and complicated situation, as this is the result already achieved by the foreign decision which must take effect at least within one territory. On the other hand, it seems a good legislative policy to restrict the assertion of jurisdiction in matters relating to status which are connected with foreign countries. Cf. Eek in *Sv.J.T.* 1957, pp. 536 f.

[20] It must be mentioned, however, that in Sweden the spouses may jointly apply for separation when because of profound and lasting disruption they consider themselves unable to continue cohabitation. This situation is not foreseen in the Act of 1904. According to the Marriage Code ch. 15, sec. 4 *in fine,* the proper *forum* for a joint application for separation is the court of the domicile of both parties or any of them or the court of the place where the spouses had their last common domicile. By analogy it seems reasonable to conclude that a Swedish court would entertain jurisdiction with respect to a joint application for separation of spouses who are foreign citizens whenever any of them is domiciled in Sweden and also when the spouses had their last common domicile in Sweden.

country.[21] Under the special provisions concerning domicile (above pp. 135 ff.), a Swedish woman, although domiciled in Sweden according to the Swedish municipal rules, will be regarded as having her relevant domicile in the same country as her husband if she cannot have a separate domicile under the law of the country to which the couple are held to belong.

Jurisdiction

A Swedish court will always assume jurisdiction when the spouses are Swedish citizens even if domiciled abroad. This seems to apply also in the case where one of the spouses does not actually hold Swedish citizenship but both, according to the transformation rule, are to be regarded as belonging to Sweden.

When the spouses are foreign, Swedish courts entertain jurisdiction if the defendant party[22] is domiciled in Sweden, and also if both spouses once had domicile in Sweden and the defendant has deserted his spouse or has left the country after a cause for divorce arose. There are some exceptions to this rule. If a foreign state claims exclusive jurisdiction of divorce with respect to its citizens, a Swedish court may not exercise jurisdiction.[23] Here, there is however, an exception: if the marriage is regarded as void in the home country, jurisdiction is assumed according to the general rule. These rules are contained in chapter 3, section 1, of the Act of 1904.

In 1934, the Act of 1904 was amended by the introduction of another exception to the general rule on jurisdiction. The exception is to be found in chapter 7:2 (2). If one of the spouses is a Swedish citizen (but not a stateless person domiciled in Sweden) and has been domiciled in Sweden for at least one year, he or she may initiate proceedings for divorce or separation in Sweden. This rule makes it possible, for instance, for a Swedish wife, returning from Italy, where she has an Italian husband, to start divorce proceedings in Sweden in spite of the fact that under the transformation rule the couple must be regarded as Italian. Moreover, it is provided that the question

[21] It should, however, be recalled that the rules in ch. 3. secs. 5 to 7 inclusive of the 1904 Act concerning recognition of foreign decrees on divorce or separation apply also to Swedish citizens.

[22] Cf. 1908 *N.J.A.* 190.

[23] 1956 *N.J.A.* 601.

whether there is a ground for divorce shall be decided by application of Swedish law.[24]

Applicable Law

The general rule is that a Swedish court applies the national law of the spouses cumulatively with Swedish law. (Cp. above pp. 122 f.). The national law in principle controls both the permissibility of divorce or separation and the ground for granting divorce or separation. There must also, however, be a ground according to Swedish law, but not necessarily the same one as in the national law.

Recognition of Foreign Divorce

The Act of 1904 contains different rules for two different categories of foreign divorces. If the divorce was granted by a court (or administrative agency) in a country to which both spouses belonged as citizens, the divorce must be recognized in Sweden; no special requirements of *exequatur* or confirmation exist (ch. 3, sec. 4).[25] This simple rule is, of course, based on the national test; the foreign authority was competent and presumably applied *lex fori* (the *lex patriae* of the spouses). If, on the other hand, a foreign authority has dissolved a marriage between spouses of another nationality than that of the authority, the Act of 1904 defines more in detail the requirements of "the national test" (ch. 3, sec. 5).

In such a case recognition is granted, (I) if the foreign authority's jurisdiction rested on requirements consistent with those laid down for Swedish courts in chapter 3:1 of the Act, and (II) if there was a ground for divorce in the *lex patriae* of the spouses. In addition, a divorce decree by an administrative agency is recognized only if recognized by the latter law. The jurisdictional requirement refers only to chapter 3. Therefore, a foreign divorce will not be recognized in Sweden if the foreign authority had assumed jurisdiction on the

[24] Cf. 1929 *N.J.A. 1* (before the amendment) and 1952 *N.J.A.* 471 (after the amendment).

[25] 1927 *N.J.A.* 130; 1956 *N.J.A.* 337. Cp. 1956 *Sv.J.T.* 65. A request for confirmation of a foreign divorce was rejected as not necessary in a case where a German court had granted a divorce of a marriage where the husband was German and the wife probably Swedish. The wife would in any case be regarded as German under the transformation rule.

basis of circumstances such as those described in chapter 7:2 (2), of the Act of 1904. In an exceptional case, namely with respect to Swiss divorces, recognition will be granted even where the Swiss court had assumed jurisdiction under circumstances such as those envisaged in chapter 7 (Cp. above p. 85 note 68). The jurisdictional rule is exemplified by the following case[26]. Two Swedes married in Sweden in 1920. Later the man left his wife and emigrated to the United States. He became a United States citizen in 1931 and was, in 1952, granted a divorce by the Chancery Court for Grundy County in Tennessee. The wife who had remained in Sweden applied for a confirmation of the American divorce by the Stockholm Court of Appeal. This was denied. The spouses, being of different nationality, were to be regarded under the transformation rule as citizens of the country to which they had both belonged at the same time (Sweden). Under these circumstances chapter 3:5 was applicable and the American court was not to be regarded as competent under chapter 3 of the 1904 Act. But if the man had moved to Switzerland and had acquired Swiss citizenship, a Swiss divorce would have been recognized in Sweden if there was a cause for divorce according to Swedish law.

Recognition means that the foreign divorce will have the same effect as to matrimonial status as a divorce granted in Sweden. However, if the foreign divorce is of the second category, a Swedish marriage is prohibited until one or both of the former spouses have applied for and received a confirmation *(exequatur)* of the foreign divorce decree by the Stockholm Court of Appeal.

The 1902 Convention from which the Swedish rules were taken has been understood to mean that the courts and other authorities in states parties to the Convention were not allowed to recognize a divorce if the treaty requirements were not satisfied.[27] It has been argued however, that it might be necessary, or at least reasonable, to recognize foreign divorces even in some cases where the requirements of the Act of 1904 are not satisfied, for instance when either of the

[26] 1956 *Sv.J.T.* 65 — It should be noted that according to the 1964 statute mentioned below (p. 248) the Stockholm Court of Apeal has the authority to issue a confirmation of a foreign decree on divorce or separation when the foreign authority has entertained jurisdiction on the basis of rules corresponding to those contained in ch. 7:2:2 of the Act of 1904. Such decisions will, however, have no effect at all in Sweden until confirmation has been granted.
[27] Cf. Rabel. I, p. 517.

spouses of the dissolved marriage has entered into a new marriage in a country where the divorce is recognized.[28] Undén suggests that an *exequatur* should be obtainable in such cases in spite of the wording of the Act.[29] This, however, is doubtful, and a person receiving a foreign divorce decree incompatible with the rules of chapter 3:5 probably could not be married in Sweden.[30] But in other respects nothing prevents a construction of the Swedish law which would permit recognition of the foreign divorce. Proceedings for annulment or a trial for bigamy, for instance, might not be possible in Sweden in case one of the parties settles in Sweden after having been married again abroad.

Stateless Persons and Political Refugees

A statute dealing mainly with the problem of jurisdiction in divorce and separation cases involving stateless persons and political refugees was adopted in 1954 and came into force 1 January 1965. It provides that the rules of the Act of 1904 shall not prevent Swedish jurisdiction, a) if one of the spouses is stateless and has been domiciled in Sweden for at least one year, b) if one of the spouses is a political refugee and has been domiciled in Sweden for at least two years and c) if one of the spouses has been domiciled in Sweden for at least two years and it is not known whether the other spouse is alive or where he or she lives. In addition, the King in Council may always give a special dispensation allowing the courts to entertain jurisdiction when one of the spouses has been domiciled in Sweden for two years. In cases of this kind, Swedish law shall in principle apply, but the courts may also take foreign law into account when this is necessary in order to protect the interests of the defendant spouse or children of the marriage. Questions concerning support to children and custodianship in cases of this kind will be decided in accordance with the rules of Swedish law if the child lives in Sweden. Foreign decisions based on

[28] Cf. Undén, pp. 93 and 56. Cf. also 1947 *N.J.A.* 346, discussed by Philip in *Recueil*, p. 533.

[29] Undén p. 92.

[30] Cf. however, 1958, *Sv.J.T.* 27. See Eek in *Scandinavian Studies in Law*, 1959, p. 47.

rules corresponding to those included in the draft statute may be recognized in Sweden after *exequatur* granted by the Stockholm Court of Appeal. They will have no effect in Sweden until *exequatur* has been granted.

D. HUSBAND AND WIFE

The provisions of the Swedish Act of 1912 correspond to those in the 1905 Hague Convention concerning the Conflict of Laws relating to the Effects of Marriage on the Rights and Duties and on the Property of the Spouses. As explained above, (pp. 36 f.) the statute is now supposed to contain the "general rules" in contradistinction to the "Nordic rules," even though its applicability was originally regarded as more limited.[31]

Personal Effects of Marriage

The personal relations between husband and wife are governed by the law of the country to which they belong as citizens. If both spouses acquire a new nationality, their new *lex patriae* shall apply. If the spouses should happen to become citizens of different countries, the law of the last nationality common to the spouses shall govern. There is no rule for the situation where the spouses did not belong to the same country either at the time of the marriage ceremony or after it. It might be assumed, however, that the *lex patriae* of the husband would govern. (Cf. above p. 133 note 181). It should be noted that rights and duties can not be enforced by means other than those permitted by Swedish law even if a foreign law applies in principle.

There are few cases relating to the question of the scope of "personal relations" and legal writing is scarce on this subject. Questions concerning the duty of spouses to support one another belong without any doubt to the personal relations to be governed by the *lex patriae*. Moreover, this rule has been applied also to questions of alimony raised during divorce proceedings or after the conclusion of such proceedings, Swedish or foreign.[32]

[31] 1915 *N.J.A.* 391; 1930 *N.J.A.* 692; 1931 *N.J.A.* 495.
[32] See 1934 *N.J.A.* 77. Cf. 1927 *N.J.A.*, 130; 1930 *N.J.A.*, 692.

Effects of Marriage on Property

In the absence of a marriage settlement the effects of marriage on property are governed by the law of the country to which the husband belonged as a citizen at the time of the marriage. While alterations in this law must be recognized (cf. above pp. 151 ff.), a change in the national status of the husband does not lead to a change of applicable law.[33] In other words, the Act upholds the principle of immutability. The choice of law rule relates to both movables and immovables, with the exception that special rules of a foreign country relating to special types of real property within that country may be applied.

The Act provides (sec. 2, para. 1) that where foreign law is applicable it may not be invoked against a third party unless its applicability has been recorded with a Swedish court. In the absence of such recording a third party can rely on Swedish law.[34]

A new marriage settlement may be concluded if permitted by a new *lex patriae* of both spouses. It cannot, however, have any retroactive effect with respect to a third party. As to the form of a marriage settlement either the *lex loci actus* or the national law or laws of the parties must be observed. If one of the parties is a Swedish citizen, the Swedish rules relating to formalities must, however, always be observed.

Procedural Questions

Jurisdiction. Questions concerning matrimonial rights and duties may be raised in proceedings for separation or divorce. With respect to jurisdiction cases which do not involve separation or divorce, Swedish courts would always entertain jurisdiction when both spouses are Swedish nationals. If only one of the spouses is a Swedish citizen, jurisdiction will be entertained, at least if the defendant is domiciled in Sweden[35], and probably also in some other cases where another

[33] 1915 *N.J.A.* 391; 1931 *N.J.A.* 495; 1937 *N.J.A.* 438. Cf. also 1931 *N.J.A.* 403 and the two cases 1929 *N.J.A.* 1 and 1929 *N.J.A.* 532 concerning the same marriage. The three cases, however, are not clear with respect to either law or facts.

[34] Cf. Karlgren, p. 124; Undén, pp. 110 f.

[35] In 1931 *N.J.A.* 403 the defendant spouse was a Swedish citizen but it was doubtful whether he could be regarded as domiciled in Sweden. The other spouse (the wife) had been a Swedish citizen and was either a British subject or stateless and was domiciled in South Africa. Cf. 1929 *N.J.A.* 532, and 1929 *N.J.A.* 1.

jurisdiction (in the international sense) is not available or not easily available. If both spouses are foreigners it must be assumed that a Swedish court would assume jurisdiction if both have a domicile in Sweden[36]. By analogy from chapter 3:1 of the Act of 1904 it would probably suffice if the defendant spouse is domiciled in Sweden,[37] and it would probably be safe to assume that this would also be the case where the spouses have had a common domicile in Sweden, but the defendant spouse has deserted the other and left the country. Jurisdiction will always be entertained in cases concerning support if the defendant spouse has property in Sweden.[38]

Recognition. In principle "the national test" will apply but its application is not easy as the Swedish rules with respect to jurisdiction have not been laid down in any statutory text or been clearly settled by case law. Where the foreign court has been found competent according to the Swedish jurisdictional rules, "the national test" would further require that it had applied the law which constituted the *lex causae* according to the choice of law rules in the Act of 1912. It seems doubtful whether this latter requirement would be observed in all cases, particularly when the foreign decision does not interfere with the rights or duties of spouses of Swedish nationality.

Recognition means that the foreign decision is put on the same footing as a Swedish decision. A Swedish decision is necessary, however, in order to make enforcement measures possible if such are required. In 1927 *N.J.A.*, 130 a Hungarian decision was recognized as the basis of the duty of the husband to support his wife, but a Swedish decision was necessary in order to make the enforcement of the foreign judgement possible in Sweden.[39]

36 1934 *N.J.A.* 77.

37 1927 *N.J.A.* 130 concerned support during separation. Both spouses were Hungarian citizens. The wife lived in Hungary and the man, the defendant spouse, lived in Stockholm but was not registered as a resident of Sweden.

38 1930 *N.J.A.* 692; 1950 *N.J.A.* 464. 1936 *Sv.J.T.* 27 Jurisdiction was accepted in a case concerning support. Both spouses were German citizens, the wife was living in Germany and the man in Helsinki. The court made itself available as the defendant spouse (the man) from time to time visited Sweden where he was carrying on business; he had also received summons in Sweden.

39 The case also concerned an increase of the amount of support due to raised living-costs in Hungary.

E. PARENTS AND CHILDREN

The conflict rules concerning parents and children—i.e. concerning legitimacy, custodianship, support, paternity and all rights and duties which relate to parenthood—are largely unsettled in Sweden. There are only a few court decisions to quote, and divergent recommendations for conflict solution appear in legal writing. The principle of nationality, which is still said to prevail in Sweden, may indicate a preference for the *lex patriae* of the various *propositi*, but in the field of parental relations the trend towards the principle of domicile or towards the application of the *lex fori* is clearly noticeable and throws doubt on many presumptions for the application of the *lex patriae*. Here we shall only deal with a few of the many questions or problems which occur in the field of parental relations and base ourselves mainly on the authority of the few Supreme Court decisions rendered.

Legitimacy

As to legitimacy it is clear that Swedish courts have jurisdiction where the parties, i.e., the child and the husband of its mother, are Swedish citizens. General principles of justice support the assumption of jurisdiction also in cases where the child is domiciled in Sweden,[40] probably even if the defendant is not domiciled there. Those principles would also support the entertainment of jurisdiction when only the husband of the mother is domiciled in Sweden.

According to a number of court decisions,[41] the national law of the parties or, if they belong to different countries, the *lex patriae* of the husband of the mother at the time of the birth of the child will be applied. This law should govern not only cases where the child or the husband of its mother wants a decision to the effect that the man is not the father of the child but also cases where the claimant wants a confirmation of the status of legitimacy. However, in 1964 the Supreme Court reversed or at least modified its previous practice. The claimant in case was a child who wanted a decision that the French husband of his mother was not his father. Swedish law was applied, as the mother was Swedish and domiciled in Sweden at the time of

40 1953 *N.J.A.* 4 (above p. 71) and 1962 *N.J.A.* 123 (above p. 72).
41 See the preceding footnote and also 1957 *N.J.A.* 135 (above p. 218 ff.)

the child's birth, and, in addition, the child was domiciled in Sweden at the time of the action.[42]

Custodianship

In Swedish municipal law a clear distinction has existed since 1920 between guardianship, which relates to the administration of the property of an infant, and custodianship, which relates to the personal care of a child. The 1902 Hague Convention to Regulate the Guardianship of Minors does not concern the *patria potestas* or *puissance paternelle,* but does concern both personal care and guardianship with respect to property in cases where a special custodian or guardian has to be appointed. The Act of 1904, however, is worded as if it concerned only guardianship with respect to property.[43] Since Sweden has left the Convention, the Act may be construed as referring only to guardianship in the Swedish municipal sense. In this section we are dealing with custodianship, and mainly with disputes between husband and wife concerning the right to custody. Guardianship will be dealt with later.

Jurisdiction. The municipal forum rules provide that a dispute concerning custody shall be settled by the court of the domicile of the party who actually is in charge of the child. In two cases where one of the spouses claimed that Swedish courts could not entertain jurisdiction the Supreme Court took jurisdiction as the mother and the child (aliens) were living in Sweden.[44] It has been assumed that Swedish courts would always be available if the child is domiciled in Sweden. The same would apply when both spouses are Swedish citizens even if domiciled abroad.

The applicable law is, in principle, the national law of the family if husband, wife and child belong to the same country.[45] Legal writers have variously recommended that where the members of the family belong to different countries, the applicable law should be the national law of the father, the national law of the child, or the *lex fori.* Exceptions based on public policy are, of course, possible, for instance where

[42] 1964 *N.J.A.* 1. See Dennemark in *Festskrift tillägnad Hjalmar Karlgren,* pp. 49 ff.

[43] This fact may explain the attitude taken by Swedish authorities in the *Boll Case.* See Eek in *Festschrift Schätzel,* pp. 119 ff.

[44] 1952 *N.J.A.* 471; 1956 *N.J.A.* 337.

[45] 1956 *N.J.A.* 337. Cf. above pp. 233 f.

the foreign law of the family gives the right of custody to the father but he, according to Swedish standards, is unsuitable as a custodian.

It has been argued that questions concerning custody raised in proceedings for separation or divorce should be governed by the law which applies to the divorce or separation. One case gives some support to this theory, but its import is disputed.[46]

Support

Jurisdiction in cases concerning support is assumed where the defendant is domiciled in Sweden or has property in Sweden and this would probably also be true where the child for whom support is claimed is domiciled in Sweden. Swedish courts are always available when the parties are Swedish citizens.

The choice of law issue is not settled. When the parties belong to the same foreign country, it might be argued that the national law of the family should apply in principle. However, in custodianship cases an inclination towards *lex fori* has been noticeable. It can be assumed that such cases would normally concern children domiciled in Sweden. In cases concerning support, however, it is not unusual that the child is domiciled in a foreign country. Then, the *lex fori* must lose its interest. Instead it seems reasonable to apply the *lex domicilii;* by its application the child would get support according to the rules which prevail within its social *milieu.* It may be recalled that the draft Hague convention concerning support (1956) expresses itself in favour of the law of the country where the child has its "*résidence habituelle.*"

Paternity

Cases concerning paternity generally concern two questions, namely the question whether the defendant is to be declared the father of a child and the question of the amount of support he has to pay to the child if declared its father.

As to jurisdiction, the Supreme Court in two rather recent cases (apparently followed by lower courts subsequently) assumed jurisdiction when the only connexion with Sweden was the fact that the child and its mother lived in Sweden. The first case concerned a child born in Sweden to a refugee from the Soviet Union; the action was

[46] 1952 *N.J.A.* 471.

brought against a Norwegian citizen, living in Norway, and the intercourse was said to have taken place in Oslo.[47] In the second case suit was brought on behalf of a child born in Sweden of a Swedish mother against a person from Afghanistan; the intercourse had taken place in San Francisco.[48] In both cases, jurisdiction was assumed as both mother and child were living in Sweden. It seems reasonable to assume, however, that if only the child was connected with Sweden in this way, jurisdiction would be entertained on grounds of public policy.[49] Swedish jurisdiction is also available if the parties are Swedish citizens, if the defendant is domiciled in Sweden and, probably, if the intercourse took place in Sweden and the circumstances of the case present some additional connexion with Sweden.

In an early paternity case the Supreme Court applied the law of the place of the intercourse.[50] It has been said that this rule has been replaced by the personal law of the child or the *lex fori*.[51] It has also been argued that where the mother, the child and the defendant belong to the same foreign country, the law of that country should apply, while in at least some other cases the *lex fori* might be the applicable law.[52] Arguments have also been put forward in favour of the application of the national law of the mother at the time of conception.[53] In one case concerning two Norwegian citizens living in Sweden the Supreme Court applied Swedish law. The decision was unanimous and one of the judges outlined in detail why in his view *lex fori* should apply in all cases in Sweden concerning paternity (as well as support to children born out of wedlock).[54] It seems doubtful whether this decision and its sweeping *ratio* will continue to be the law. It may in future appear reasonable to restrict the application of Swedish law to the question of support. While the *lex domicilii* recommends itself in questions of support, the application of the personal law of the mother and the defendant, or of the child if they do

47 1956 *N.J.A.* 410.

48 1957 *N.J.A.* 430.

49 It seems that in both cases the Supreme Court neglected reasonable interests of the defendant.

50 1915 *N.J.A.* 1.

51 Beckman, p. 69.

52 Karlgren, pp. 130 f.

53 Wallin, *op.cit.*, p. 532.

54 1946 *N.J.A.* 310. Cf. the later case 1963 *N.J.A.* 489.

not all belong to the same country, seems more desirable where only the status question is at issue.

Questions relating to the effect of a later marriage on the status of an illegitimate child, or concerning its recognition, have not been dealt with in decisions of the Supreme Court. The principle of nationality might be followed in such cases since they directly concern status.

Recognition of Foreign Decisions

Foreign judgments concerning support to children must be confirmed by a Swedish judgment in order to be executed in Sweden. However, under certain conditions they may be accepted by Swedish courts without any scrutiny, particularly when emanating from courts in countries to which the parties belong.[55]

As to foreign decisions concerning status—legitimacy, custodianship, paternity and legitimation—the national test should apply. Its application in the field of parental relations is not always easy. A foreign decision determining the legitimacy of a child would, according to the national test, be recognized in Sweden if the decision had been taken by a court in the country to which the persons belonged as citizens and was based on their *lex patriae*. But if the foreign court had assumed jurisdiction only because the child was domiciled in the country of thė court, recognition seems more doubtful, even if the *lex patriae* of the mother's husband was applied, particularly if one or more of the persons concerned were Swedish citizens. The national test, however, speaks in favour of recognition. A foreign decision concerning custodianship would according to the national test be recognized if rendered by the court of the country to which the child belonged as at national or where it had its domicile, provided that the foreign court had applied the law to which the Swedish conflict rules refer. But it is uncertain whether this law is the national law of the family, that of the father or of the child or is, rather, the *lex fori*.

In paternity cases Swedish courts have assumed jurisdiction where the child is domiciled in Sweden and have applied the *lex fori*. The national test would, for instance, result in the recognition of an American decision, based on *lex fori,* to the effect that a Swede X was not the father of the Swedish child Y, residing with his mother in the United States, and as *res judicata* the decision would prevent

55 Cf. above p. 251.

litigation in Sweden. If the national test seems to go astray with respect to paternity, the reason may be that the Swedish jurisdictional rules are too liberal towards the child and that the indiscriminate application of the *lex fori* to all cases in Sweden is unsound.

F. ADOPTION

Some questions relating to adoption have been dealt with above (pp. 55 ff.). It was explained that Sweden assumes jurisdiction on condition that the applicant has domicile in Sweden. If the applicant is a Swedish citizen it must be assumed that Swedish courts will consider his application even if he is domiciled abroad. No jurisdictional rules relate to the nationality or domicile of the person who is to be adopted.

The applicable law is Swedish law. The Act of 1904 (ch. 6, sec. 1) however, prohibits adoption in Sweden unless the decision will be recognized in the countries to which the various parties belong as citizens.

As to the recognition of foreign adoptions, the national test implies that an adoption between foreigners in their own national state will be recognized and, in addition, an adoption between foreigners in the country where the adopter was domiciled. A Swedish citizen can not adopt or be adopted abroad without permission by the King in Council, given either with respect to a particular state or *in casu*. Therefore, a foreign decision contrary to this rule will not be recognized in Sweden even if the adopter was domiciled in the country of adoption. The requirement of permission does not imply that the King of Council applies the substantive Swedish law relating to adoption when granting or refusing an application for permission.[56] The King is free to act as it pleases him, but the general principles in the substantive law on adoption will naturally play a role when individual applications are being considered.

The recognition of a foreign adoption means acceptance of a change in status; if legal questions which relate to the persons concerned have to be resolved in Sweden, the status of "adoption" must in principle be accepted. But "relationships based on 'adoption' may have little in common but the name."[57] It would seem reasonable

[56] 1960 *R.Å.* Ju 49.
[57] Ehrenzweig, p. 182.

then to assume that when the conditions for recognition are present, the rights and duties of the adopter and the child should be those laid down by the law of the country where adoption occurred. In Swedish legal writing, however, it has been stated that the legal relationship between the adopter and the adopted person are governed by the *lex patriae* of the adopter.[58] Inheritance rights, however, are governed by the *lex patriae* of the person whose estate is concerned.

Under Swedish municipal law the relationship between the adopter and the adopted person can be dissolved by a court decision. No cases can be cited concerning the jurisdictional and choice of law issues.[59] The only statutory rules governing this situation are found in chapter 6:2 of the Act of 1904. There it is provided that a Swedish court cannot dissolve an adoption when the adopter is a foreign citizen unless the decision will be recognized in the country to which he belongs. It is also provided that a foreign dissolution of an adoption where the adopter is a Swedish citizen will not be recognized in Sweden if permission for the dissolution had not been given by the King in Council.

G. GUARDIANSHIP

The general capacity to have rights and duties, including the capacity to sue and be sued, is generally said to be governed by the personal law of an individual, i.e., in Sweden his *lex patriae*. But it might be argued that it is rather the *lex fori* that applies, as a Swedish court would probably never apply a foreign rule depriving a person of general capacity, for example in the case of slavery or civil death. As to the limitations of a person's capacity to engage in transactions on his own behalf (e.g., effects of infancy and interdiction), the *lex patriae* applies.

The Act of 1904, in chapters 4 and 5, provides for questions relating to the appointment of guardians for infants (ch. 4) and for persons

[58] Karlgren, p. 136.—In the Nordic system the country of the domicile of the adopter entertains jurisdiction in cases concerning adoption and the legal relationship so created is governed by the law of the country where the adopter is domiciled.

[59] According to Walin, *op.cit.*, p. 564, Swedish substantive law applies when the court has to decide whether the requirements for dissolution exist.

under interdiction (ch. 5). These rules are based on the relevant Hague Conventions of 1902 and 1905; the principle of nationality prevails. Both chapters, however, contain general rules which do not entirely correspond to those of the Conventions. While Sweden was still a party to the Conventions, special statutes, therefore, introduced rules in accordance with the Conventions for application in relation to the other parties.[60] The special statute relating to chapter 4 was repealed but the special statute relating to chapter 5 is in force. These special rules will not be dealt with here.[61]

Jurisdiction

The appointment of a guardian for a minor of Swedish nationality or for a person of Swedish nationality declared incapable is a matter for the courts in Sweden, even where the person concerned is domiciled abroad.[62] In exceptional cases, however, Swedish courts may also assume jurisdiction where the *propositus* is a foreigner with domicile in Sweden if no guardianship is arranged in his home country.[63] Swedish courts are competent to re-establish full capacity in the case of a Swedish citizen who has been subject to foreign interdiction, but other foreign interdictions can not be revised in Sweden. As concerns Swedish citizens domiciled abroad who are minors or possibly subject to interdiction, a Swedish court may decide that action shall not be taken in Sweden under Swedish law if guardianship is under consideration in the country of domicile.

Applicable Law

Wherever a Swedish court decides a case concerning guardianship and interdiction or re-establishment of capacity, it applies Swedish law except that the *lex patriae* governs the question whether there is need for a guardian for a minor.

Recognition. Capacity

Recognition a of foreign decision concerning interdiction or the appointment of a guardian means that the limitations imposed with

[60] Germany, Hungary, Italy, Netherlands, Portugal and Rumania.

[61] It is assumed that the special statute relating to ch. 5 will soon be repealed.

[62] 1915 *N.J.A.* 395.

[63] 1915 *N.J.A.* 321.

respect to capacity are regarded as valid in Sweden, and that the powers of the appointed guardian must be respected. If, on the other hand, a foreign decision cannot be recognized, it is to be regarded in Sweden as nonexistent. These principles are expressed in the Act of 1904 which provides that the effects of the appointment of a guardian and of interdiction shall be governed by the law of the country where guardianship was established.[64] This law would normally be identical to the *lex patriae* of the person under guardianship. However, guardianship can exceptionally be arranged for a Swedish citizen in the country of his domicile, and a Swedish court may have to decide questions of the kind just mentioned with respect to a foreigner for whom guardianship has been established in a country other than that to which he belongs as a citizen. The statutory provision therefore makes possible the determination of capacity by another law than the *lex patriae* when a guardian has been appointed, while the *lex patriae* would always apply with respect to an infant for whom no guardian has been appointed.[65]

Which foreign decisions concerning guardianship are recognized in Sweden?[66] A foreign decision will always be recognized if taken by an authority in the country to which the *propositus* belonged as a citizen; in most such cases it can be assumed that the *lex fori* was applied. A decision concerning a foreign citizen taken by an authority in his country of domicile, applying the *lex patriae* with respect to the grounds for the decision, would be recognized, and the same would

[64] The Act includes some protective rules which make a contract relating to property matters valid, if concluded in Sweden by a person under guardianship with a party who did not know, or did not have reason to know, of the lack in capacity. Special rules apply to bills of exchange and checks since Sweden is a party to the 1930 Geneva conventions on negotiable documents.

[65] According to the Act, however, the *lex patriae* shall always determine the question whether there is a need to appoint a guardian for a minor. For instance, if a person has been supplied with a guardian in country X where people attain majority at the age of 23, but his *lex patriae* provides for majority at the age of 21, no need for a guardian exists. (A possible question of interdiction must be dealt with separately.) The consequence seems to be that the person concerned should in Sweden be regarded as having reached majority even if the foreign appointment of a guardian has not been formally repealed. But the matter is not settled.

[66] The general rules apply to Swiss decisions as the convention between Sweden and Switzerland excludes "*décisions rendues en matière de tutelle et d'interdiction.*"

probably also be the case where the *lex fori* was applied instead of the *lex patriae*. A foreign decision concerning a Swedish citizen taken by an authority in his country of domicile will be recognized in the sense that in Sweden the consequences of the decision will be those prescribed by the law of the foreign country, unless nullified by a Swedish decision to appoint a guardian or re-establish capacity.[67] Moreover, the Act might be construed to mean that recognition of a foreign decision concerning a Swede presupposes that a Swedish court has decided that guardianship shall not be established under Swedish law.

H. INHERITANCE

Administration of a decedent's estate by an administrator appointed by a court is compulsory in Sweden only in a limited number of situations. Therefore, the "heirs," broadly interpreted, may themselves settle an estate. The courts can, however, and must in some cases, appoint an administrator or executor. In all cases the result of the settlement or administration is a document providing for the final distribution of the estate. If the "heirs" disagree concerning the distribution, the dispute may be brought to a court.

Conflict rules relating to the law of succession and the administration of decedents' estates are to be found in the Act of 1937 referred to many times in the previous chapters. The Act is based on the principle of nationality with respect to succession, but with respect to administration the domicile is of equal importance. The rules express the principle that administration in Sweden covers all the assets of the decedent, even those located abroad. But this claim can, of course, not always be maintained, as in other countries different rules apply and the Swedish claims may not be recognized.

Jurisdiction

Chapter 2:10 of the Act of 1937 provides that disputes concerning succession, wills and the claims of a surviving spouse against the dece-

[67] It might be argued that the foreign decision should be recognized in Sweden only if the foreign authority had applied the *lex patriae* (Swedish law) with respect to the grounds for the appointment of a guardian and interdiction. Cf. Walin *op.cit.*, p. 553. "The national test," however, strictly applied would speak against such arguments.

dent's estate belong to Swedish jurisdiction if the decedent was a Swedish citizen or was domiciled in Sweden. Jurisdiction shall also be entertained in a dispute concerning succession to property located in Sweden. In the exceptional case where assets have been transmitted to an administrator abroad there is no Swedish jurisdiction.

If a person was a Swedish citizen at the time of death or had domicile in Sweden, his estate shall be administered in accordance with the procedures of Swedish law, and the administration shall in principle apply to all assets in Sweden or abroad.[68] However, if the decedent was a national of a foreign country, administration may, if the interested parties agree, be transferred from Sweden to the decedent's home country at the stage when all debts have been paid.[69] If a national of a foreign country domiciled outside Sweden at his death has assets in Sweden, administration may be established in Sweden with respect to those assets and "Swedish" debts. In this case also, administration may be transferred to the home country for effecting distribution.[70]

Applicable law of Inheritance

Chapter 1 of the Act contains choice of law rules; a few are also to be found in chapter 2. The *lex patriae* of the decedent at the time of death governs the right of succession, i.e. the distribution of the estate (sec. 1), and this rule, with very special exceptions, also applies to imovables.[71] One exception to section 1 provides that assets in Sweden belonging to the estate of a deceased foreigner shall be assigned to the Swedish State if by applying the *lex patrie* they would become the property of a foreign state or a municipality or a public foundation or institution in a foreign state. The *lex patriae* also governs the question whether an heir can claim support from the estate (sec. 1). Questions concerning the effect of arrangements *mortis causa,* e.g. contracts, gifts, etc., between the decedent and his heirs are governed by the *lex patriae* of the decedent at the time the arrangement was made (secs. 7 and 8).[72]

[68] Cf. 1933 *N.J.A.* 514; 1915 *N.J.A.* 395.
[69] A similar rule applies to Swedish citizens with domicile abroad.
[70] Cf. 1957 *N.J.A.* 441.
[71] Sec. 2. Cf. 1919 *N.J.A.* 546.
[72] Cf. 1934 *N.J.A.* 320.

The choice of law rules concerning wills are contained in chapter 1. The form of wills is governed either by the *lex loci actus* or by the *lex patriae* of the testator at the time when the will was made or revoked (sec. 4). The same *lex patriae* governs questions concerning testamentary capacity (sec. 3). The rule is qualified by a provision in the same section which makes revocation of a will valid in Sweden in those cases where revocation was permissible according to the *lex patriae* at the time of the execution even though revocation was not permissible under the *lex patriae* at the time of the act of revocation. The *lex patriae* at the time of execution or revocation also governs questions of invalidity due to lunacy, undue influence, mistake etc. The question whether or not a will is valid according to rules relating to the substantive requirements of wills, for instance concerning the testator's power of disposing of his property, is governed by the *lex patriae* of the decedent at the time of death (sec. 5). With respect to immovables, however, a will in favour of a person not born will not be regarded as valid if it is not valid under the *lex rei sitae*.

Chapter 2 of the Act contains in section 7 a choice of law rule, i.e., that Swedish law shall apply to questions concerning liability for the debts of the estate. However, if the administration in Sweden concerns the property in Sweden of a foreigner domiciled abroad such debts are considered only where the creditor is Swedish or domiciled in Sweden. Swedish law also governs the limitation on inheritance rights (sec. 8).

Recognition

Provisions concerning recognition are included in sections 11—13 of the Act. Distribution abroad by a public authority, an appointed administrator or a court, if formally valid (sec. 11), will according to to section 12 be recognized in Sweden under the following main conditions:[73]

(i) that the decedent was at national of or domiciled in the country where distribution was made;

(ii) that distribution did not concern property which was subject to administration in Sweden or which should have been distributed by administration in Sweden;

[73] The question of recognition of judgments *in absentia* has been left out.

(iii) that distribution is final;

(iv) that distribution was governed by a law the provisions of which are not contrary to the substantive rules referred to by the choice of law rules contained in chapter 1 of the Swedish Act of 1937;

(v) that the distribution effected is not contrary to *ordre public;* The foreign distribution decree may be enforced in Sweden on the condition of an *exequatur* by the Stockholm Court of Appeal (sec. 13).

§ 15. Property Law

A few words must be said in order to explain the use of the term "property law" in the heading of this paragraph as it does not corresponds to English terminological usage. In contemporary Swedish legal writing private law is generally divided into two main branches of law: family law and property law *(förmögenhetsrätt)*. "Family law," broadly used, includes the law of inheritance, but the latter is sometimes regarded as a third branch of private law. Property relations between spouses belong to the field of family law.

Earlier, "property law" was treated as including two main sub-branches: *obligationsrätt,* i.e., the law of obligations and *sakrätt,* the latter comprising all rules relating to proprietary rights *in rem,* that is rights available against persons generally. At present, a Swedish textbook on "property law" will deal with a number of subjects, such as contracts in general, sales, insurance, securities, agency, gifts etc., and for each subject both rights *in personam* and rights *in rem* will be discussed. In other words, questions concerning rights *in rem,* especially relations to third parties, will be dealt with by reference to special rules which govern them but which are greatly influenced by the particular rules relating to the various types of situations (sales, agency, etc.) which create rights *in personam*. This manner of presenting the rules of Swedish property law corresponds to changes which have gradually occurred in the various substantive rules of private law. These changes make it unrealistic to present Swedish conflict rules in the field of "property law" under such traditional headings as *statuta personalia* and *statuta realia,* respectively.

The discussion of conflict solution below begins with "the proper law" which will mainly concern the general part of the law of contracts. The application of the doctrine of the proper law is wide and we are using the term contract in a comparatively extensive sense, deviating thereby, perhaps, from English terminology. In fact, the application of conflict rules other than the proper law, for instance the *lex loci delicti commissi* or the *lex rei sitae* seems to be exceptional in the field of property relations. A comprehensive presentation of the Swedish conflict rules would, of course, have to deal with a number of specialized forms of contracts and other specific property relations which are omitted in this resumé. Companies and bankruptcy, for instance, are such subjects; they give rise to problems of a complex nature. Other examples are to be found in areas where economic relations are governed in part by rules laid down in treaties, e.g. relating to negotiable instruments, copyright, patents, trade marks, transportation of goods and persons. It must be mentioned, however, that in such areas also the doctrine of the proper law plays an important role.

A résumé of legal rules relating to conflict cases in the field of property law is hampered by the fact that in Sweden very few cases exist from which conclusions can be drawn; at the same time statutory provisions are extremely scarce (above pp. 28 f.). The judge may find himself in a situation where he has to "make" a conflict rule, basing himself on the nature of the dispute and its objects, and on whatever recommendations he can find in legal writing. The method used by the judge is therefore of primary interest; the legal rules remain to a large extent elusive. Problems relating to judicial methods in conflict cases have been discussed in previous chapters of this book.[74] The following pages contain a summary of that discussion as it relates to property law and a brief description of the present law in Sweden in so far as it can be ascertained.

A. THE PROPER LAW

Swedish case-law before 1937 does not give any clear indication of the law which should govern disputes concerning contracts. In early days the *lex loci contractus* was sometimes applied[76], while in some

[74] See for instance pp. 108 f. and 128 ("centre of gravity method"); pp. 62 f., 140, 216 f. and 224 f. (choice of law clause).

[75] Cf. Ole Lando, *Kontraktstatuttet*, København 1962, with an extensive summary in English.

[76] For instance in 1879 *N.J.A.* 185; 1904 *N.J.A.* 384.

cases the choice of law issue was not noticed[77]. A case from 1912 was in favour of the *lex domicilii debitoris.*[78] In 1937, however, the Supreme Court decided a case between a Swedish insurance company and the Swedish State concerning bonds issued by the Swedish State on the American market; the bonds were found to be subject to the United States Joint Resolution of 1933 concerning gold clauses in the law of the state of New York.[79] This decision is now looked upon as authority for the proper law of the contract under the Swedish conflict of laws: a) the law chosen by the parties, and, in the absence of such a choice, b) the law of the country with which the contract is most closely connected ("the centre of gravity method" or "the individualizing method"). However, by the Act on international sales of movables, which was adopted in 1964 and has entered into force, the rules embodied in the 1951 Hague Convention on the international sales of movables apply in Sweden. This means that when the parties to an "international" contract have not agreed on a choice of law the *lex causae* is normally the law of the country where the seller was domiciled at the time when the received the order.

The Choice of Law Clause

In its decision of 1937 (1937 *N.J.A.* 1) the Supreme Court stated that the bonds in question did not contain any choice of law clause, nor anything else which could be interpreted as expressing any intention as to the choice of law. In consequence, the choice of the proper law had to be made by weighing against each other the various objective elements which might point in one direction or the other, that is, towards Swedish law or the law of the state of New York.

From this statement the conclusion has been drawn that the court would have bowed to a choice of law clause if included in the bonds, that a tacit (but not merely presumed or hypothetical) expression of intention as to the applicable law would have been accepted, but that in the absence of such a choice the proper law must be found by an "objective" scrutiny of all facts present. In Swedish legal writing it is generally accepted that the express intention of the parties determines

77 For instance 1911 *N.J.A.* 467.

78 1912 *N.J.A.* 231. Cf. 1930 *N.J.A.* 507.

79 1937 *N.J.A.* 1. Cf. 1937 *N.J.A.* 17; 1939 *N.J.A.* 247; 1942 *N.J.A.* p. 389; 1956 *N.J.A.* 150.

the proper law. It may even be said that an unwritten choice of law rule exists to the effect that the will of the parties constitutes the connecting factor.[80]

There are, however, in all legal systems where the principle of party autonomy is accepted, some limitations on the exercise of this autonomy. The Supreme Court decision of 1937 has nothing to say in this respect. In Swedish legal writing it is generally held that a contract must have a certain connection with the legal system chosen. Professor Nial has argued that this connection must be of considerable strength not only in itself but also as compared to connections with other legal systems,[81] but not all writers demand so much.[82] In Scandinavian legal writing emphazis has been put on what commercial interests demand, a point of view which leads to the acceptance in principle of the choice of law clause; the only exceptions occur in cases where the clause appears to be meaningless or frivolous.[83] This issue is, however, now settled in Swedish law at least for the field where the liberal rules from the 1951 Hague Convention apply.

The Individualizing Method

In Swedish legal writing there is strong resistance to the search for a presumed or hypothetical intention of the parties in the absence of a real intention, explicitly expressed or implied. Support for this view is sought in the absence from the 1937 Supreme Court decisions of any mention of a possible presumed intention.[84] Writers look upon the doctrine of the presumed intention as fictitious and recommend instead a direct search for the proper law by finding the "centre of gravity" of the legal relations concerned; this is the "individualizing method."

In principle the search for the "centre of gravity" should be conducted without prejudice in favour of any one of the laws which, as it were, present themselves for possible application. It seems, at least to the present author, that one should not at the beginning of the search rely on any presumptions or *prima facie* rules. Only at the stage when the weighing of the various connecting factors has failed

[80] Cf. Eek in 13 *American Journal of Comparative Law* (1964), pp. 173 ff.
[81] Nial, p. 19.
[82] Karlgren, p. 95.
[83] Cf. above pp. 216 f.
[84] Cf. however 1941 *N.J.A.* 350.

to give result, should the judge rely in "presumptions."[85] These are in Swedish legal writing called "in dubio rules" which indicates that they do not operate *prima facie* but are brought into function not at the beginning but at the end of the process of choosing the proper law. When, however, in-dubio-rules become well established by case law or commercial practice or by strong support in legal writing, they tend gradually to assume the role of *prima facie* rules and to create a certain amount of predictability (cf. above pp. 108 f.).

In Swedish legal writing, partly supported by case law, various in dubio rules are recommended; they are generally adapted to the type of legal relationship concerned. With respect to sales of goods, for instance, the in dubio rule is said to point to the *lex domicilii* of the seller. For unilateral obligations such as surety[86] or loans the in dubio rule points to the *lex domicilii debitoris.* Unilateral contracts such as gifts or donations would in dubio be governed by the *lex patriae* of the donor[87], contracts for labour and service by the law of the country where the work is performed,[88] mass bargaining by the law of the enterprise, transactions at markets, fairs and auctions by the *lex loci actus,* etc.

The Scope of the Proper Law

As already indicated the methods just outlined for finding the proper law may extend further within the field of property law than to the law of contract, narrowly defined. The existence of fixed rules such as those referring to the *lex rei sitae* appears to be exceptional.[89]

The scope of the proper law is limited, however, with respect to some matters incidental to a contract. Formalities are in the first instance governed by the law of the contract. But in accordance with the old rule *locus regit actum,* a contract will as a rule be regarded as valid if the formal requirements of the *lex loci contractus* have been followed, even where the demands of the law of the contract are different or more severe. (Cf. above pp. 123 f.). Questions concerning capacity in general are governed by the *lex patriae.* Questions con-

85 Cf. Knoph in *T.f.R.* 1938, pp. 46 ff.

86 Cf. 1912 *N.J.A.* 231.

87 Cf. 1934 *N.J.A.* 320.

88 Cf. 1911 *N.J.A.* 467.

89 Special rules refer to conflict problems in the field of maritime law. See for instance Stig Jägerskiöld, *Arkiv for Sjørett,* Tome 2, 1954 pp. 8 ff.

cerning the mode of payment are governed by the law of the place of performance (cf. above pp. 135 f.), etc.[90]

B. TORTS

Torts whether committed by fault, that is intentionally or negligently, or without fault, are governed by the law of the place where the alleged tort occurred *(lex loci delicti commissi)*. This rule is generally accepted in Swedish legal writing and supported by case law.[91] The substantive rules of the *lex loci* govern the rights and liabilities of the parties including both the prerequisites and the evaluation of liability and the assessment of damages. As the only source of the obligation for tort, the *lex loci* must be assumed also to govern capacity to commit tort.

The question has been raised, however, whether the "individualizing method" might not in the future extend its field of application to torts.[92] Such a development might be brought about by increasingly characterizing the basis of certain actions as contractual rather than as tortious liability.[93] But it may at the same time be assumed that the *lex loci* would not be applied in certain cases closely connected to the *lex fori,* for instance in a case where a Swedish citizen has caused damage to another Swedish citizen and the place of the wrong is outside Sweden.

C. LEX REI SITAE

Real Property

Whether a thing is movable or immovable is determined by application of the law of the country where the thing is located (the *lex rei sitae*). All incidents to a thing classified as an immovable except the general capacity of persons are subject to the *lex situs* of the immovable. This law, in other words, applies also to the relations between the parties to a contract and it has been assumed that as a consequence a choice of law clause contained in a contract concerning

[90] See further Nial, pp. 46 ff. and 54 f. Cf. also 1928 *N.J.A.* 252; 1930 *N.J.A.* 507; 1951 *N.J.A.* 444 and 1952 *N.J.A.* 41 and 382.

[91] 1932 *N.J.A.*, 267; 1933 *N.J.A.*, 364; 1935 *N.J.A.*, 585; 1936 *N.J.A.*, 291.

[92] Karlgren p. 111.

[93] See concerning this problem Strömholm, pp. 144 ff. and Eek in *Festskrift til Borum,* pp. 127 ff.

the sale of real property and referring to another law than the *lex situs,* is valid only in so far as allowed by that law.[94]

The principle of *locus regit actum* does not extend to contracts concerning real property.

It should be added that Swedish courts will only exceptionally entertain jurisdiction in cases relating to real property abroad.[95]

Movables

The field of application of the *lex rei sitae* to movables is limited to questions concerning rights *in rem,* but not all questions relating to the acquisition and transfer of title to movables are governed by the *lex situs.* Issues between the parties to a transfer, in the case, for *lex situs.* Issues between the parties to a transfer, for instance, in the case of a sale or a mortgage, will be governed by the proper law of the contract.

Consequently, it does not seem correct to state that, under the present Swedish conflict of laws, disputes concerning rights *in rem* are governed by the *lex rei sitae,* or that this law governs the aquisition and transfer of movables in general. The position of the Swedish law is, rather, that while the proper law of the contract governs the relations between the parties, the *lex rei sitae* applies to the relations between one of the parties and third persons. In addition, the *lex rei sitae* applies to some special questions concerning title to property, for instance, in the case of property found. Professor Nial, accordingly, in his textbook on Swedish international property law, deals separately with specific types of situations where the *lex rei sitae* applies: the protection of the buyer against the creditors of the seller, the protection of the seller against the creditors of the buyer, the divestment of title in favour of third parties who have acquired goods *bona fide* from holders of possession without a title, etc.[96]

The few Swedish cases relating to the application of the *lex rei sitae* are not significant.[97] Unsettled questions concern, *inter alia,* the applicable law with respect to *res in transitu* and the *situs* of intangible movables.

[94] Nial, p. 81.
[95] Cf. above pp. 74 f. and 80 f., and 1923 *N.J.A.* 669; 1929 *N.J.A.* 466.
[96] Nial, pp. 81. *Vide* also Nial in *Recueil.* 1960, pp. 265 ff. and *Liber amicorum,* pp. 155 ff.
[97] 1895 *N.J.A.* 208; 1931 *N.J.A.* 172.

Chapter V
Conflict Avoidance

§ 16. An Excursus

Our résumé of conflict rules in the field of Swedish international property law was extremely brief, and the reason is that material in the form of court decisions is scarce. This part of the law appears to be undeveloped. But the scarcity of court decisions is at least partly explained by the fact that more and more attention is devoted today to conflict avoidance. Efforts are made to avoid, by various means situations where courts have to decide whether a dispute shall be settled by rules chosen from one or another of several legal systems.

It is characteristic of international civil actions that they proceed by two successive stages. The first question—apart from that of the jurisdiction of the court, which arises in all cases—concerns the applicable substantive law, i.e. the so-called conflict of laws. Once that has been answered, the action enters a second phase which concerns the construction and application of the chosen substantive rules. A person has, for example, bought a consignment of goods abroad, which turns out to be faulty, whereupon he engages in a dispute with the vendor on the quality of the goods and the vendor's promises in this respect. It is perhaps only when the matter has come to court that the buyer discovers that in the vendor's home country the case might be decided under other substantive rules than those upon which the buyer has based his claim. Thus, in the first stage of the action, he has to argue with the vendor the question of the applicable law, and the solution of that conflict influences the outcome of the action as a whole, although several disputed elements may remain after "the conflict of laws" has been resolved. Sometimes, however, the solution of this conflict exhausts the issues in the case. The method followed by the judge when solving a "conflict of laws", the subject of the preceding chapters of this work and of most books on private international law, has been described as the "clinical" method.[98] Its purpose is to find the best possible solution of the acute case at bar. This is a typical judicial task. But conflict rules may also be considered from another point of view: that of counsel. The latter asks himself the question how, on the basis of the conflict rules of the countries concerned (and with knowledge of their substantive law), he should plan a contemplated transaction so that no doubt can conceivably arise as to the legal system under which any possible future dispute with regard to the transaction shall be decided. This is the "preventive" method in private international law, which has the purpose of avoiding law conflicts ("conflict avoidance").

The rules and principles which characterize the "clinical" method are not wholly satisfactory. Different countries apply different jurisdictional rules and this occasionally makes it possible for a clever party to an international business affair to choose the *forum* of an action, and thereby, also, the conflict rules which will be applied in the choice of law; for conflict rules also vary from one legal system to another. We have found that even identical conflict rules in two countries do not always produce the same result in the choice of the substantive law regardless of the country in which the action is brought. If, for example, a rule has been agreed upon, according to which actions concerning international sales of goods shall be governed by the law of the vendor's domicile, the courts of the various countries may nevertheless have different opinions on the construction of the expressions "international sales of goods" or "the vendor's domicile." The relatively high degree of uncertainty about the outcome of a possible conflict of laws makes measures for conflict avoidance both desirable from the private point of view and beneficial to the preservation of confidence in the judicial process. Planning for the purpose of conflict avoidance has now become increasingly common. For obvious reasons, the scope for such planning in the field of family law is limited, although it is not wholly unknown in that branch of the law. In

[98] "In the conflict of laws, two approaches to the disposal of a conflict problem are possible: the preventive method of conflict avoidance and the clinical method of conflict solution." Schmitthoff in *Law and Contemporary Problems*, 1956, p. 429.

contract and property, on the other hand, and particularly within the domain of international big business, measures for conflict avoidance have been developed to such a point that future works on international contracts and property rights are likely to deal principally with such measures, while the traditional conflict problems are most likely to arise in connection with incidental legal transactions of smaller economic importance. It is not only the legal advisers of big business who plan for conflict avoidance. This purpose is also pursued through legislative measures, both internal and international, above all these for the unification of private law. National legislatures, as well as judges, may further promote conflict avoidance by a liberal attitude to the validity of choice of law by the parties. Certain international bodies have contributed to the endeavours towards conflict avoidance by elaborating standard contracts and by promoting the development of private arbitration agreements. In Swedish legal writing, these questions seem to have received relatively little attention as part of the conflict of laws. The survey given in the present work is an incomplete summary, an excursus which does not attempt a systematic analysis of the various individual problems. An important contribution to the study of the problem of conflict avoidance is made by papers on the preventive law of conflicts collected in vol. 21 (1956) of *Law and Contemporary Problems*.[99]

The following survey deals first with a number of public legislative measures. Subsequently, we shall indicate some different types of arrangements which may be undertaken by private parties on the basis of existing legislation, possibly with recourse also to the "services" of international institutions. The question of arbitral awards has been singled out for specal treatment. It is only natural that a particular interest in conflict avoidance has developed in those countries where private enterprise prevails. However, similar problems arise also in countries with socialist economic systems; therefore, we shall give a little attention to the legal regulation of international trade in the European communist states.

[99] Notice also the survey of these problems given by Vallindas in *T.f.R.* 1960, pp. 134 ff., Schmitthoff in *Current Law and Social Problems* 1961, pp. 129 ff. and *Proceedings of the American Society of International Law*, Washington, 1960, pp. 48 ff.

10 — 637386. Eek

A. PUBLIC LEGISLATIVE MEASURES

Uniform Law

If the national legal systems in two different countries, A and B, have the same substantive rules in a certain field of law, a court in A or B has no reason for undertaking a choice of law in an action within that field as long as the legal system of a third country is not involved. Instead conflicts are avoided by applying uniform rules of private law. This has been the case in Scandinavia. As the substantive rules of one field of law after another have become identical or at least very close to each other, law conflicts have been avoided between the Nordic countries. In a case arising in Sweden, it would not be really necessary to discuss the question of the applicable Nordic law on the sale of goods, but if, for example, German law should also claim to be applicable, a conflict would have materialized. Partial conflict avoidance has been achieved where states in other parts of the world have attained legal unity or a close legal affinity within the field of private law. Illustrations are furnished by the cooperation between the Benelux countries and within South America, the reception of the French civil code in other countries, e.g. in Asia, and the endeavours to bring about legal unity on the part of the states of the United States of America through the preparation of unofficial drafts of "uniform acts".

The importance of regional unification measures should not be underestimated as the intercourse between countries comprising a particular geographical or political region may well represent a high proportion of the total international business of these countries. In spite of such measures, the possibility of law conflicts remains, however. It would be completely eliminated only if one single system of private law, comprising all the states of the earth, were achieved. It is obvious that the need for uniform law is most strongly felt within special fields of law, where wide-spread international connections are natural. In these fields the common interests of all states, or a majority of them, in having uniform regulations, is manifest, and to the extent that this is achieved, the number of potential legal conflicts is materially reduced. It is natural, therefore, that the endeavours towards unification commenced, and have been crowned with the greatest success, in the fields of copyright, industrial property, and carriage of goods. In the first two branches of law mentioned, cooperation started with the Paris convention on industrial property in 1883 and the Berne convention on copyright in 1886; it has been carried on energetically ever since. A multilateral treaty on carriage by rail was concluded at Berne in 1890. In the field of maritime law, conventions on collisions at sea, etc. were adopted in 1910, and others have followed. Cooperation in air law began with a convention concluded in Warsaw in 1929. A complete unification of private law rules has not been achieved within these fields of law, and the convention technique has its peculiarities, particularly in copyright and industrial property. Nor have all the states of the world taken part in this cooperation. Its results are considerable, however. It is possible that progress in other fields of the law could be promoted by investigation of the legislative techniques which have been developed in the special areas mentiond.

The problems of international payments and of international big business are found also to demand uniform rules.[100] The needed uniformity has been achieved to some extent by the conventions of 1930 and 1931 on uniform laws concerning bills of exchange and cheques.

> Further urgent projects of unification have been studied and elaborated by the International Institute for the Unification of Private Law, which began its work in 1928, under the auspices of the League of Nations. The Institute has prepared a draft for a uniform law on international sales of movables (sales of goods), a matter on which the need for a uniform law is obvious. Among the drafts elaborated by the Rome Institute, mention should also be made of draft conventions containing rules on such contracts of carriage as have not already been dealt with in international agreements (carriage by road, carriage of goods on territorial waters and combined transport).[101] Since 1948, the Institute has issued a series of *Annuaires* with continuous information about the endeavours towards uniform private law.

[100] Cf. Matteucci in *J.B.L.* 1960, pp. 137 ff.

[101] *Vide* on this topic Prodromidès in *Liber amicorum*, pp. 180 ff. On the accession of Sweden to the convention on road transport elaborated in 1956 by the E.C.E., *vide Sv.J.T.* 1961, p. 150.

Since the creation of the Rome Institute, a discussion of some intensity has been carried on in conflict writing about the methods and the procedure which should preferably be adopted for the realization of uniform law.[102] The method of comparative legal research, which is a prerequisite for uniform legislation, has attracted considerable interest. In the course of time, however, the centre of gravity in this discussion has moved towards questions concerning the application and construction of uniform legal rules. The increasingly intimate economic cooperation in Western Europe has become a strong impetus in this development, since that cooperation necessitates a harmonization of the legal systems of the participating countries.

International Corporations

Attempts have been made to create supernational public enterprises or corporations intended to operate under their own body of international rules. Certain intergovernmental bodies within the United Nations system have this character to some extent, e.g. the *International Bank for Reconstruction and Development* in Washington, which is a specialized agency of the United Nations, and the associated *International Finance Corporation*. The laws under which such bodies operate are laid down in international instruments; special agreements, furthermore, are needed to create rules outside national legal systems to govern their relations with individual countries or private enterprises.

As one of the first corporations of a partly international character, may be mentioned the *Bank for International Settlements* in Basle; its members are the central banks of European states. The corporation was created by a convention in the Hague in 1930, and subsequently an agreement was concluded between the participating states and Switzerland, where the bank was to have its domicile. Through the agreement, the bank was granted a special position from the point of view of company law, but it should nevertheless be considered as a Swiss juridical person and it is registered in Switzerland. As a further illustration of existing "international"

[102] *Vide* the footnotes of Vallinda's paper in *T.f.R.* 1960 (above, note 99).

enterprises, mention should be made of the *Scandinavian Airlines System* (SAS) which was created by a cooperation agreement between the participating companies.[103] They included an arbitration clause in the agreement for settling disputes between them.[104] *Eurofima* and *Eurochemic* are enterprises which have been granted certain privileges in multilateral conventions but which have not been wholly exempted from the company law of the countries of incorporation (Switzerland and Belgium respectively).[105]

Several efforts have been made to devise a type of international company, governed by its own substantive law, which would apply in all actions to which the company was a party. So far, these attempts have not been successful.[106] The Council of Europe, in particular, has busied itself with this problem, without managing to solve it, however. Reports on its studies were published in 1948 and

[103] *Vide Royal Proposition* No. 260, 1950.

[104] Sec. 17 of the cooperation agreement reads as follows:

"1. Disputes concerning the construction or application of this agreement shall not be brought before the courts of justice but shall be referred to arbitrators whose decision shall be final.

2. If the parties cannot agree upon the choice of arbitrator or arbitrators for the settling of the dispute, it shall be decided by an arbitration board composed of three arbitrators, one of whom is appointed by the President of the Supreme Court of Denmark, one by the Justiciar of the Supreme Court of Norway and one by the President of the Supreme Court of Sweden.

3. The board elects its chairman and decides upon the procedure to be adopted, including the place where the board shall have its seat and the question what legal rules from the three countries shall be applied. It is incumbent upon the board to render its award in such form that it can be enforced against the losing party under that party's national law." On the SAS, *vide* further *Arkiv for Luftrett* 1961, pp. 199 ff.

[105] On these and similar enterprises, *vide* Adam, *Les établissements publics internationaux,* Paris 1957, and Seidl-Hohenveldern in *J.B.L.* 1959, pp. 120 ff. *Eurofima* is also described in a most interesting memorandum published by the Council of Europe, *International public enterprises in industry and commerce,* 1957. It also contains accounts of the *Bank for International Settlements,* the Franco-Swiss public enterprise *Aéroport de Bâle-Mulhouse* and two companies incorporated in Belgium, *Interfrigo* with various national railway companies as shareholders and *La Compagnie Internationale des Wagons-Lits et des Grands Express Européens.* The convention which is the legal basis of Eurochemic is published in *Clunet* 1961, pp. 250 ff. Cf. on *Eurofima, Royal Proposition* No. 211, 1955, and on *Eurochemic* No. 59, 1958, and 186, 1959.

[106] *Vide* Seidl-Hohenveldern, *op.cit.,* and Vallindas in *Festschrift Schätzel,* 1960, pp. 495 ff.

1952 by the International Law Association, containing outlines of statutes for international "chartered companies." These should be created by multilateral conventions containing detailed rules on all questions concerning these enterprises and their operation, so that there should be no need to resort to national rules for the purpose of settling disputes involving these enterprises. The idea is unrealistic.[107] Such regulations could never be so complete that there would be no need for application of supplementary rules from any national legal system. Nor can it be assumed that the courts of countries which were not parties to the convention upon which the corporation was based would always apply the corporation's "own" law in relation to third parties. The subject has not been exhaustively dealt with, however. It is possible that certain forms of international enterprise can be created within the framevork of a group of legal systems which have been gradually unified, and tendencies in that direction are already visible in the European Economic Community.[108]

B. MEASURES BY PRIVATE PARTIES

Standard Contracts

It has become increasingly common for large enterprises to indicate —often on printed forms—the uniform conditions on which they are willing to conclude contracts.[109] It is also usual for organizations

[107] Cf. Batiffol in *Law and Contemporary Problems*, 1956, p. 579. However, new light on the subject may be thrown by C. Wilfred Jenks in his forthcoming study on "Corporate Personality for International Purposes."

[108] *Vide* Seidl-Hohenveldern, *op.cit.*, pp. 127 f. on the German *Internationale Mosel-Gesellschaft G.m.b.H.* and the Franco-German *Union charbonnière Rhénane;* ibid., p. 125 on the legal possibility of special enterprises within the *Euratom,* which is part of the European Community. Cf. also Calon in *Clunet* 1961, pp. 694 ff.

[109] On this habit in Swedish law, *vide* Grönfors in *Juridikens källmaterial* (at pp. 126 ff.) and in *Rättsvetenskapliga studier ägnade minnet av Phillips Hult* (at pp. 148 ff.). Cf. also Nial in *Minnesskrift,* pp. 195 ff. and Salmonson in *Orientering kring exportproblemen,* 1945, pp. 242 ff. We can also refer to the discussion at the twenty-first Inter-Nordic lawyers' meeting in Helsingfors (in *Förhandlingarna å det tjugoförsta nordiska juristmötet i Helsingfors,* 1957, pp. 152 ff.) on the basis of the work *Verkan av avtalsklausuler i standardformulär* by C. Olsson.

representing a number of enterprises in the same branch of industry to lay down such conditions. The individual contracts, therefore, conform to a standard. Such contracts have a particular importance for international intercourse. In so far as freedom of contract is recognized by countries in which litigation arises over a particular transaction, the detailed substantive provisions of the contract normally decide the outcome of the action. The possibility that a conflict of law issue will arise is limited by the detailed nature of the standard contract.[110] In the international field these contracts are often drafted with the explicit purpose of avoiding a conflict of law, since in the event of a conflict its solution could mean for either party submission to foreign rules, the import of which might be difficult to assess beforehand. Some of the international standard contracts while originally drawn up by a particular enterprise or organization of enterprises for their own use, have gained such general recognition that they are used without exception by enterprises of all countries to regulate the kind of transaction to which they are applicable.

International standard contracts exist in great number and embrace most branches of economic life. Some of them are drafted unilaterally by big enterprises or by branch organizations. Others are the result of the work of international bodies. Thus the so-called York-Antwerp rules (1950) were given their present form by the International Law Association; forms for charter-parties and bills of lading usually contain a clause to the effect that average contributions shall be calculated in accordance with these rules. In 1953, the International Chamber of Commerce elaborated a number of rules for the construction of trade terms, *Incoterms,* to which parties often refer in their contracts. In so far as a standard contract has been formulated by a big company, by an organization representing a branch of industry or in a particular country which holds a predominant position in the branch of business concerned, there is always a risk of

[110] The case 1954 *N.J.A.* 573 was decided on the basis of a certain construction of a standard charter-party, *China Clay Association Approved Form of Charter Party,* which, according to the report of the case, was used without exception for transport of china clay. The "law conflict" which was visible in the case was therefore not decisive for the issue. The parties were a Swedish freighter and a carrier domiciled in Norway. The transport had been performed by a Norwegian ship and the voyage had begun in England and ended at Gothenburg.

one-sidedness, that the stronger party will be favoured or that special emphasis will be put on purely national customs and usages. A very remarkable contribution towards the creation of impartial international standard contracts has been made, in the postwar years, by the United Nations Economic Commission for Europe.[111] This has been particularly important for the promotion of trade between Eastern and Western Europe; the Eastern States, which had earlier considered the contract forms of the West with some suspicion, have contributed to the work of the Commission towards the creation of "white"—i.e. neutral—contracts. The forms embody general conditions for the delivery of machines, rules on the mounting of delivered machinery and general conditions for the delivery of wood, citrus fruits, coal, corn and potatoes. Contract forms, which are identified by numbers to which the parties can refer in their individual contracts, are sold to business men.[112]

Choice of Law by the Parties and Submission to Certain Courts

The conclusion of an international contract upon the conditions set out in a form with detailed standard rules does not in itself exclude the possibility of conflicts of law. It is impossible to foresee all problems, and questions relating to the validity of the contract are always left open. It is usual that standard contracts contain choice of law clauses and prorogation clauses submitting disputes to a selected forum; arbitration clauses belong to the latter category.[113] These two kinds of clauses have different purposes and should be carefully distinguished. The choice of law clause only indicates the applicable law and does not include any agreement to the effect that actions arising out of the contract shall be brought within a determined jurisdiction or by a determined court or board of arbitra-

[111] *Vide* Benjamin in *J.B.L.* 1961, pp. 113 ff.

[112] *Vide* Kopelmanas in *Annuaire français de droit international,* 1955, pp. 370 ff., and Tunc in *Revue internationale de droit comparé,* 1960, pp. 108 ff.

[113] Clauses on submission to the courts of certain countries in the law of carriage by sea are treated in great detail by Siesby in *Arkiv for Sjorett* 1960, pp. 313 ff. The survey in the main work by Dennemark should also be observed.—Other arrangements for the purpose of conflict avoidance which are not treated here are clauses on payment by letter of credit or the creation of subsidiaries abroad. On such "total localization devices," *vide* Schmitthoff in *Law and Contemporary Problems,* 1956, pp. 446 ff.

tors. In some standard contracts there are choice of law clauses which are not combined with prorogation clauses. Such combinations are frequent, however. An illustration is furnished by the case 1949 *N.J.A.* 724, where the bill of lading concerned included a clause with the following text: "All claims arising out of this bill of lading shall be settled in the United Kingdom, under English law; no court in any other country shall have jurisdiction over such disputes." A great number of other examples could be given. However, we shall only mention the E.C.E. form containing general rules for the delivery and mounting of machinery (No. 188 A), to which reference was made above:

> "*28. Arbitration and Law Applicable*
> 28.1. Any dispute arising out of the Contract shall be finally settled, in accordance with the Rules of Conciliation and Arbitration of the International Chamber of Commerce, by one or more arbitrators designated in conformity with those Rules.
>
> 28.2. Unless otherwise agreed, the Contract shall, so far as is permissible under the law of the country where the Works are carried out, be governed by the law of the Contractor's country.
>
> 28.3. If the parties expressly so agree, but not otherwise, the arbitrators shall, in giving their ruling, act as *amiables compositeurs.*"

The fact that so many carefully elaborated contract forms make a clear distinction between the question of the applicable law and that of jurisdiction supports the statement that, from the mere presence in a contract of a clause to the effect that disputes arising out of the contract shall be settled, say, in Sweden, it is not permissible to conclude that the parties have also intended to designate Swedish law as the legal system applicable to the contract as a whole. This may sometimes be the case, but is not necessarily so.[114] Nevertheless, many writers contend that a prorogation clause must be held to include a choice of law, at least if it is an arbitration clause.[115]

[114] Cf. Nial, p. 27; Hambro, pp. 232 f.

[115] Schmitthoff states (*op.cit.*, p. 455): "It is widely held, and rightly so, that if the parties agree on arbitration to be held at a particular locality, this imports a

Anyone who plans a transaction with the intention of avoiding conflicts of law and therefore considers the inclusion of choice of law and/or prorogation clauses must undertake a thorough comparison of the law of the countries concerned. It may be found, for instance, that in a given case, a clause implying submission to the courts of England or to a board of arbitrators would mean an infringement of certain restrictive principles in the international procedural law of country X, where one party is domiciled and has his property, and that the execution of an English judgment or of an arbitral award could therefore not be effected there. The drafter of the contract may then have to limit it to a choice of the applicable law. However, a choice of law which is not combined with a prorogation clause is not quite safe. If English law has been chosen as *lex causae,* and the dispute is handled by a Swedish court, questions concerning the invalidity of the contract because of duress, fraud, error or similar grounds will probably be solved in accordance with the rules of the Swedish law of contract.[116] This splitting of the *lex causae* will be avoided if the parties submit to the jurisdiction of English courts. It may also be found that the *forum* country demands a certain measure—which is difficult to evaluate beforehand—of connection between the contract and the chosen law in order to accept a choice of law. A Dutch firm which has sold a consignment of tulip bulbs to a Swedish buyer and included a reference to English law in the contract might find that the Swedish courts apply Swedish or Dutch law in spite of the choice of law undertaken by the parties (although the Dutch firm may have had the bulk of its customers in England and always referred to English law in order to facilitate a uniform handling of its export business). Inclusion also of a prorogation clause is advisable in such cases. However,

choice-of-law clause, namely, an agreement that the law of the arbitration tribunal shall be the proper law of the contract." In *The English Conflict of Laws* (London 1954) tht same writer states that the circumstances of the case may contradict the assumption that an agreement on the place of the arbitral award also implies that it shall be based upon the local law. The statement is illustrated by an example: two cousins, who are partners in a London firm, refer a dispute concerning their partnership to an uncle who, after reaching the age of retiring, has taken up his residence at Nice. Here it may be assumed that the law of England, not that of France, shall be applicable. See *op.cit.* pp. . . .

[116] Cf. Nial, pp. 23 ff.

its binding effect—in Holland, England and Sweden—would have to be examined.

In order to promote conflict avoidance by means of measures of the kind now discussed it should obviously be recommend to national courts to adopt a liberal attitude towards the question whether choice of law or prorogation clauses can be accepted.[117] As we have already stated (above, at p. 216), however, some sort of *fraus legis* mechanism may be necessary as a safety valve in those exceptional cases where the choice of law is meaningless, disloyal or frivolous, e.g. not founded upon a natural business interest. The basic purpose of measures for "conflict avoidance" is to create certainty, before a dispute has arisen between the parties, as to the substantive rules which will be applicable in case of disagreement. In itself, this purpose cannot be called "evasive." One can speak of evasion only in connection with a particular choice of law by the parties. A court confronted by the question whether a choice of law is valid should consider as evasive devices which have the immediate purpose of avoiding the application of a specific rule in the *lex fori*—and similar considerations would seem to be relevant with regard to prorogaton clauses—but only, in the persent author's view, where a clear public interest in the *forum* country calls for the application of the rule which it is sought to avoid.

Evasion means that the parties have tried to circumvent certain substantive rules with the help of a conflict rule which recognizes the principle of a choice of law by the parties. The reaction of courts is to modify that conflict rule *in casu*. The court disregards the evasive device, i.e. the choice of law of the parties.[118] Similarly, a prorogation clause is set aside if it is intended to make any judicial

117 Cf. above, p. 216.

118 This is not the same situation as where the law chosen by the parties without any disloyal purpose is applied as *lex causae* although subject to the modification implied by the simultaneous application of certain rules of the *lex fori*. An evasive choice of law may be illustrated by a contract between a Swedish and an English businessman on a partnership in gambling, where it is laid down that the validity of the contract shall be governed by the law of Monaco, other questions by the law of England. On the other hand, a reference to the legal system of Monaco should probably not be set aside as disloyal, devoid of sense, or frivolous if the contract concerns future activities at the Bank of Monte Carlo. Here, if necessary, corrections could be undertaken with the help of the mechanism of *ordre public*. Cf. Schmitthoff. *op.cit.*, pp. 115 f.

trial of a dispute impossible by referring to the courts of a country where, for legal or practical reasons, an action cannot be brought. To contract out of all national laws is not in itself evasive, however.[119]

C. ARBITRATION

Standard contracts frequently contain clauses providing for arbitration of disputes arising out of the contract. Such clauses often include a choice of law, i.e., a clause which determines the law upon which arbitrators shall base their decisions. By this means full certainty is reached concerning both jurisdiction and the applicable law —in so far, that is, as it is known that the arbitration clause will be respected in the countries affected by the contract. At the same time, the parties will have secured the advantages usually mentioned in favour of arbitration clauses: a cheaper and more rapid procedure, a business-like appraisal of the issues, etc. Furthermore, while considerable difficulty is still encountered in securing the enforcement of foreign civil judgements, states extensively permit executon of foreign arbitral awards.

Arbitration has been promoted in various ways both through legislative measures in many states and on the initiative and with the help of private bodies. Under the auspices of the League of Nations, a protocol on the validity of agreements by private parties to refer their disputes to arbitrators instead of to courts was signed in 1923.[120] Subsequently, in 1927, a Convention was concluded on the enforcement of foreign arbitral awards.[121] The International Chamber of Commerce had played an important part in the creation of these agreements which, in the course of time, have been adopted by some thirty states.[122] The Swedish Act on foreign arbitration

[119] Cf. the above-mentioned clause in form 188 A of the E.C.E. (sec. 283) and the examples given by Hambro (at pp. 10 f.) from the fields of Inter-Nordic reinsurance business and the artificial manure trade.

[120] *S.Ö.* 1929, No. 27.

[121] *S.Ö.* 1929, No. 28 and 1931, No. 32. The standpoint of Swedish law before the introduction of the Act on the enforcement of foreign arbitral awards, 1929, has been studied by Professor Hassler in *Sv.J.T.* 1929, pp. 197 ff.

[122] Surveys of the present state of the law in various countries are given in *Arbitrage international commercial,* publ. by the Union Internationale des Avocats, Paris 1960, and in *Commercial Arbitration and the Law throughout the World,*

agreements and arbitral awards, 1929, is based upon the protocol and convention. The sphere of application of this Act is general and thus embraces even arbitral awards rendered in states which are not parties to the convention and which do not enforce Swedish arbitral awards.

States and many international organizations have continued to take part in the development of international arbitration. Thus a Convention on the recognition and enforcement of foreign arbitral awards was adopted in New York in 1958 on the initiative of the International Chamber of Commerce; it is intended to replace both the Geneva protocol of 1923 and the Convention of 1927.[123] It is hoped that the Convention will be ratified by a great number of States; on the other hand, difficulties are undoubtendly to be expected since the Convention goes much further than the earlier agreements, *inter alia* by abolishing the condition of reciprocity laid down in the 1927 Convention and by setting aside the "principle of territoriality" in a number of cases.[124]

Other conventions relating to arbitration have recently been drafted. Thus the United Nations Economic Commission for Europe (E.C.E.) has worked for a number of years on the draft of a convention on procedural questions; the draft was completed in 1961.[125] The Rome Institute has elaborated a draft uniform law on arbitral awards in international disputes falling within the field of private law, which has been discussed in the Council of Europe. The Rome draft deals both with the question of execution, which is regulated by the 1958 Convention, and with procedural matters, which are dealt with in the E.C.E. draft convention.[126]

publ. by the International Chamber of Commerce, Basle 1958. *Vide* also *International Trade Arbitration. A Road to World-Wide Cooperation,* publ. by Domke *et al., New York* 1958, and Schönke, *Die Schiedsgerichtsbarkeit in Zivil- und Handelssachen in Europa,* vol. 1, Berlin 1944, vol. 2, Berlin 1948.

123 The text of the convention is published in *J.B.L.* 1958, pp. 393 ff.

124 On the 1958 Convention, *vide* Pisar in *J.B.L.,* 1959, pp. 219 ff. and 342 ff.; Sultan in 53 *A.J.I.L.* (1959), pp. 807 ff.: Bredin in *Clunet* 1960, pp. 1003 and Sanders in *NeT.I.R.,* 1959, pp. 43 ff.

125 *Vide* Sv.J.T. 1961, pp. 526 ff.

126 On these matters, *vide* Pisar, *op.cit.,* p. 232, note 32. The draft Convention of the E.C.E. is studied in *Tidskrift för Sveriges Advokatsamfund* 1959, pp. 184 ff. and 1960, pp. 152 ff. The Rome draft is discussed by Matteucci in Domke *et al., op. cit.,* pp. 189 ff., and in *T.S.A.* 1962, pp. 657 ff.

To promote recourse to arbitration, international organizations have created permanent boards of arbitrators for the use of private parties. Thus the International Chamber of Commerce has put several bodies at the disposal of trade and industry in order to facilitate the settlement of disputes. A number of other bodies —arbitration commissions, chambers of commerce, etc.—are also available. A tendency all over the world for parties to contracts to prefer arbitration bodies in their own countries has often made agreement on the locality of the arbitration proceedings and the applicable law difficult. This has been combated by the adoption of ingenious agreements between arbitration bodies in different countries, which are intended to make decisions possible concerning these questions even where they have been left open in the arbitration clauses of contracts.[127]

D. THE COMMUNIST STATES OF EUROPE.

Internal trade in the individual Eastern European States is governed by what are called "general rules on delivery of goods" which, however, function as a uniform sales of goods act.[128] In these countries, foreign trade is a state monopoly administered by the ministries for foreign trade. The various national "enterprises" engaged in foreign trade are adminstratively subordinate to these ministries. The business transactions between the enterprises and foreign vendors or buyers are thus subject to formal requirements and conditions laid down in regulations issued by the ministry. The commercial intercourse between the different Eastern States was in 1949 given a stricter organization through the creation of a Council for mutual economic assistance—CEMA, sometimes called *Comecon*—; it has the character of a special international body but without any supernational elements in its legal structure.[129] The individual business transactions between parties belonging to these states

[127] *Vide* P. Benjamin in 8 *I.C.L.Q.* (1959), pp. 289 ff.

[128] On the law of contract in Eastern Europe, *vide Government, Law and Courts in the Soviet Union and Eastern Europe,* II (pp. 1125 ff.), publ. by Grovski and Grzybowski, London 1959.

[129] *Vide* Tokareva in *S.Y.I.L.* 1959, pp. 169 ff.

were regulated, until 1958, by bilateral "protocols" founded upon certain general principles laid down in the form of advisory opinions by the Council in 1951. In 1958, these rules were replaced by general rules on delivery of goods in foreign trade, which include rules on the contract of sale and are applicable in principle to all sales between the countries which are members of CEMA, i.e. all communist states in Europe except Yugoslavia. These countries have thus achieved the creation of a uniform law in the field of international sales as between the member states.[130] The uniform "sales of goods legislation" came into force on 1 January, 1958. A German version and East German schedules on the application of the rules were published in the review *Osteuropa-Recht* at the beginning of 1960 (pp. 49—73).[131]

The rules of the uniform sales legislation, which have been incorporated into the national law of the member states are mainly compulsory. Exceptions from the rules are admitted only where goods or deliveries of a particular character are concerned or where the legislation itself lays down as an exception that a provision may be put aside by the parties (e.g., a rule on the packing of goods). In all other cases, the individual contracts shall be construed and applied in accordance with the uniform rules and these override rules to the contrary in the national laws of the members states, even those which have a compulsory character for internal purposes. On the other hand, the uniform legislation is only valid, as we have already pointed out, with regard to contracts of sale between enterprises in different countries, e.g., Russia and Rumania.

If the rules of the uniform law are thus compulsory, it should be pointed out, on the other hand, that they do not comprise a full regulation of all the legal questions which may arise out of international contracts of sale within Eastern Europe. In some

[130] Cf. Loeber in *Osteuropa-Recht* 1960, p. 39. Our survey of the topic is very largely based upon Loeber's paper. *Vide* also, however, Boguslavski in *Clunet* 1960, pp. 881 ff. It is most interesting to compare the draft for a uniform Act elaborated by the Rome Institute and the uniform sales legislation of the communist states. Such a comparison is undertaken by Bystricki and Landa in *Review of Contemporary Law* 1959, pp. 67 ff.

[131] Cf. Grodecki in 9 *I.C.L.Q.* 1960, pp. 185 f.

cases, therefore, rules from the internal commercial law of a member state may have serve as a complement to the uniform rules.[132] Thus conflicts are not wholly "avoided" as a result of the uniform legislation. It is provided in the uniform law itself that questions which are not fully regulated by its rules or in the individual contracts shall be decided in accordance with the vendor's national law. Nor has an international Eastern European arbitration body been created in connection with the adoption of the uniform legislation.[133] It is true that the uniform legislation provides that all disputes shall be settled by arbitration, but for this purpose recourse shall be had to the arbitration bodies of the defendant's country unless it is agreed in the individual contract that an arbitration tribunal in a third country shall be resorted to.[134] All the members of CEMA have created permanent arbitration bodies.[135] These do not seem to be organized in the same way in all the communist states, but it is a characteristic feature that the actions are decided by persons appointed in each case from a panel of arbitrators. The parties are not entitled to nominate arbitrators who do not belong to the panel.

Trade with the "Capitalist" World

The communist states conclude an increasing number of trade agreements or similar treaties with states in the West. These agreements serve as a framework within which individual transactions may be carried out.[136] When individual contracts are

[132] *Vide* Lunz in *S.Y.I.L.* 1959, p. 82.

[133] It should be observed, however, that Poland, Czechoslovakia and Eastern Germany have created a joint arbitration tribunal for settling disputes arising in connection with the naval traffic in the port of Gdynia. Vide *Osteuropa-Recht* 1960, pp. 74 ff.

[134] In *Clunet* 1960, p. 881 an arbitral award rendered in Moscow between the Czech enterprise Metallimex and the Rumanian agency Rudmetall is reported. In their contract, the parties had submitted future disputes to the arbitration tribunal in Moscow.

[135] *Vide* Benjamin in *Revue de l'arbitrage* 1957, p. 114 and 1958, pp. 2 ff. and, concerning the Polish arbitration system, Grodecki, *op.cit.*

[136] Cf., e.g., article 3 in the agreement between Sweden and the Soviet Union on exchange of goods and payment, 1940, *S.Ö.* 1956, No. 22, where it is laid down that "general conditions of delivery and payment shall be normal on both sides." Cf. also Jokela in *Scandinavian Studies in Law* 1962, pp. 185 ff.

under negotiation and questions arise which had been left open in the relevant trade agreement, the Eastern European enterprises seem to be bound by internal administrative law to insist on certain conditions laid down by the ministries for foreign trade. Since arbitration has become the normal way of settling commercial disputes in the communist states they usually as a matter of course demand the inclusion of an arbitration clause in their contracts. For example, in the absence of a treaty provision, a Russian enterprise would normally demand that the award be rendered in Moscow by the arbitration board established by the Chamber of Commerce for the Soviet Union established there. Apparently, the transaction would often fail to materialize at all unless this condition is accepted by the party from the "capitalist" country.

The latter party will undoubtendly consider it a disadvantage that by accepting such an arbitration clause he submits to Soviet procedure which means, *inter alia,* that he must appoint a Soviet citizen from a permanent panel as an arbitrator and that all arbitrators will have the same nationality as the opposite party. Moreover, it has been assumed by Western observers that since Soviet enterprises are governed or supervised by public authorities, if not formally state-owned, it will be difficult for a Soviet citizen acting as arbitrator to take an objective position. The machinery of his own state is a party to the action, and more often than not he is part of that machinery himself, in one capacity or another.[137] However, there does not seem to be any clear evidence of partiality in arbitral awards.[138] Professor Hazard states that out of 29 reported cases from the arbitration tribunal in Moscow before the Second World War, the foreign party's action was sustained in 10 cases and the Soviet party's in 15, while in

[137] On the legal position of aliens in Soviet civil procedure, *vide* Boguslavsky and Rubanov in *S.Y.I.L.* 1959, pp. 181 ff.

[138] Pisar states (in Domke *et al., op.cit.,* p. 107, note 16) that "there is no evidence in the available reports of cases heard by the Foreign Trade Arbitration Commission (in Moscow) to indicate manifest unfairness or partiality." Cf., however, Domke, in 53 *A.J.I.L.* (1959), pp. 787 ff. on the arbitration award rendered in Moscow in July, 1958, in the Israeli-Russian oil dispute.

4 cases, the foreign party was successful on one point and the Soviet party on one or more points.[139]

In treaties with some states, the Soviet Union has given up the unconditional requirement that arbitration shall take place in Moscow.[140] The first example was the agreement with Sweden on exchange of goods and payments, 1940.[141] In article 14 it is "expected" that disputes arising out of Swedish-Russian business transactions will be settled by arbitration, and in article 15 the parties engage themselves mutually to recognize and enforce arbitral awards upon certain conditions. To the agreement was attached a protocol with special provisions, *inter alia,* on the locality of and the conditions for the arbitration procedure. The parties are free from any restrictions in their choice of arbitrators. As regards the place of arbitration if the plaintiff is a Swedish institution, organization, firm or person, the seat of the board of arbitration shall be Stockholm; correspondingly, it shall be Moscow if the plaintiff is the Commercial Delegation of the Soviet Union in Stockholm or a Soviet economic organization. The arbitration clauses in the various treaties of the Soviet Union are not uniform, however. Thus an agreement between the Soviet Union and Japan contains a clause providing that the arbitration procedure shall take place in the defendant's country of domicile. It would obviously be gratifying if the situation could be stabilized in such a way that the Eastern states could, on certain conditions, always recognize clauses providing for arbitration at a locality outside the communist countries, and, would allow the enforcement of awards rendered on the basis of such clauses. There are certain signs which seem to indicate the possibility of such a development. Thus, even in some cases not covered by international agreements, the Soviet Union has not required that arbitration shall take place in Moscow.[142] Lawyers from the Eastern states took part in a meeting in Rome in 1958, concerning "legal aspects of trade between planned and free enterprise economies", where certain

139 Hazard in Domke *et al., op.cit.*, p. 95.

140 *Vide* Benjamin in 53 *A.J.I.L.* (1959), pp. 882 ff.

141 *S.Ö.* 1946, nr 22.

142 *Vide* Domke in 53 *A.J.I.L.* (1959), pp. 798 f.

proposals were made for multilateral agreements between various arbitration bodies in Europe, and also participated at a similar meeting in Helsingfors in 1960.[143] It also remains to be seen what the importance may be for contracts between Eastern and Western Europe of the 1958 arbitration convention and the 1961 European convention which gives particular attention to East-West trade.

Conflicts of law are not avoided by arbitration clauses. If, however, the clause refers disputes to a specific arbitration tribunal or to a tribunal within a specific jurisdiction—e.g., Belgium rather than "the plaintiff's home country"—while certainty is not achieved as to the rules which will be applied in the settlement of a possible dispute, still the parties know at least from what legal system choice of law rules will be taken in order to find the applicable substantive provisions. A party who has made a contract with, say, a Soviet enterprise containing a clause stipulating that arbitration shall take place in Moscow, can, however, avoid conflicts, if he succeeds in having a choice of law clause in the contract. It does not seem to be required by the Eastern European states that their own substantive law be made applicable. In the cases where no choice of law has been made, the arbitration tribunals in the communist states apply the conflict rules of the *lex fori;* the result is that foreign substantive law can be applied.[144]

[143] *Vide* Tunc in *Revue internationale de droit comparé,* 1958, and Jokela, *loc.cit.*

[144] *Vide* e.g. Romzaitsev in *S.Y.I.L.* 1958, pp. 475 ff. In the absence of a choice of law clause the *lex loci contractus* governs contracts of sale in the Soviet Union. Cf. the case reported in *Clunet* 1960, p. 879. It concerned a dispute between the Russian agency *Prodintorg* and a Belgian firm, *Nectone,* which had delivered a cargo of herring f.o.b. Ostende. The contract had been concluded in Belgium, but Prodintorg contended that the goods had been finally received in the Soviet Union and that Soviet law should therefore be taken into consideration to some extent. The Moscow arbitration tribunal declined to accept this argument. Belgian law was held exclusively applicable by virtue of "la pratique solidement établie . . . selon laquelle en absence d'accord entre les parties quant à la loi applicable à leurs rapports de droit, c'est le système juridique du lieu de conclusion du contract qu'il convient d'appliquer." *Prodintorg's* action was dismissed in accordance with sec. 1139 of the Belgian civil code.

Table of Swedish Cases

Nytt juridiskt arkiv

Bibliography

Books.

ABRAHAMSON, P. *Sveriges Rikes Landslag.* Stockholm 1726.

AGGE, IVAR. *Den svenska straffrättens allmänna del i huvuddrag, 1.* Stockholm 1944.

AGGE, IVAR. *Valda kapitel ur den allmänna rättsläran.* Kompendium. Stockholm 1956.

ALEXANDERSON, N. *Under vilka förutsättningar bör verkställighet av dom eller skiljedom, meddelad i något av de nordiska länderna kunna erhållas i de övriga.* Stockholm 1919.

ALMÉN, TORE. *Om köp och byte av lös egendom. Kommentar till lagen 20 juni 1905.* 4th partly revised ed. by Rudolf Eklund. Stockholm 1960.

BECKMAN, NILS. *Svensk domstolspraxis i internationell rätt.* Stockholm 1959.

BERGLUND, HADAR. *Svensk eller främmande lag?* Göteborg 1946.

BJÖRLING, JOHAN and LINDENCRONA, GUSTAF. *Utlänningslagen jämte dithörande författningar med kommentar.* Stockholm 1955.

BLIX, HANS. *Statsmyndigheternas internationalla förbindelser.* Stockholm 1964.

BLOMBERG, HUGO. *Om svenskt statsborgarskap.* Uppsala 1891.

BOLDING, PER OLOF. *Bevisbördan och den juridiska tekniken.* Uppsala 1951.

BOLDING, PER OLOF. *Skiljeförfarande och rättegång. En studie i processuell organisation och rättstillämäpningsmetodik.* Stockholm 1956.

DENNEMARK, SIGURD. *Om svensk domstols behörighet i internationnellt förmögenhetsrättsliga mål.* Stockholm 1961.

EBERSTEIN, G. *Den svenska författarrätten, 1.* Stockholm 1923.

EEK, HILDING. *Socialpolitiken inför internationellt forum.* Stockholm 1951.

EEK, HILDING. *Om främlingskap. En undersökning av principerna för främlingskapets rättsliga reglering i fredstid.* Stockholm 1955.

EEK, HILDING. *Studiet av folkrätt.* Stockholm 1956.

EKELÖF, PER OLOF. *Rättegång.* Stockholm 1957—1963.

EKSTRÖM, F. W. *Sju internationellt privaträttsliga uppsatser.* Helsingfors 1920.

FLINTBERG, J. A. *Lagfarenhetsbibliotek.* Strängnäs 1807.

GEIJER, ERLAND. *Om beskattning i Sverige vid in- och utflyttning samt vistelse i utlandet.* 7th revised and enlarged ed. Stockholm 1959.

GIHL, TORSTEN. *Den internationella privaträttens historia och allmänna principer.* Stockholm 1951.

GIHL, TORSTEN. *Studier i internationell rätt.* Stockholm 1955.

GIHL, TORSTEN. *Huvuddragen av den allmänna folkrätten.* Stockholm 1956.

GRÖNFORS, KURT. *Om trafikskadeansvar utanför kontraktsförhållanden. Studier över skadeståndsproblem vid trafik till lands, tills sjöss och i luften.* Stockholm 1952.

HASSLER, ÅKE. *Internationella adoptivförhållanden. En studie till 26 och 27 §§ adoptionslagen.* Lund 1923.

HASSLER, ÅKE. *Civilprocessrätt. Huvuddragen av domstolsväsendet och rättegången i tvistemål enligt RB, I.* Stockholm 1956.
HASSLER, ÅKE. *Utsökningsrätt.* 2nd ed. Stockholm 1960.
HELLNER, JAN. *Om obehörig vinst särskilt utanför kontraktsförhållanden. Ett civilrättsligt problem i komparativ belysning.* Uppsala 1950.
HELLNER, JAN. *Köprätt. Kortfattad lärobok.* Stockholm 1961.
HELMERS, DAG. *Kringgående av skattelag, Studier i svensk och utländsk beskattningsrätt.* Stockholm 1956.
HJERNER, LARS A. E. *Främmande valutalag och internationell privaträtt. Studier i de främmande offentligrättsliga lagarnas tillämplighet.* Uppsala 1956.
HULT, PHILLIPS. *Föräldrar och barn enligt svensk internationell privaträtt.* Stockholm 1943.
KALLENBERG, ERNST. *Svensk civilprocessrätt I.* 2nd ed. Lund 1923—26.
KALLENBERG, ERNST. *Svensk civilprocessrätt II.* Lund 1927—39.
KARLGREN, HJ. *Kortfattad lärobok i internationell privat- och processrätt.* 2nd ed., Lund 1960.
KARLGREN, HJ. *Kutym och rättsregel. En civilrättslig undersökning.* Stockholm 1960.
KREÜGER, I. *Hufvuddragen af utländingars rättsförhållande i Sverige.* Stockholm 1867.
LAGERGREN, G. *Internationella Handelskammarens förliknings- och skiljedomsreglemente antaget vid kammarens kongress i Tokio den 15—21 maj 1955.* Stockholm 1956.
LINDBLAD, J. C. *Läran om bevisning inför rätta.* Uppsala 1842.
MALMSTRÖM, ÅKE. *Det s. k. kvalifikationsproblemet inom den internationella privaträtten. En principundersökning.* Uppsala 1938.
MALMSTRÖM, ÅKE. *Föräldrarätt.* Stockholm 1956.
MATZ, S. *Om underdomarens materiella processledning i svensk ordinär civilprocess.* Stockholm 1919.
NEHRMAN, D. *Inledning till den svenska iurisprudentiam civilem.* Lund 1729.
NEHRMAN, D. *Den svenska jurisprudentia civilis.* Stockholm 1746.
NIAL, HÅKAN. *Internationell förmögenhetsrätt.* 2nd ed. Stockholm 1953.
NIAL, HÅKAN. *Om handelsbolag och enkla bolag.* Stockholm 1955.
NORDLING, E. V. *Föreläsningar över ärvdabalken.* Uppsala 1872.
OHLSSON, L. G. and STARLAND, H. *Arbetarskyddslagstiftningen. Kommenterande redogörelse för 1949 års arbetarskyddslag och därtill hörande författningar.* Stockholm 1951.
OLIVECRONA, KARL. *Domen i tvistemål.* Lund 1943.
OLIVECRONA, KARL. *Utsökning. Föreläsningar.* 2nd ed. Lund 1955.
OLIVECRONA, KARL. *Rätt och dom.* Stockholm 1960.
RAMEL, E. *Studier i svensk internationell arvsrätt.* Uppsala and Stockholm 1930.
REUTERSKIÖLD, C. A. *Inledning till den svensk-internationella obligationsrätten.* Uppsala 1899.
REUTERSKIÖLD, C. A. *Föreläsningar över privat internationell rätt I: Om äk-*

tenskap, äktenskapsskillnad och förmynderskap enligt svensk internationell rätt. Bidrag till tolkningen av konventionerna av 12 juni 1902 och 17 juli 1905 samt lagstiftningen av 8 juli 1904. Uppsala and Stockholm 1909.

REUTERSKIÖLD, C. A. *Föreläsningar över privat internationell rätt II: Handbok i svensk privat internationell rätt (processrätt m. m.).* Uppsala and Stockholm 1907.

SANDSTRÖM, K. G. A. *Svenska dubbelbeskattningsavtal i vad de avse skatt å inkomst eller förmögenhet.* Stockholm 1949.

SCHMIDT, FOLKE. *Föreläsningar i sjörätt.* Lund 1944.

SBHMIDT, FOLKE m. fl. *Huvudlinjer i svensk frakträtt.* 2nd ed., Stockholm 1962.

SCHREVELIUS, F. *Lärobok i Sveriges allmänna nu gällande civilrätt.* Lund 1844—49.

SJÖCRONA, C. A. *Und. betänkande med förslag till författningar ang. försäkringsväsendet.* Stockholm 1883.

SKARSTEDT, S. *Lagen om försäkringsrörelse av 25 maj 1917 samt lagen om tuländsk försäkringsanstalts rätt att driva försäkringsrörelse här i riket av 24 juli 1903 jämte dithörande författningar med förklarande anmärkningar.* Stockholm 1918.

SUNDBERG, HALVAR G. F. *Lag och traktat.* 2nd ed., Uppsala 1942.

SUNDBERG, HALVAR G. F. *Folkrätt.* 2nd ed., Stockholm 1950.

v. SYDOW and ANDERSSON. *Allmänna leveransbestämmelser.* Stockholm 1955.

AF UGGLAS, S. *Samling av Kgl. Maj:ts brev.* Stockholm 1780 and 1794.

UNDÉN, ÖSTEN. *Studier i internationell äktenskapsrätt, särskilt med hänsyn till Haag-konventionerna,* I—II. Lund 1913.

UNDÉN, ÖSTEN. *Internationell äktenskapsrätt enligt gällande svensk lag.* Lund 1922.

WALIN, GÖSTA. *Föräldrabalken.* Stockholm 1952.

WALIN, GÖSTA. *Barnens ställning enligt föräldrabalken m. m. Handledning.* Stockholm 1953.

WESTRING, HJ. *Den nya giftermålsbalken jämte dithörande författningar med förklaringar.* Stockholm 1920.

WIKANDR, HUGO. *Regleringen av äktenskapets legala förmögenhetsrättsliga verkningar enl. 1912 års kompetenslag. En provföreläsning.* Uppsala and Stockholm 1913.

Articles.

Svensk Juristtidning.

BAGGE, ALGOT. »Erfarenheter och resultat från det internationella rättsarbetet», 1955.

BAGGE, ALGOT, »Internationella institutet för unifiering av privaträtten», 1960.

CAKSTE, MINTAUTS. »Till frågan om sovjetmedborgarens befogenhet att förvärva egendom», 1955.

DENNEMARK, SIGURD. »Svensk-schweizisk konvention om verkställighet av domar och skiljedomar», 1937.

DENNEMARK, SIGURD. »Om avtalsstatutet», 1943.

DENNEMARK, SIGURD. »Svensk rättspraxis. Internationell privaträtt 1941—1948», 1950.

EEK, HILDING. »Att sakna hemlandets beskydd. Några reflexioner om internationella skilsmässor», 1957.
EEK, HILDING. »Utländsk civildom», 1957.
EEK, HILDING. »Fullgörande av traktatsförpliktelser», 1959.
EEK, HILDING. »Aktuellt inom internationell familjerätt», 1962.
EKEBERG, BIRGER. »Sjätte Haagkonferensen för internationell privaträtt», 1928.
EKEBERG, BIRGER. »Två nordiska konventionsförslag», 1929.
EKEBERG, BIRGER. »Världsväxelrätten», 1930.
EKELÖF, PER OLOF. »Processkostnaderna och rättshjälpen», 1956.
FALK, SARA. »Nordiskt lagsamarbete», 1959.
FALK, SARA and FRÉDÉRICQ, L. »Lagsamarbetet inom Beneluxstaterna», 1958.
GRÖNFORS, KURT. »Om konventionstolkning», 1957.
GÄRDE, STYRBJÖRN. »Konvention i internationella dödsbofrågor?», 1959.
HALLENBORG, M. »Adoptionslagen och domicilbegreppet», 1939.
HASSLER, ÅKE. »Om verkställighet av utländsk skiljedom», 1929.
HJERNER, LARS. »Folkrättsfrågor i den inomstatliga rättsskipningen. Några anteckningar», 1956.
HOLMBÄCK, ÅKE. »Kring ett fakultetsjubileum», 1957.
JUNGEFORS, STIG. »Gränstullsrättsliga spörsmål», 1960.
KARLGREN, HJ. »Några reflexioner i anledning av en avhandling om kvalifikationsproblemet», 1954.
KARLGREN, HJ. »Svensk rättspraxis. Internationell privat-, straff- och processrätt 1949—1955», 1956.
KARLGREN, HJ. »Svensk rättspraxis. Internationell prviat-, straff- och processrätt 1956—1960», 1961.
KELLBERG, LOVE. »Om juridiska personers ställning enligt 1905 och 1954 års civilprocesskonventioner», 1961.
LIDGARD, CURT. »Europarådets konventioner», 1962.
MALMAR, FOLKE. »Om erkännande och verkställighet av utländsk dom samt om internationella verkningar av konkurs», 1927.
MALMAR, FOLKE. »Svensk rättspraxis. Internationell privaträtt 1931—1935», 1937.
MALMAR, FOLKE, »Svensk rättspraxis. Internationell privaträtt 1936—1940», 1942.
MALMSTRÖM, ÅKE. »Från den internationella privaträttens arbetsfält», 1953.
NIAL, HÅKAN and DENNEMARK, SIGURD. »Förslag till internationell köprättskonvention», 1955.
PERSSON, FOLKE. »Domstolshandräckning och delgivning i utlandet», 1953.
PETRÉN, S. »Barnavårdslagen och förmynderskapskonventionen», 1959.
ROSÉN, K. E. »Något om utländska dödsförklaringars giltighet», 1959.
SCHMIDT, FOLKE. »Asylrätt för flyktingars förmögenhet», 1944.
STENBECK, E. »Femte Haagkonferensen för internationell privaträtt», 1926.
SUNDSTRÖM, C.-E. »Om verkan av utländsk civildom», 1958.
UNDÉN, ÖSTEN. »Återförvisningsläran i internationell privaträtt», 1922.
UNDÉN, ÖSTEN. »Om utländska domars rättskraft i Sverige», 1933.

WELAMSON, LARS. »Svensk rättspraxis. Civil- och straffprocessrätt 1948—1952», 1953.
WISÉN, THORE. »Kungl. Maj:ts praxis i internationella adoptionsärenden», 1961.
Nordisk Tidskrift for International Ret
(Published in Copenhagen)
EEK, HILDING. »Kollisionsnormens struktur och staternas samarbete inom internationell privaträtt», 1954.
ENG, BRYNOLF. »Tillämpning av internationella överenskommelser i intern svensk rätt», 1938.
GRÖNFORS, KURT. »Det andra internationella rymdrättskollokviet i London 1959», 1959.
SIDENBLADH, KARL. »Tredje kollokviet i Stockholm 1960», 1960.
STRÖMBERG, HÅKAN. »Främmande statschefers civilprocessuella immunitet jämförd med statens och diplomaters immunitet». 1958.
NIR. Nordiskt immateriellt rättsskydd.
BERGSTRÖM, SVANTE. »Ett konventionsarbete i slutfasen. Haagförslaget om droits voisins», 1960.
LJUNGMAN, SEVE. »Revision av Haagöverenskommelsen rörande internationell anmälan av mönster och modeller», 1961.
Tidskrift för Sveriges Advokatsamfund
HELLNERS, VIDAR. »Utrikesdepartementets medverkan vid utredning angående utländsk rätt», 1964.
RUMSTEDT, HÅKAN, »Om den gemensamma europeiska marknadens juridiska problem», 1959.
Tidsskrift for Rettsvitenskap
(Published in Oslo)
BAGGE, ALGOT. »Den amerikanska guldklausullagstiftningens internationella verkningar i fråga om obligationslån utfärdade av icke-amerikansk gäldenär i dollarvaluta», 1937.
BENTZON, VIGGO. »Fem nordiske rets-konventioner», 1934.
EEK, HILDING. »Lex causae okänd storhet», 1955.
GRÖNFORS, KURT. »Sjörätt och lufträtt. Till frågan om rättsanalogiens betydelse», 1959.
HJERNER LARS. »Rättstillämpningen och Ordre Public», 1953.
KARLGREN, HJ. »Några anmärkningar om 'tillämpning' av utländsk rätt och om kvalifikationsspörsmålet inom den internationella privaträtten», 1951.
KARLGREN, HJ. »Om rättstillämpning m. m. En slutreplik», 1952.
STRÖMHOLM, STIG. »Skadeståndsproblem i den internationella privaträtten», 1960.
Other articles.
ALMQUIST, J. E. »Den moderna romanistikens metoder och deras genombrott i Sverige vid början av 1900-talet». In *Minnesskrift utg. av Juridiska fakulteten i Stockholm vid dess femtioårsjubileum,* Stockholm 1957.
BAGGE, ALGOT. »En preskriptionsfråga inom den internationella privaträtten». In *Festskrift tillägnad Erik Marks von Würtemberg,* Stockholm 1931.

BOMGREN, GUNNAR. »Forum mot utlänningar i tvistemål». In *Festskrift tillägnad Karl Schlyter,* Stockholm 1949.

DENNEMARK, SIGURD. »Om tillämplig lag i mål rörande äktenskaplig börd». In *Festskrift tillägnad Hjalmar Karlgren,* Stockholm 1964.

EBERSTEIN, GÖSTA. »Immaterialrätten under det senaste halvseklet». In *Minnesskrift utg. av Juridiska fakulteten i Stockholm vid dess femtioårsjubileum,* Stockholm 1957.

EEK, HILDING. »Nya stater och nya regimer». In *Skrifter åt minnet av C. A. Reuterskiöld,* Helsingfors 1945.

EEK, HILDING. »Makten över utrikes ärendena». In *Statsvetenskaplig tidskrift,* Lund 1954.

EEK, HILDING. »Sverige och den internationella rätten». In *Minnesskrift utg. av Juridiska fakulteten i Stockholm vid dess femtioårsjubileum,* Stockholm 1957.

EEK, HILDING. »Svensk medborgares skydd i utlandet, en fråga om förhållandet mellan den enskilde och det allmänna». In *Festskrift tillägnad Halvar Sundberg,* Uppsala 1959.

EEK, HILDING. »Hemlandsprovet». In *Festskrift tillägnad Hjalmar Karlgren,* Stockholm 1964.

EEK, HILDING. »Den ovissa räjongen». In *Festskrift til professor, Dr. juris O. A. Borum,* Copenhagen 1964.

GRÖNFORS, KURT. »Några utvecklingslinjer i internationell luftfartslagstiftning». In *Festskrift tillägnad Nils Herlitz,* Stockholm 1955.

GRÖNFORS, KURT. »Handelsbruk och annan sedvänja». In *Juridikens källmaterial,* Stockholm 1959.

GRÖNFORS, KURT. »Avtalsreglering och tvångsreglering av sjötransporter». In *Rättsvetenskapliga studier ägnade minnet av Phillips Hult,* Uppsala 1960.

HELLNER, JOH. »Om giltigheten av utomlands ingångna äktenskap». In *Förhandlingar å det åttonde nordiska juristmötet,* Stockholm 1896.

HULT, PHILLIPS. »Kvalifikationsproblemet i den internationella privaträtten. En strid om påvens skägg, en gåta för mindre begåvade — eller vad?» In *Festskrift tillägnad Halvar Sundberg.* Uppsala 1959. Also in English in *NTIR* 1960.

KELLBERG, LOVE. »Internationella adoptionsärenden». In *UD:s aktstycken, ny serie II: 14,* Stockholm 1961.

MALMAR, FOLKE. »Återförvisningsläran ännu en gång». In *Festskrift tillägnad Erik Marks von Würtemberg,* Stockholm 1931.

MALMSTRÖM, ÅKE. »Några anteckningar till domicilprincipens historia inom internationell privaträtt». In *Rättsvetenskapliga studier ägnade minnet av Phillips Hult,* Uppsala 1960.

NIAL, HÅKAN. »Några reflexioner om utländska aktiebolags rättsställning i Sverige». In *Festskrift tillägnad Nils Herlitz,* Stockholm 1955.

NIAL, HÅKAN. »Från individualism till kollektivism — en utvecklingslinje i avtalsrätten under ett halvt sekel». In *Minnesskrift utgiven av Juridiska fakulteten i Stockholm vid dess femtioårsjubileum,* Stockholm 1957.

OLSSON, CURT. »Verkan av avtalsklausuler i standardformulär». In *Bilaga till Förhandlingarna å 21 nordiska juristmötet i Helsingfors,* Vammala 1957.

RODHE, KNUT. »Exportörens rättsskydd gentemot mottagaren». In *Orientering kring exportproblemen,* Stockholm 1946.

SALMONSSON, SVEN. »Praktiska erfarenheter i exporthandelns rättsfrågor». In *Orientering kring exportproblemen,* Stockholm 1946.

SCHMIDT, FOLKE. »Nationalitetsprincipen och domicilprincipen i svensk internationell privaträtt». In *Festskrift tillägnad Birger Ekeberg,* Stockholm 1950.

Index

Errata

Page 7, line 15,
should read: "country or the territory in which the judicial decision was rendered."

Page 7, footnote 15:
substitute "foreseen" for "presupposed".

Page 49, line 9 from the bottom:
delete "examine".

Page 62, first line
should read: "to" Swedish law. Two constructions are possible. According to one".

Page 90, end of line 20:
add: "be desirable, since the recognition of foreign judgments creates greater security for legal rights, facilitates the work of courts and provides a basis for reciprocity in favour of Swedish judgments abroad. *82/* If the matter is considered from a wider international".

Page 115, second line:
substitute "obvious" for "obviously".

Page 237, line 12 from the bottom:
substitute "couple" for "coupled".

Page 248, line 14:
substitute "1964" for "1954".

Page 249, first line
delete "draft".

Page 270, line 10 and 11:
delete: "Issues between the parties to a transfer, in the case, for *lex situs.*"

GPSR Compliance

The European Union's (EU) General Product Safety Regulation (GPSR) is a set of rules that requires consumer products to be safe and our obligations to ensure this.

If you have any concerns about our products, you can contact us on ProductSafety@springernature.com

In case Publisher is established outside the EU, the EU authorized representative is:

Springer Nature Customer Service Center GmbH
Europaplatz 3
69115 Heidelberg, Germany

Batch number: 10830935

Printed by Printforce, the Netherlands